I…I finally did it. I ate the world's stinkiest food: Surströmming!! To be honest, this little guy was worse than I imagined! The stench exceeded my expectations! The first whiff smelled like a really deadly fart mixed with rotten fish, fresh garbage and lots of other stuff. In other words, the most indescribably putrid smell ever!! I've never been so taken aback by a food in my life! I swear. And because I ate it without soaking it in a strong alcohol like vodka first (doing so is supposed to lessen its rankness), the taste was, well…not good. It felt like a punch to the gut. No joke… But at least it was a cool experience. It earned me as many experience points as beating twenty Metal Slimes in **Dragon Quest**. (My current weight is 70 kg!! Hm, well, not bad!! Right?)

–Mitsutoshi Shimabukuro, 2012

Mitsutoshi Shimabukuro made his debut in **Weekly Shonen Jump** in 1996. He is best known for **Seikimatsu Leader Den Takeshi!** for which he won the 46th Shogakukan Manga Award for children's manga in 2001. His current series, **Toriko**, began serialization in Japan in 2008.

TORIKO VOL. 20
SHONEN JUMP Manga Edition

STORY AND ART BY **MITSUTOSHI SHIMABUKURO**

Translation/Christine Dashiell
Weekly Shonen Jump Lettering/Erika Terriquez
Graphic Novel Touch-Up Art & Lettering/Elena Diaz
Design/Matt Hinrichs
Editor/Hope Donovan

Printed in the U.S.A.

Published by VIZ Media, LLC
P.O. Box 77010
San Francisco, CA 94107

10 9 8 7 6 5 4 3 2 1
First printing, February 2014

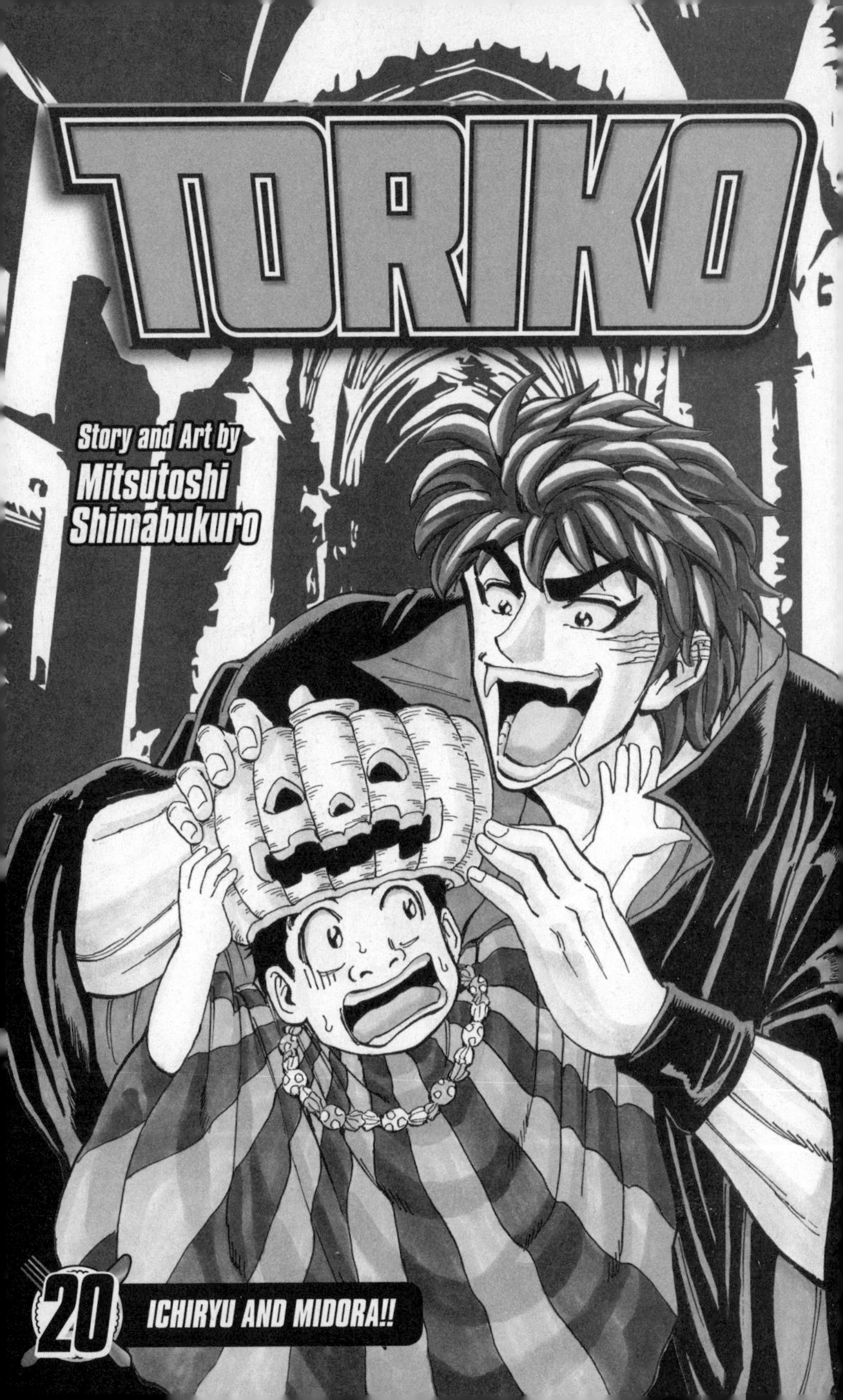
TORIKO
Story and Art by
Mitsutoshi Shimabukuro
20
ICHIRYU AND MIDORA!!

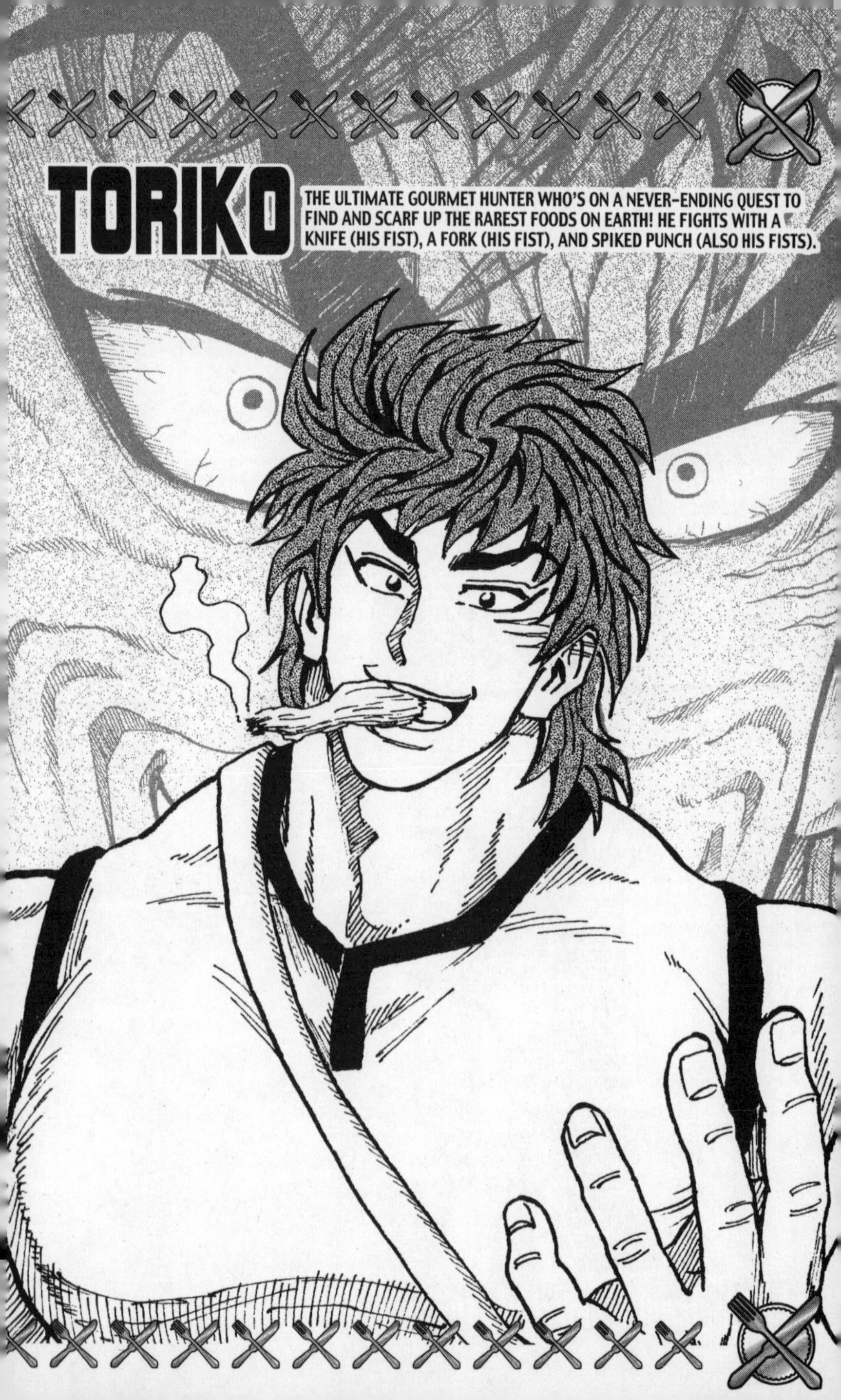
TORIKO
THE ULTIMATE GOURMET HUNTER WHO'S ON A NEVER-ENDING QUEST TO FIND AND SCARF UP THE RAREST FOODS ON EARTH! HE FIGHTS WITH A KNIFE (HIS FIST), A FORK (HIS FIST), AND SPIKED PUNCH (ALSO HIS FISTS).

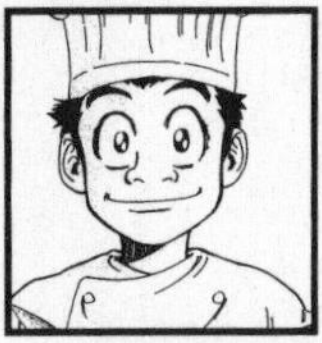

●KOMATSU
TALENTED IGO HOTEL CHEF AND TORIKO'S #1 FAN.

●ICHIRYU
HARDY IGO PRESIDENT AND DISCIPLE OF THE LATE GOURMET GOD ACACIA.

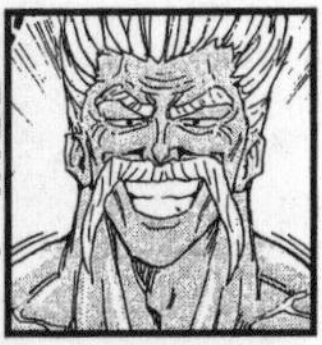

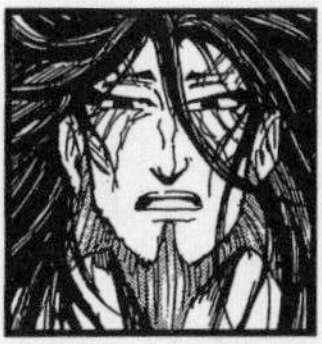

●MIDORA
BOSS OF GOURMET CORP. AND DISCIPLE OF ACACIA. LOOKING FOR GOD.

●COCO
ONE OF THE FOUR KINGS, THOUGH HE IS ALSO A FORTUNETELLER. SPECIAL ABILITY: POISON FLOWS IN HIS VEINS.

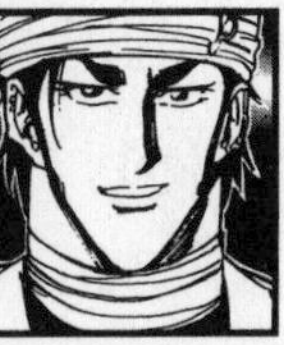

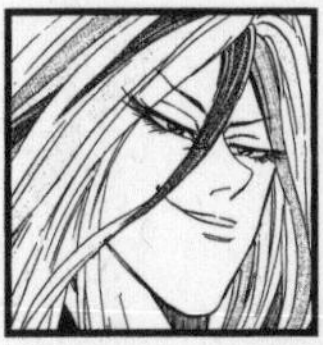

●SUNNY
A GOURMET HUNTER AND ONE OF THE FOUR KINGS. SENSORS IN HIS LONG HAIR ENABLE HIM TO "TASTE" THE WORLD. OBSESSED WITH ALL THAT IS BEAUTIFUL.

●ZEBRA
A GOURMET HUNTER AND ONE OF THE FOUR KINGS. A DANGEROUS INDIVIDUAL WITH SUPERHUMAN HEARING AND VOCAL POWERS.

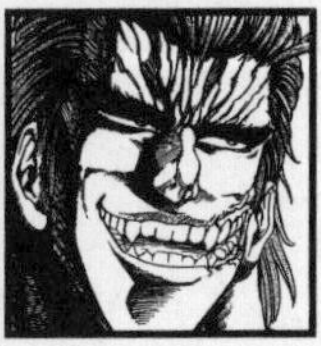

WHAT'S FOR DINNER

IT'S THE AGE OF GOURMET! KOMATSU, THE HEAD CHEF AT THE HOTEL OWNED BY THE IGO (INTERNATIONAL GOURMET ORGANIZATION), BECAME FAST FRIENDS WITH THE LEGENDARY GOURMET HUNTER TORIKO WHILE GATOR HUNTING. NOW KOMATSU ACCOMPANIES TORIKO ON HIS LIFELONG QUEST TO CREATE THE PERFECT FULL-COURSE MEAL.

WHILE TORIKO AND KOMATSU TRAVEL THE WORLD IN SEARCH OF DELICIOUS FOODS, TENSIONS GROW BETWEEN THE IGO AND THE NEFARIOUS GOURMET CORP. THINGS WEREN'T ALWAYS SO BAD. ONCE UPON A TIME, IGO PRESIDENT ICHIRYU, KNOCKING MASTER JIRO AND GOURMET CORP. BOSS MIDORA WERE ALL GOURMET GOD ACACIA'S DISCIPLES TOGETHER. BUT NOW ICHIRYU BELIEVES THAT WHEN GOD, THE MIRACULOUS FOOD THAT ACACIA DISCOVERED, REAPPEARS, IT WILL CAUSE ALL-OUT WAR BETWEEN THE IGO AND GOURMET CORP. KNOWING THAT, TORIKO VOWS TO FIND GOD HIMSELF. WITH HIS CHEF PARTNER KOMATSU AT HIS SIDE, THEY BEGIN TRAINING TO ENTER THE DEADLY GOURMET WORLD. BY TACKLING ONE ITEM AT A TIME FROM THE TRAINING LIST ICHIRYU PROVIDED, AND SOMETIMES JOINING FORCES WITH THE OTHER FOUR KINGS, THEY SLOWLY BUT SURELY CLEAR EACH TASK...

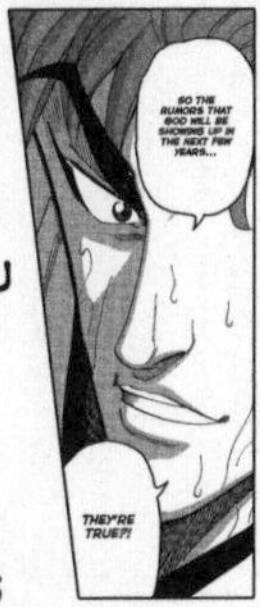
SO THE RUMORS THAT GOD WILL BE SHOWING UP IN THE NEXT FEW YEARS...
THEY'RE TRUE?!

MEANWHILE, ICHIRYU ENTERS THE GOURMET WORLD ALONE WITH THE INTENTION OF SEEING MIDORA, ONLY TO BE MET BY A LEGION OF GOURMET CORP. FLUNKIES BENT ON STOPPING HIM.

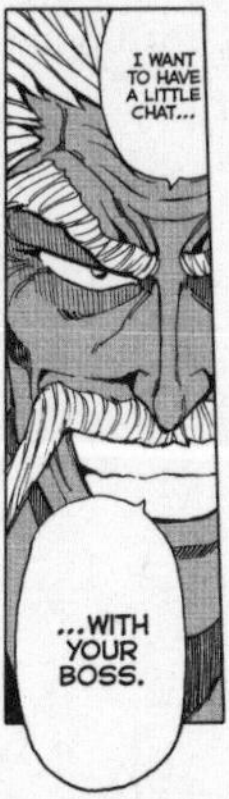
I WANT TO HAVE A LITTLE CHAT...
...WITH YOUR BOSS.

Contents

TORIKO

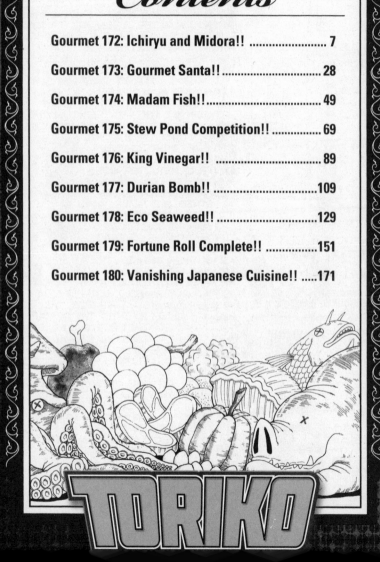

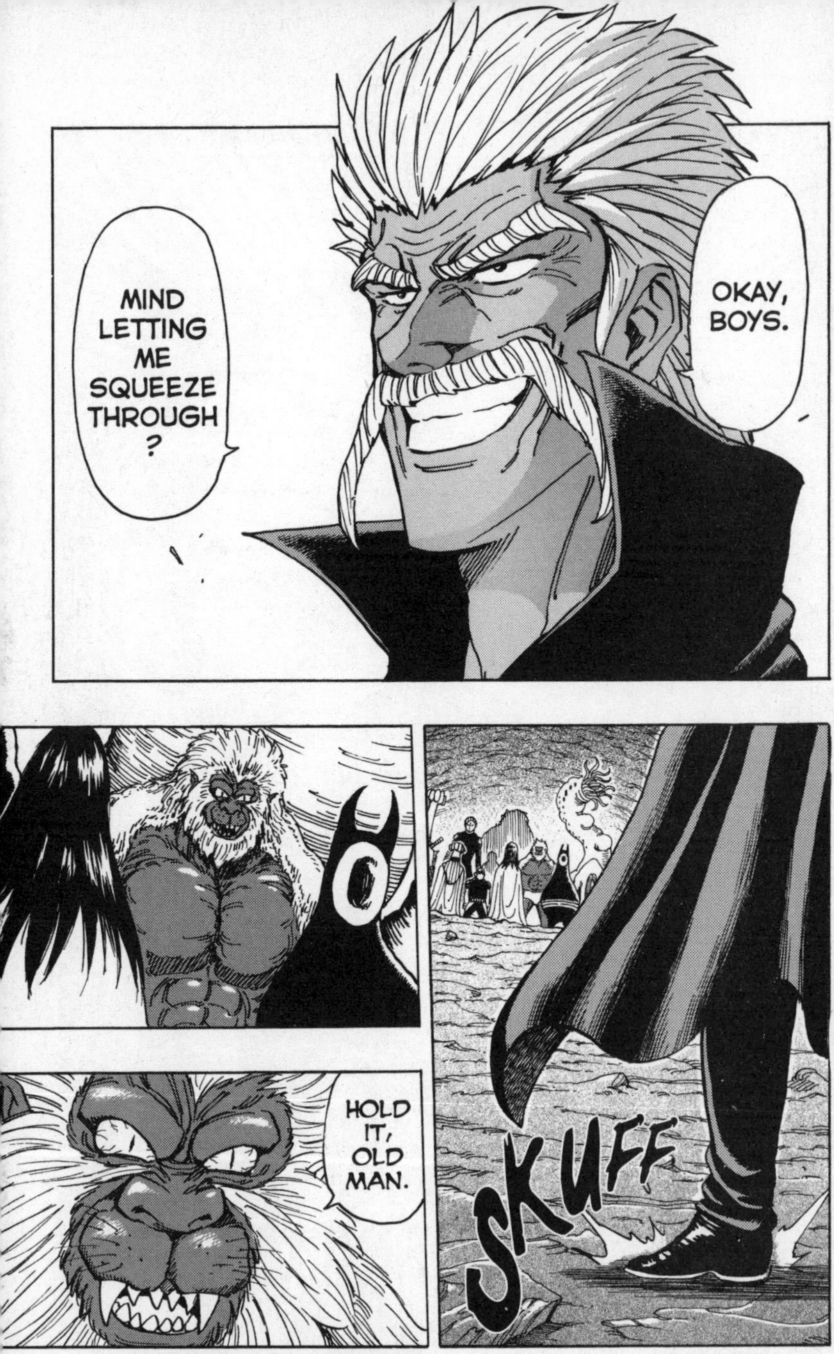
OKAY, BOYS.
MIND LETTING ME SQUEEZE THROUGH?
SKUFF
HOLD IT, OLD MAN.

GOURMET 172: ICHIRYU AND MIDORA!!

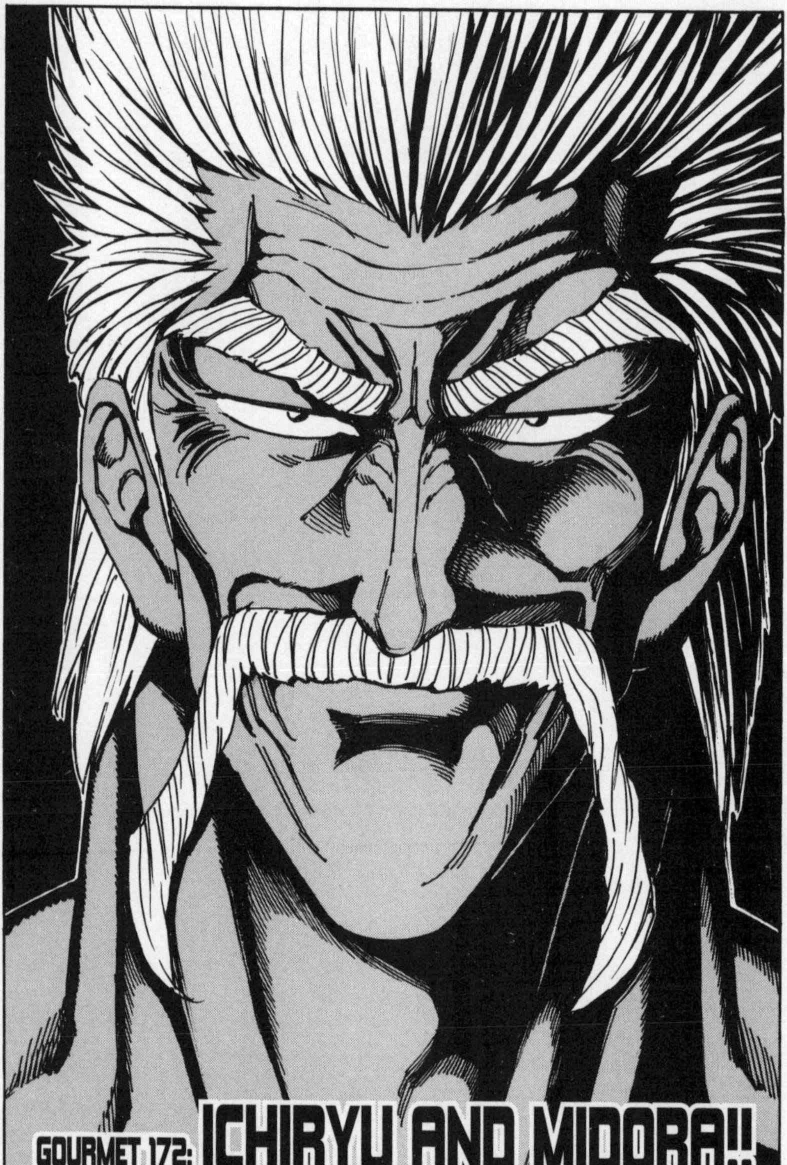
GOURMET 172: ICHIRYU AND MIDORA!!

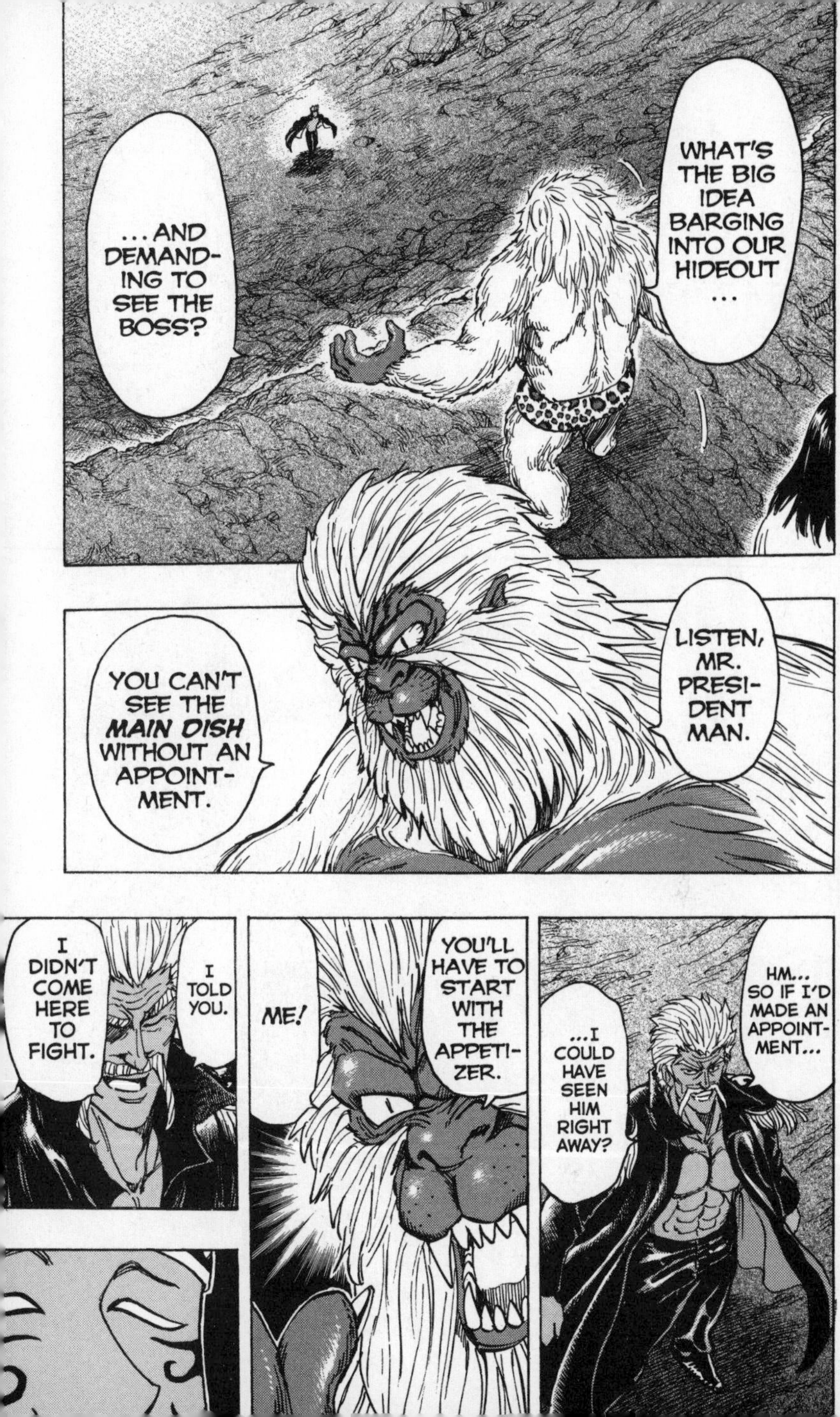
WHAT'S THE BIG IDEA BARGING INTO OUR HIDEOUT ...
...AND DEMANDING TO SEE THE BOSS?
LISTEN, MR. PRESIDENT MAN.
YOU CAN'T SEE THE *MAIN DISH* WITHOUT AN APPOINTMENT.
HM... SO IF I'D MADE AN APPOINTMENT...
...I COULD HAVE SEEN HIM RIGHT AWAY?
YOU'LL HAVE TO START WITH THE APPETIZER.
ME!
I TOLD YOU.
I DIDN'T COME HERE TO FIGHT.

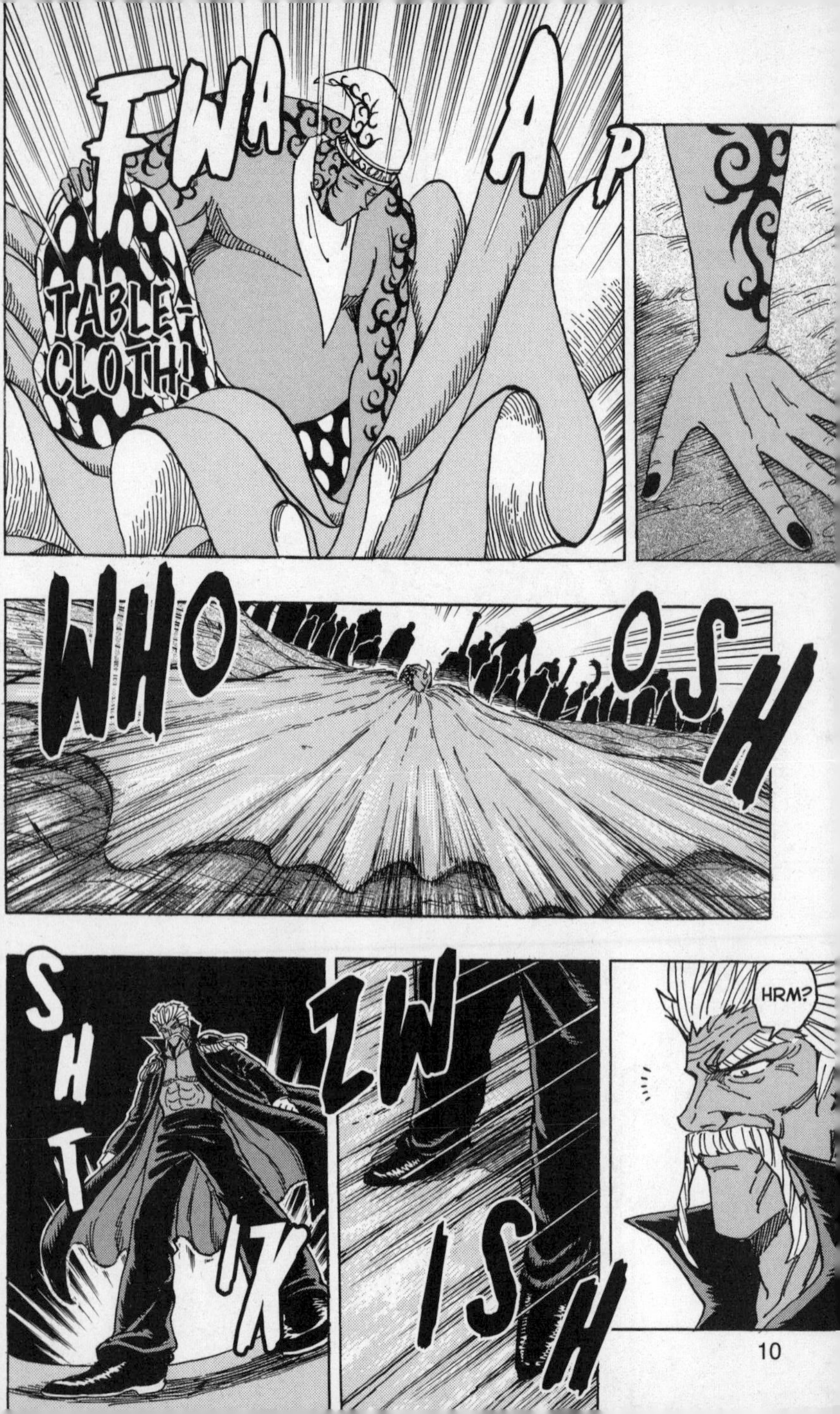
FWAAP
TABLE-CLOTH!
WHOOSH
HRM?
ZWISH
SHTIK

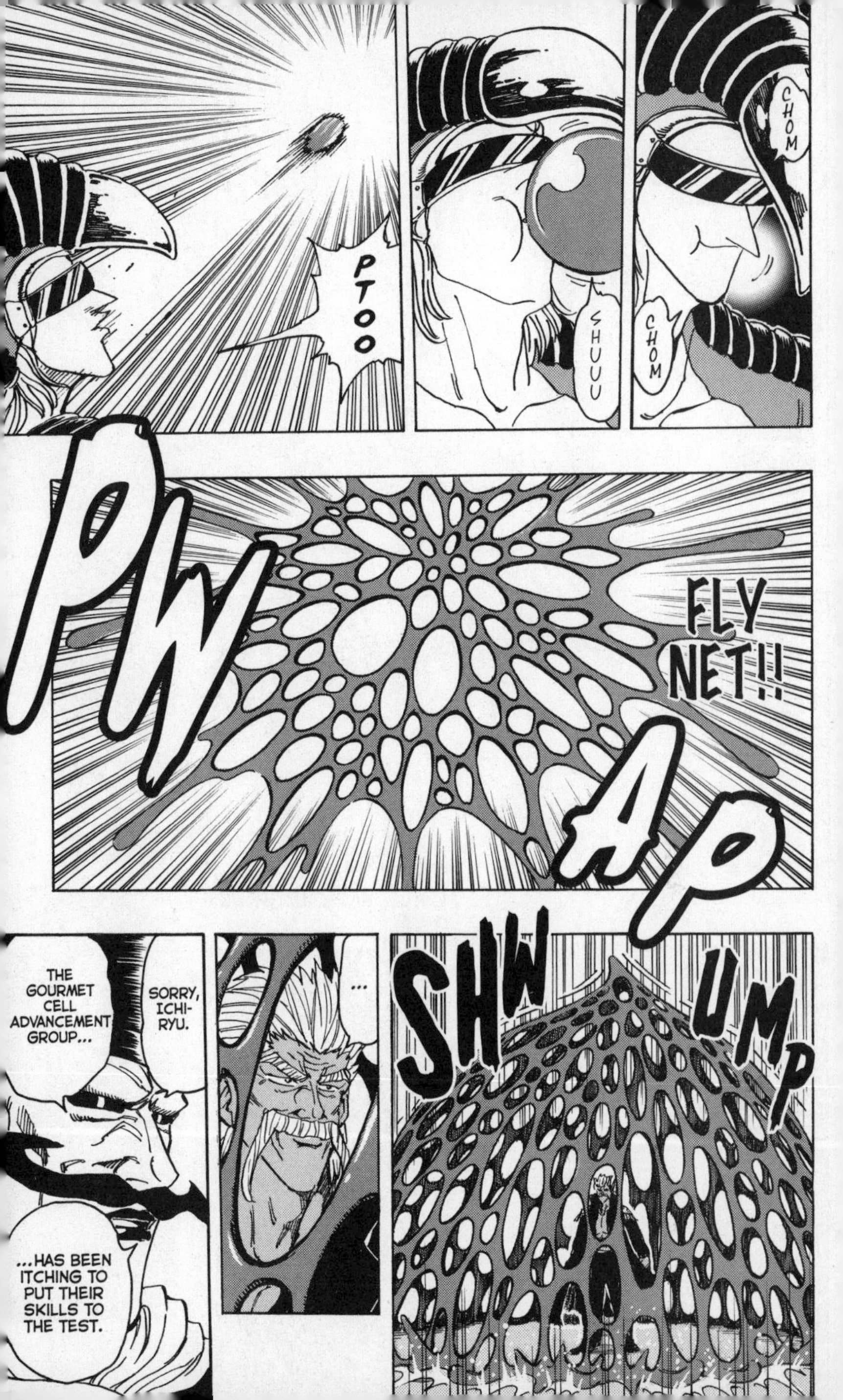
CHOM
CHOM
SHUUU
PTOO
PWAP
FLY NET!!
SHWUMP
...
SORRY, ICHIRYU.
THE GOURMET CELL ADVANCEMENT GROUP...
...HAS BEEN ITCHING TO PUT THEIR SKILLS TO THE TEST.

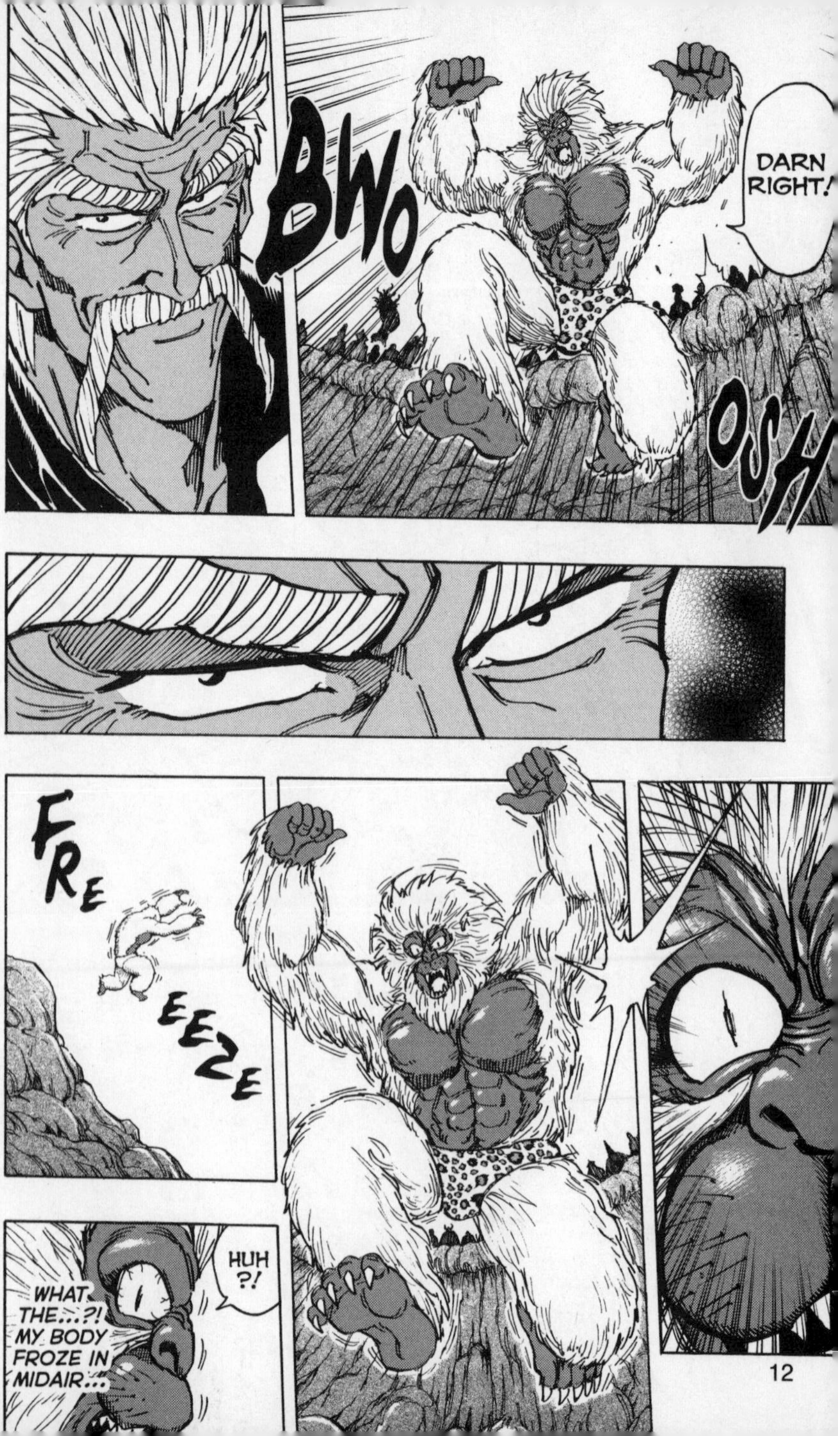

DARN RIGHT!
BWOOSH
FREEEZE
HUH ?!
WHAT THE...?! MY BODY FROZE IN MIDAIR...

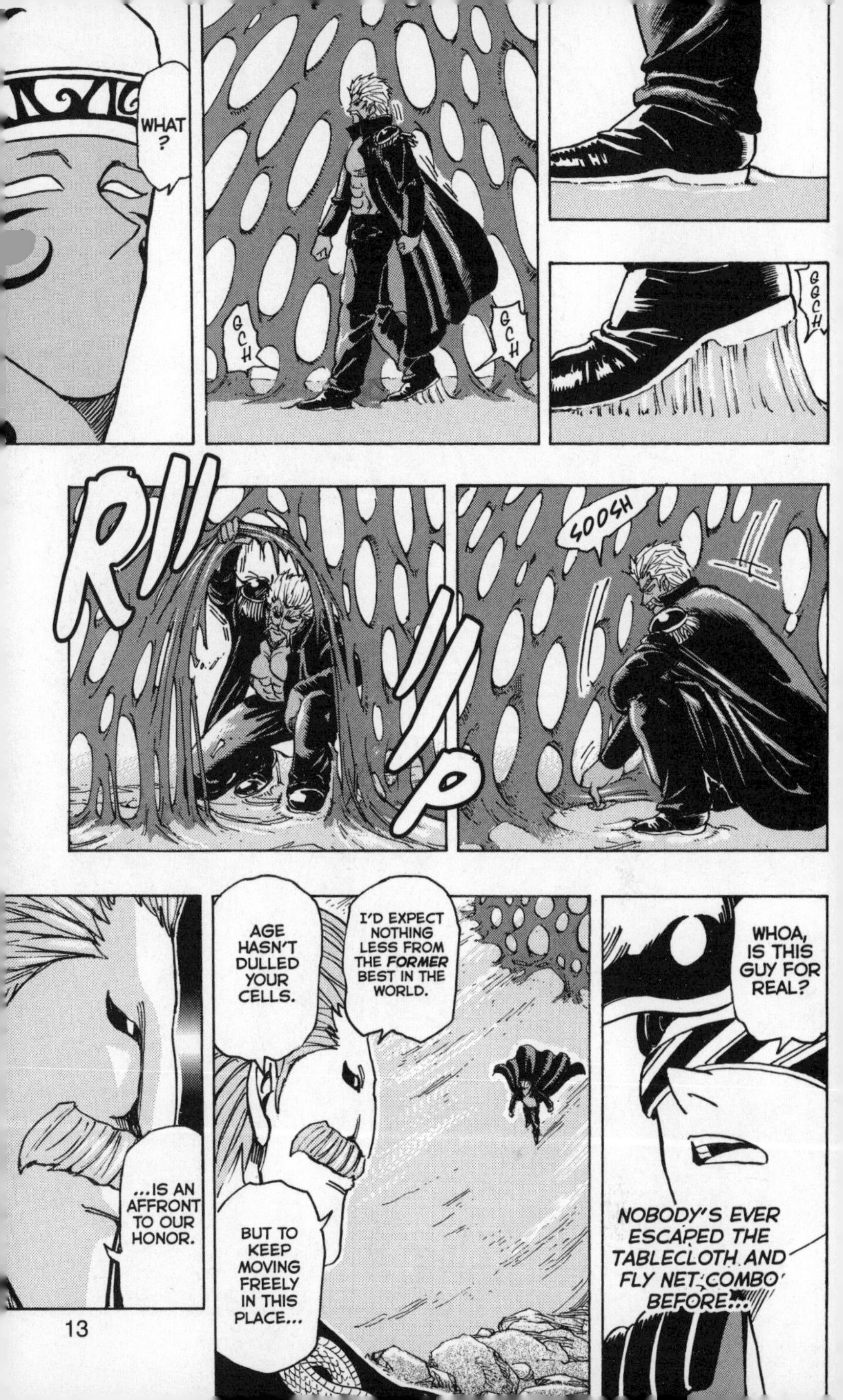
GGCH
GCH
GCH
WHAT?
SOOSH
RIIP
WHOA, IS THIS GUY FOR REAL?
NOBODY'S EVER ESCAPED THE TABLECLOTH AND FLY NET COMBO BEFORE...
I'D EXPECT NOTHING LESS FROM THE *FORMER* BEST IN THE WORLD.
AGE HASN'T DULLED YOUR CELLS.
BUT TO KEEP MOVING FREELY IN THIS PLACE...
...IS AN AFFRONT TO OUR HONOR.

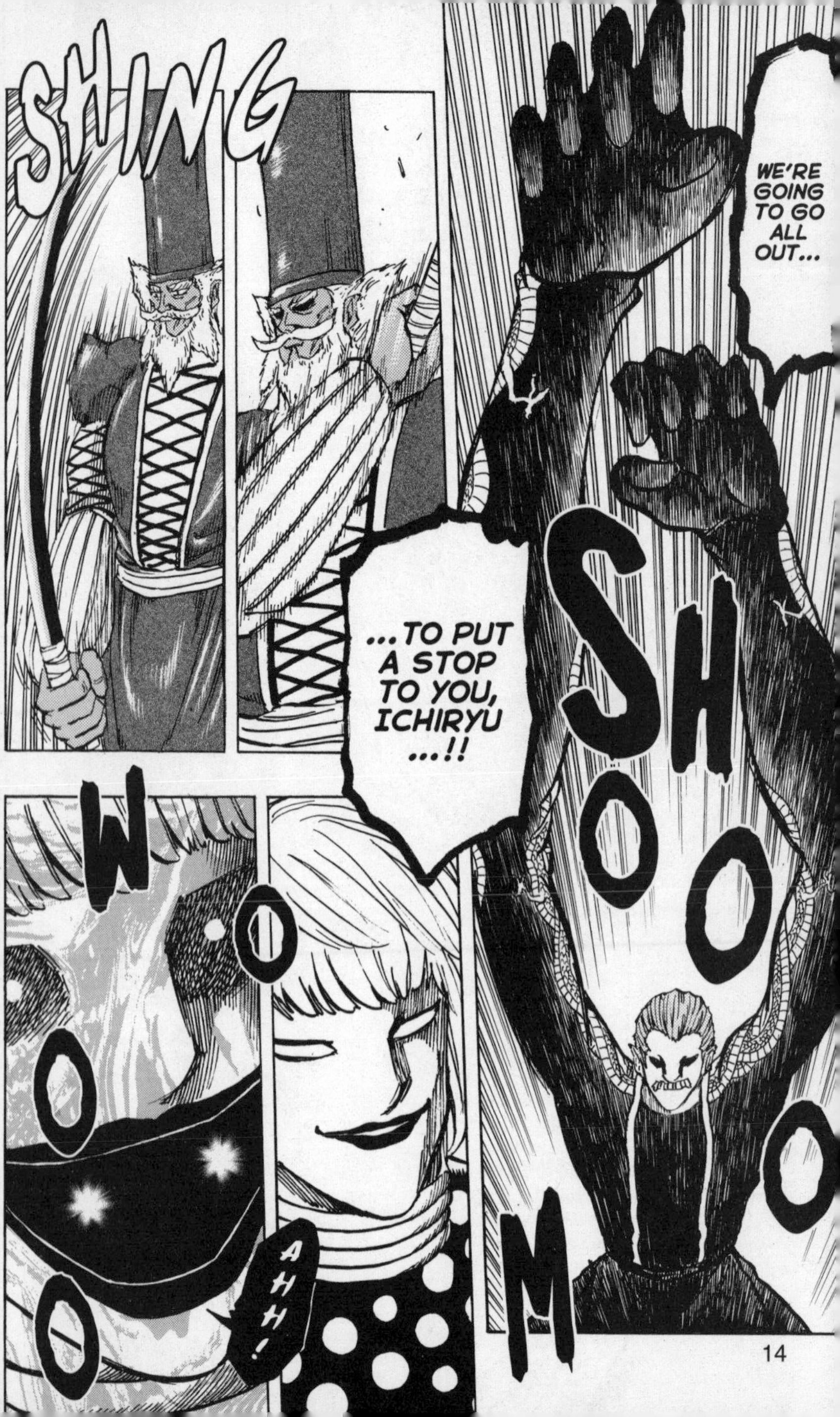
WE'RE GOING TO GO ALL OUT...
SHOOOOM
SHING
...TO PUT A STOP TO YOU, ICHIRYU ...!!
AHH!
WOOO

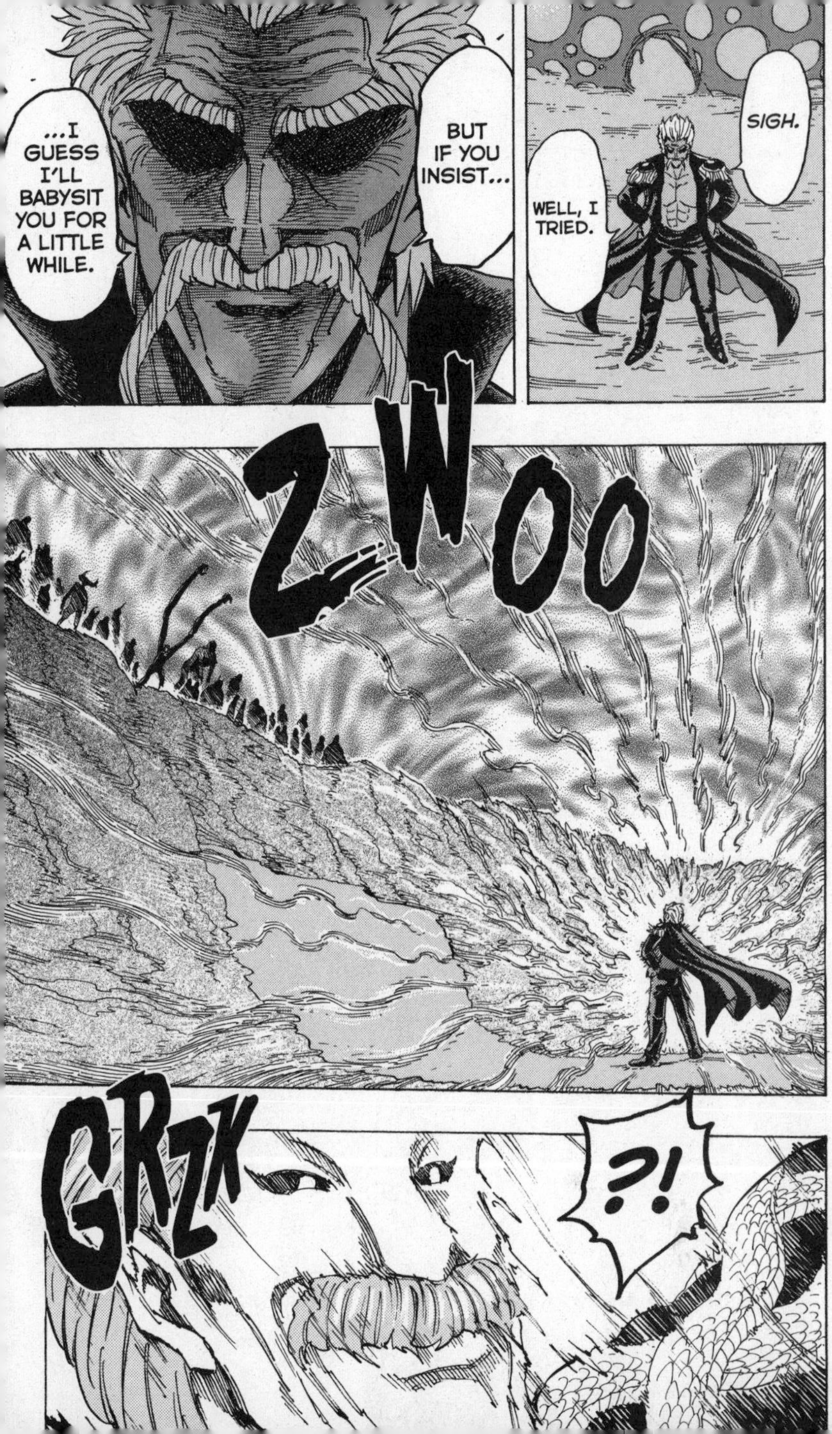
SIGH.
WELL, I TRIED.
BUT IF YOU INSIST...
...I GUESS I'LL BABYSIT YOU FOR A LITTLE WHILE.
ZWOO
?!
GRZK

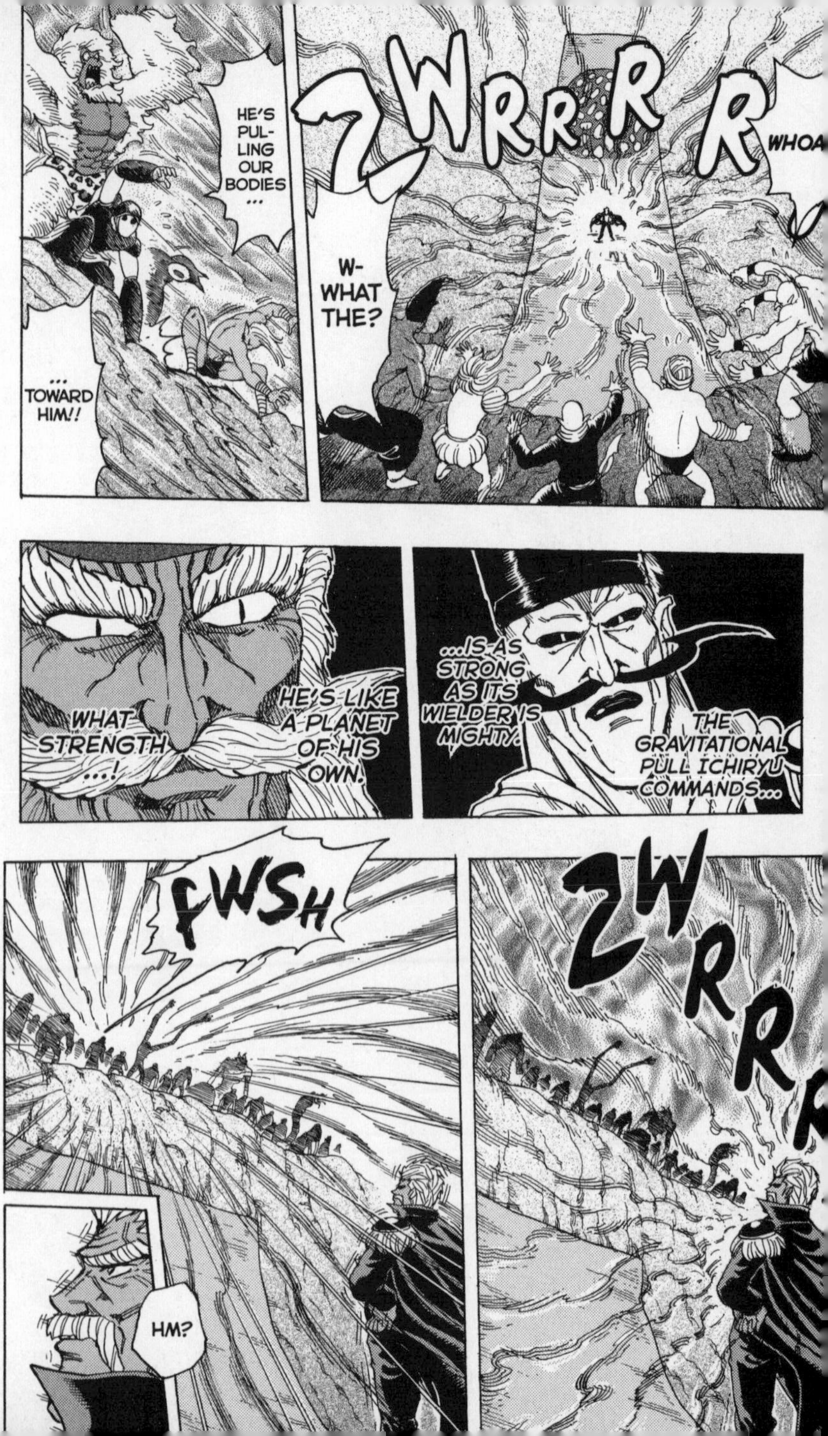
ZWRRR R R
WHOA
W-WHAT THE?
HE'S PUL-LING OUR BODIES...
...TOWARD HIM!!
THE GRAVITATIONAL PULL ICHIRYU COMMANDS...
...IS AS STRONG AS ITS WIELDER IS MIGHTY.
HE'S LIKE A PLANET OF HIS OWN.
WHAT STRENGTH...!
ZWRRR
FWSH
HM?

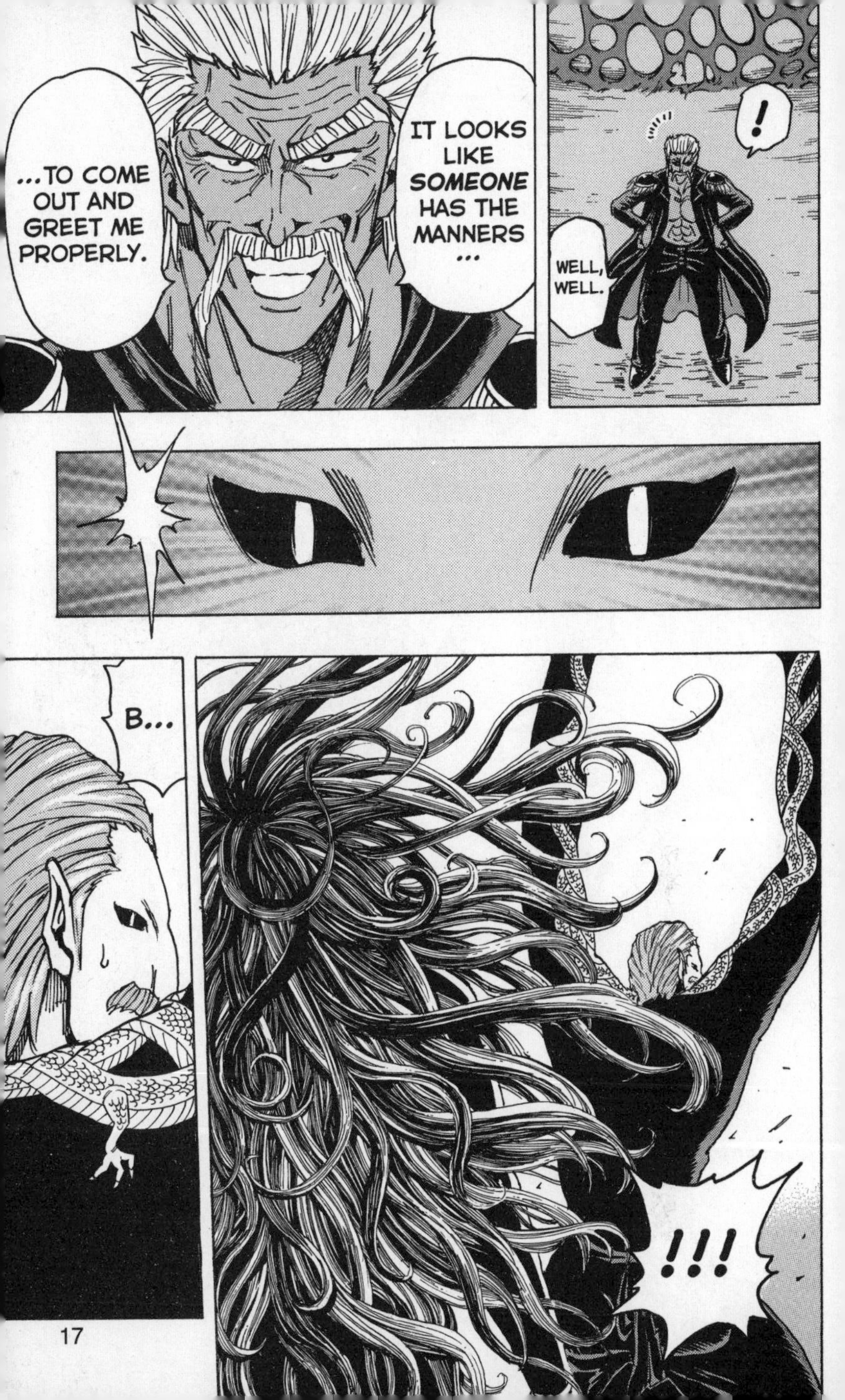
!
WELL, WELL.
IT LOOKS LIKE SOMEONE HAS THE MANNERS...
...TO COME OUT AND GREET ME PROPERLY.
!!!
B...

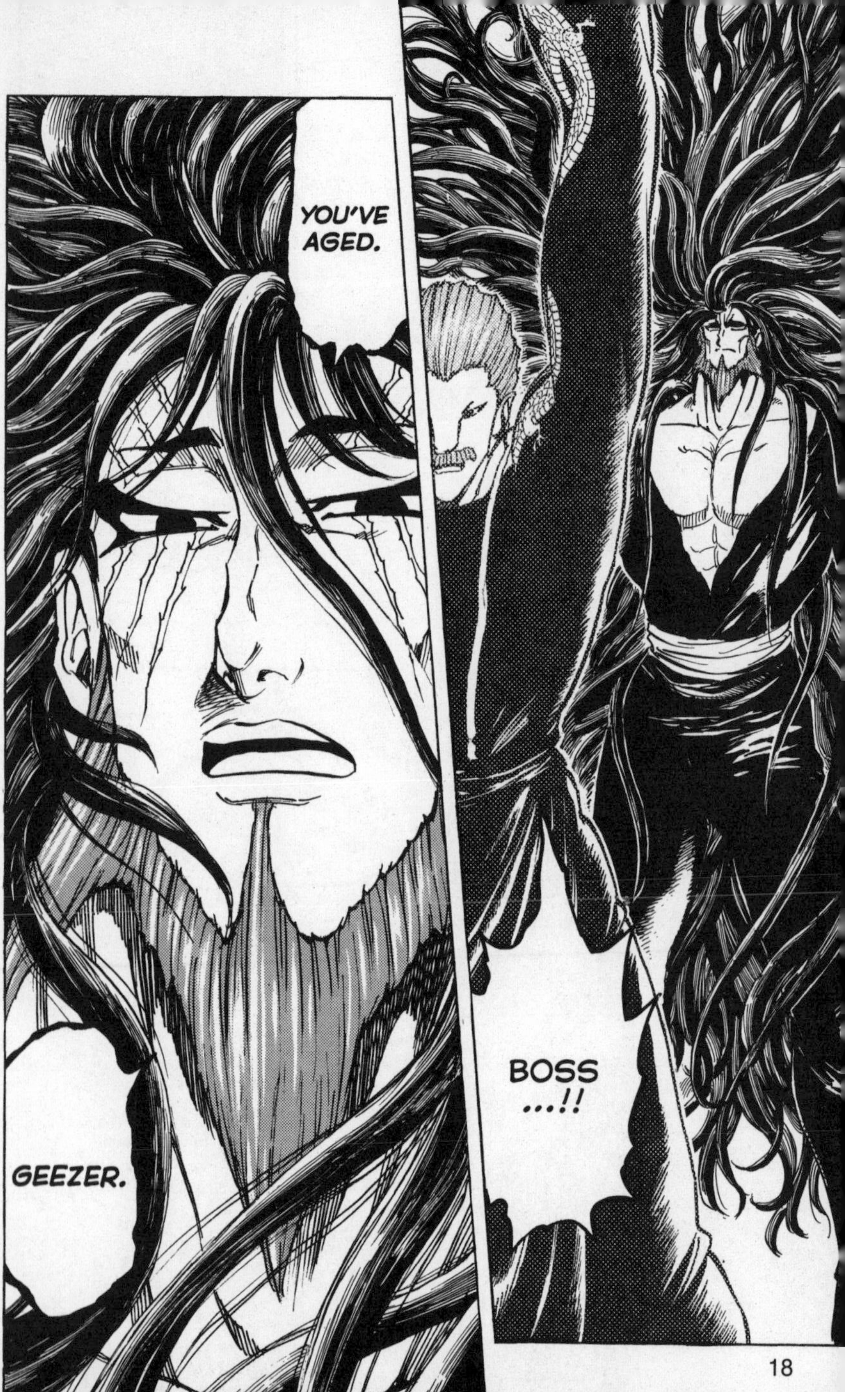
BOSS
...!!
YOU'VE
AGED.
GEEZER.

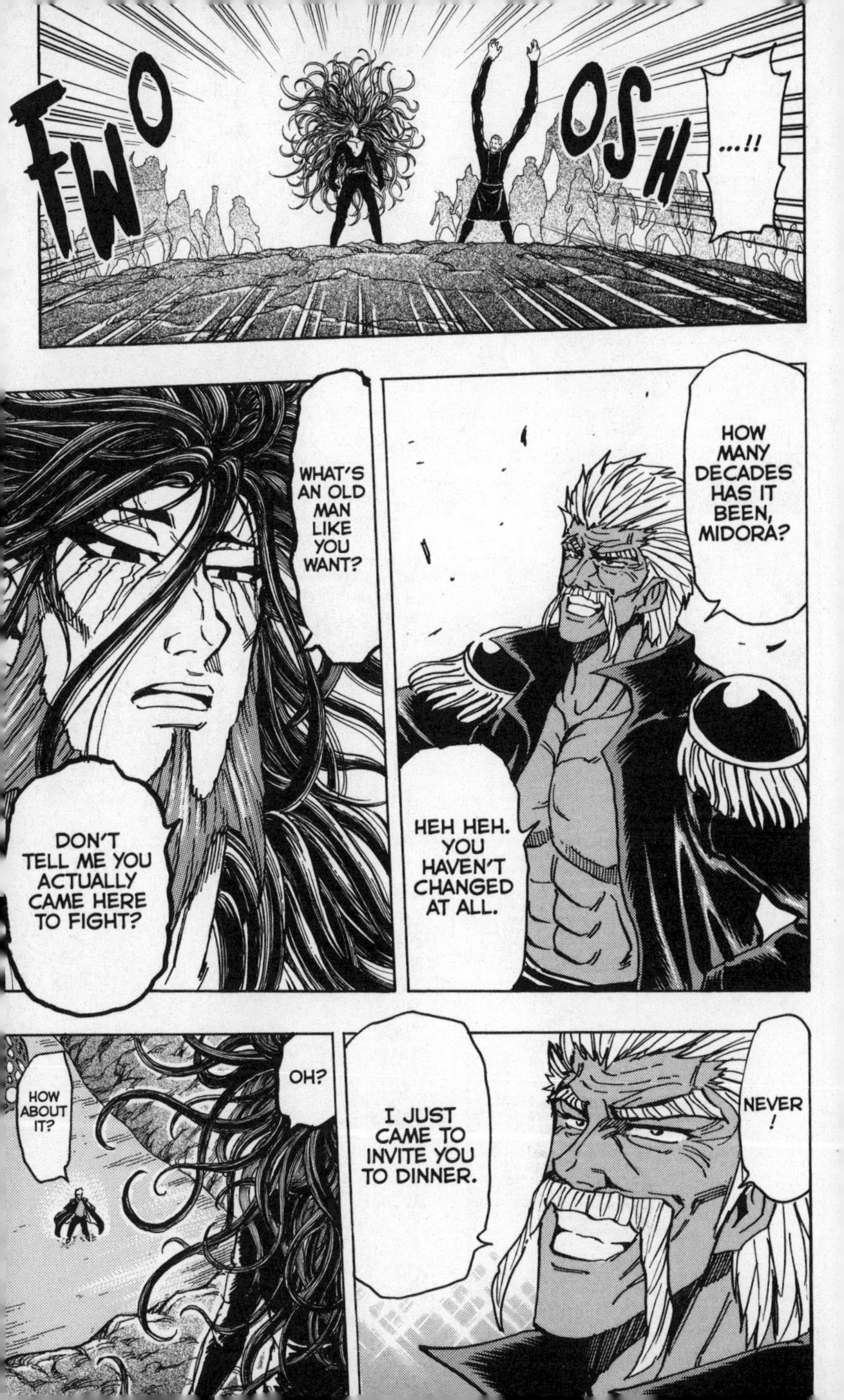
...!!
FWOOSH
HOW MANY DECADES HAS IT BEEN, MIDORA?
HEH HEH. YOU HAVEN'T CHANGED AT ALL.
WHAT'S AN OLD MAN LIKE YOU WANT?
DON'T TELL ME YOU ACTUALLY CAME HERE TO FIGHT?
NEVER!
I JUST CAME TO INVITE YOU TO DINNER.
OH?
HOW ABOUT IT?

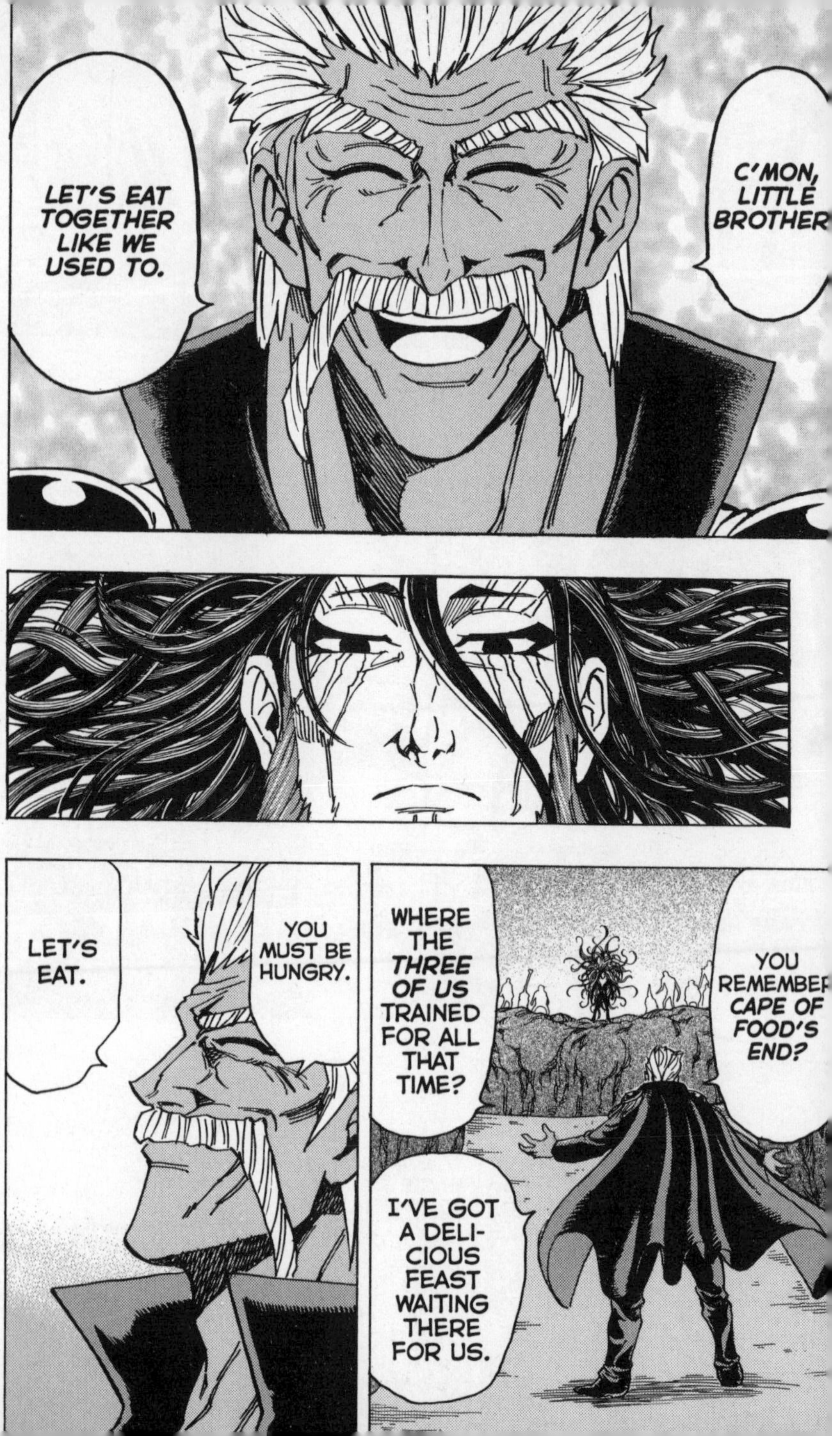
C'MON, LITTLE BROTHER
LET'S EAT TOGETHER LIKE WE USED TO.
YOU REMEMBER CAPE OF FOOD'S END?
WHERE THE *THREE OF US* TRAINED FOR ALL THAT TIME?
I'VE GOT A DELICIOUS FEAST WAITING THERE FOR US.
YOU MUST BE HUNGRY.
LET'S EAT.

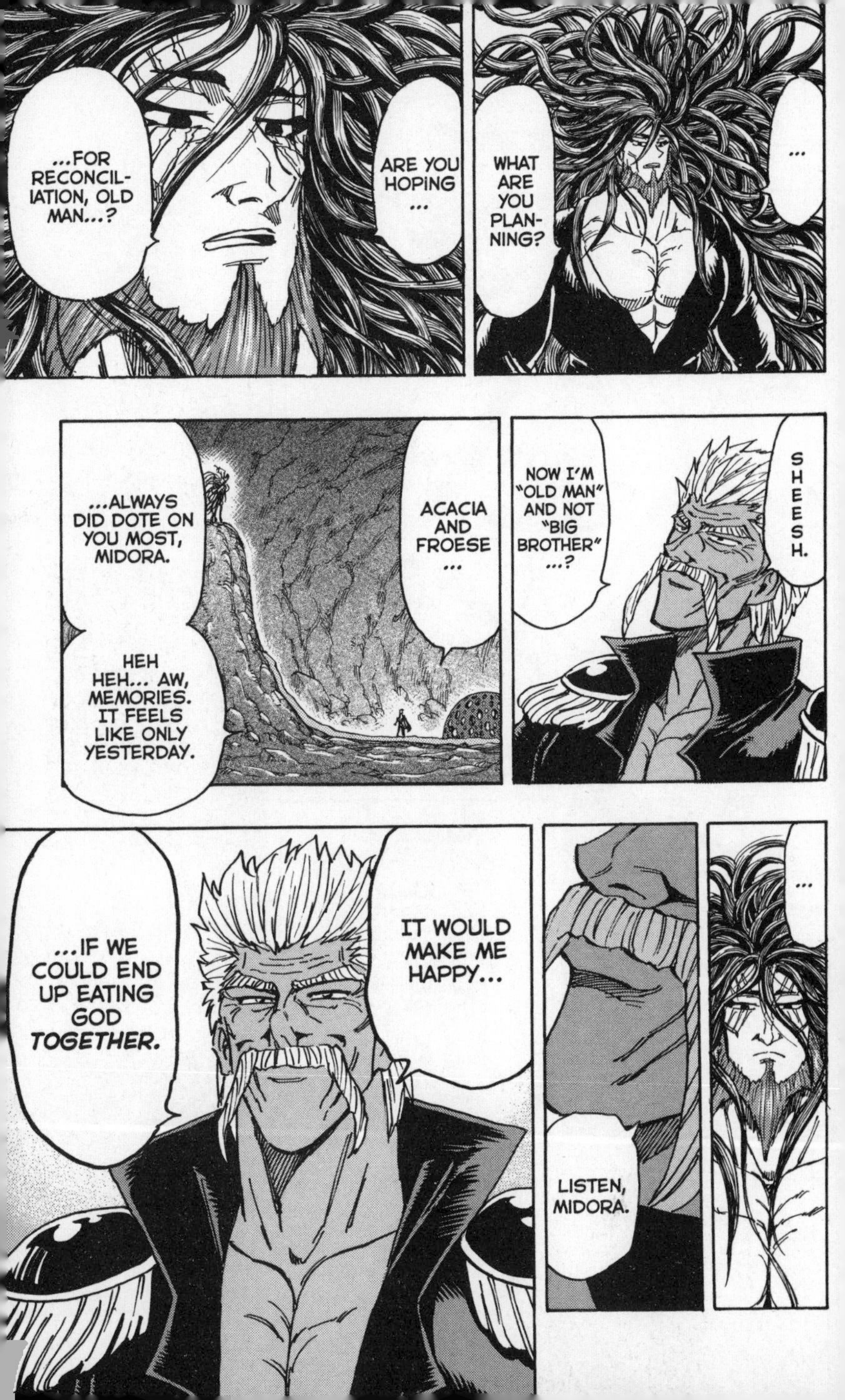
...
WHAT ARE YOU PLANNING?
ARE YOU HOPING ...
...FOR RECONCILIATION, OLD MAN...?
SHEESH.
NOW I'M "OLD MAN" AND NOT "BIG BROTHER" ...?
ACACIA AND FROESE ...
...ALWAYS DID DOTE ON YOU MOST, MIDORA.
HEH HEH... AW, MEMORIES. IT FEELS LIKE ONLY YESTERDAY.
...
LISTEN, MIDORA.
IT WOULD MAKE ME HAPPY...
...IF WE COULD END UP EATING GOD *TOGETHER.*

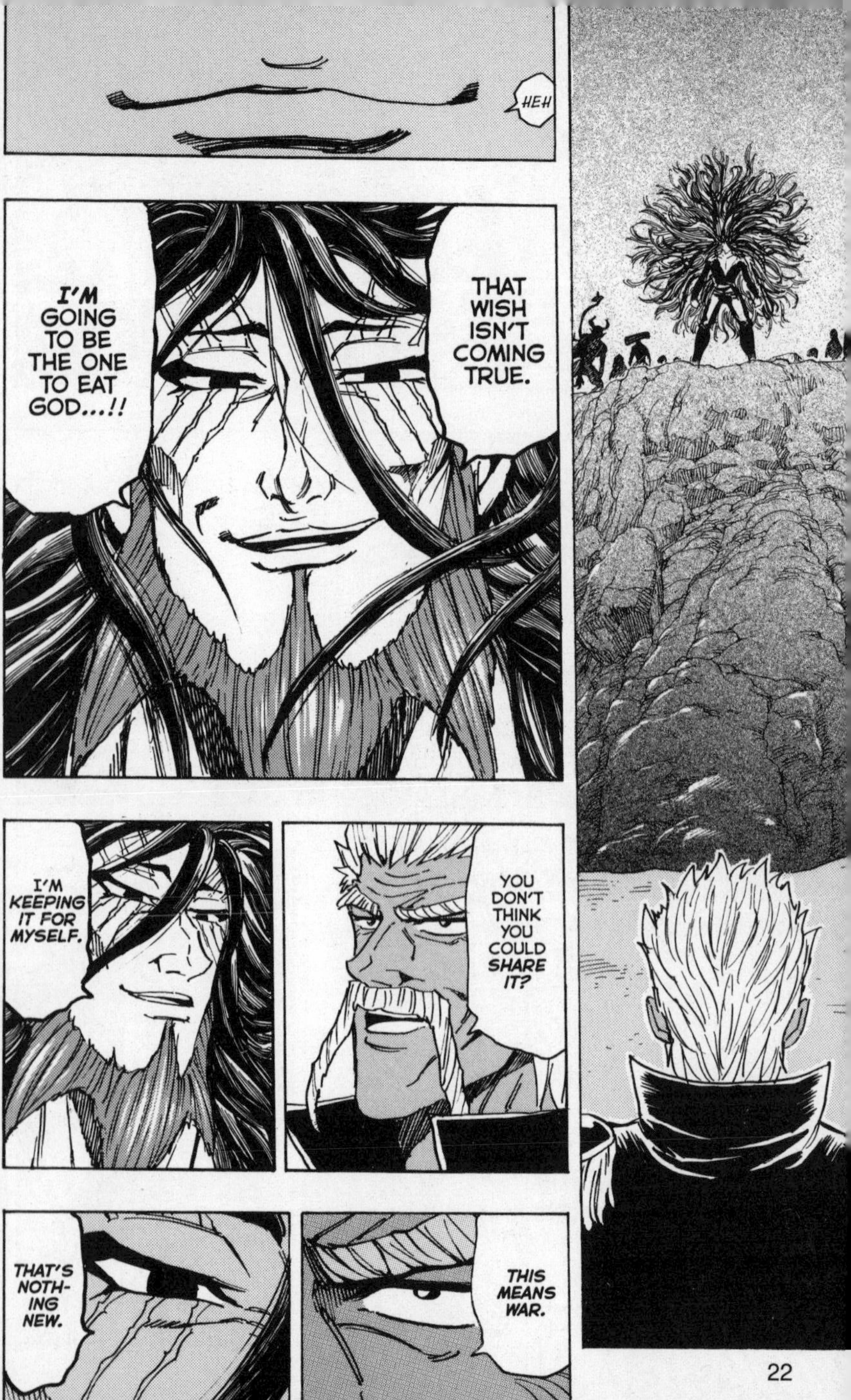
HEH
THAT WISH ISN'T COMING TRUE.
I'M GOING TO BE THE ONE TO EAT GOD...!!
YOU DON'T THINK YOU COULD SHARE IT?
I'M KEEPING IT FOR MYSELF.
THIS MEANS WAR.
THAT'S NOTHING NEW.

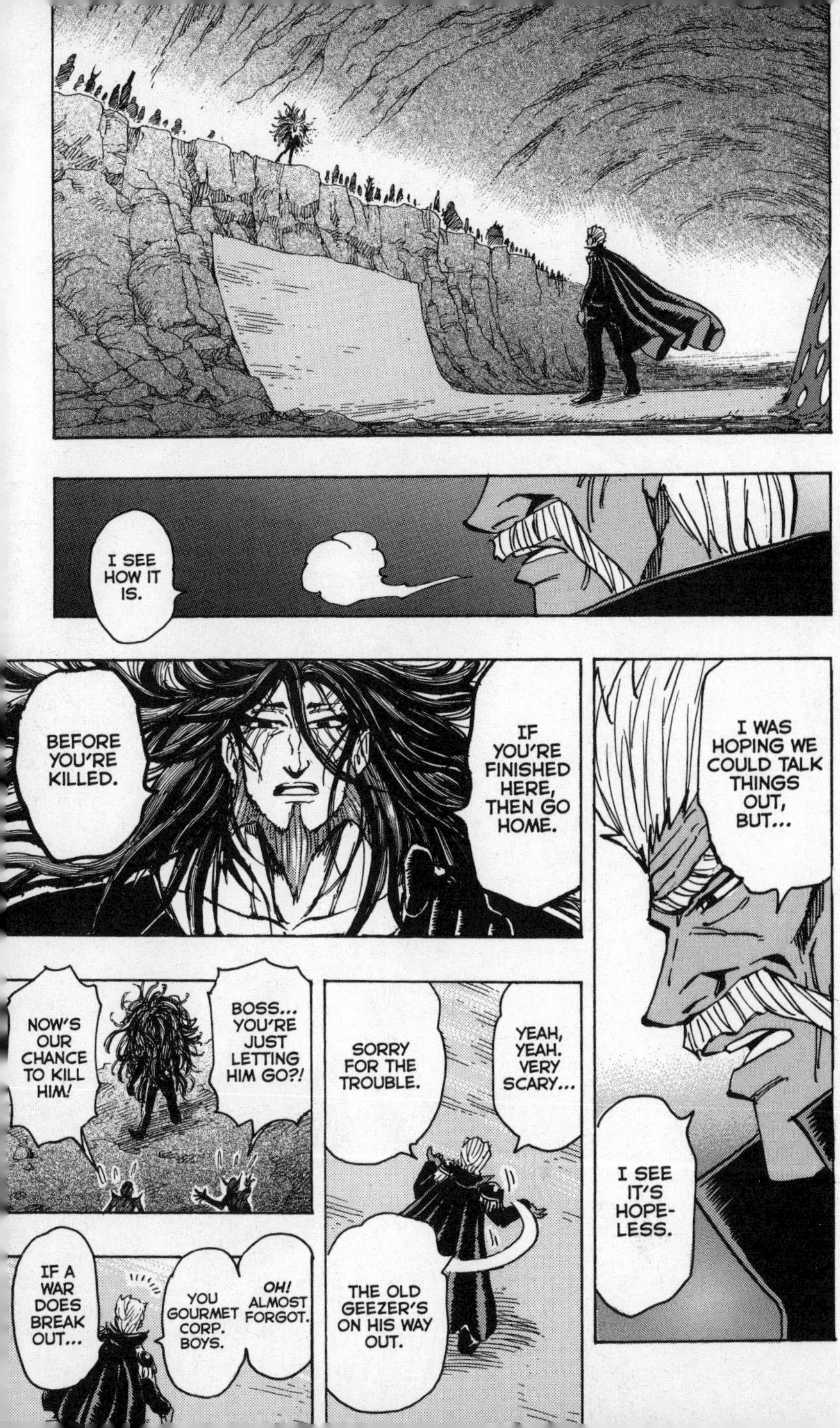
I SEE HOW IT IS.
I WAS HOPING WE COULD TALK THINGS OUT, BUT...
I SEE IT'S HOPE-LESS.
IF YOU'RE FINISHED HERE, THEN GO HOME.
BEFORE YOU'RE KILLED.
YEAH, YEAH. VERY SCARY...
SORRY FOR THE TROUBLE.
THE OLD GEEZER'S ON HIS WAY OUT.
BOSS... YOU'RE JUST LETTING HIM GO?!
NOW'S OUR CHANCE TO KILL HIM!
OH! ALMOST FORGOT.
YOU GOURMET CORP. BOYS.
IF A WAR DOES BREAK OUT...

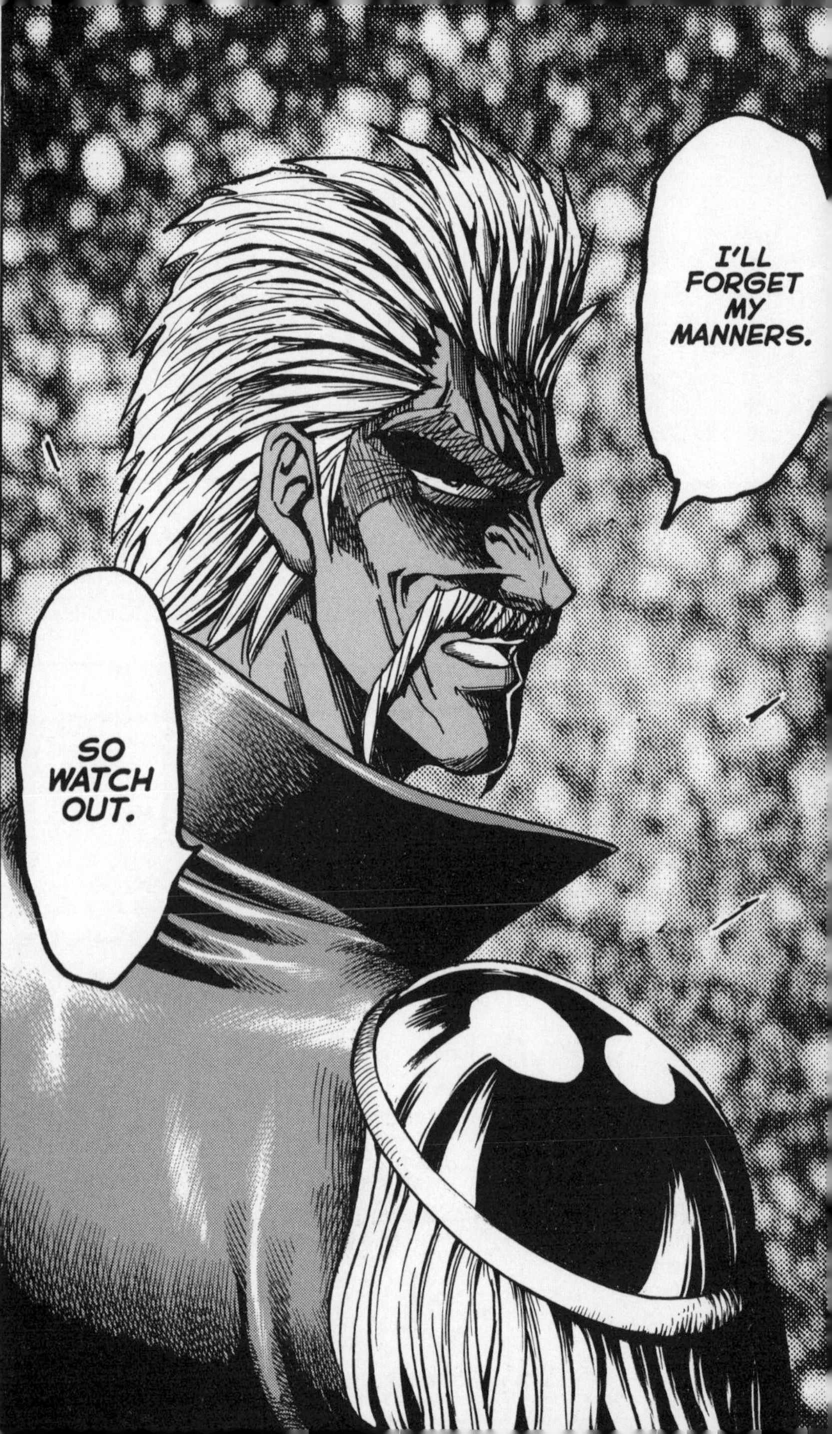
I'LL FORGET MY MANNERS.
SO WATCH OUT.

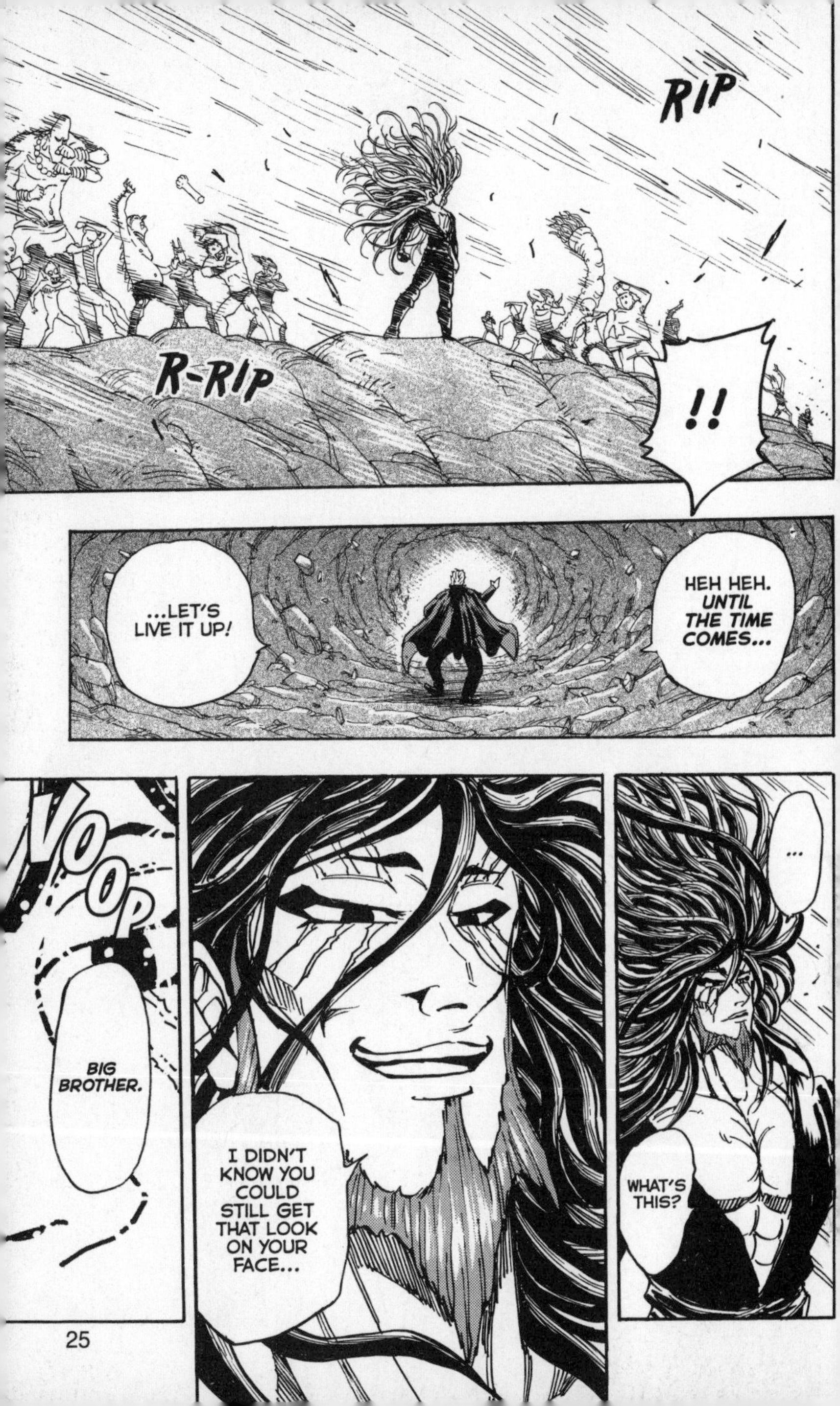

RIP
!!
R-RIP
HEH HEH. UNTIL THE TIME COMES...
...LET'S LIVE IT UP!
...
WHAT'S THIS?
I DIDN'T KNOW YOU COULD STILL GET THAT LOOK ON YOUR FACE...
VOOP
BIG BROTHER.

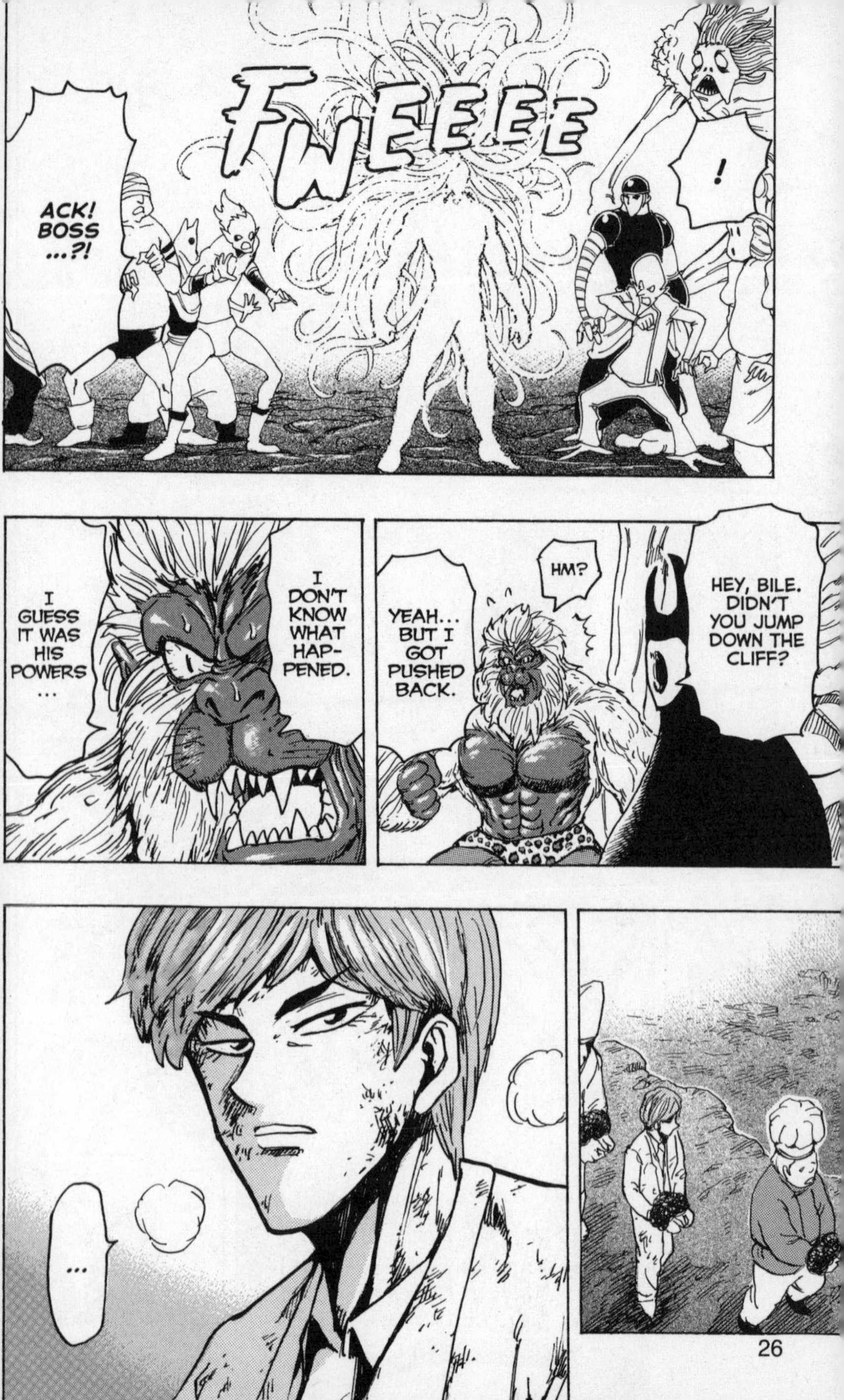
!
FWEEEE
ACK! BOSS ...?!
HEY, BILE. DIDN'T YOU JUMP DOWN THE CLIFF?
HM?
YEAH... BUT I GOT PUSHED BACK.
I DON'T KNOW WHAT HAP-PENED.
I GUESS IT WAS HIS POWERS ...
...

FL AP

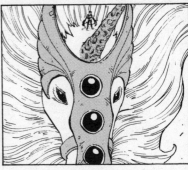

FLAp

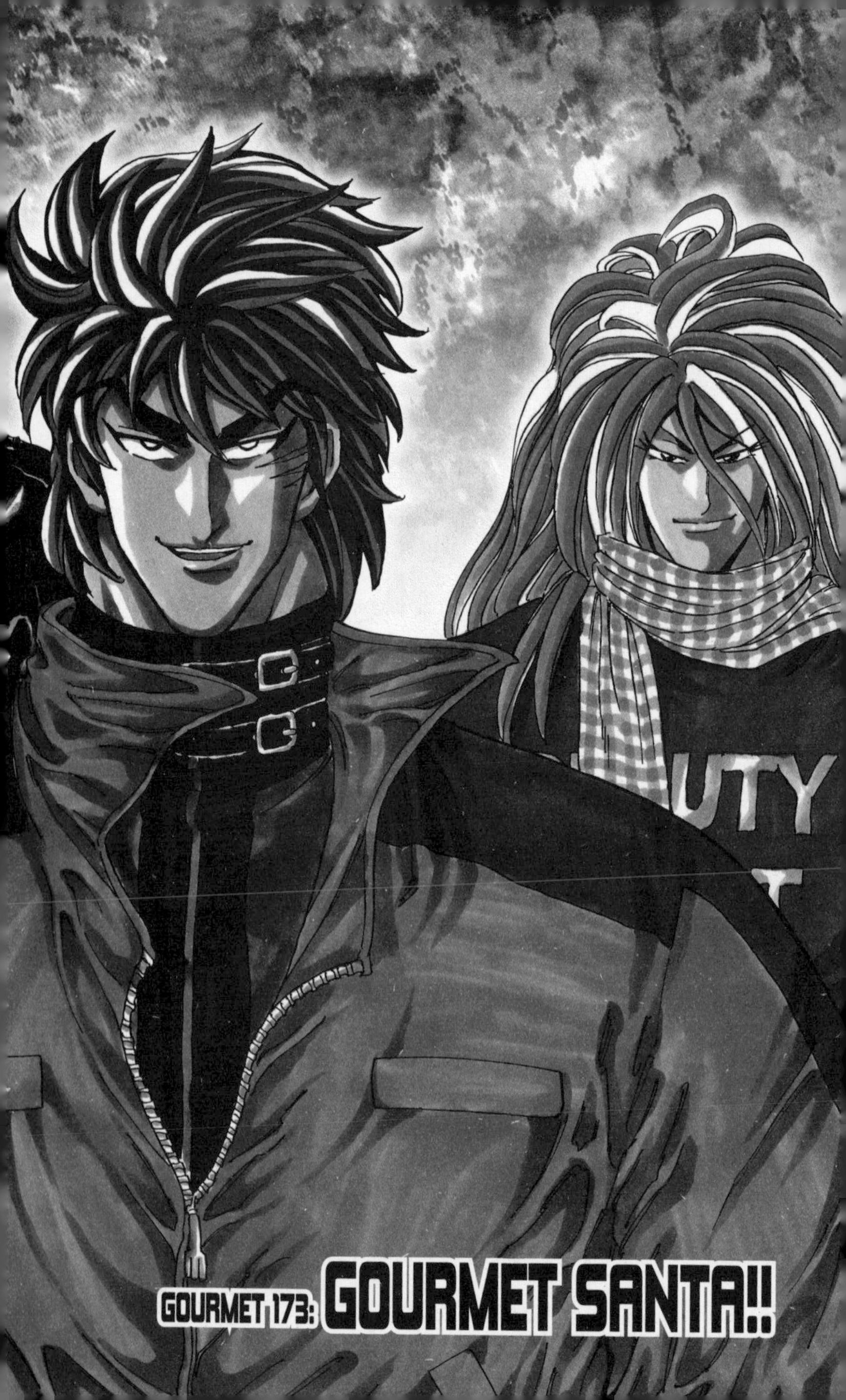
UTY
GOURMET 173: GOURMET SANTA!!

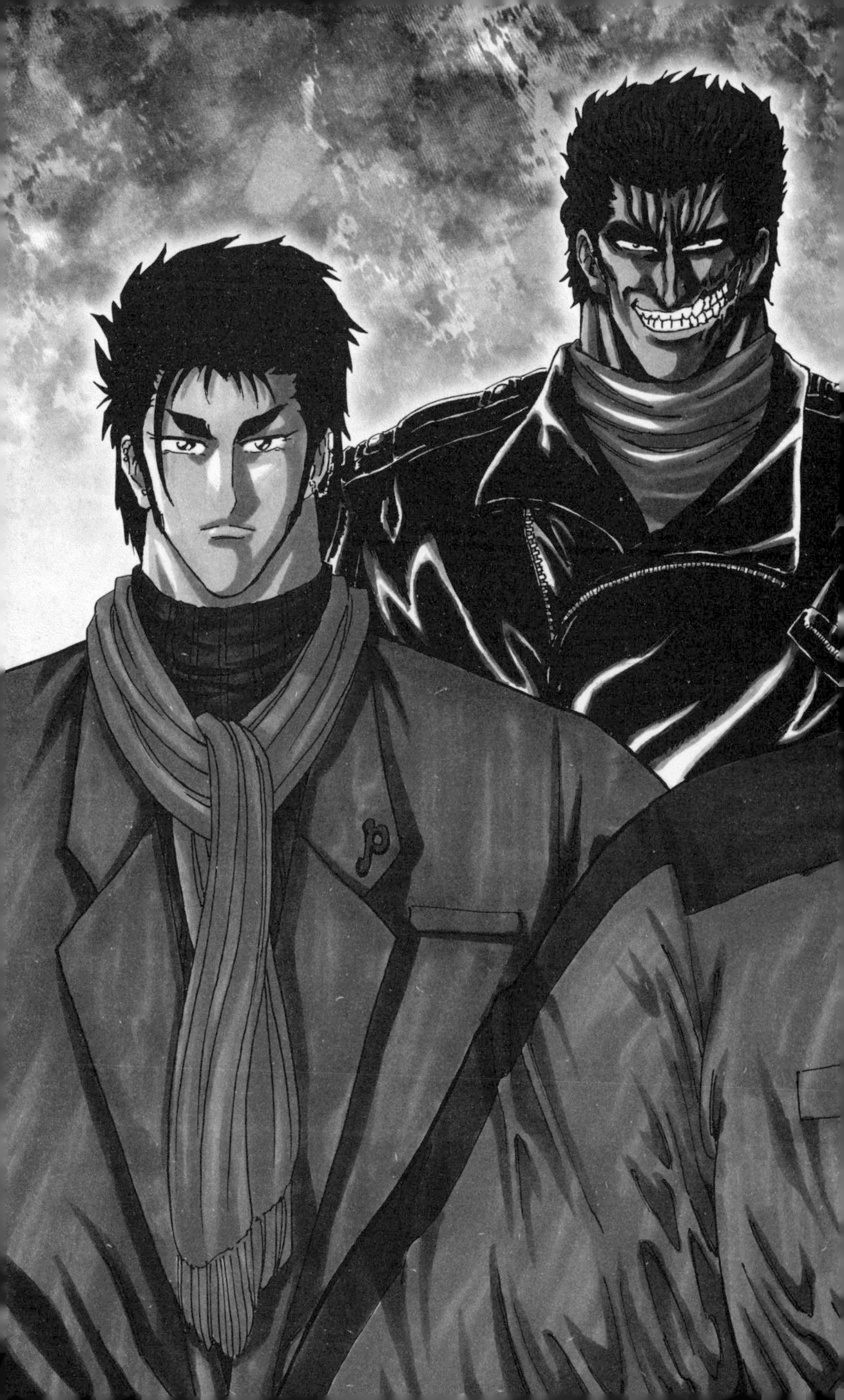

TORIKO

GOURMET CHECKLIST

Vol. 201

MELLOW COLA
(BEVERAGE)

CAPTURE LEVEL: 92

HABITAT: SALAMANDER SPHINX

LENGTH: ---

HEIGHT: ---

WEIGHT: ---

PRICE: 350 ML CAN / 1.2 MILLION YEN

SCALE

MELLOW COLA IS THE SALAMANDER SPHINX'S TEARS. TO GET TECHNICAL, MELLOW COLA IS THE D-GLUCOSE STORED IN THE SALAMANDER SPHINX'S LACRIMAL GLANDS. NOT ONLY DOES THE SPHINX HAVE A HIGH CAPTURE LEVEL, BUT LIKE THE OTHER BEASTS THAT RESIDE WITHIN GOURMET PYRAMID, UNLESS IT TAKES DAMAGE IN A PRECISE ORDER AND BY A CERTAIN TECHNIQUE, IT WON'T YIELD ITS TASTY SPOILS. IN THE SPHINX'S CASE, WITHOUT THE PROPER PRECISE POUNDING, ITS LACRIMAL GLANDS WON'T BE STIMULATED ENOUGH TO RELEASE MELLOW COLA. IF THAT WASN'T HARD ENOUGH, YOU NEED INCREDIBLE STRENGTH TO PULL THE ATTACKS OFF! BECAUSE IT'S SO RARE AND SO DELICIOUS, MELLOW COLA REALLY IS THE WORLD'S BEST COLA. IT IS ALSO THE FIRST ITEM ZEBRA PUT IN HIS FULL-COURSE MEAL.

GOURMET 173: GOURMET SANTA!!

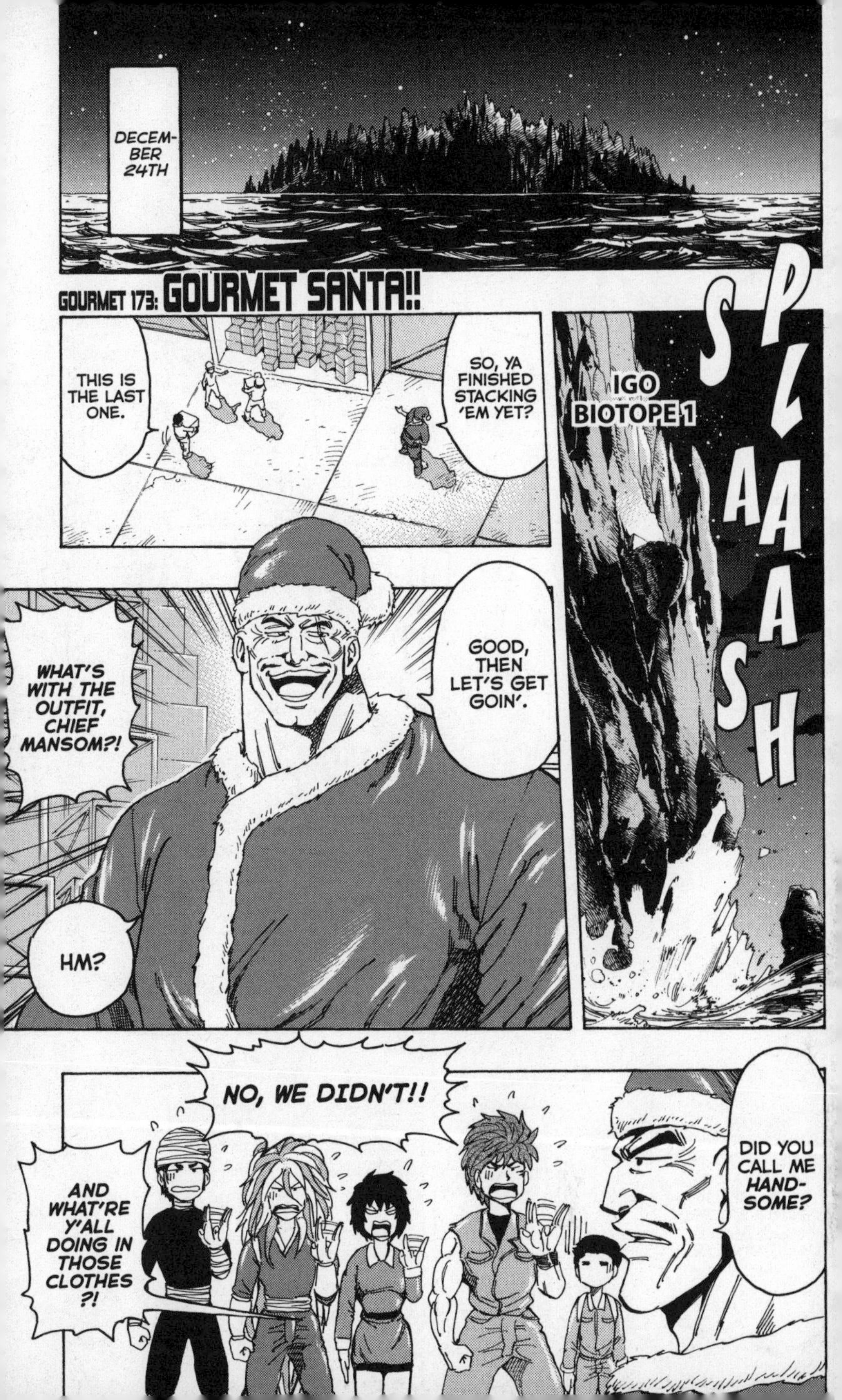
DECEMBER 24TH
IGO BIOTOPE 1
SPLAAASH
SO, YA FINISHED STACKING 'EM YET?
THIS IS THE LAST ONE.
GOOD, THEN LET'S GET GOIN'.
WHAT'S WITH THE OUTFIT, CHIEF MANSOM?!
HM?
DID YOU CALL ME HANDSOME?
NO, WE DIDN'T!!
AND WHAT'RE Y'ALL DOING IN THOSE CLOTHES?!

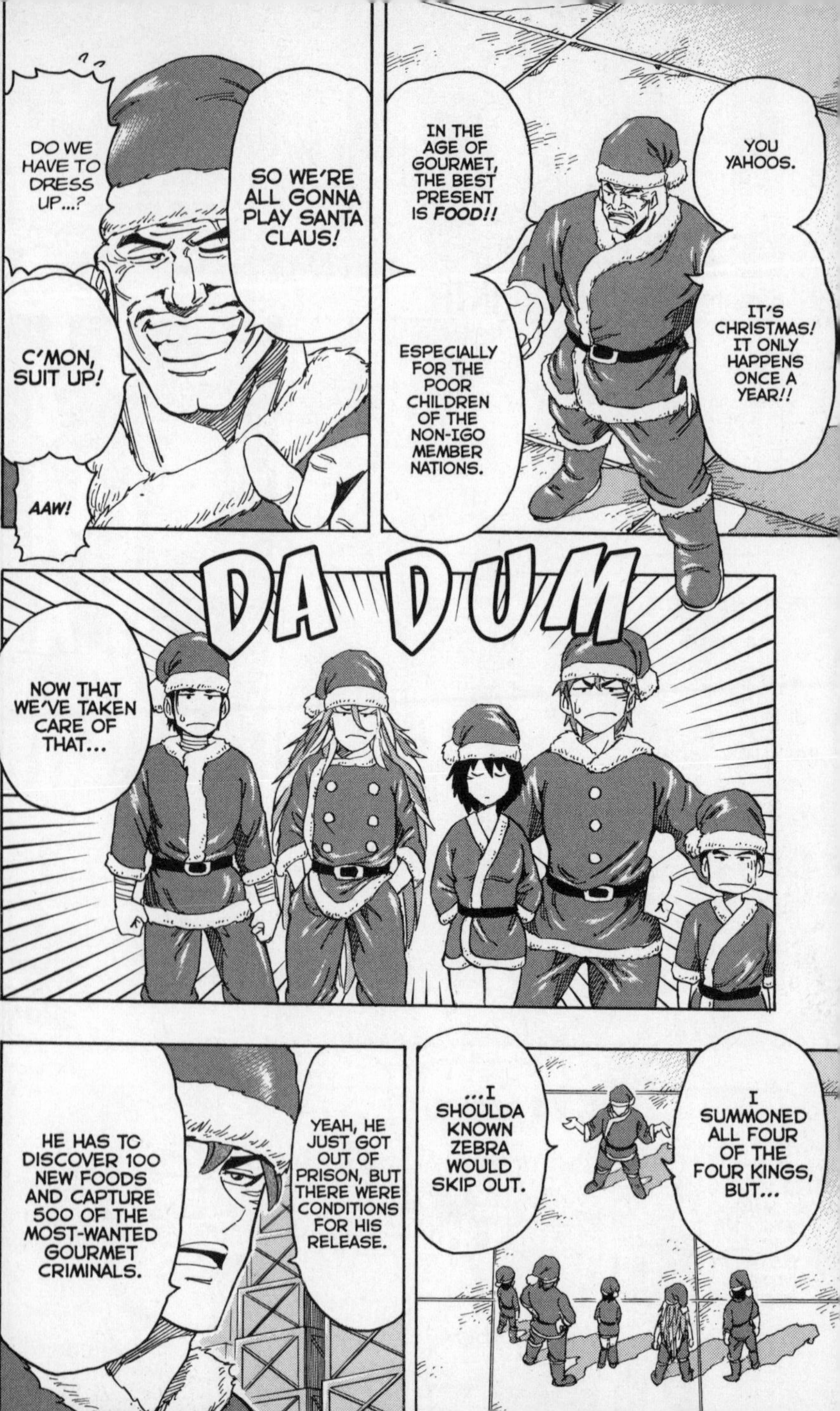
YOU YAHOOS.
IT'S CHRISTMAS! IT ONLY HAPPENS ONCE A YEAR!!
IN THE AGE OF GOURMET, THE BEST PRESENT IS *FOOD!!*
ESPECIALLY FOR THE POOR CHILDREN OF THE NON-IGO MEMBER NATIONS.
SO WE'RE ALL GONNA PLAY SANTA CLAUS!
DO WE HAVE TO DRESS UP...?
C'MON, SUIT UP!
AAW!
DA DUM
NOW THAT WE'VE TAKEN CARE OF THAT...
I SUMMONED ALL FOUR OF THE FOUR KINGS, BUT...
...I SHOULDA KNOWN ZEBRA WOULD SKIP OUT.
YEAH, HE JUST GOT OUT OF PRISON, BUT THERE WERE CONDITIONS FOR HIS RELEASE.
HE HAS TO DISCOVER 100 NEW FOODS AND CAPTURE 500 OF THE MOST-WANTED GOURMET CRIMINALS.

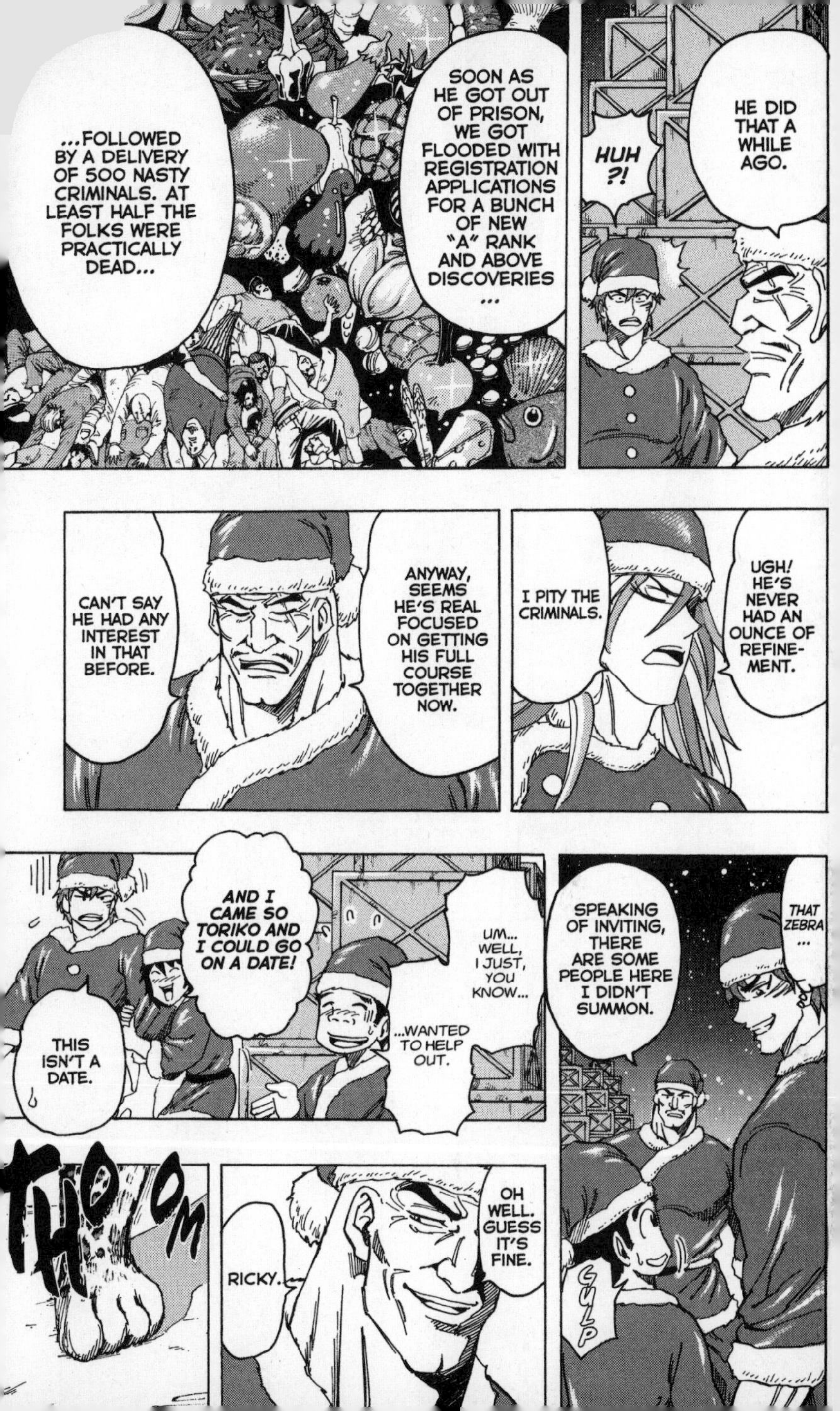
HE DID THAT A WHILE AGO.
HUH ?!
SOON AS HE GOT OUT OF PRISON, WE GOT FLOODED WITH REGISTRATION APPLICATIONS FOR A BUNCH OF NEW "A" RANK AND ABOVE DISCOVERIES ...
...FOLLOWED BY A DELIVERY OF 500 NASTY CRIMINALS. AT LEAST HALF THE FOLKS WERE PRACTICALLY DEAD...
UGH! HE'S NEVER HAD AN OUNCE OF REFINE- MENT.
I PITY THE CRIMINALS.
ANYWAY, SEEMS HE'S REAL FOCUSED ON GETTING HIS FULL COURSE TOGETHER NOW.
CAN'T SAY HE HAD ANY INTEREST IN THAT BEFORE.
THAT ZEBRA ...
SPEAKING OF INVITING, THERE ARE SOME PEOPLE HERE I DIDN'T SUMMON.
GULP
AND I CAME SO TORIKO AND I COULD GO ON A DATE!
UM... WELL, I JUST, YOU KNOW...
...WANTED TO HELP OUT.
THIS ISN'T A DATE.
OH WELL. GUESS IT'S FINE.
RICKY.
THOOM

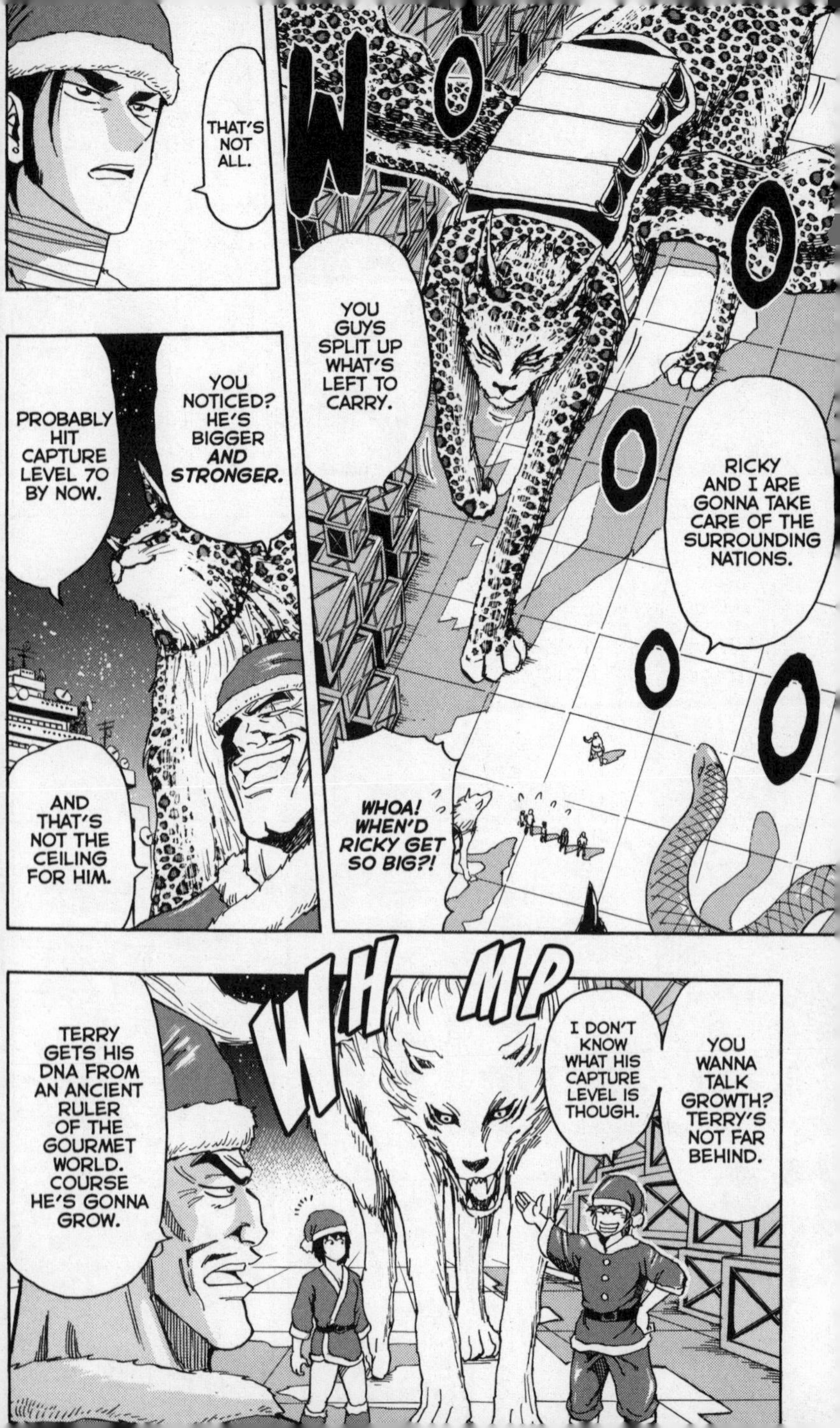
WOOOOOO
RICKY AND I ARE GONNA TAKE CARE OF THE SURROUNDING NATIONS.
YOU GUYS SPLIT UP WHAT'S LEFT TO CARRY.
WHOA! WHEN'D RICKY GET SO BIG?!
THAT'S NOT ALL.
YOU NOTICED? HE'S BIGGER AND STRONGER.
PROBABLY HIT CAPTURE LEVEL 70 BY NOW.
AND THAT'S NOT THE CEILING FOR HIM.
WHMP
YOU WANNA TALK GROWTH? TERRY'S NOT FAR BEHIND.
I DON'T KNOW WHAT HIS CAPTURE LEVEL IS THOUGH.
TERRY GETS HIS DNA FROM AN ANCIENT RULER OF THE GOURMET WORLD. COURSE HE'S GONNA GROW.

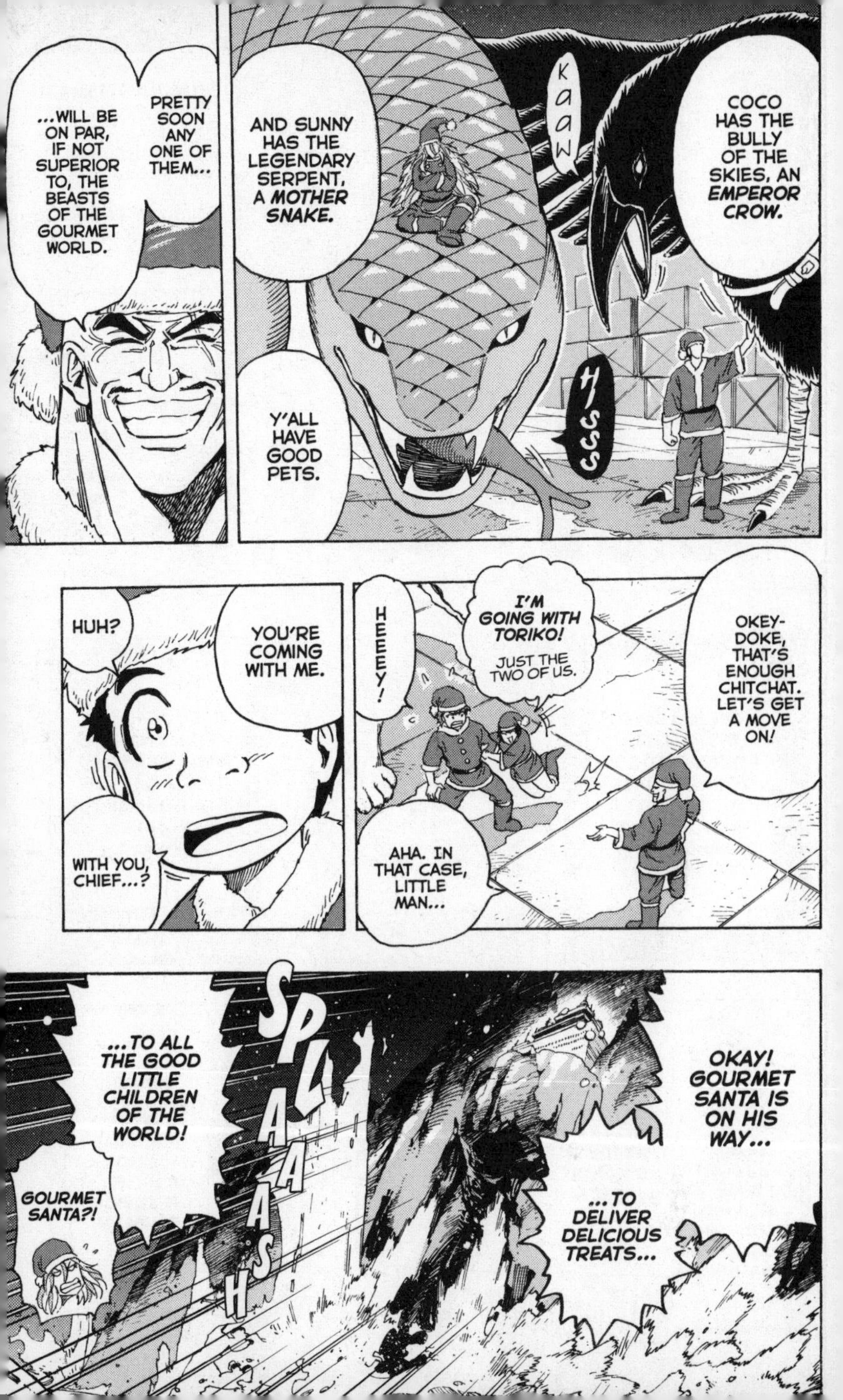

COCO HAS THE BULLY OF THE SKIES, AN *EMPEROR CROW.*
KAAW
AND SUNNY HAS THE LEGENDARY SERPENT, A *MOTHER SNAKE.*
HISSS
Y'ALL HAVE GOOD PETS.
PRETTY SOON ANY ONE OF THEM...
...WILL BE ON PAR, IF NOT SUPERIOR TO, THE BEASTS OF THE GOURMET WORLD.
OKEY-DOKE, THAT'S ENOUGH CHITCHAT. LET'S GET A MOVE ON!
I'M GOING WITH TORIKO!
JUST THE TWO OF US.
HEEEY!
AHA. IN THAT CASE, LITTLE MAN...
YOU'RE COMING WITH ME.
HUH?
WITH YOU, CHIEF...?
OKAY! GOURMET SANTA IS ON HIS WAY...
...TO DELIVER DELICIOUS TREATS...
SPLAAASH
...TO ALL THE GOOD LITTLE CHILDREN OF THE WORLD!
GOURMET SANTA?!

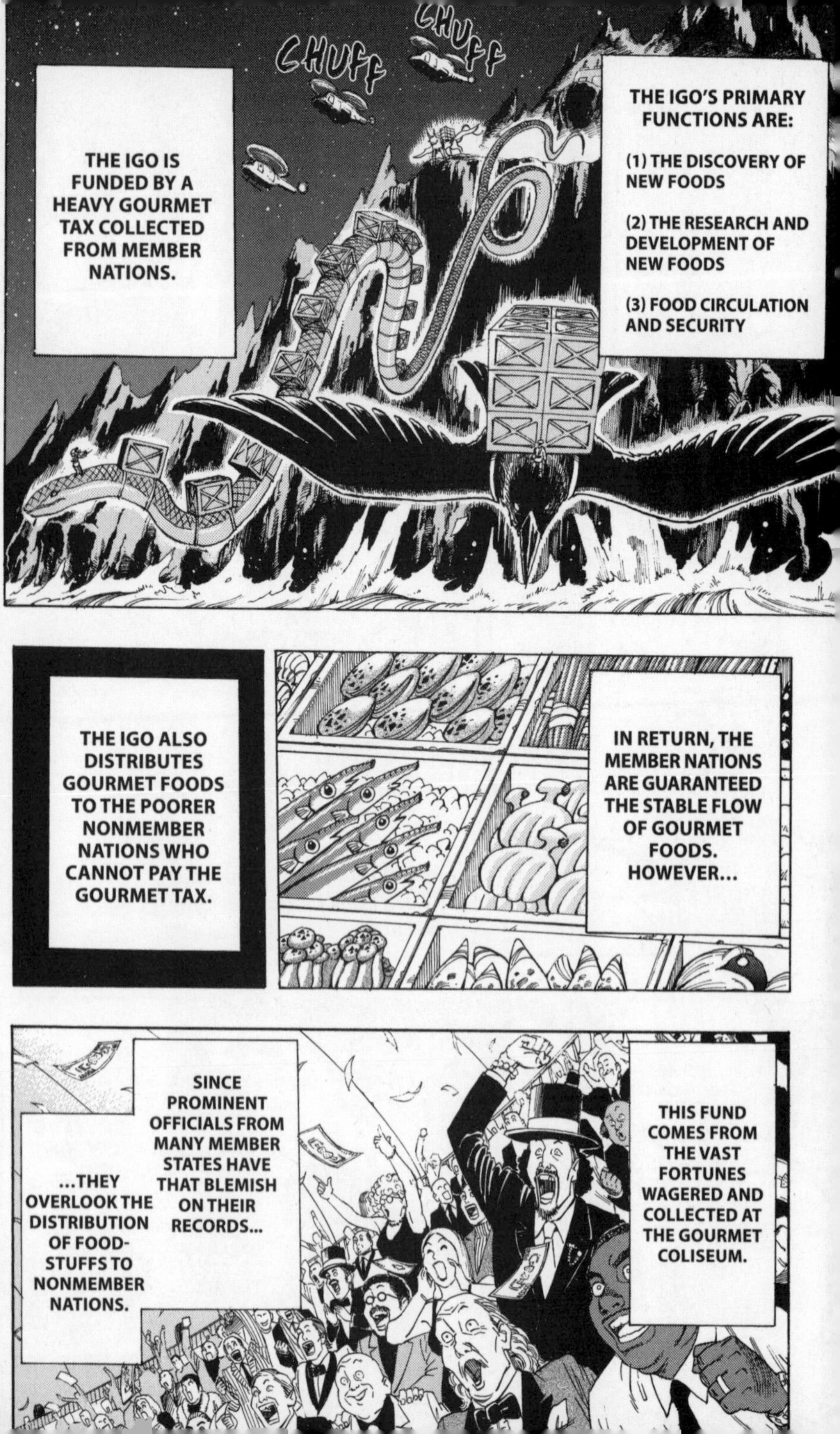
CHUFF
CHUFF
THE IGO'S PRIMARY FUNCTIONS ARE:
(1) THE DISCOVERY OF NEW FOODS
(2) THE RESEARCH AND DEVELOPMENT OF NEW FOODS
(3) FOOD CIRCULATION AND SECURITY
THE IGO IS FUNDED BY A HEAVY GOURMET TAX COLLECTED FROM MEMBER NATIONS.
IN RETURN, THE MEMBER NATIONS ARE GUARANTEED THE STABLE FLOW OF GOURMET FOODS. HOWEVER...
THE IGO ALSO DISTRIBUTES GOURMET FOODS TO THE POORER NONMEMBER NATIONS WHO CANNOT PAY THE GOURMET TAX.
THIS FUND COMES FROM THE VAST FORTUNES WAGERED AND COLLECTED AT THE GOURMET COLISEUM.
SINCE PROMINENT OFFICIALS FROM MANY MEMBER STATES HAVE THAT BLEMISH ON THEIR RECORDS...
...THEY OVERLOOK THE DISTRIBUTION OF FOOD-STUFFS TO NONMEMBER NATIONS.

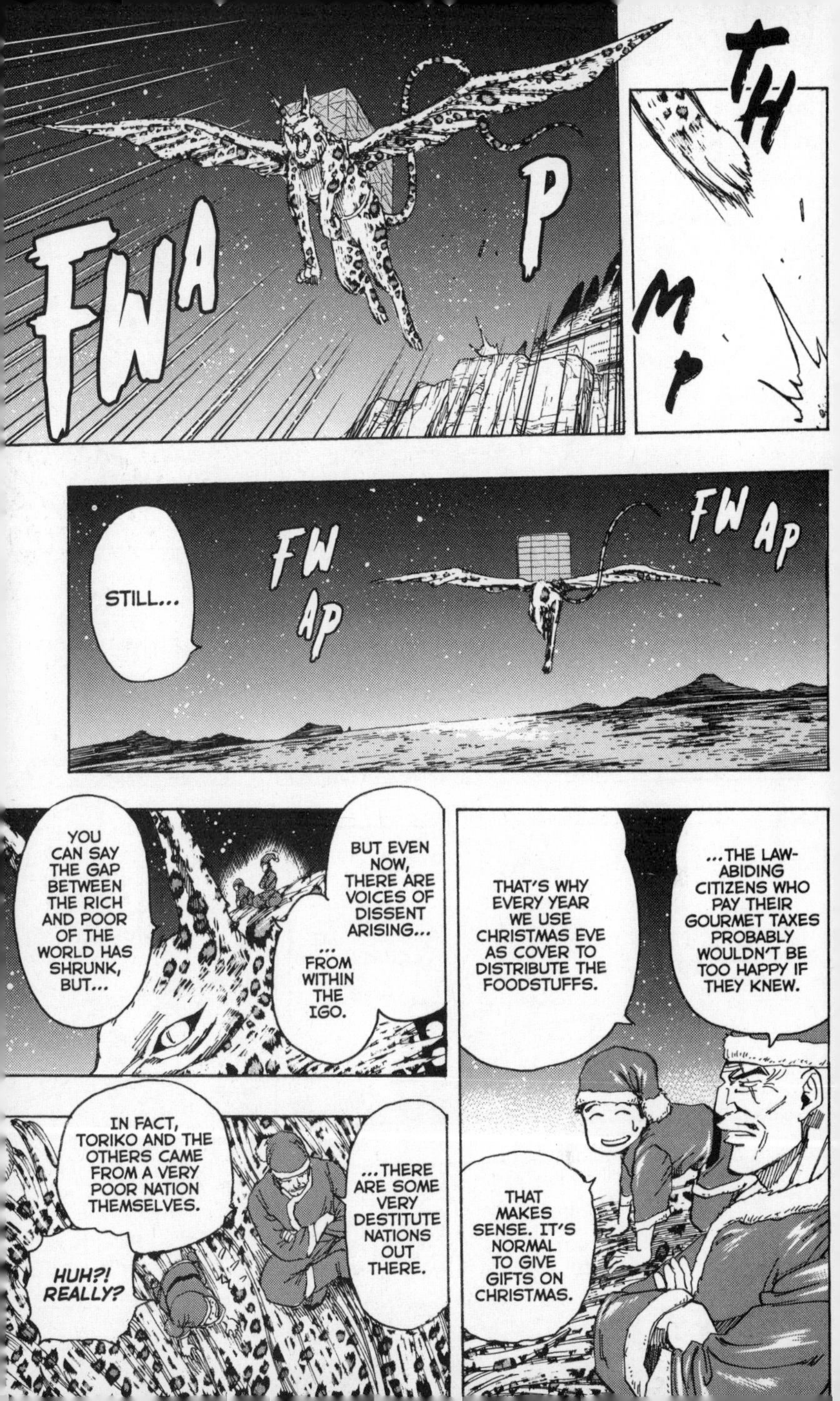
THMP
FWAP
STILL...
FWAP
FWAP
...THE LAW-ABIDING CITIZENS WHO PAY THEIR GOURMET TAXES PROBABLY WOULDN'T BE TOO HAPPY IF THEY KNEW.
THAT'S WHY EVERY YEAR WE USE CHRISTMAS EVE AS COVER TO DISTRIBUTE THE FOODSTUFFS.
THAT MAKES SENSE. IT'S NORMAL TO GIVE GIFTS ON CHRISTMAS.
YOU CAN SAY THE GAP BETWEEN THE RICH AND POOR OF THE WORLD HAS SHRUNK, BUT...
BUT EVEN NOW, THERE ARE VOICES OF DISSENT ARISING...
...FROM WITHIN THE IGO.
...THERE ARE SOME VERY DESTITUTE NATIONS OUT THERE.
IN FACT, TORIKO AND THE OTHERS CAME FROM A VERY POOR NATION THEMSELVES.
HUH?! REALLY?

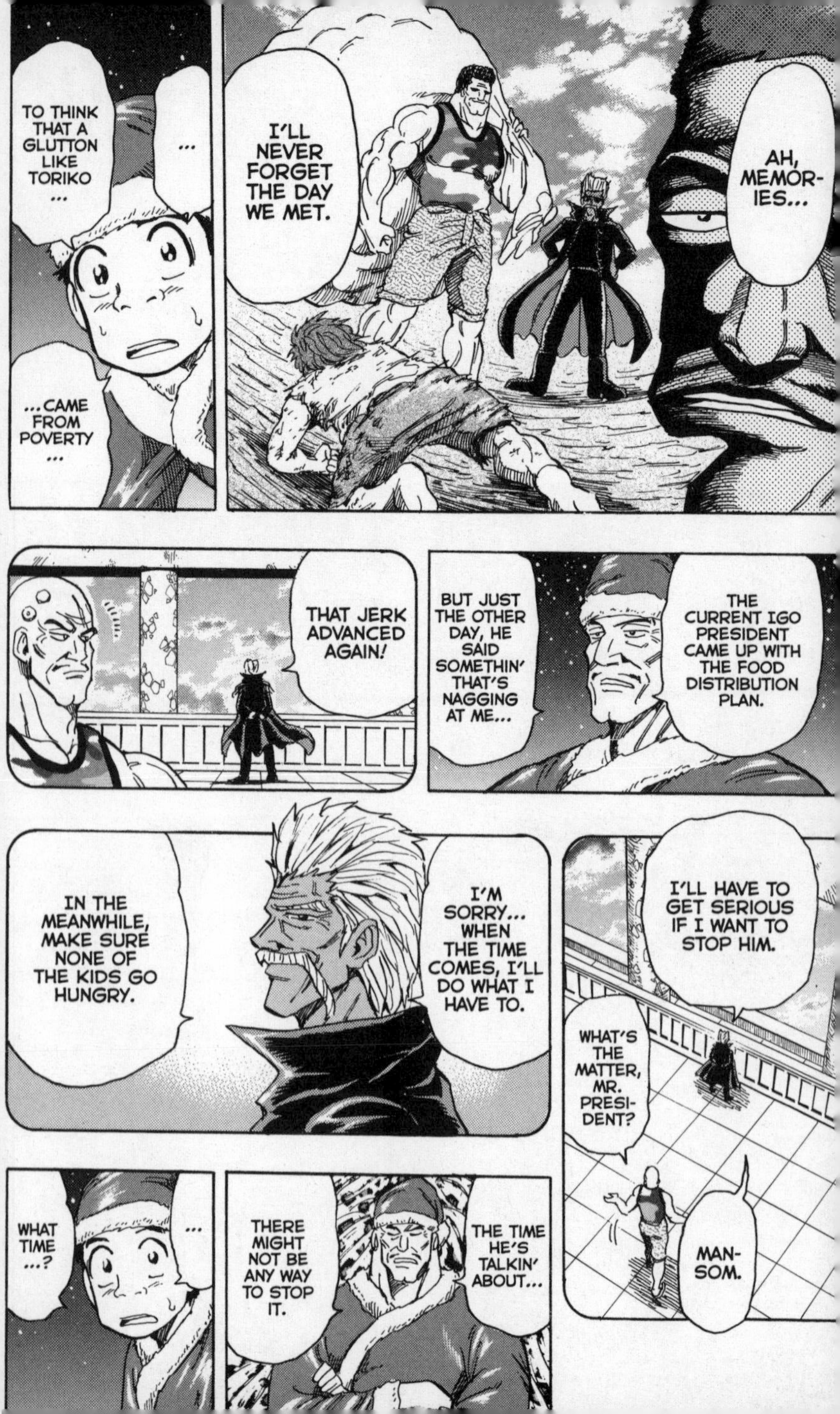
AH, MEMORIES...
I'LL NEVER FORGET THE DAY WE MET.
...
TO THINK THAT A GLUTTON LIKE TORIKO...
...CAME FROM POVERTY...
THE CURRENT IGO PRESIDENT CAME UP WITH THE FOOD DISTRIBUTION PLAN.
BUT JUST THE OTHER DAY, HE SAID SOMETHIN' THAT'S NAGGING AT ME...
THAT JERK ADVANCED AGAIN!
I'LL HAVE TO GET SERIOUS IF I WANT TO STOP HIM.
WHAT'S THE MATTER, MR. PRESIDENT?
MAN-SOM.
I'M SORRY... WHEN THE TIME COMES, I'LL DO WHAT I HAVE TO.
IN THE MEANWHILE, MAKE SURE NONE OF THE KIDS GO HUNGRY.
THE TIME HE'S TALKIN' ABOUT...
THERE MIGHT NOT BE ANY WAY TO STOP IT.
...
WHAT TIME...?

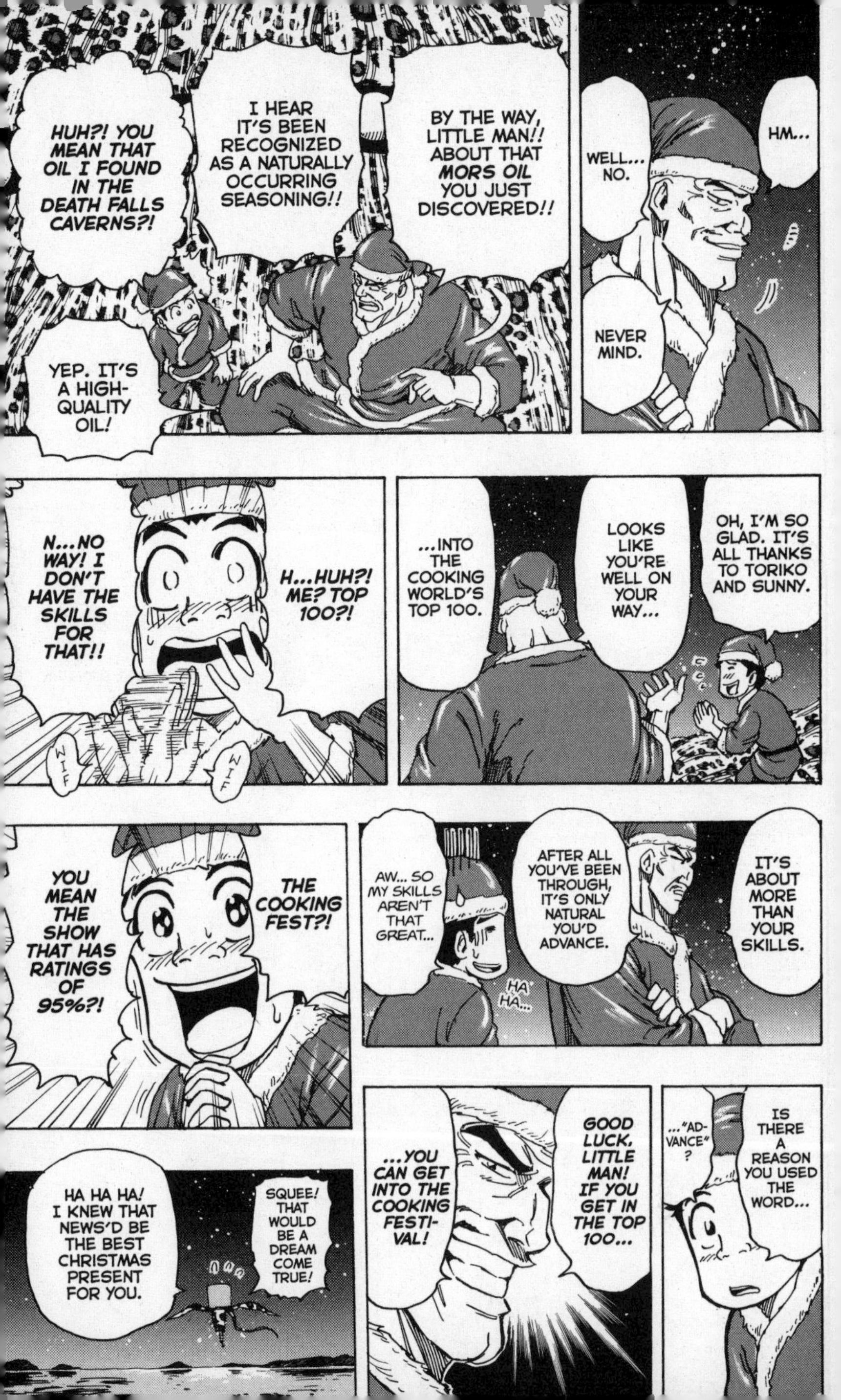
HM...
WELL... NO.
NEVER MIND.
BY THE WAY, LITTLE MAN!! ABOUT THAT MORS OIL YOU JUST DISCOVERED!!
I HEAR IT'S BEEN RECOGNIZED AS A NATURALLY OCCURRING SEASONING!!
HUH?! YOU MEAN THAT OIL I FOUND IN THE DEATH FALLS CAVERNS?!
YEP. IT'S A HIGH-QUALITY OIL!
OH, I'M SO GLAD. IT'S ALL THANKS TO TORIKO AND SUNNY.
LOOKS LIKE YOU'RE WELL ON YOUR WAY...
...INTO THE COOKING WORLD'S TOP 100.
H...HUH?! ME? TOP 100?!
N...NO WAY! I DON'T HAVE THE SKILLS FOR THAT!!
WIF
WIF
IT'S ABOUT MORE THAN YOUR SKILLS.
AFTER ALL YOU'VE BEEN THROUGH, IT'S ONLY NATURAL YOU'D ADVANCE.
AW... SO MY SKILLS AREN'T THAT GREAT...
HA HA...
IS THERE A REASON YOU USED THE WORD...
..."ADVANCE"?
GOOD LUCK, LITTLE MAN! IF YOU GET IN THE TOP 100...
...YOU CAN GET INTO THE COOKING FESTI-VAL!
THE COOKING FEST?!
YOU MEAN THE SHOW THAT HAS RATINGS OF 95%?!
SQUEE! THAT WOULD BE A DREAM COME TRUE!
HA HA HA! I KNEW THAT NEWS'D BE THE BEST CHRISTMAS PRESENT FOR YOU.

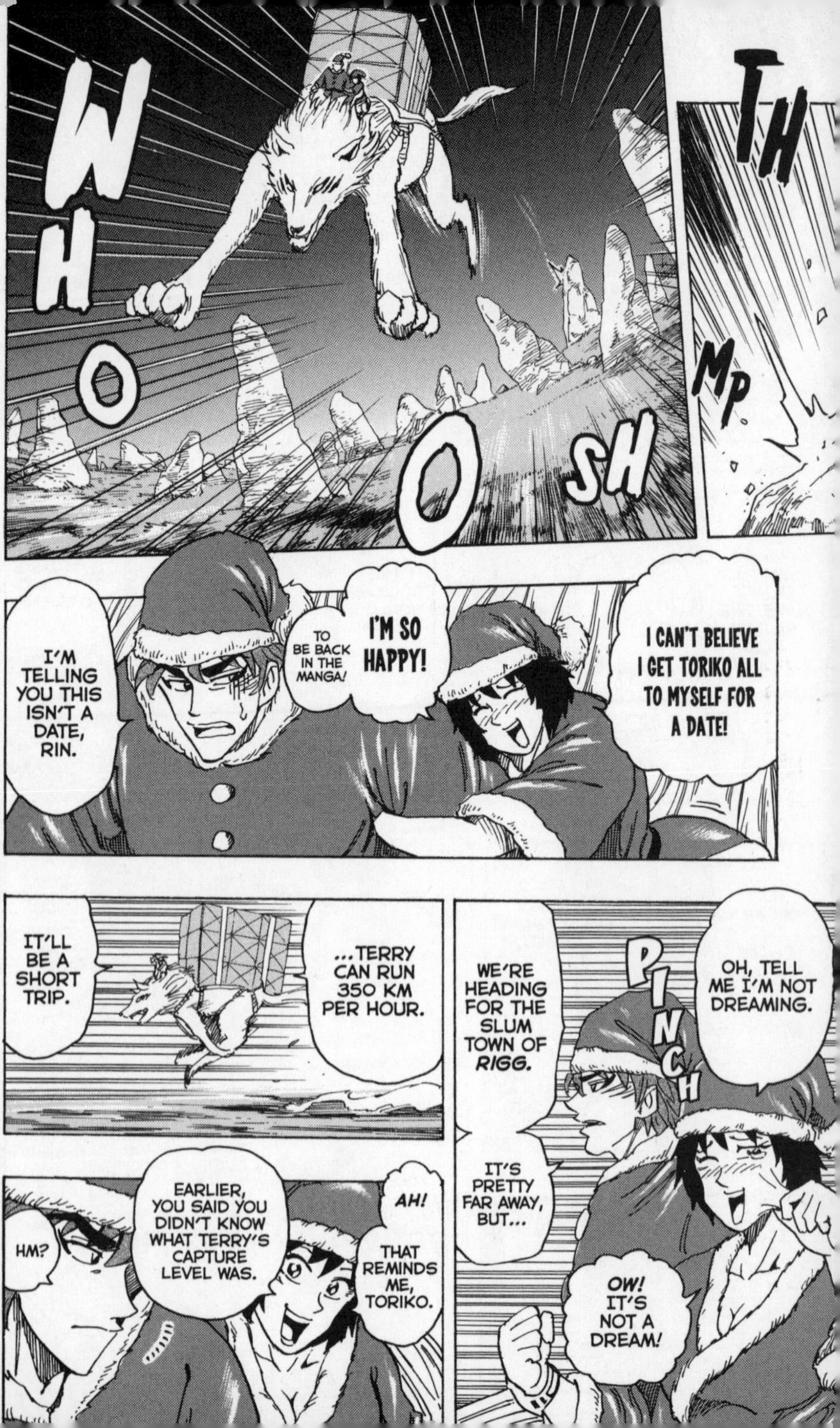
THUMP
WHOOOSH
I CAN'T BELIEVE I GET TORIKO ALL TO MYSELF FOR A DATE!
I'M SO HAPPY!
TO BE BACK IN THE MANGA!
I'M TELLING YOU THIS ISN'T A DATE, RIN.
OH, TELL ME I'M NOT DREAMING.
PINCH
WE'RE HEADING FOR THE SLUM TOWN OF *RIGG.*
IT'S PRETTY FAR AWAY, BUT...
OW! IT'S NOT A DREAM!
...TERRY CAN RUN 350 KM PER HOUR.
IT'LL BE A SHORT TRIP.
AH!
THAT REMINDS ME, TORIKO.
EARLIER, YOU SAID YOU DIDN'T KNOW WHAT TERRY'S CAPTURE LEVEL WAS.
HM?

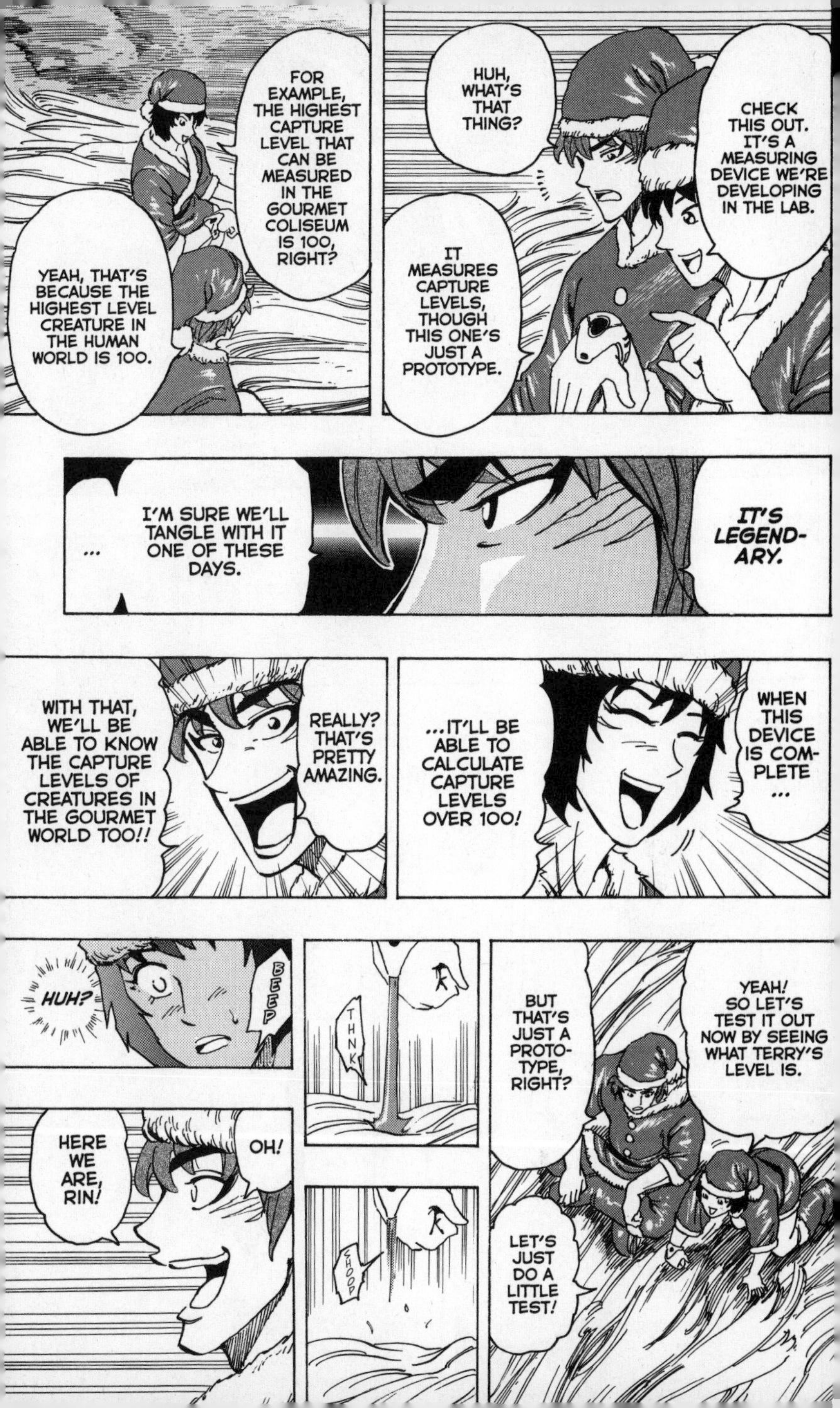

CHECK THIS OUT. IT'S A MEASURING DEVICE WE'RE DEVELOPING IN THE LAB.
HUH, WHAT'S THAT THING?
IT MEASURES CAPTURE LEVELS, THOUGH THIS ONE'S JUST A PROTOTYPE.
FOR EXAMPLE, THE HIGHEST CAPTURE LEVEL THAT CAN BE MEASURED IN THE GOURMET COLISEUM IS 100, RIGHT?
YEAH, THAT'S BECAUSE THE HIGHEST LEVEL CREATURE IN THE HUMAN WORLD IS 100.
IT'S LEGENDARY.
I'M SURE WE'LL TANGLE WITH IT ONE OF THESE DAYS.
...
WHEN THIS DEVICE IS COMPLETE...
...IT'LL BE ABLE TO CALCULATE CAPTURE LEVELS OVER 100!
REALLY? THAT'S PRETTY AMAZING.
WITH THAT, WE'LL BE ABLE TO KNOW THE CAPTURE LEVELS OF CREATURES IN THE GOURMET WORLD TOO!!
YEAH! SO LET'S TEST IT OUT NOW BY SEEING WHAT TERRY'S LEVEL IS.
BUT THAT'S JUST A PROTOTYPE, RIGHT?
LET'S JUST DO A LITTLE TEST!
THNK
SHOOP
BEEP
HUH?
OH!
HERE WE ARE, RIN!

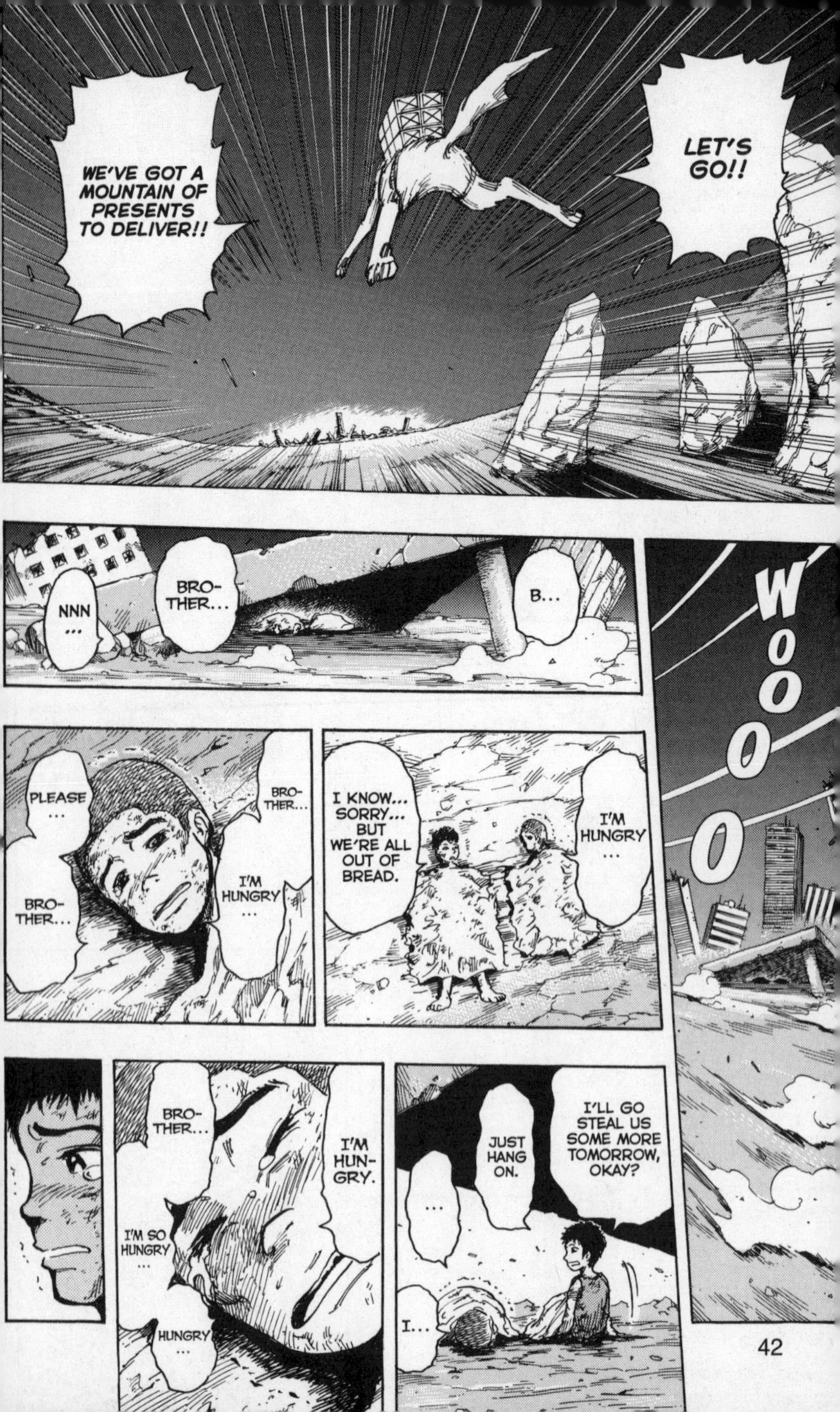
LET'S GO!!
WE'VE GOT A MOUNTAIN OF PRESENTS TO DELIVER!!
WOOOOO
B...
BROTHER...
NNN...
I'M HUNGRY...
I KNOW... SORRY... BUT WE'RE ALL OUT OF BREAD.
BROTHER...
I'M HUNGRY...
PLEASE...
BROTHER...
I'LL GO STEAL US SOME MORE TOMORROW, OKAY?
JUST HANG ON.
...
I...
I'M HUNGRY.
BROTHER...
I'M SO HUNGRY...
HUNGRY...

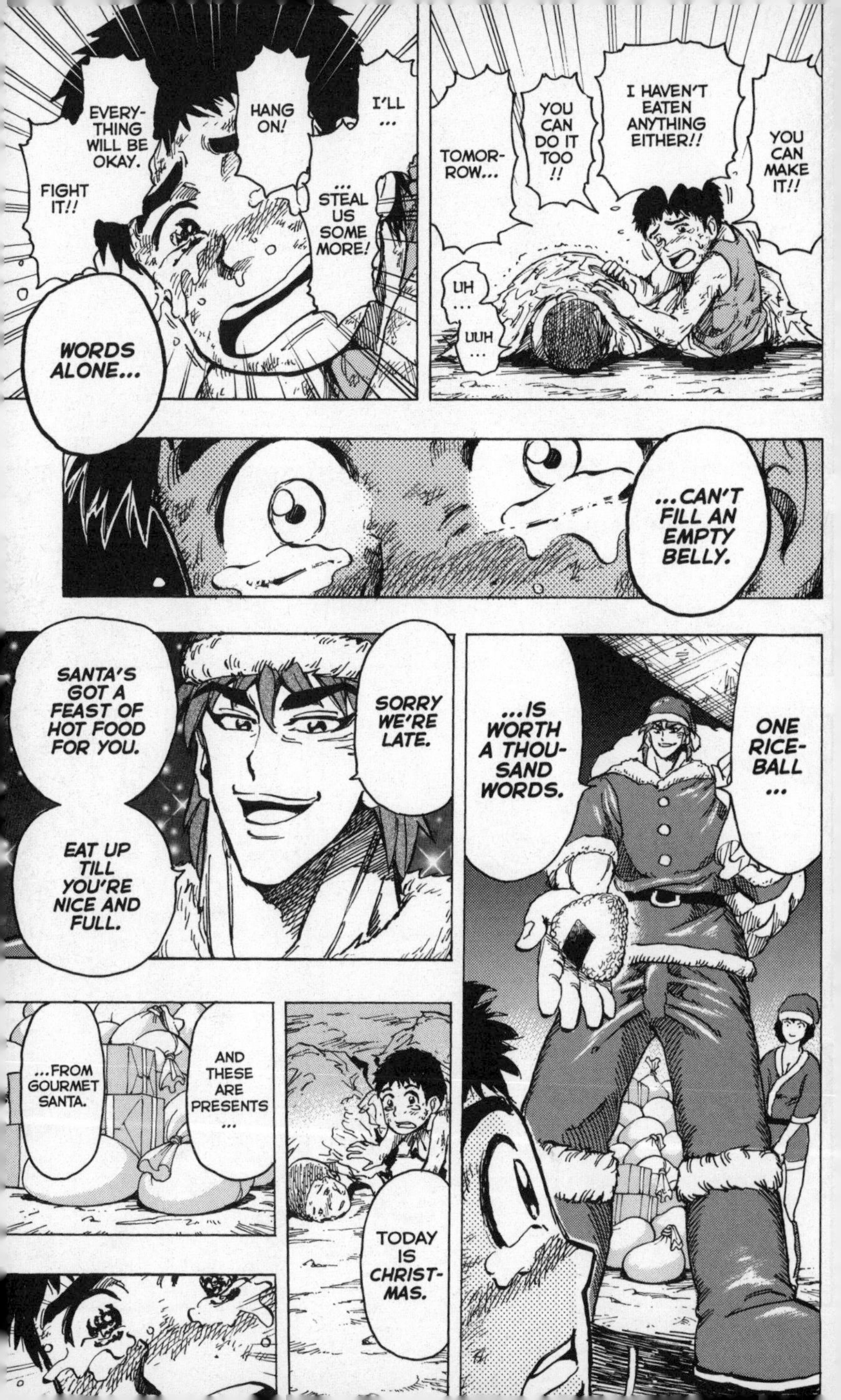
YOU CAN MAKE IT!!
I HAVEN'T EATEN ANYTHING EITHER!!
YOU CAN DO IT TOO!!
TOMORROW...
UH... UUH...
I'LL...
...STEAL US SOME MORE!
HANG ON!
EVERYTHING WILL BE OKAY.
FIGHT IT!!
WORDS ALONE...
...CAN'T FILL AN EMPTY BELLY.
ONE RICE-BALL...
...IS WORTH A THOUSAND WORDS.
SORRY WE'RE LATE.
SANTA'S GOT A FEAST OF HOT FOOD FOR YOU.
EAT UP TILL YOU'RE NICE AND FULL.
TODAY IS CHRISTMAS.
AND THESE ARE PRESENTS...
...FROM GOURMET SANTA.

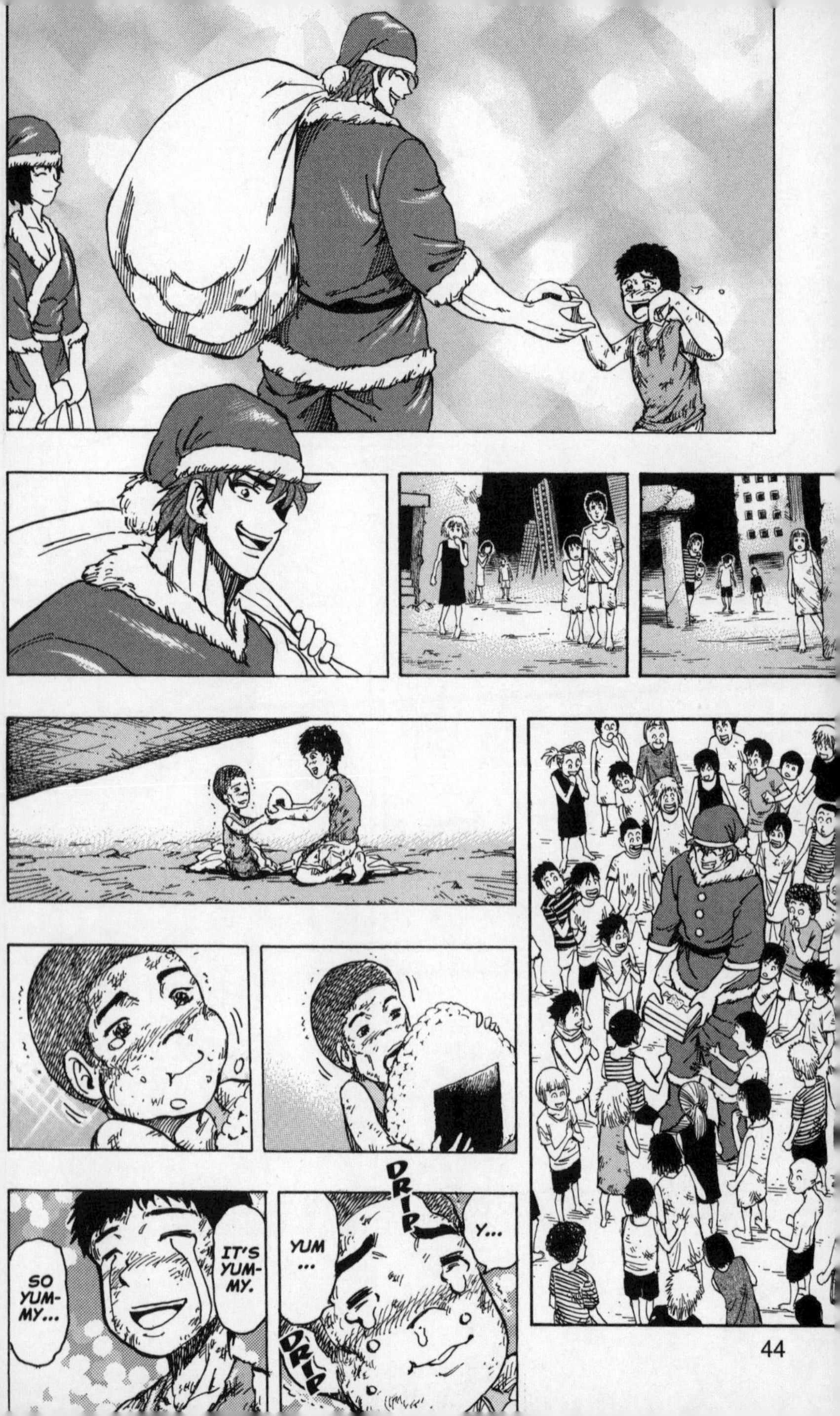
DRIP
Y...
YUM ...
DRIP
IT'S YUMMY.
SO YUMMY...

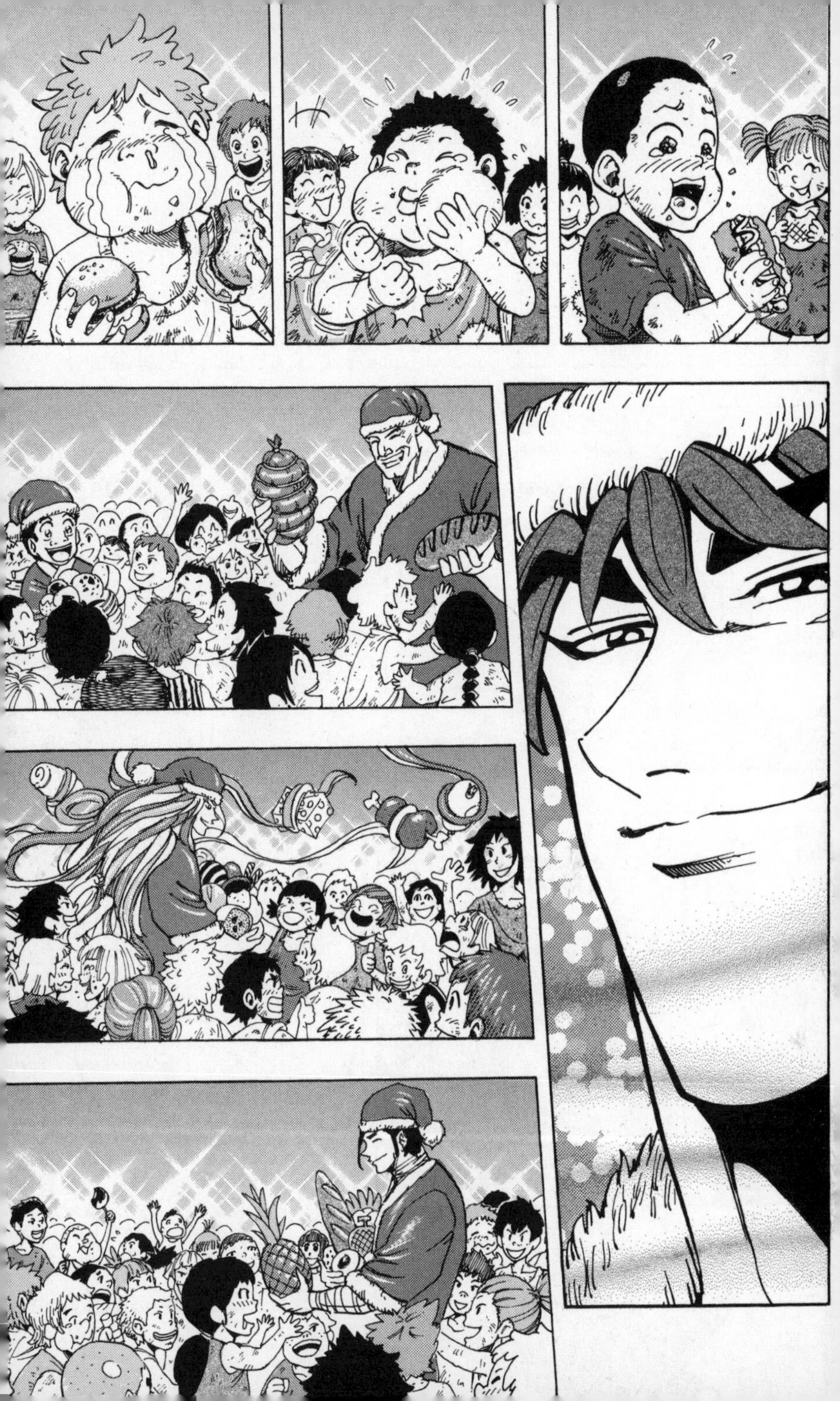

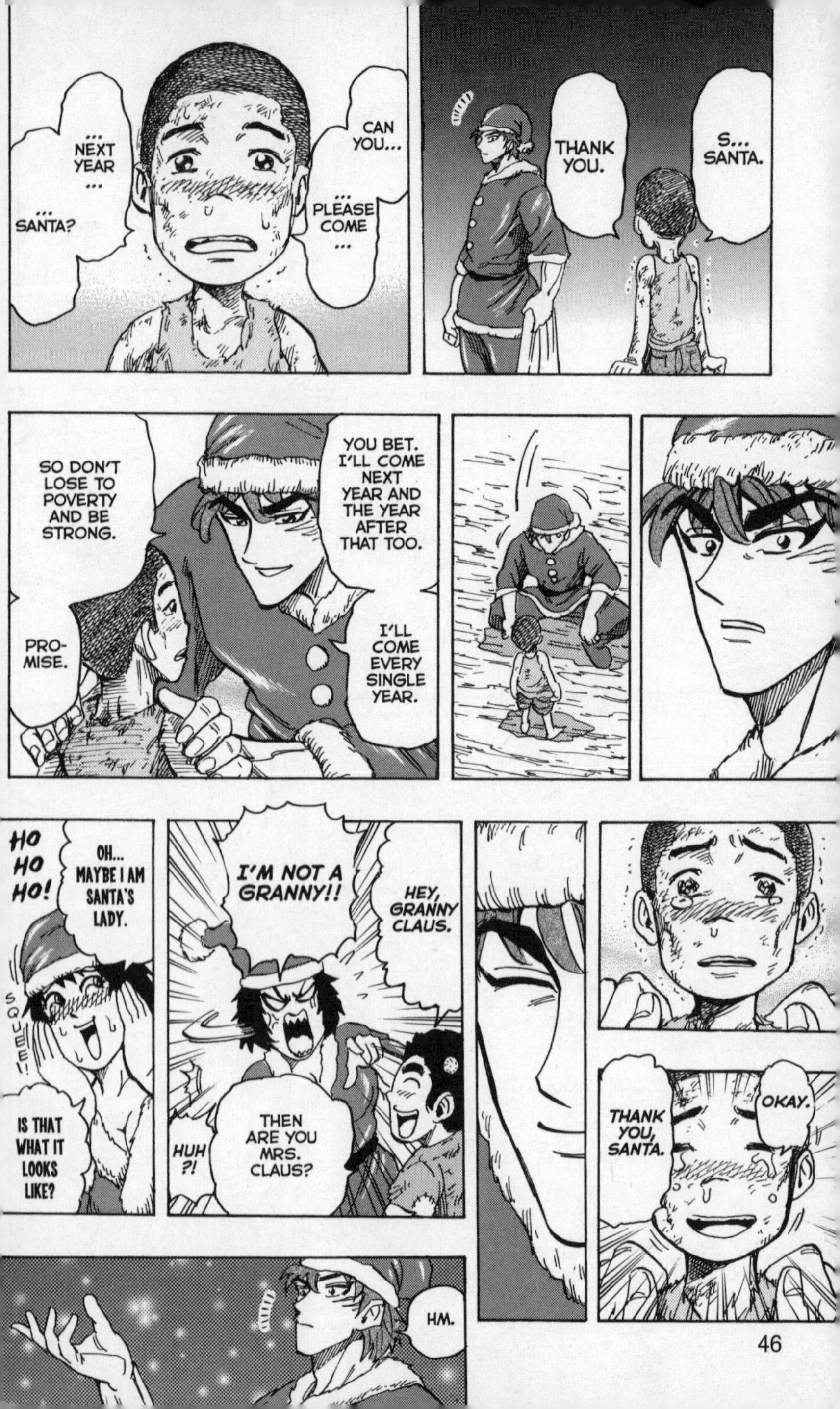
S... SANTA.
THANK YOU.
CAN YOU...
...PLEASE COME...
...NEXT YEAR...
...SANTA?
YOU BET. I'LL COME NEXT YEAR AND THE YEAR AFTER THAT TOO.
I'LL COME EVERY SINGLE YEAR.
SO DON'T LOSE TO POVERTY AND BE STRONG.
PRO-MISE.
OKAY.
THANK YOU, SANTA.
HEY, GRANNY CLAUS.
I'M NOT A GRANNY!!
THEN ARE YOU MRS. CLAUS?
HUH ?!
HO HO HO!
OH... MAYBE I AM SANTA'S LADY.
SQUEE!
IS THAT WHAT IT LOOKS LIKE?
HM.

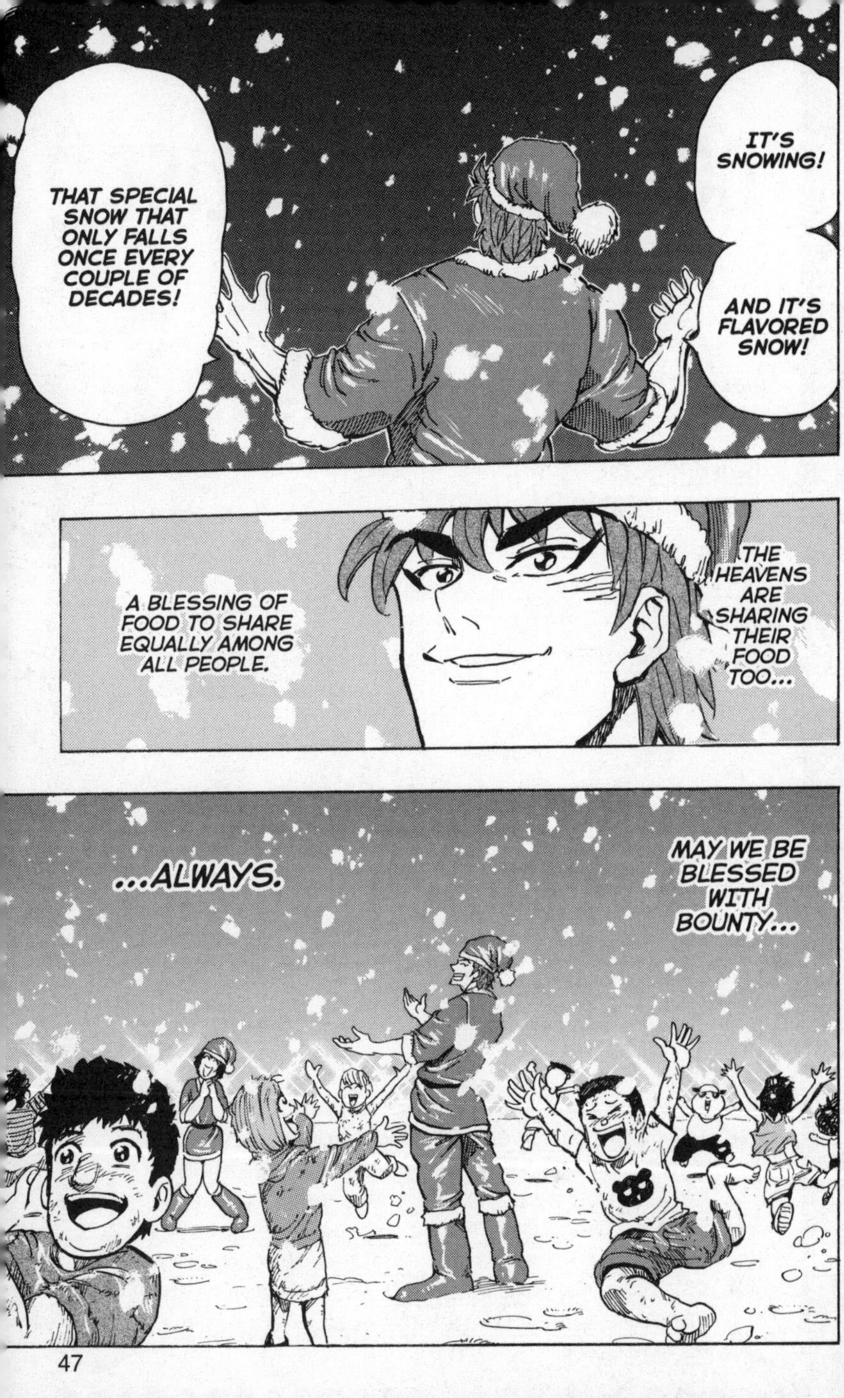
IT'S SNOWING!
AND IT'S FLAVORED SNOW!
THAT SPECIAL SNOW THAT ONLY FALLS ONCE EVERY COUPLE OF DECADES!
THE HEAVENS ARE SHARING THEIR FOOD TOO...
A BLESSING OF FOOD TO SHARE EQUALLY AMONG ALL PEOPLE.
MAY WE BE BLESSED WITH BOUNTY...
...ALWAYS.

TORIKO

GOURMET CHECKLIST

Vol. 202

JET BLACK RICE
(GRAIN)

CAPTURE LEVEL: 30
HABITAT: ARCTIC ZONES
LENGTH: ---
HEIGHT: ---
WEIGHT: ---
PRICE: 1 KG / 80,000 YEN

...WE SPRINKLE THAT ON THE JET BLACK RICE.

NEXT...

SHK SHK SHK

SCALE

A GRAIN THAT TYPICALLY GROWS ONLY IN ARCTIC CLIMATES. BECAUSE THE EXTREME COLD FORCES IT TO GROW SLOWLY, IT ABSORBS AND STORES AN ABUNDANCE OF NUTRIENTS, MAKING IT QUITE NUTRITIOUS. JET BLACK RICE TASTES SUPERB RAW, BAKED OR STEAMED. IT HAS A HIGHER SUGAR CONTENT THAN TYPICAL RICE, AS WELL AS A CRISPY CRUMBLINESS WHEN BAKED, AND A CHEWY GOODNESS WHEN BOILED. IT TASTES SO GOOD THAT YOU COULD GO FOR SECONDS, THIRDS...AND FOURTHS...WITHOUT HAVING A SINGLE SIDE DISH WITH IT. BUT WHEN SPRINKLED WITH SOMETHING LIKE JEWEL MEAT JERKY, YOU REALLY WON'T BE ABLE TO TEAR YOUR CHOPSTICKS AWAY.

GOURMET 174: MADAM FISH!!

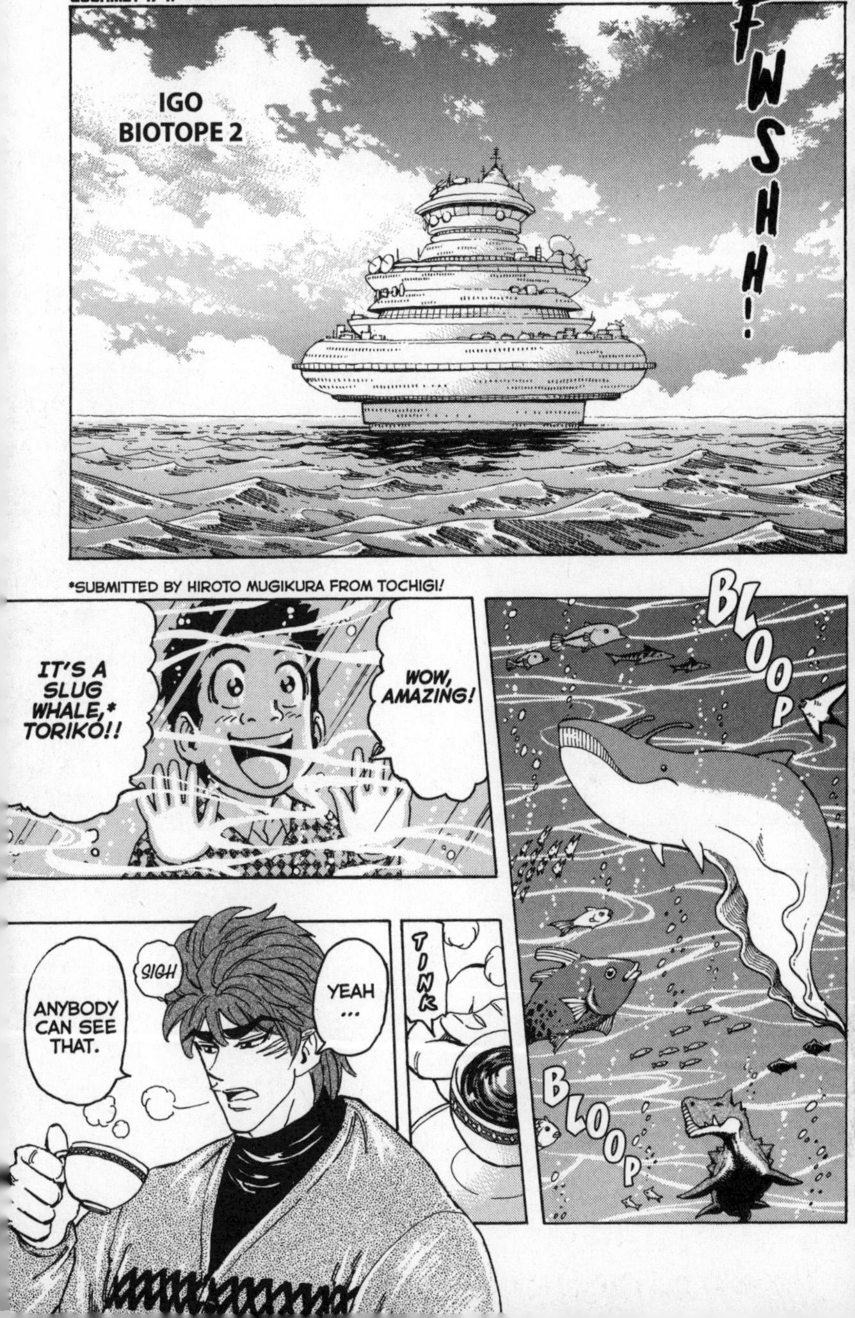
IGO BIOTOPE 2
FWSHH!
BLOOP
BLOOP
WOW, AMAZING!
IT'S A SLUG WHALE,* TORIKO!!
TINK
SIGH
YEAH...
ANYBODY CAN SEE THAT.
*SUBMITTED BY HIROTO MUGIKURA FROM TOCHIGI!

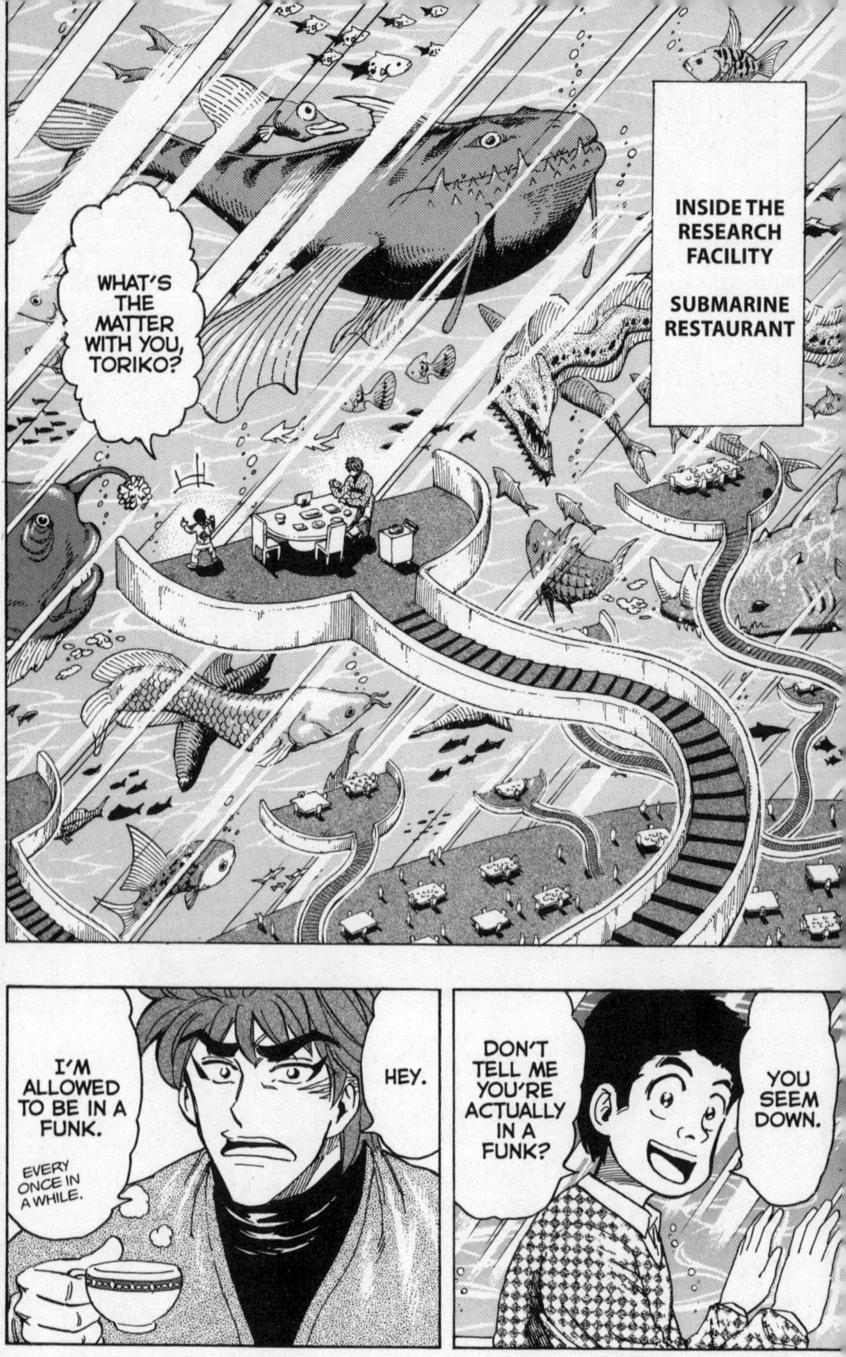
INSIDE THE RESEARCH FACILITY
SUBMARINE RESTAURANT
WHAT'S THE MATTER WITH YOU, TORIKO?
YOU SEEM DOWN.
DON'T TELL ME YOU'RE ACTUALLY IN A FUNK?
HEY.
I'M ALLOWED TO BE IN A FUNK.
EVERY ONCE IN A WHILE.

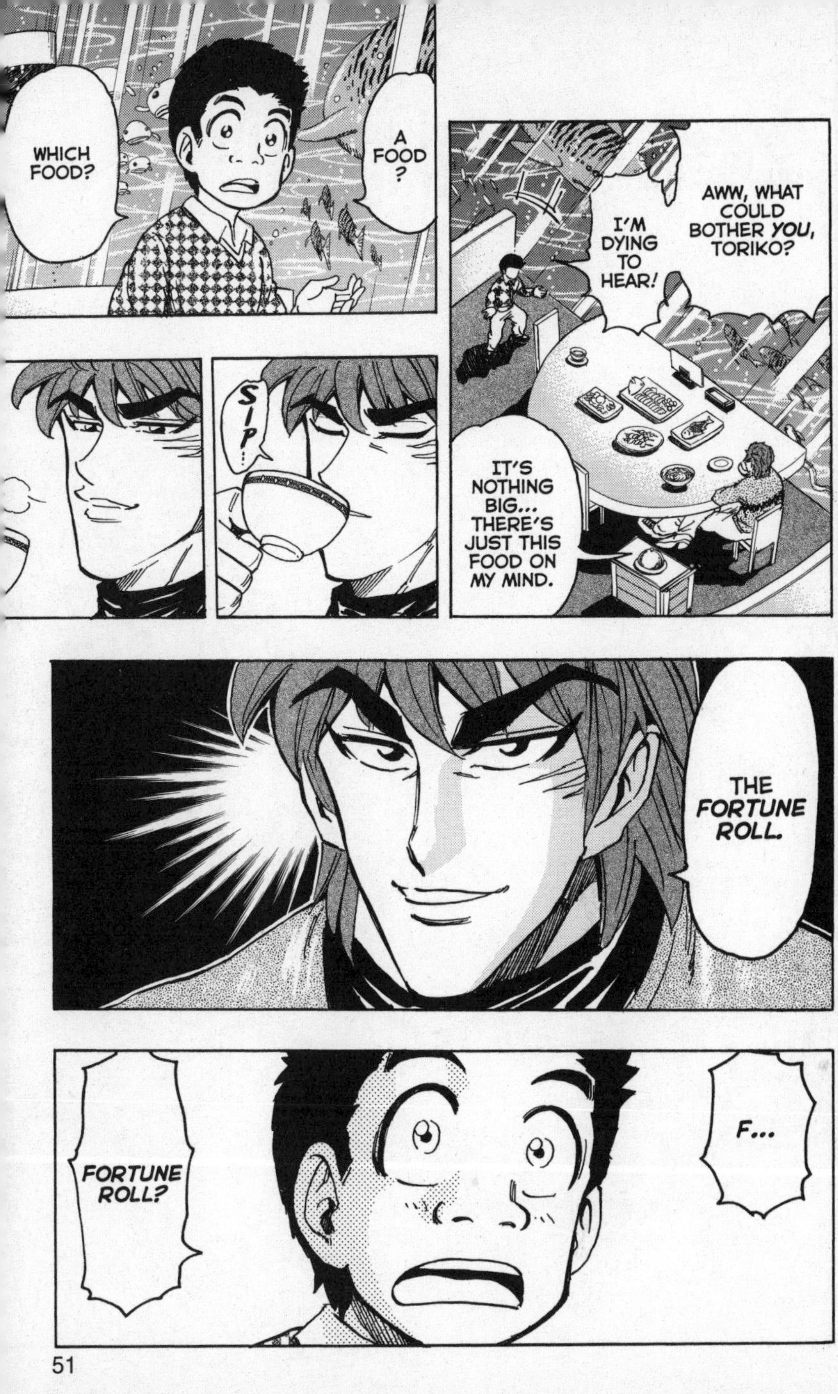
AWW, WHAT COULD BOTHER *YOU*, TORIKO?
I'M DYING TO HEAR!
IT'S NOTHING BIG... THERE'S JUST THIS FOOD ON MY MIND.
A FOOD?
WHICH FOOD?
SIP...
THE *FORTUNE ROLL*.
F...
FORTUNE ROLL?

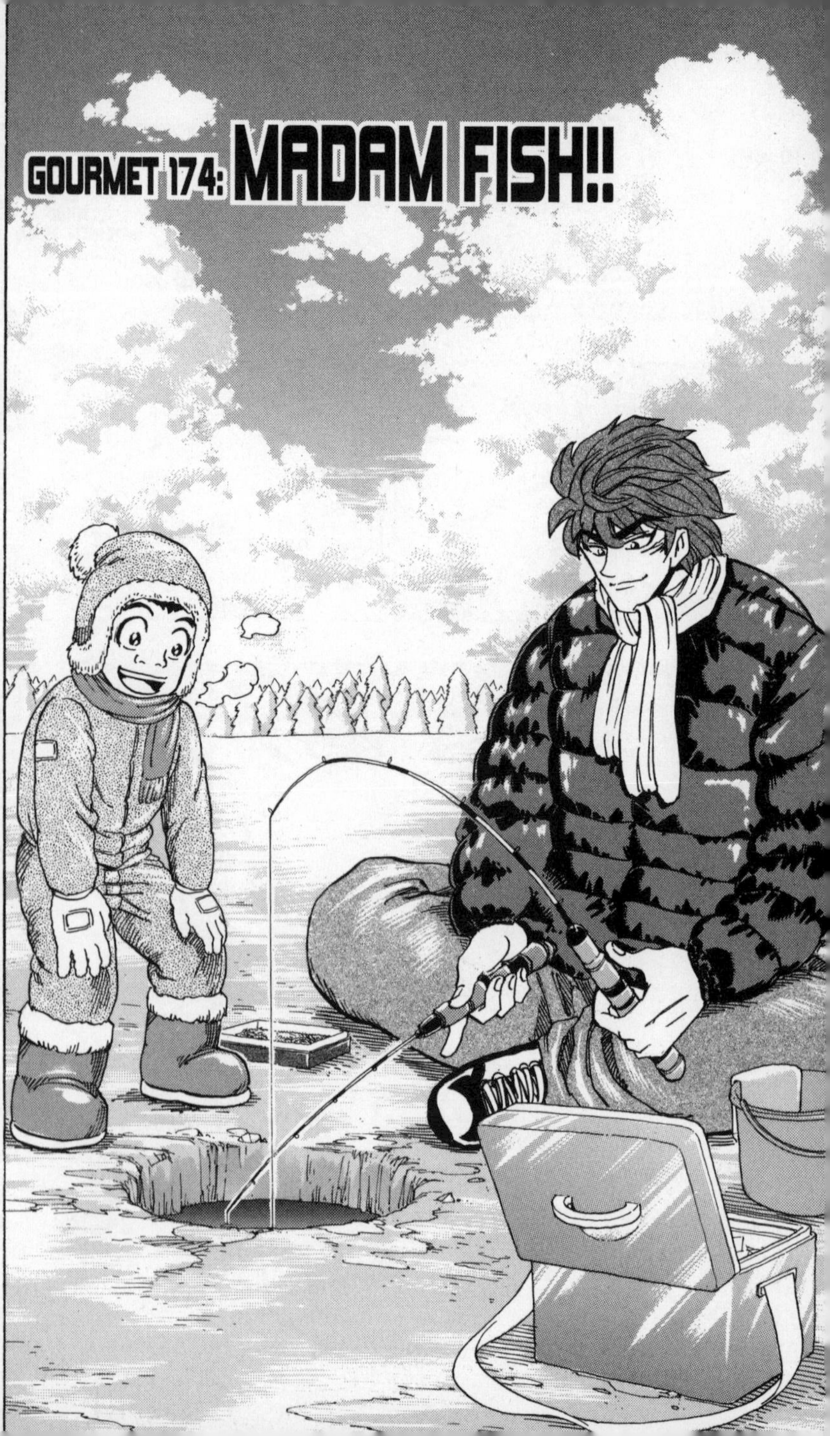
GOURMET 174: MADAM FISH!!

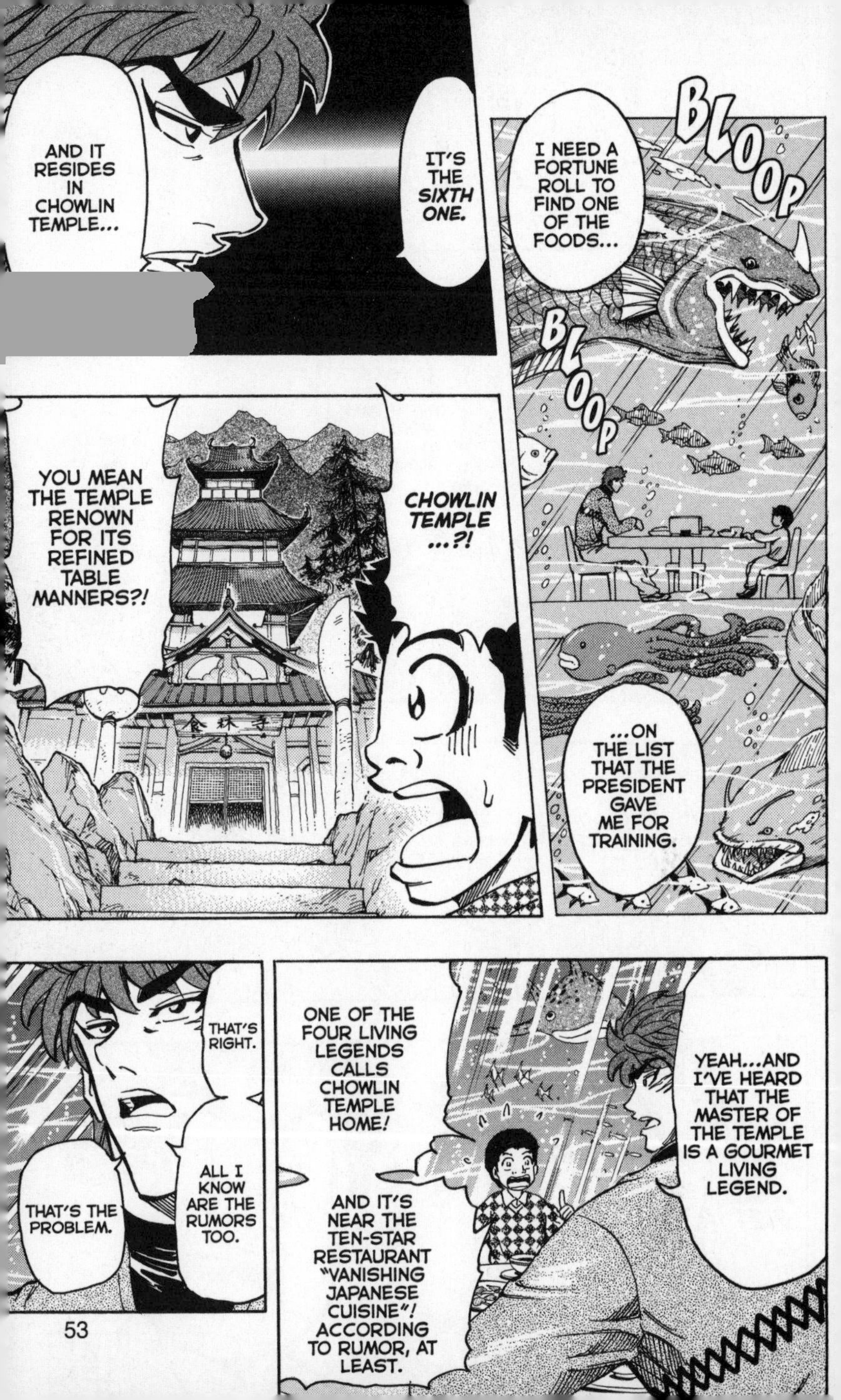

BLOOP
I NEED A FORTUNE ROLL TO FIND ONE OF THE FOODS...
BLOOP
...ON THE LIST THAT THE PRESIDENT GAVE ME FOR TRAINING.
IT'S THE SIXTH ONE.
AND IT RESIDES IN CHOWLIN TEMPLE...
CHOWLIN TEMPLE ...?!
YOU MEAN THE TEMPLE RENOWN FOR ITS REFINED TABLE MANNERS?!
食林寺
YEAH...AND I'VE HEARD THAT THE MASTER OF THE TEMPLE IS A GOURMET LIVING LEGEND.
ONE OF THE FOUR LIVING LEGENDS CALLS CHOWLIN TEMPLE HOME!
AND IT'S NEAR THE TEN-STAR RESTAURANT "VANISHING JAPANESE CUISINE"! ACCORDING TO RUMOR, AT LEAST.
THAT'S RIGHT.
ALL I KNOW ARE THE RUMORS TOO.
THAT'S THE PROBLEM.

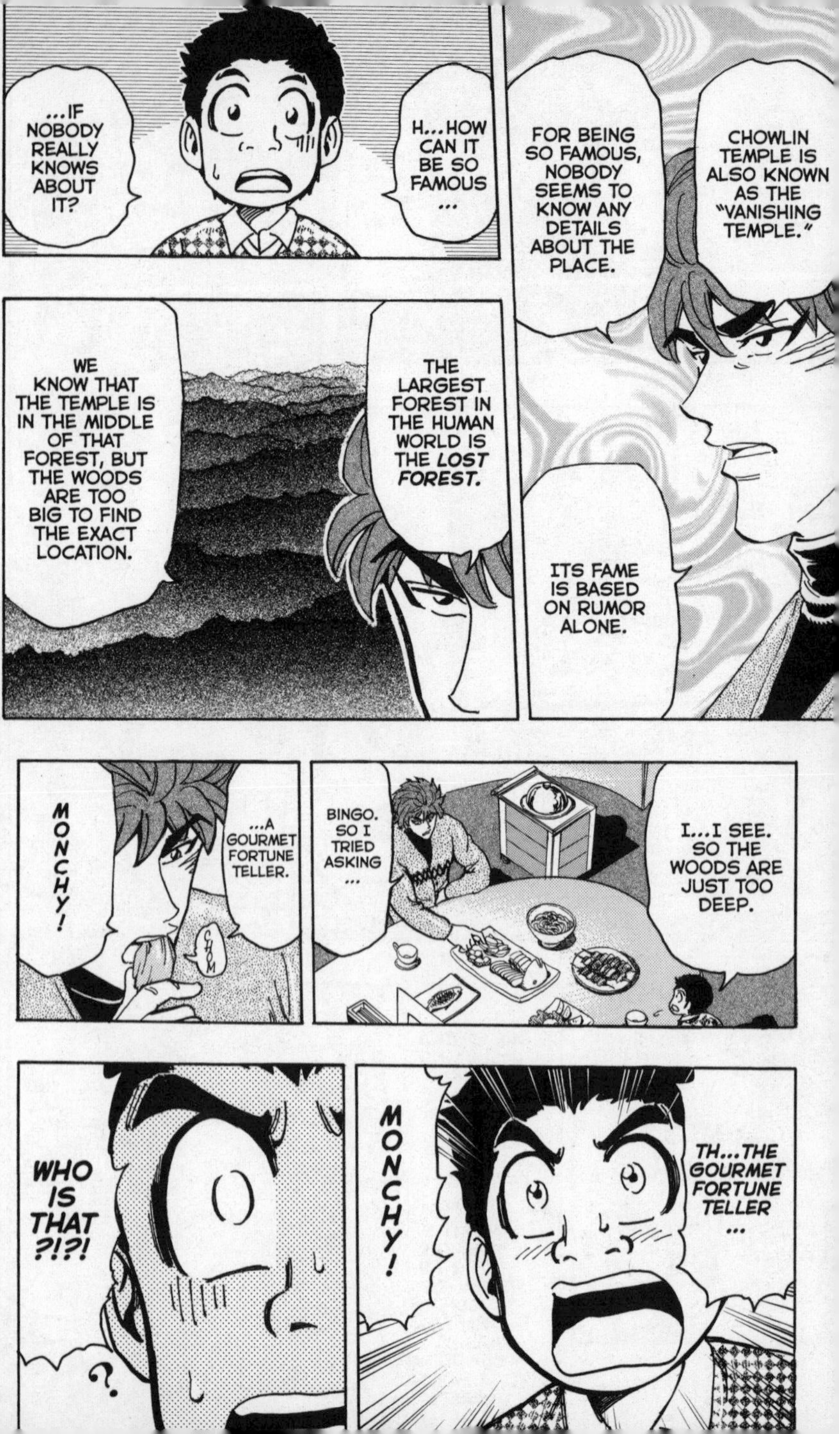
CHOWLIN TEMPLE IS ALSO KNOWN AS THE "VANISHING TEMPLE."
FOR BEING SO FAMOUS, NOBODY SEEMS TO KNOW ANY DETAILS ABOUT THE PLACE.
ITS FAME IS BASED ON RUMOR ALONE.
H...HOW CAN IT BE SO FAMOUS ...
...IF NOBODY REALLY KNOWS ABOUT IT?
THE LARGEST FOREST IN THE HUMAN WORLD IS THE *LOST FOREST.*
WE KNOW THAT THE TEMPLE IS IN THE MIDDLE OF THAT FOREST, BUT THE WOODS ARE TOO BIG TO FIND THE EXACT LOCATION.
I...I SEE. SO THE WOODS ARE JUST TOO DEEP.
BINGO. SO I TRIED ASKING ...
...A GOURMET FORTUNE TELLER.
MONCHY!
CHOM
TH...THE GOURMET FORTUNE TELLER ...
MONCHY!
WHO IS THAT ?!?!
?

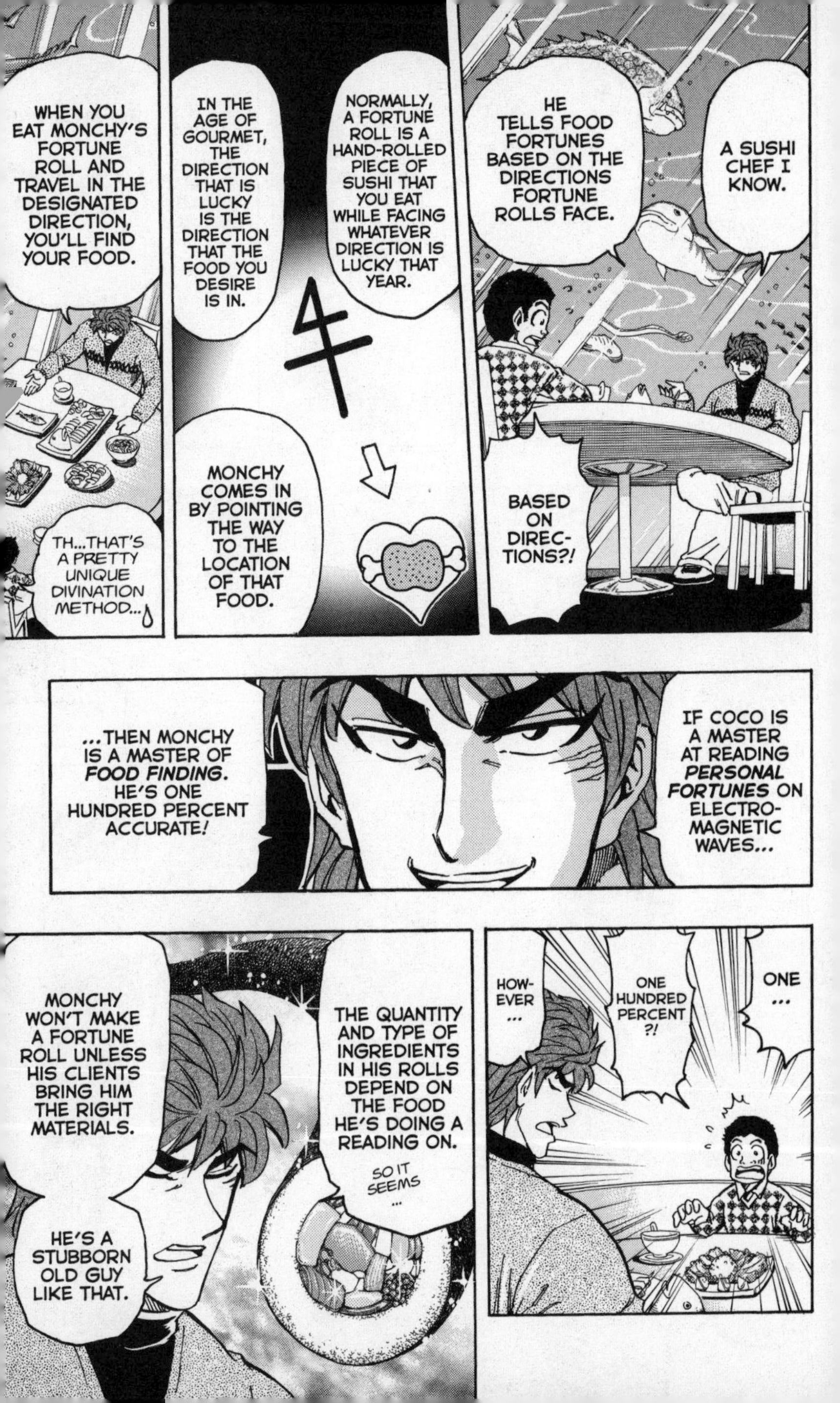
A SUSHI CHEF I KNOW.
HE TELLS FOOD FORTUNES BASED ON THE DIRECTIONS FORTUNE ROLLS FACE.
BASED ON DIREC-TIONS?!
NORMALLY, A FORTUNE ROLL IS A HAND-ROLLED PIECE OF SUSHI THAT YOU EAT WHILE FACING WHATEVER DIRECTION IS LUCKY THAT YEAR.
IN THE AGE OF GOURMET, THE DIRECTION THAT IS LUCKY IS THE DIRECTION THAT THE FOOD YOU DESIRE IS IN.
MONCHY COMES IN BY POINTING THE WAY TO THE LOCATION OF THAT FOOD.
WHEN YOU EAT MONCHY'S FORTUNE ROLL AND TRAVEL IN THE DESIGNATED DIRECTION, YOU'LL FIND YOUR FOOD.
TH...THAT'S A PRETTY UNIQUE DIVINATION METHOD...
IF COCO IS A MASTER AT READING *PERSONAL FORTUNES* ON ELECTRO-MAGNETIC WAVES...
...THEN MONCHY IS A MASTER OF *FOOD FINDING*. HE'S ONE HUNDRED PERCENT ACCURATE!
ONE...
ONE HUNDRED PERCENT ?!
HOW-EVER...
THE QUANTITY AND TYPE OF INGREDIENTS IN HIS ROLLS DEPEND ON THE FOOD HE'S DOING A READING ON.
SO IT SEEMS...
MONCHY WON'T MAKE A FORTUNE ROLL UNLESS HIS CLIENTS BRING HIM THE RIGHT MATERIALS.
HE'S A STUBBORN OLD GUY LIKE THAT.

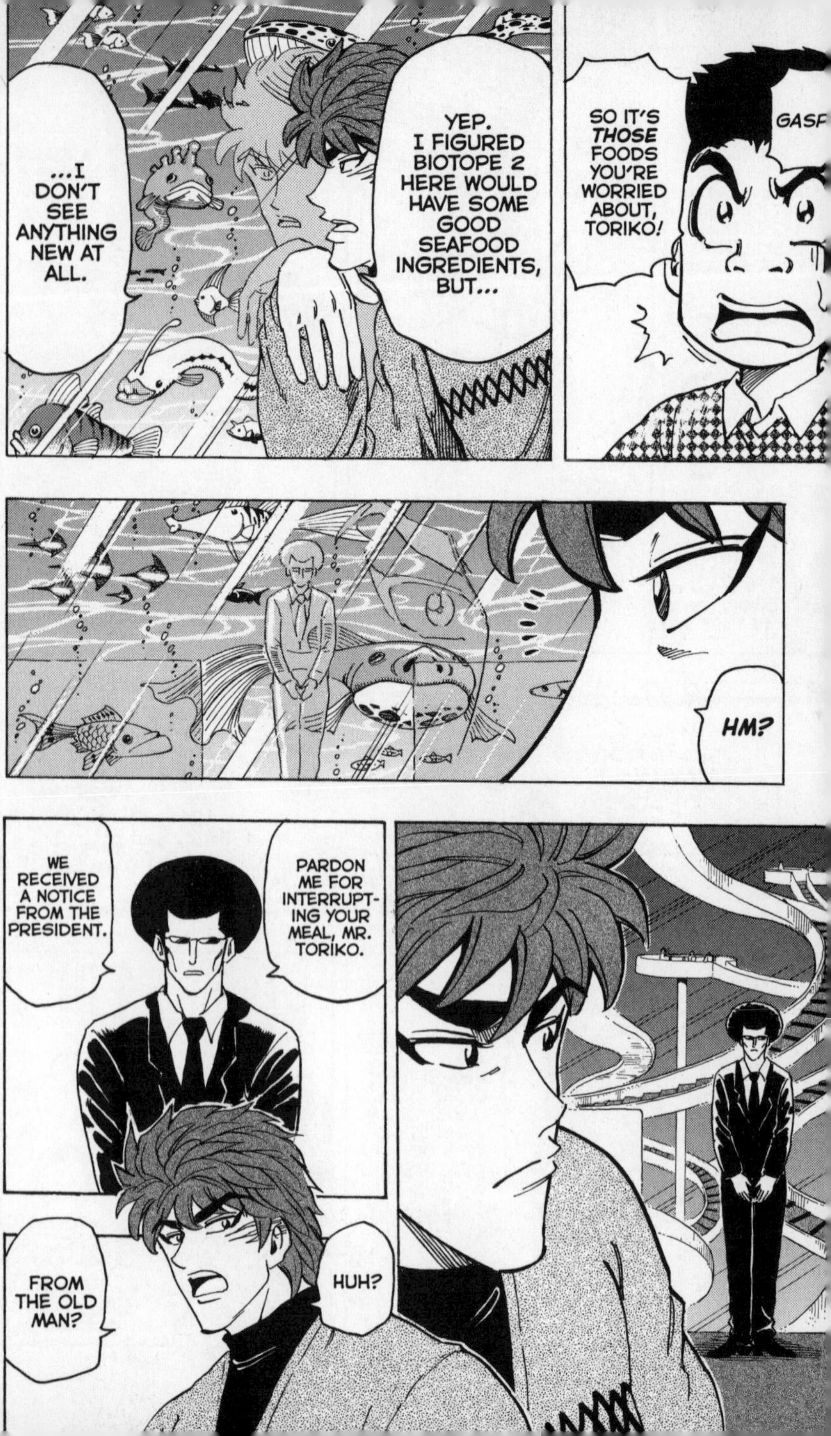
GASP
SO IT'S *THOSE* FOODS YOU'RE WORRIED ABOUT, TORIKO!
YEP. I FIGURED BIOTOPE 2 HERE WOULD HAVE SOME GOOD SEAFOOD INGREDIENTS, BUT...
...I DON'T SEE ANYTHING NEW AT ALL.
HM?
PARDON ME FOR INTERRUPTING YOUR MEAL, MR. TORIKO.
WE RECEIVED A NOTICE FROM THE PRESIDENT.
HUH?
FROM THE OLD MAN?

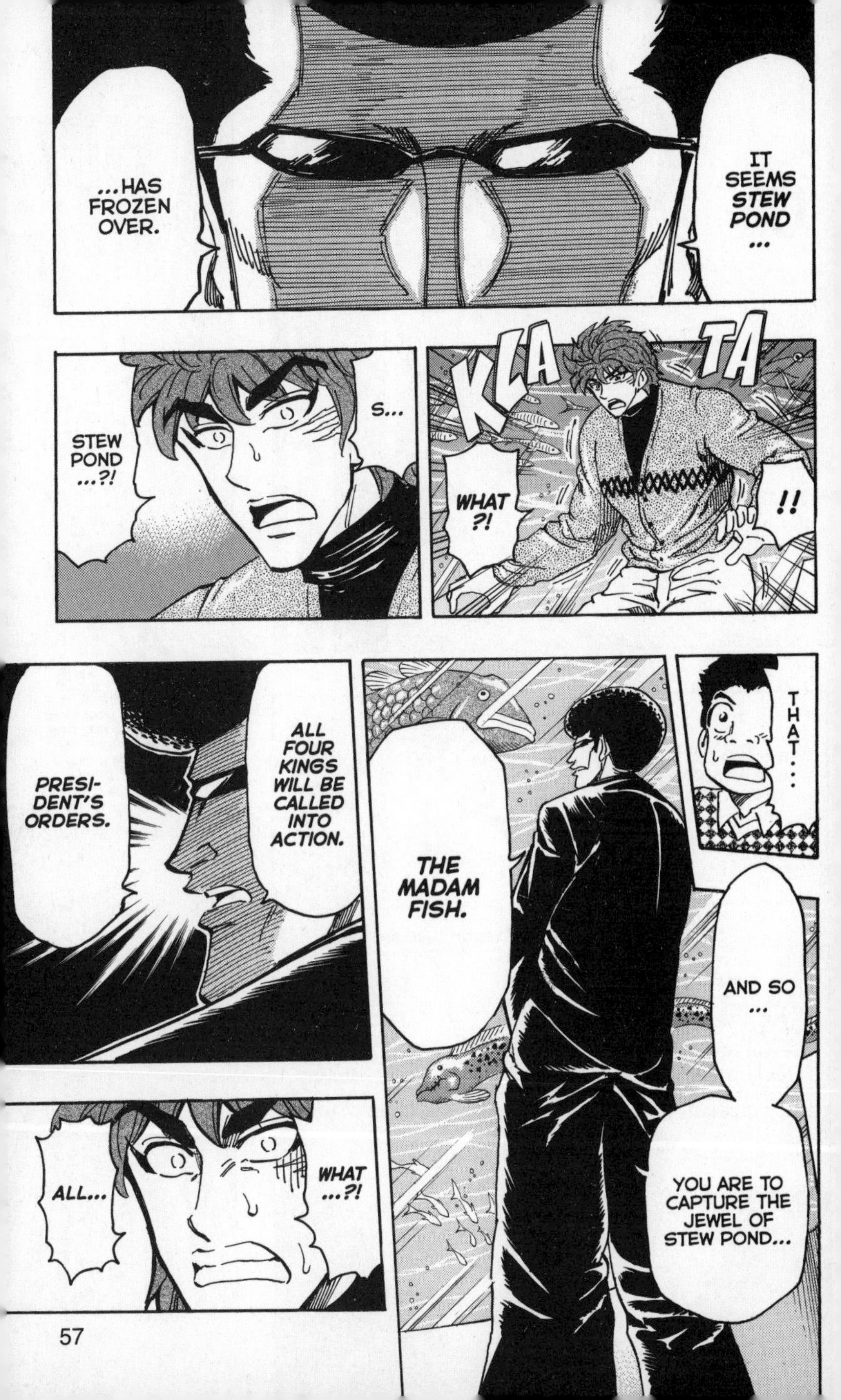
IT SEEMS STEW POND ...
...HAS FROZEN OVER.
KLA
TA
!!
WHAT ?!
S...
STEW POND ...?!
THAT...
AND SO ...
YOU ARE TO CAPTURE THE JEWEL OF STEW POND...
THE MADAM FISH.
ALL FOUR KINGS WILL BE CALLED INTO ACTION.
PRESI-DENT'S ORDERS.
WHAT ...?!
ALL...

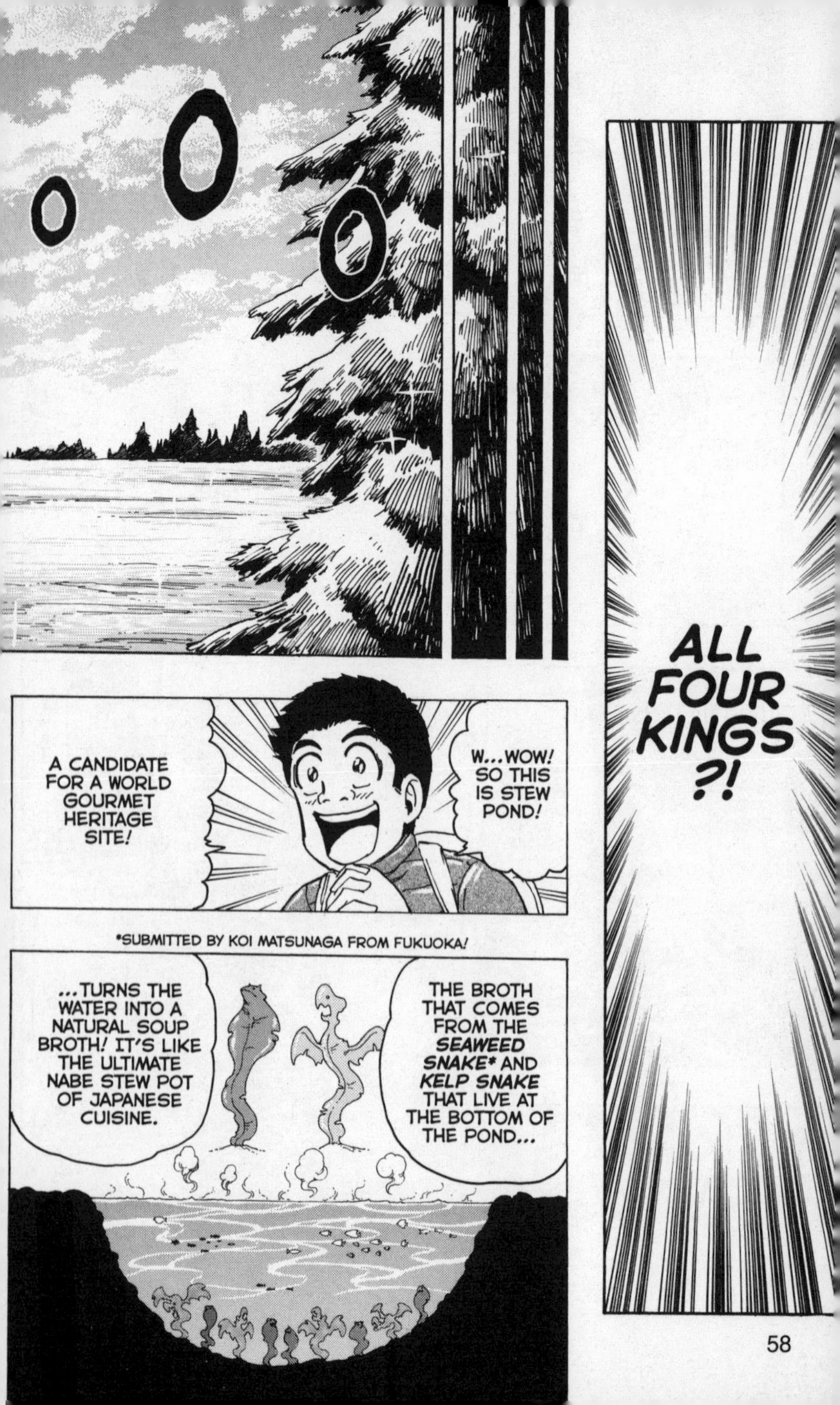
ALL FOUR KINGS ?!
W...WOW! SO THIS IS STEW POND!
A CANDIDATE FOR A WORLD GOURMET HERITAGE SITE!
THE BROTH THAT COMES FROM THE *SEAWEED SNAKE** AND *KELP SNAKE* THAT LIVE AT THE BOTTOM OF THE POND...
...TURNS THE WATER INTO A NATURAL SOUP BROTH! IT'S LIKE THE ULTIMATE NABE STEW POT OF JAPANESE CUISINE.

*SUBMITTED BY KOI MATSUNAGA FROM FUKUOKA!

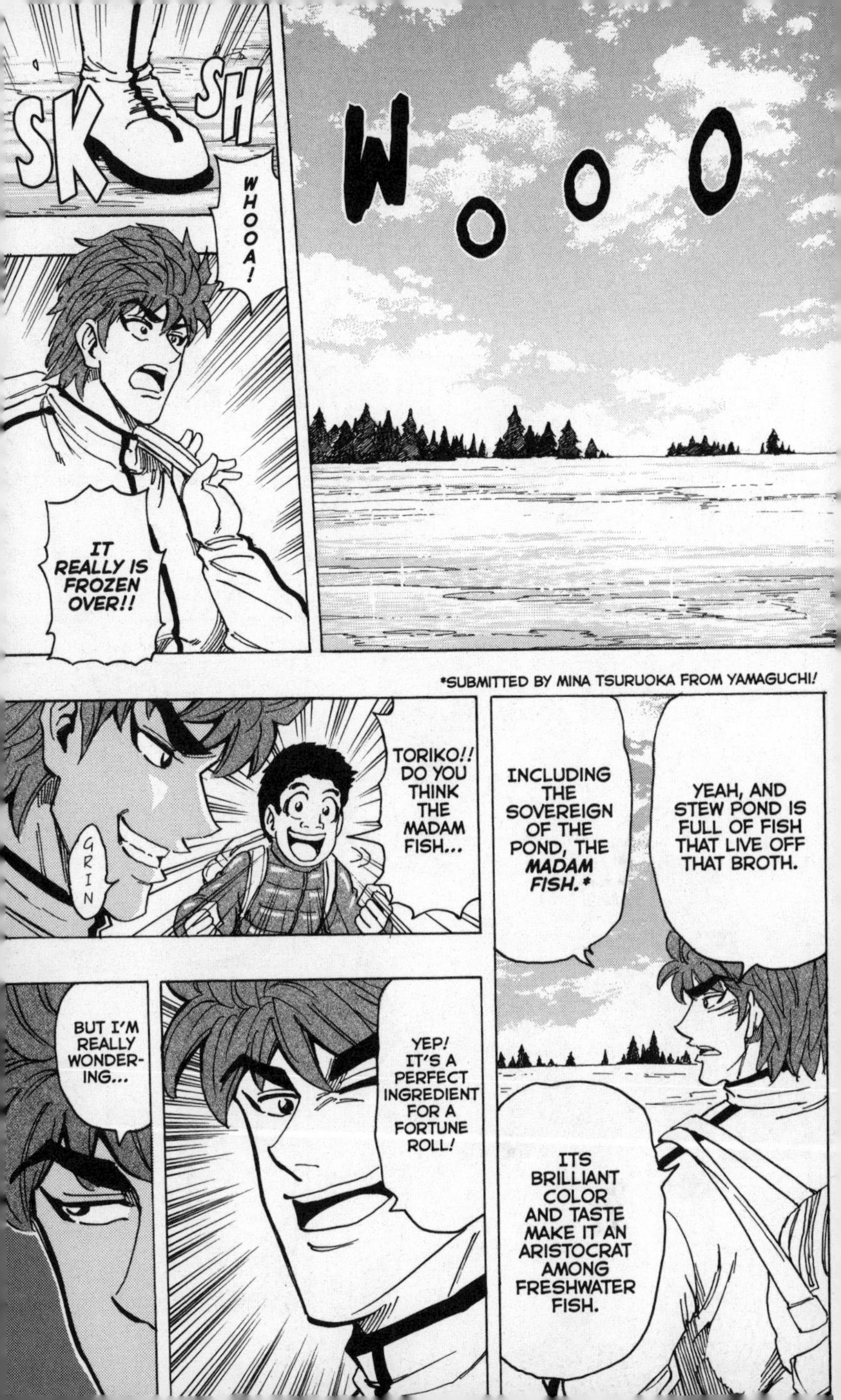
WOOO
SKSH
WHOOA!
IT REALLY IS FROZEN OVER!!
*SUBMITTED BY MINA TSURUOKA FROM YAMAGUCHI!
YEAH, AND STEW POND IS FULL OF FISH THAT LIVE OFF THAT BROTH.
INCLUDING THE SOVEREIGN OF THE POND, THE *MADAM FISH.**
ITS BRILLIANT COLOR AND TASTE MAKE IT AN ARISTOCRAT AMONG FRESHWATER FISH.
TORIKO!! DO YOU THINK THE MADAM FISH...
GRIN
YEP! IT'S A PERFECT INGREDIENT FOR A FORTUNE ROLL!
BUT I'M REALLY WONDERING...

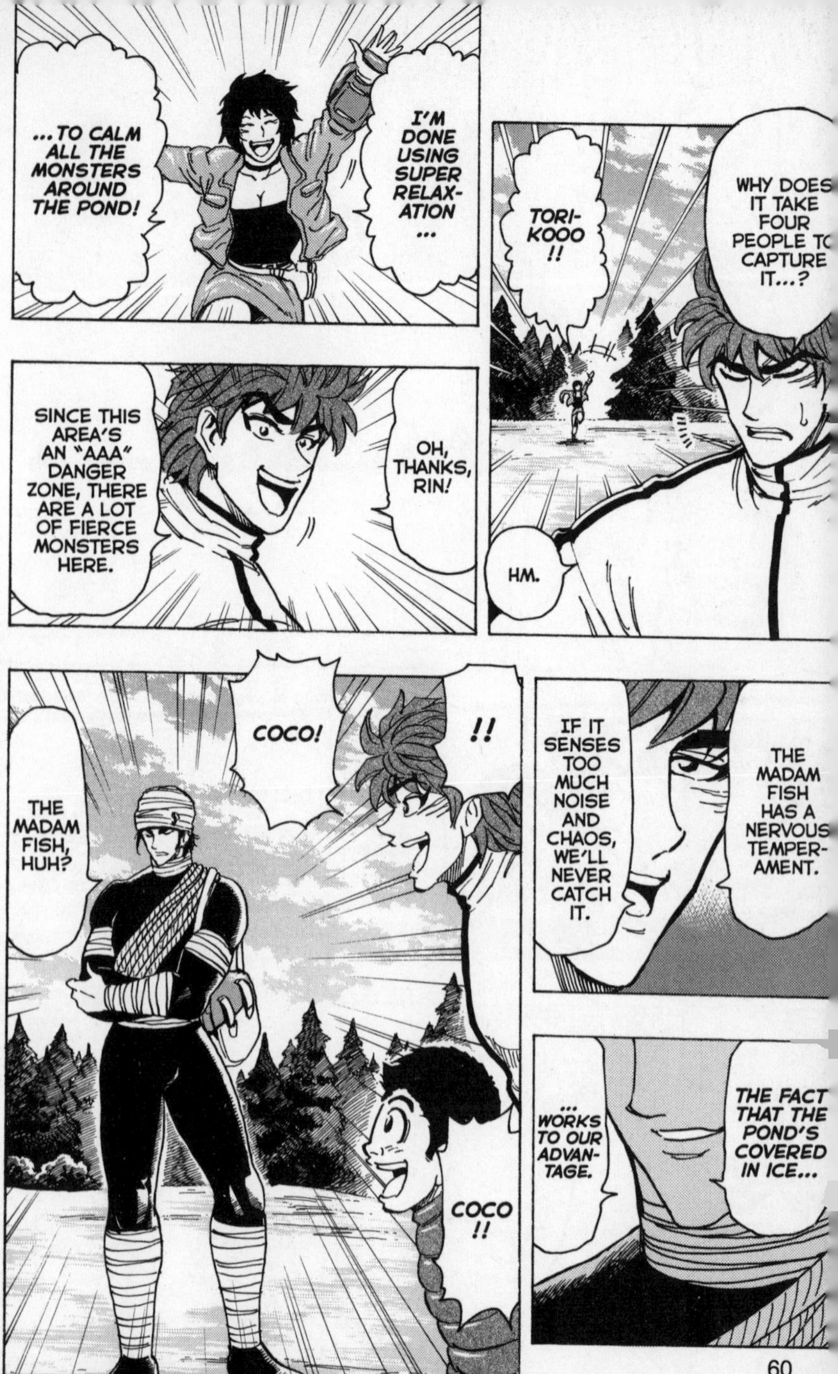
WHY DOES IT TAKE FOUR PEOPLE TO CAPTURE IT...?
TORI-KOOO!!
HM.
I'M DONE USING SUPER RELAX-ATION...
...TO CALM ALL THE MONSTERS AROUND THE POND!
OH, THANKS, RIN!
SINCE THIS AREA'S AN "AAA" DANGER ZONE, THERE ARE A LOT OF FIERCE MONSTERS HERE.
THE MADAM FISH HAS A NERVOUS TEMPER-AMENT.
IF IT SENSES TOO MUCH NOISE AND CHAOS, WE'LL NEVER CATCH IT.
THE FACT THAT THE POND'S COVERED IN ICE...
...WORKS TO OUR ADVAN-TAGE.
!!
COCO!
THE MADAM FISH, HUH?
COCO!!

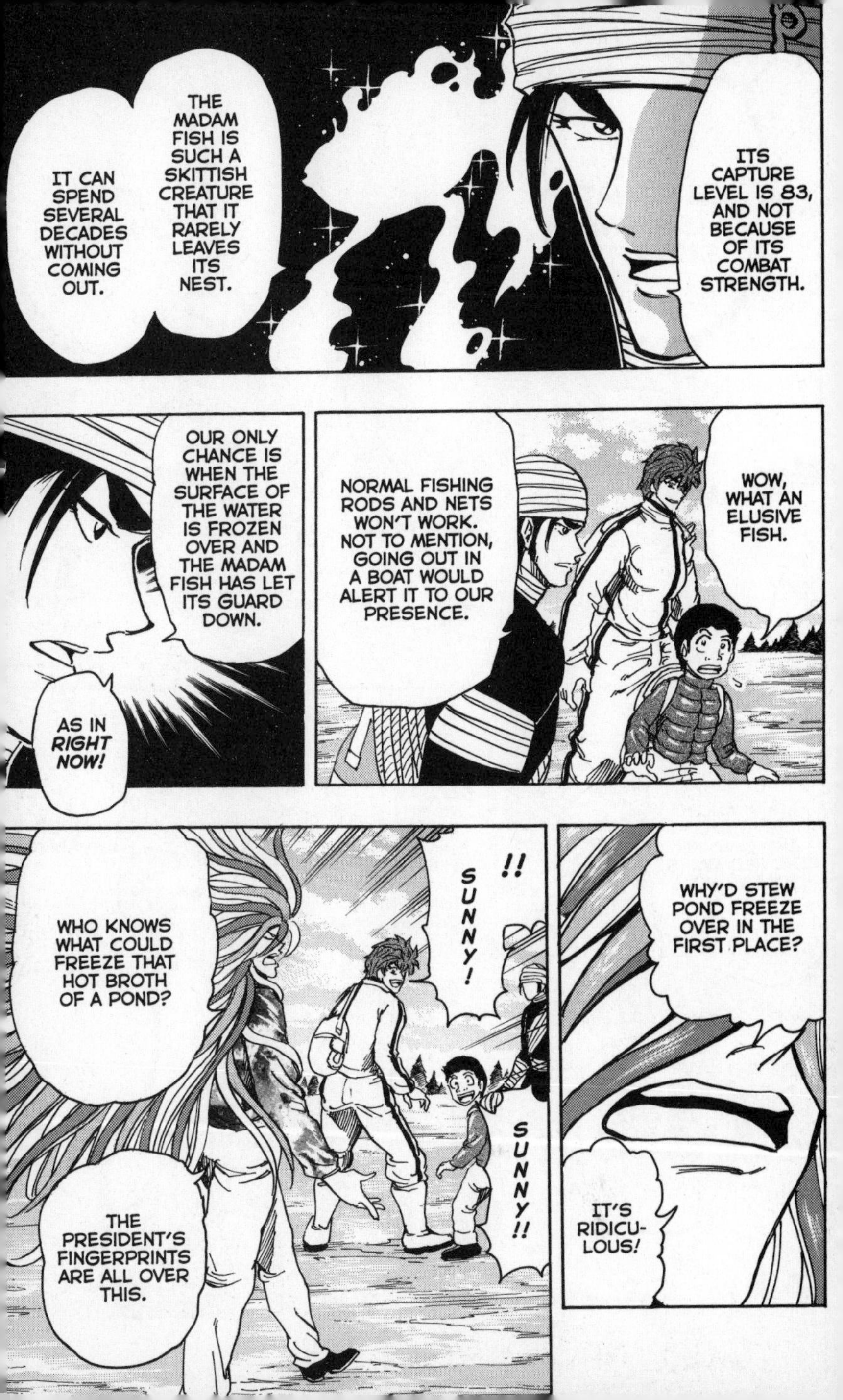
ITS CAPTURE LEVEL IS 83, AND NOT BECAUSE OF ITS COMBAT STRENGTH.
THE MADAM FISH IS SUCH A SKITTISH CREATURE THAT IT RARELY LEAVES ITS NEST.
IT CAN SPEND SEVERAL DECADES WITHOUT COMING OUT.
WOW, WHAT AN ELUSIVE FISH.
NORMAL FISHING RODS AND NETS WON'T WORK. NOT TO MENTION, GOING OUT IN A BOAT WOULD ALERT IT TO OUR PRESENCE.
OUR ONLY CHANCE IS WHEN THE SURFACE OF THE WATER IS FROZEN OVER AND THE MADAM FISH HAS LET ITS GUARD DOWN.
AS IN *RIGHT NOW!*
WHY'D STEW POND FREEZE OVER IN THE FIRST PLACE?
IT'S RIDICULOUS!
!!
SUNNY!
WHO KNOWS WHAT COULD FREEZE THAT HOT BROTH OF A POND?
SUNNY!!
THE PRESIDENT'S FINGERPRINTS ARE ALL OVER THIS.

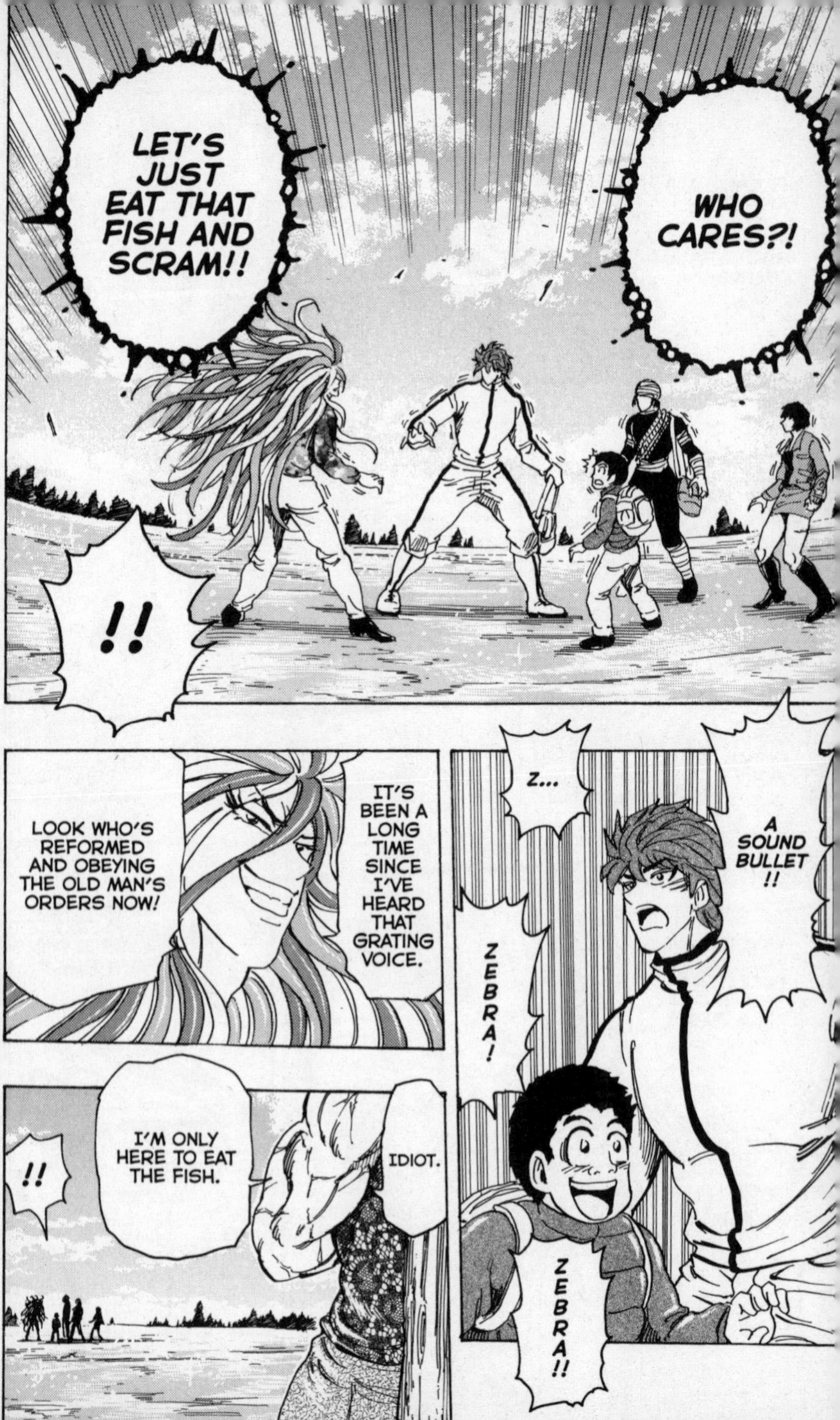
WHO CARES?!
LET'S JUST EAT THAT FISH AND SCRAM!!
!!
A SOUND BULLET!!
Z...
ZEBRA!
ZEBRA!!
IT'S BEEN A LONG TIME SINCE I'VE HEARD THAT GRATING VOICE.
LOOK WHO'S REFORMED AND OBEYING THE OLD MAN'S ORDERS NOW!
IDIOT.
I'M ONLY HERE TO EAT THE FISH.
!!

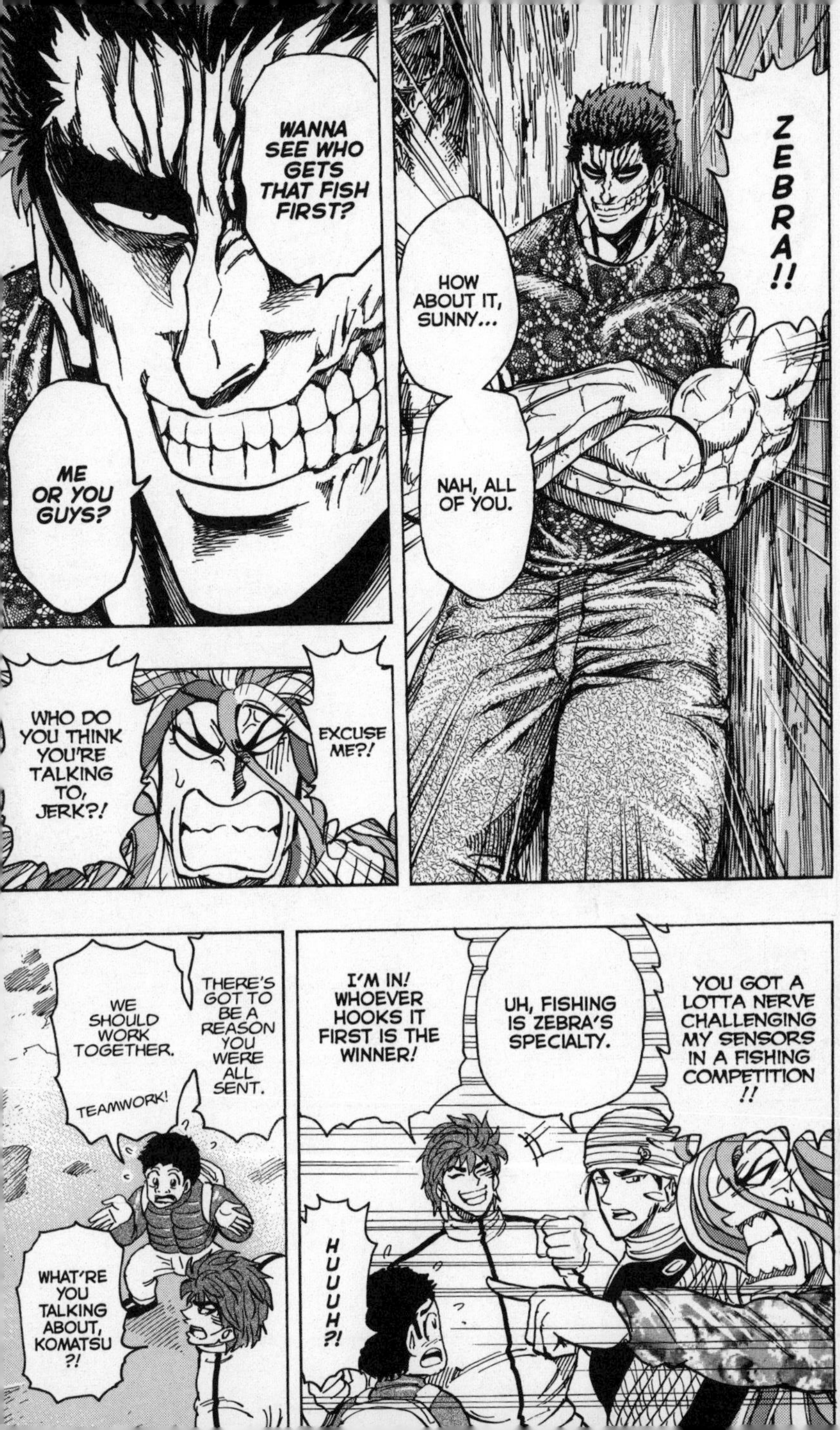
ZEBRA!!
HOW ABOUT IT, SUNNY...
NAH, ALL OF YOU.
WANNA SEE WHO GETS THAT FISH FIRST?
ME OR YOU GUYS?
EXCUSE ME?!
WHO DO YOU THINK YOU'RE TALKING TO, JERK?!
YOU GOT A LOTTA NERVE CHALLENGING MY SENSORS IN A FISHING COMPETITION!!
UH, FISHING IS ZEBRA'S SPECIALTY.
I'M IN! WHOEVER HOOKS IT FIRST IS THE WINNER!
HUUUH?!
THERE'S GOT TO BE A REASON YOU WERE ALL SENT.
WE SHOULD WORK TOGETHER.
TEAMWORK!
WHAT'RE YOU TALKING ABOUT, KOMATSU?!

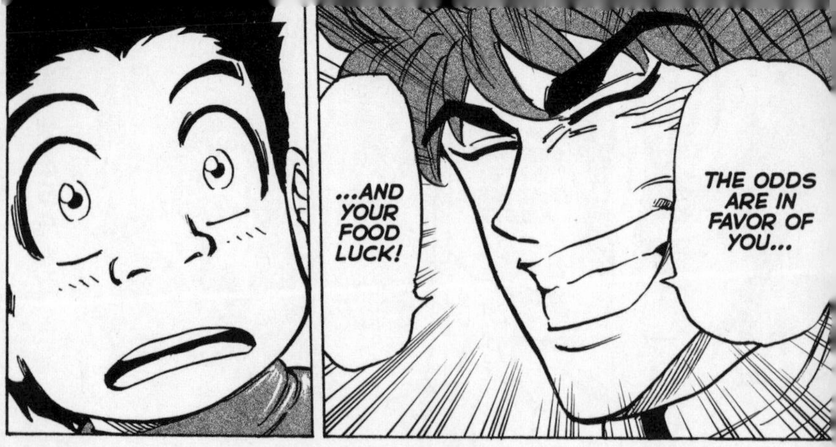
THE ODDS ARE IN FAVOR OF YOU...
...AND YOUR FOOD LUCK!

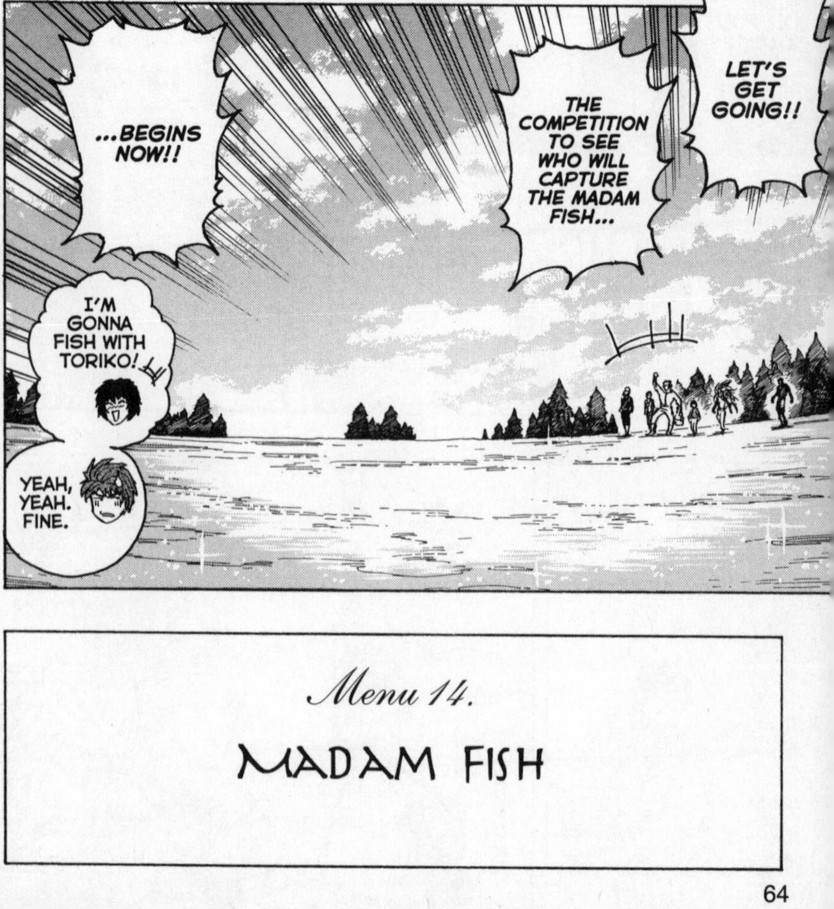
LET'S GET GOING!!
THE COMPETITION TO SEE WHO WILL CAPTURE THE MADAM FISH...
...BEGINS NOW!!
I'M GONNA FISH WITH TORIKO!
YEAH, YEAH. FINE.

Menu 14.

MADAM FISH

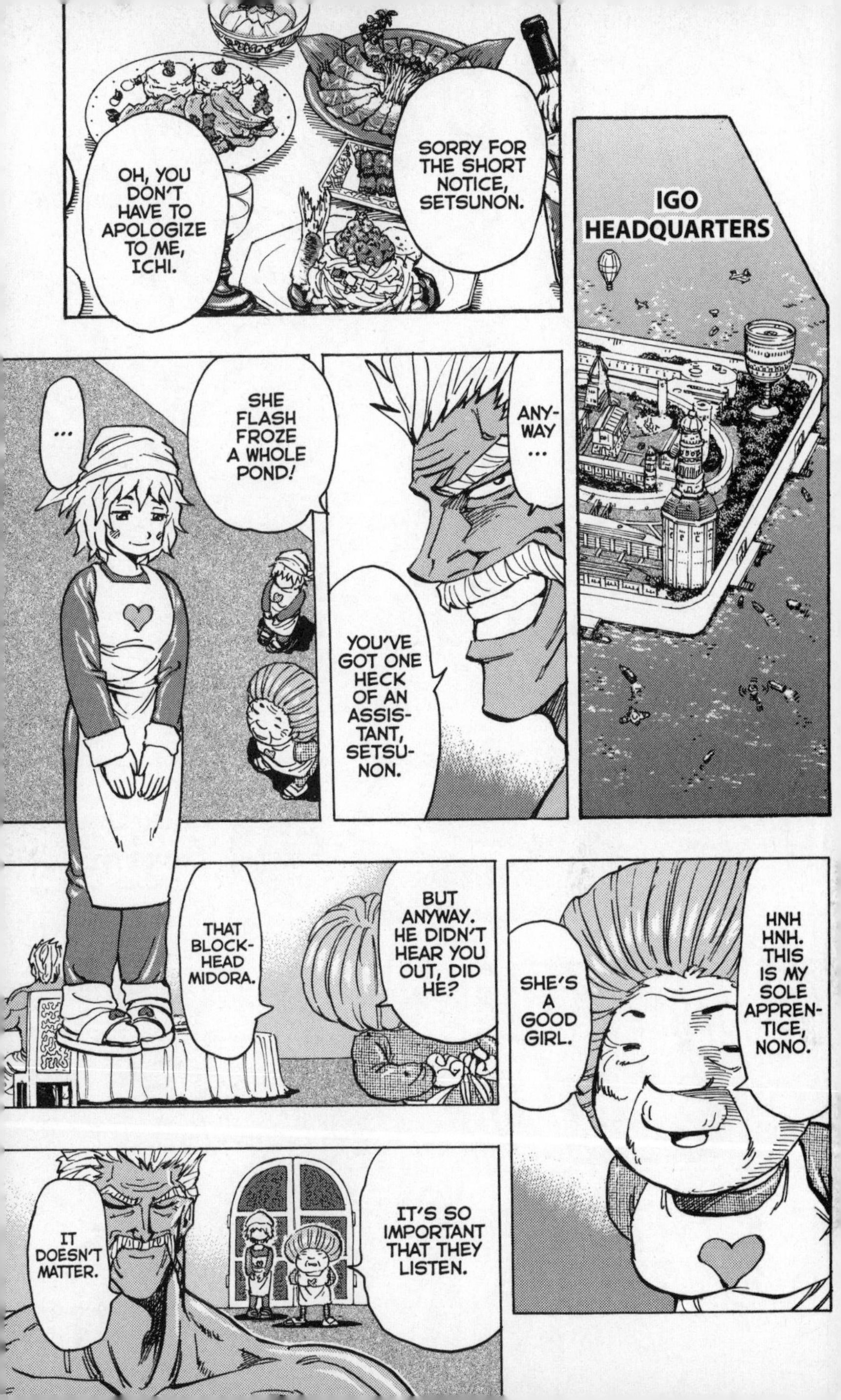
IGO HEADQUARTERS
SORRY FOR THE SHORT NOTICE, SETSUNON.
OH, YOU DON'T HAVE TO APOLOGIZE TO ME, ICHI.
ANYWAY ...
YOU'VE GOT ONE HECK OF AN ASSISTANT, SETSUNON.
SHE FLASH FROZE A WHOLE POND!
...
HNH HNH. THIS IS MY SOLE APPRENTICE, NONO.
SHE'S A GOOD GIRL.
BUT ANYWAY. HE DIDN'T HEAR YOU OUT, DID HE?
THAT BLOCKHEAD MIDORA.
IT'S SO IMPORTANT THAT THEY LISTEN.
IT DOESN'T MATTER.

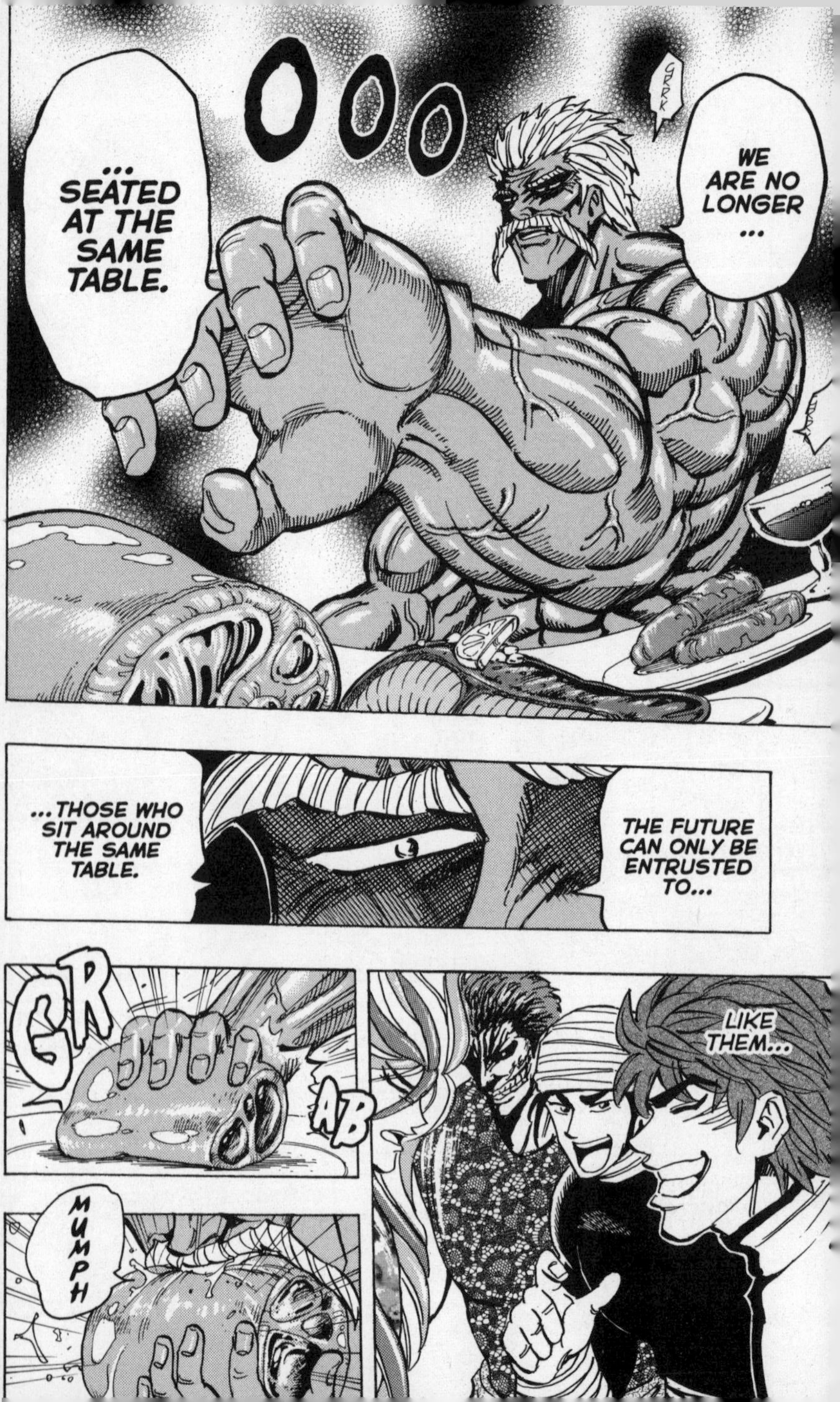

GRRK
WE ARE NO LONGER ...
OOO
... SEATED AT THE SAME TABLE.
THE FUTURE CAN ONLY BE ENTRUSTED TO...
...THOSE WHO SIT AROUND THE SAME TABLE.
LIKE THEM...
GR
AB
MUMPH

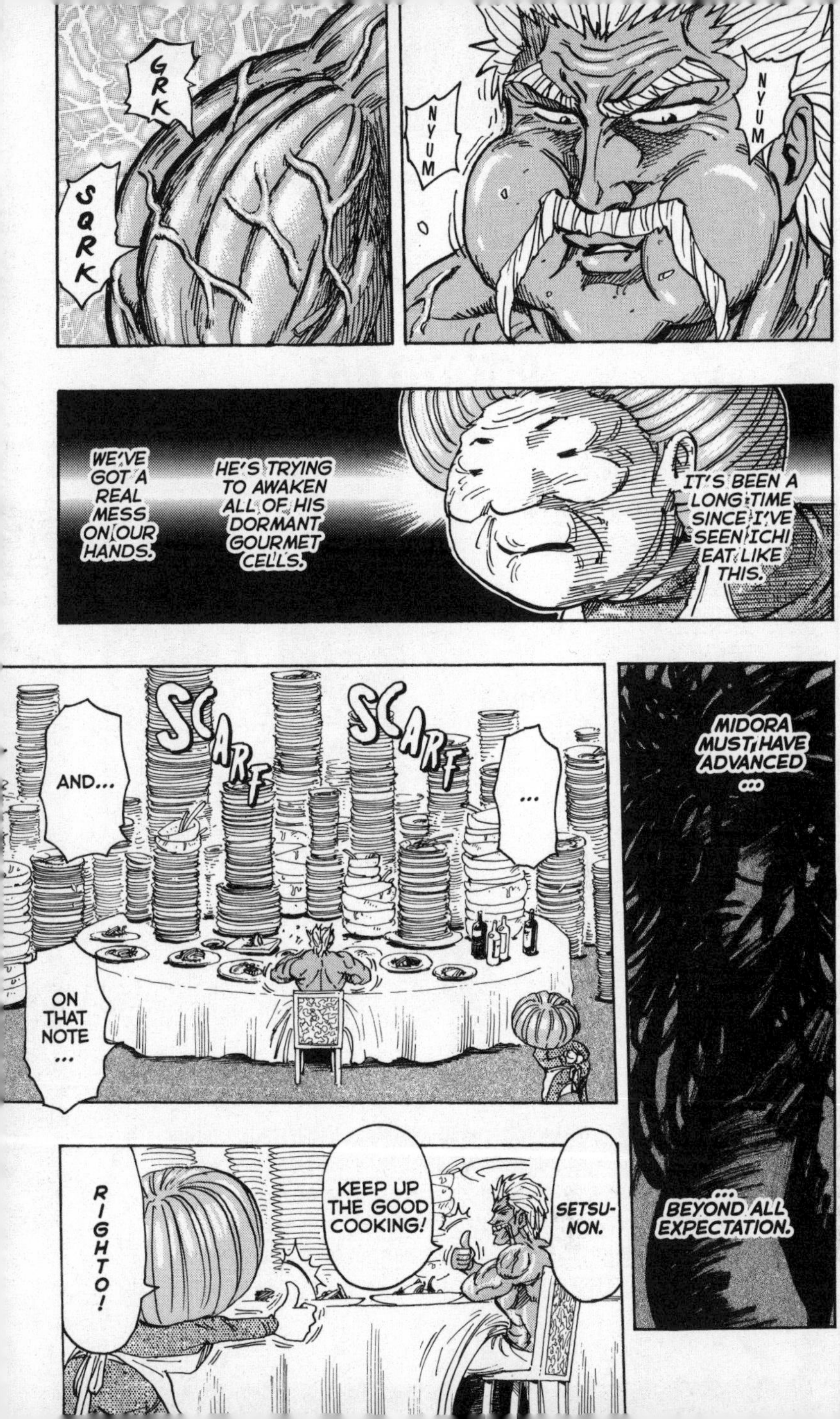
NYUM
NYUM
GRK
SQRK
IT'S BEEN A LONG TIME SINCE I'VE SEEN ICHI EAT LIKE THIS.
HE'S TRYING TO AWAKEN ALL OF HIS DORMANT GOURMET CELLS.
WE'VE GOT A REAL MESS ON OUR HANDS.
MIDORA MUST HAVE ADVANCED ...
... BEYOND ALL EXPECTATION.
SCARF
SCARF
...
AND...
ON THAT NOTE ...
SETSU-NON.
KEEP UP THE GOOD COOKING!
RIGHTO!

TORIKO

GOURMET CHECKLIST

Vol. 203

POTATO RAT
(MAMMAL)

CAPTURE LEVEL: 18
HABITAT: ANYWHERE (CAN BE
    DOMESTICATED)
LENGTH: 15 CM
HEIGHT: ---
WEIGHT: 800 G
PRICE: ABOUT 20 FRIES (ONE RAT'S
    WORTH)/ 1,200 YEN

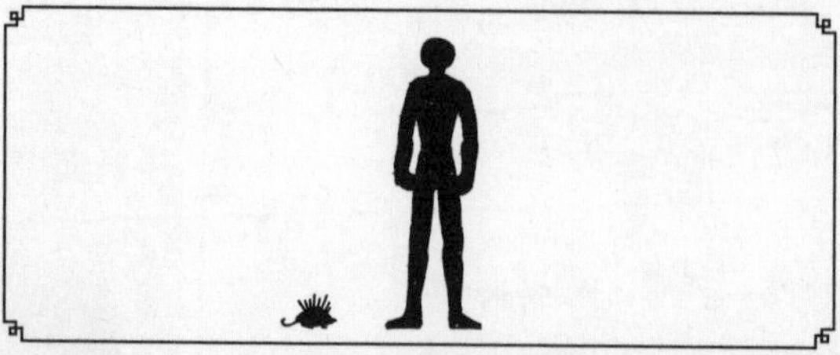

SCALE

A RARE CREATURE, THIS MAMMAL IN THE HEDGEHOG FAMILY SPROUTS FRENCH FRIES FROM
ITS BACK. THEY'RE HEATED BY ITS BODY TEMPERATURE! THE FRIES ARE DELICIOUS WHEN
HARVESTED IN A NON-STRESSFUL WAY OR IF THEY FALL OUT NATURALLY, BUT IF FORCIBLY
EXTRACTED OR REMOVED WHEN THE RAT IS IN A FOUL MOOD, THE FLAVOR IS DRASTICALLY
AFFECTED. THE POTATO RAT'S BODY IS INEDIBLE, BUT PLENTY OF PEOPLE RAISE THEM JUST
FOR THE FRENCH FRIES ON THEIR BACKS. THAT'S HOW DESIRED A FOOD THEIR FRIES ARE.

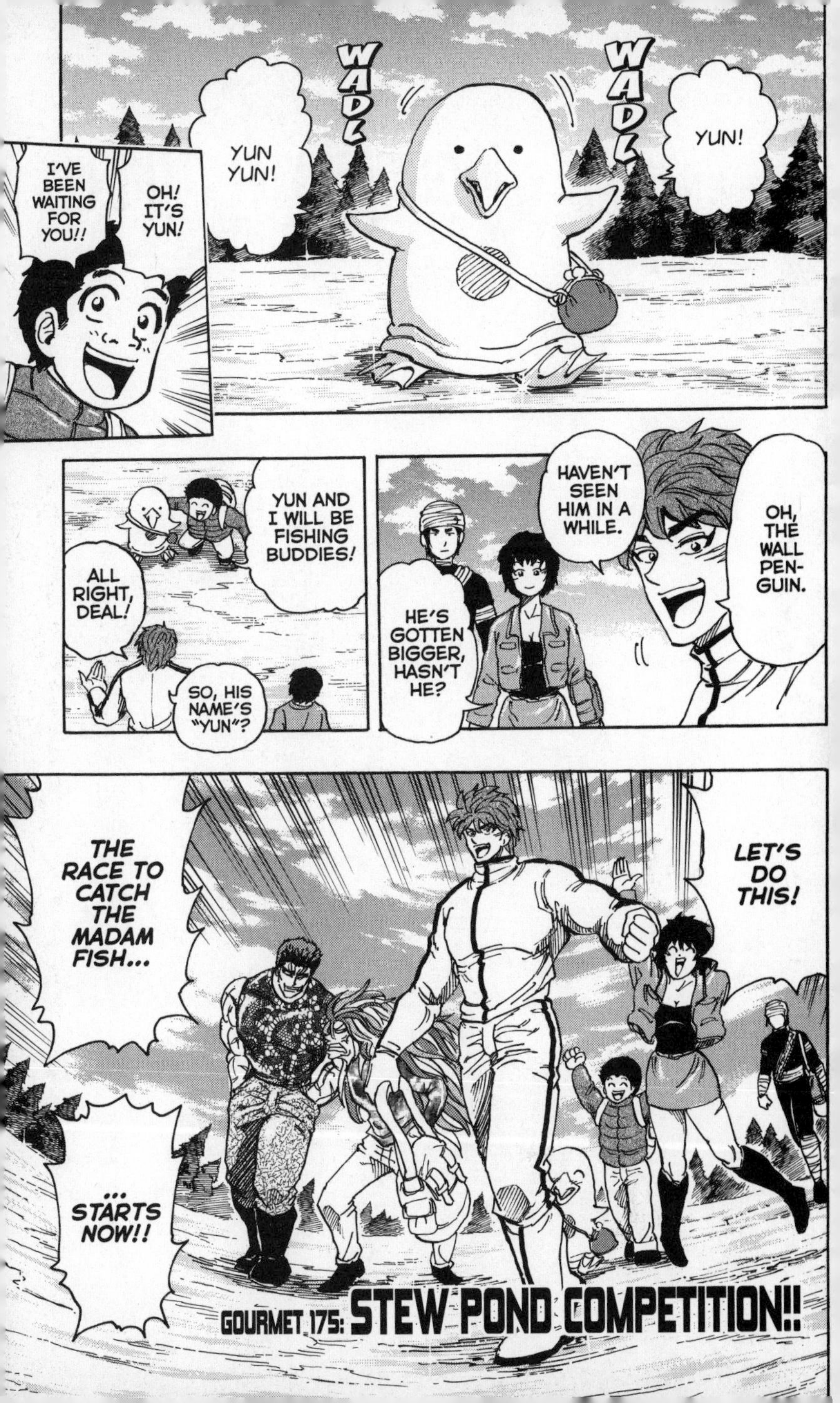
WADL
WADL
YUN!
YUN YUN!
OH! IT'S YUN!
I'VE BEEN WAITING FOR YOU!!
OH, THE WALL PEN-GUIN.
HAVEN'T SEEN HIM IN A WHILE.
HE'S GOTTEN BIGGER, HASN'T HE?
YUN AND I WILL BE FISHING BUDDIES!
ALL RIGHT, DEAL!
SO, HIS NAME'S "YUN"?
LET'S DO THIS!
THE RACE TO CATCH THE MADAM FISH...
...STARTS NOW!!
GOURMET 175: STEW POND COMPETITION!!

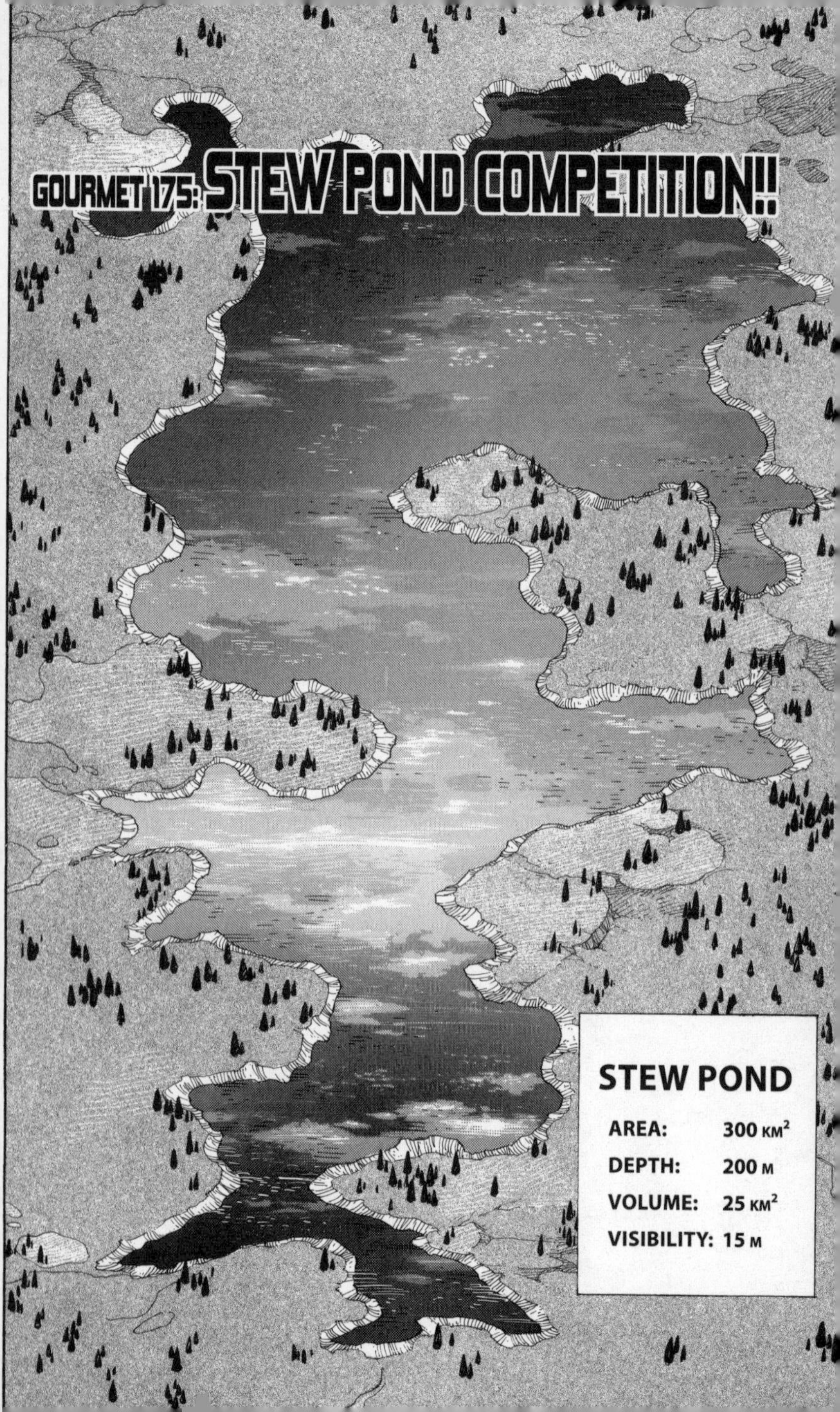
GOURMET 175: STEW POND COMPETITION!!
STEW POND
AREA: 300 KM^2
DEPTH: 200 M
VOLUME: 25 KM^2
VISIBILITY: 15 M

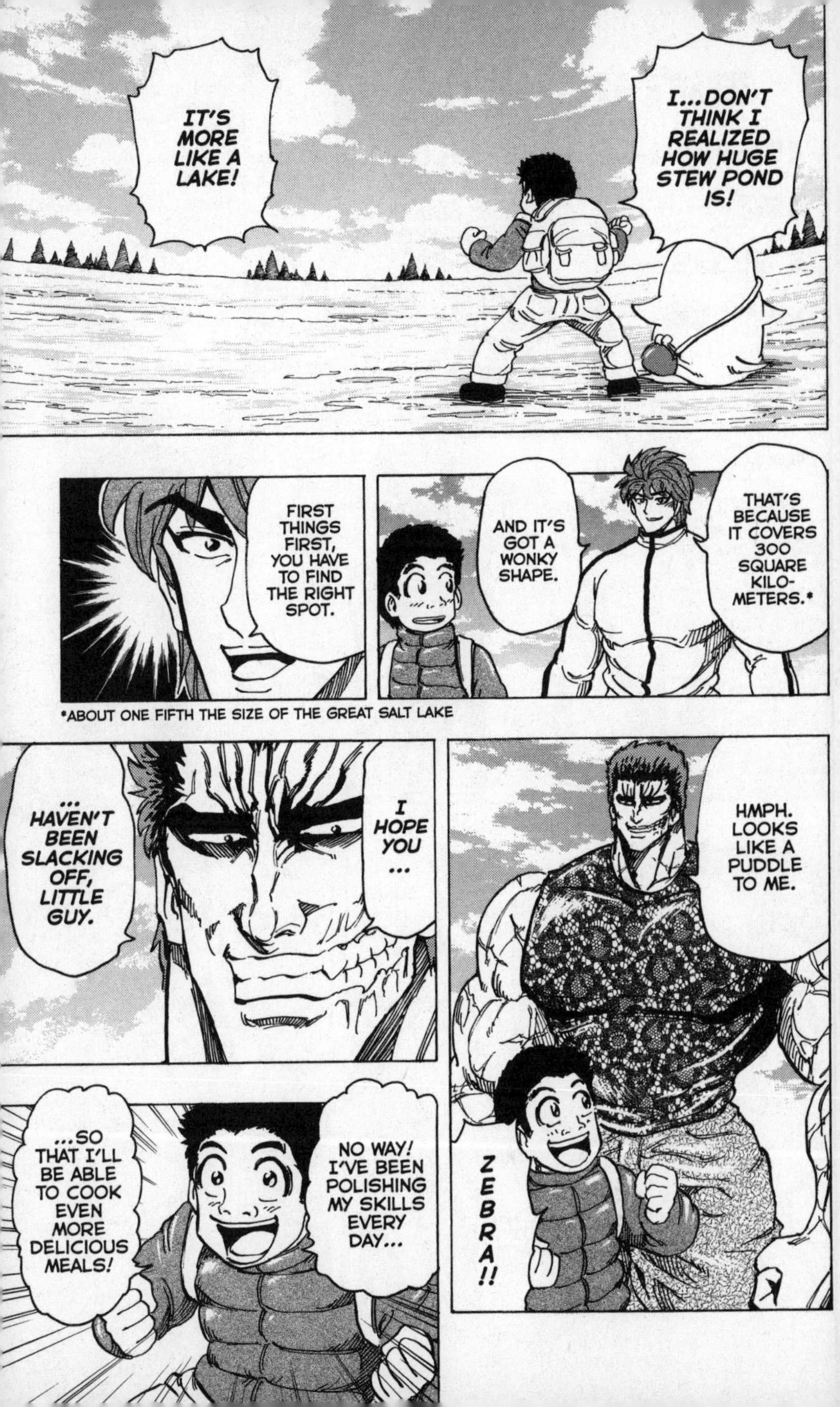
I...DON'T THINK I REALIZED HOW HUGE STEW POND IS!
IT'S MORE LIKE A LAKE!
THAT'S BECAUSE IT COVERS 300 SQUARE KILO-METERS.*
AND IT'S GOT A WONKY SHAPE.
FIRST THINGS FIRST, YOU HAVE TO FIND THE RIGHT SPOT.
*ABOUT ONE FIFTH THE SIZE OF THE GREAT SALT LAKE
HMPH. LOOKS LIKE A PUDDLE TO ME.
ZEBRA!!
I HOPE YOU ...
...HAVEN'T BEEN SLACKING OFF, LITTLE GUY.
NO WAY! I'VE BEEN POLISHING MY SKILLS EVERY DAY...
...SO THAT I'LL BE ABLE TO COOK EVEN MORE DELICIOUS MEALS!

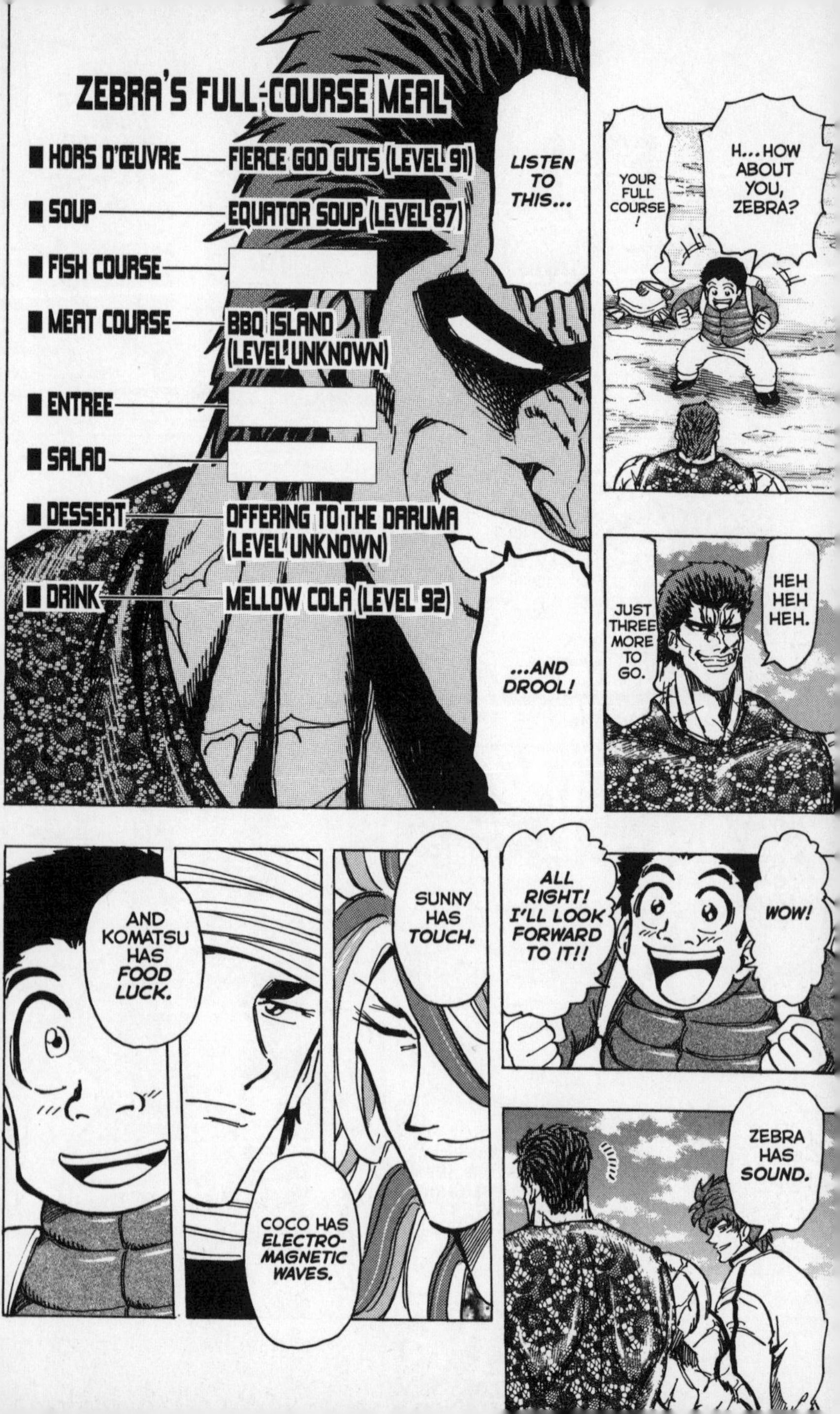
H...HOW ABOUT YOU, ZEBRA?
YOUR FULL COURSE!
HEH HEH HEH.
JUST THREE MORE TO GO.
LISTEN TO THIS...
ZEBRA'S FULL-COURSE MEAL
■ HORS D'ŒUVRE—FIERCE GOD GUTS (LEVEL 91)
■ SOUP—EQUATOR SOUP (LEVEL 87)
■ FISH COURSE—
■ MEAT COURSE—BBQ ISLAND (LEVEL UNKNOWN)
■ ENTREE—
■ SALAD—
■ DESSERT—OFFERING TO THE DARUMA (LEVEL UNKNOWN)
■ DRINK—MELLOW COLA (LEVEL 92)
...AND DROOL!
WOW!
ALL RIGHT! I'LL LOOK FORWARD TO IT!!
ZEBRA HAS SOUND.
SUNNY HAS TOUCH.
COCO HAS ELECTRO-MAGNETIC WAVES.
AND KOMATSU HAS FOOD LUCK.

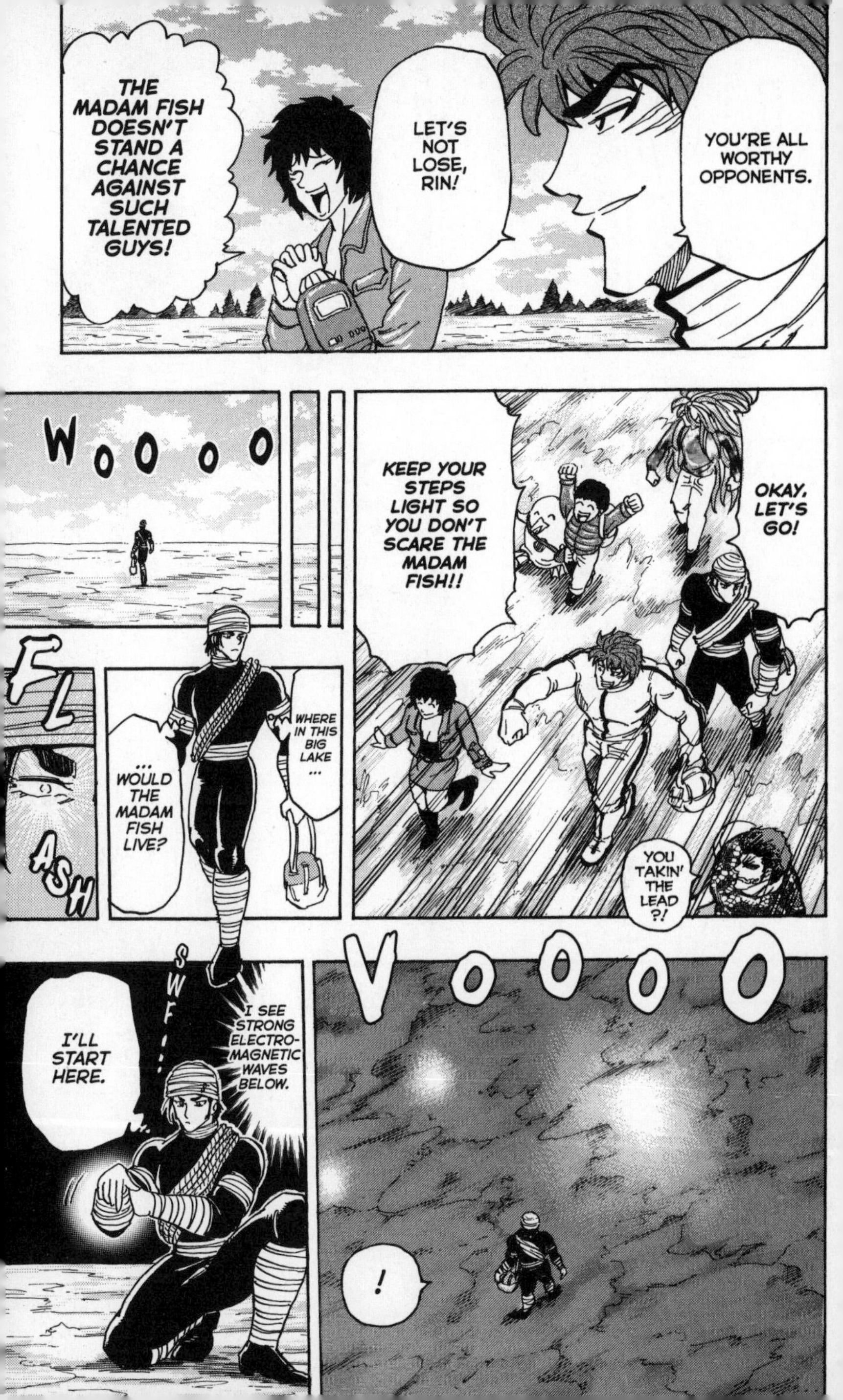
YOU'RE ALL WORTHY OPPONENTS.
LET'S NOT LOSE, RIN!
THE MADAM FISH DOESN'T STAND A CHANCE AGAINST SUCH TALENTED GUYS!
OKAY, LET'S GO!
KEEP YOUR STEPS LIGHT SO YOU DON'T SCARE THE MADAM FISH!!
YOU TAKIN' THE LEAD?!
WOOOO
WHERE IN THIS BIG LAKE ...
... WOULD THE MADAM FISH LIVE?
FLASH
VOOOO
!
SWF...
I SEE STRONG ELECTRO-MAGNETIC WAVES BELOW.
I'LL START HERE.

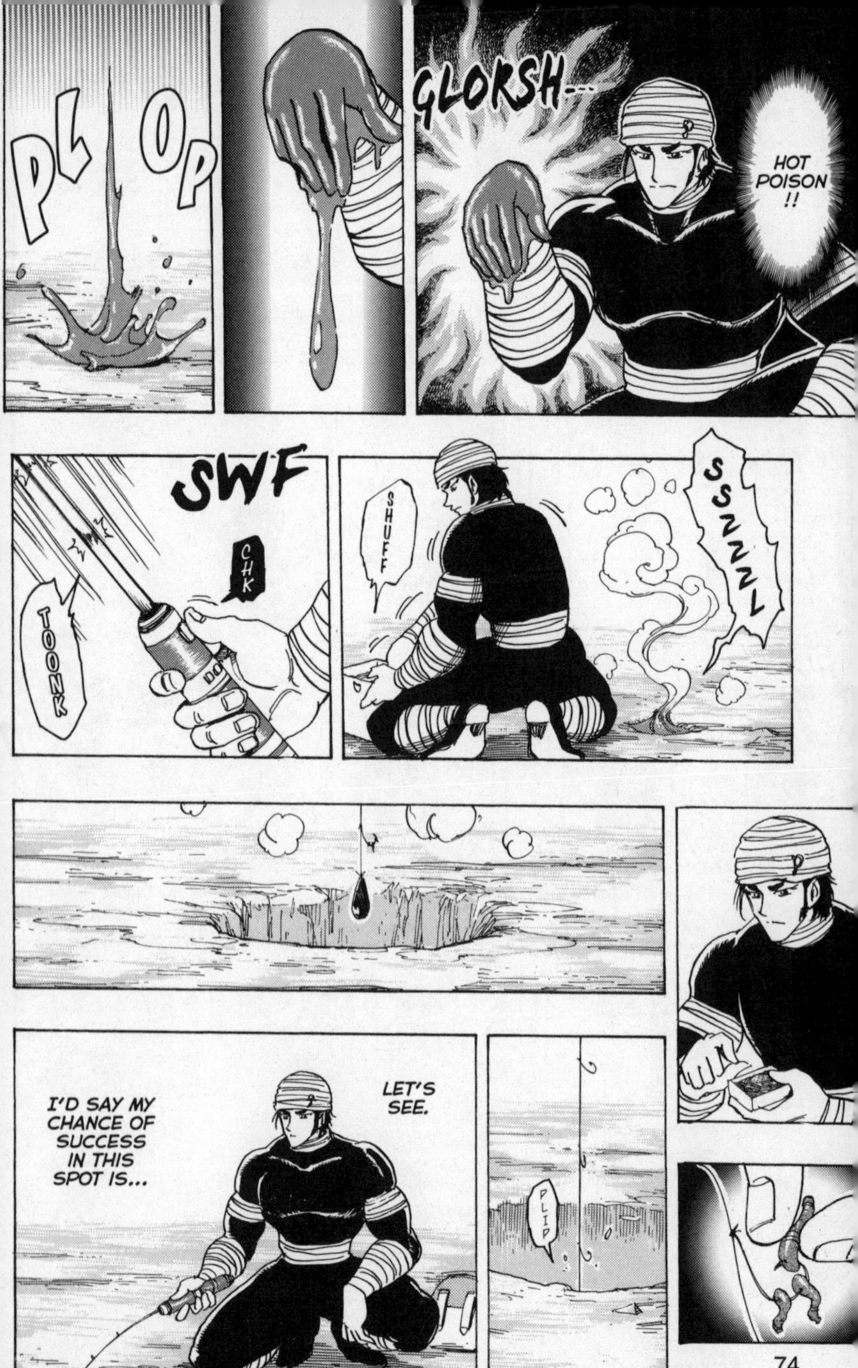
HOT POISON !!
GLORSH...
PLOP
SSZZZZ
SHUFF
SWF
CHK
TOONK
PLIP
LET'S SEE.
I'D SAY MY CHANCE OF SUCCESS IN THIS SPOT IS...

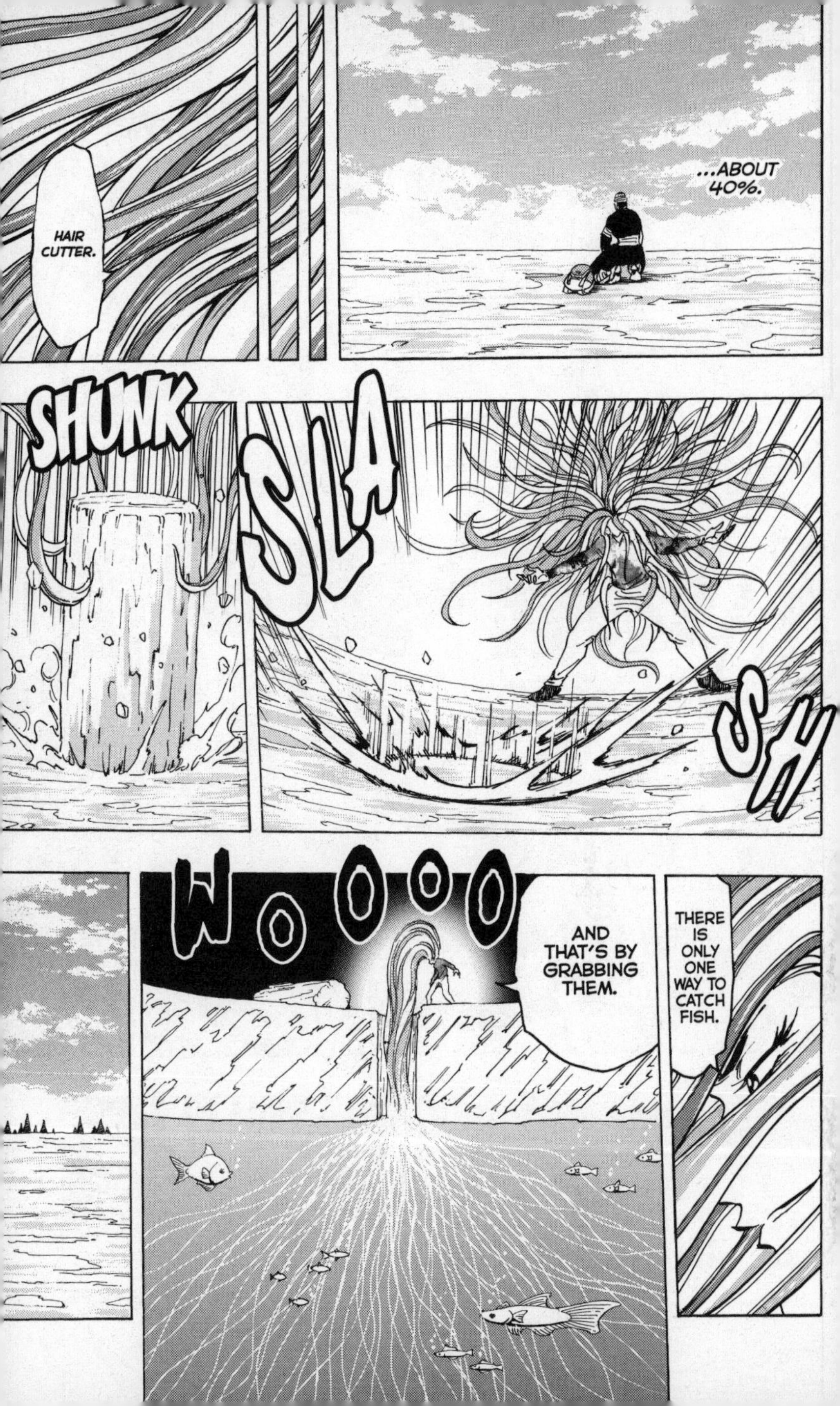
...ABOUT 40%.
HAIR CUTTER.
SLA
SH
SHUNK
THERE IS ONLY ONE WAY TO CATCH FISH.
AND THAT'S BY GRABBING THEM.
WOOOO

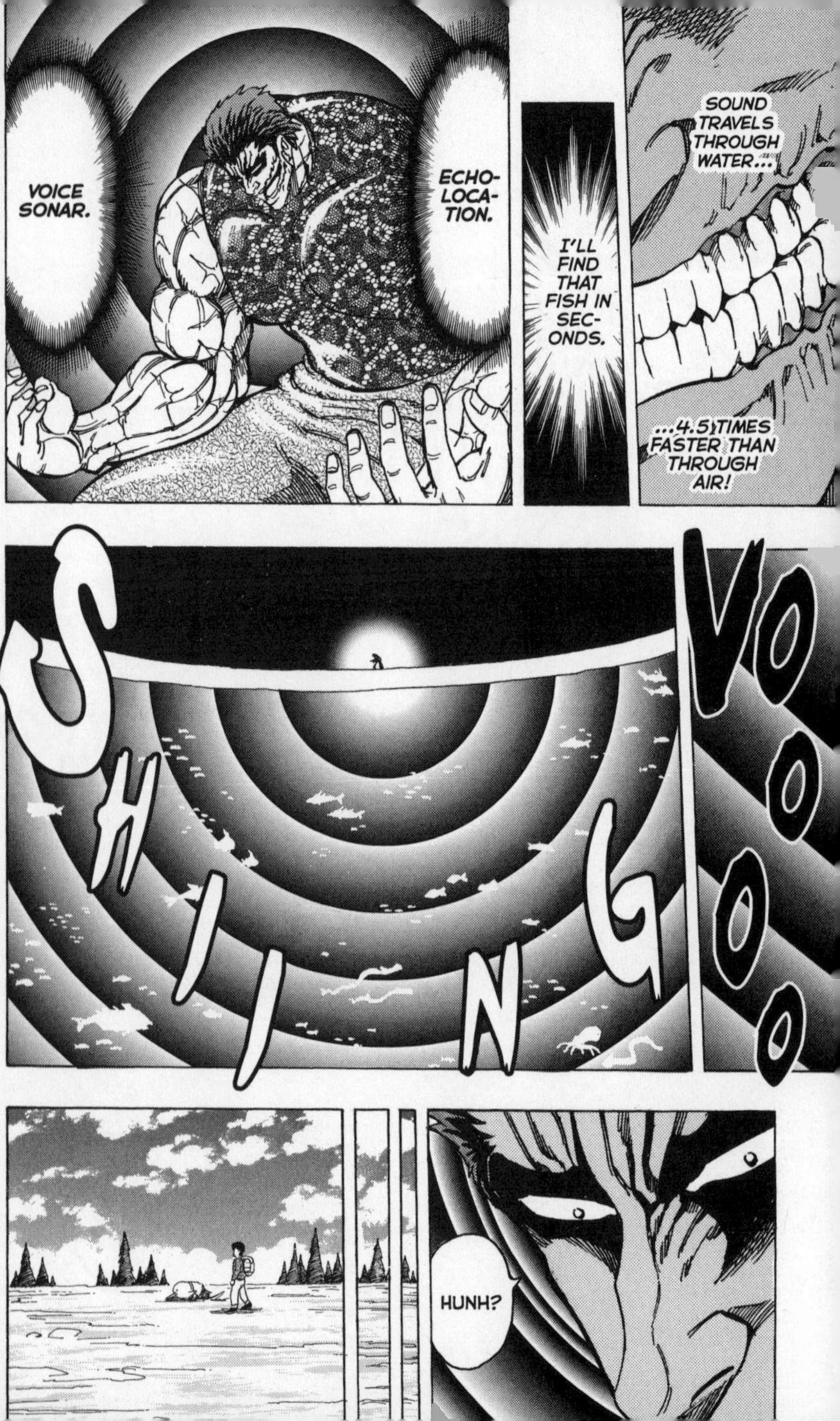
SOUND TRAVELS THROUGH WATER...
...4.5 TIMES FASTER THAN THROUGH AIR!
I'LL FIND THAT FISH IN SECONDS.
ECHOLOCATION.
VOICE SONAR.
VOOOOO
SHIING
HUNH?

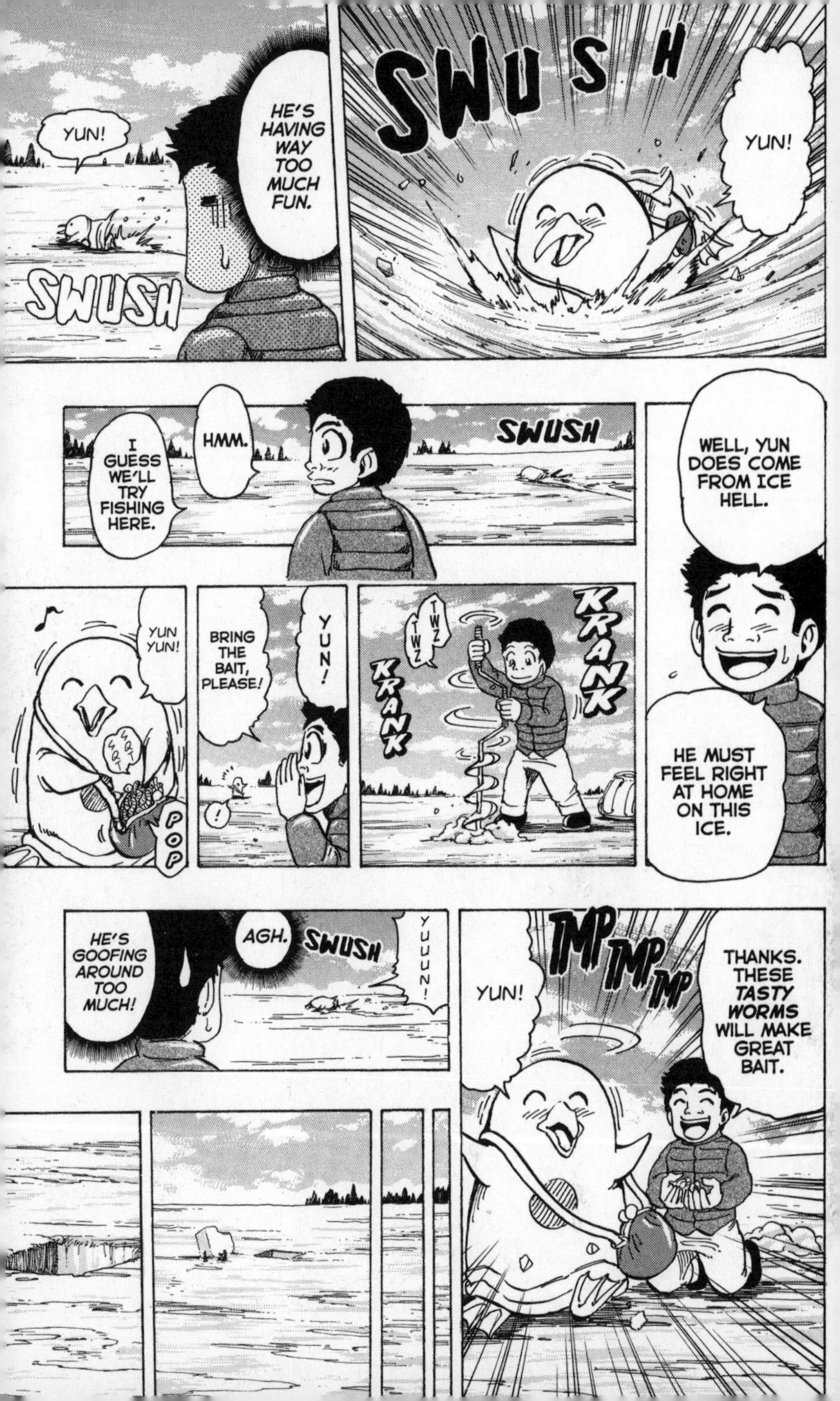
SWUSH
YUN!
HE'S HAVING WAY TOO MUCH FUN.
YUN!
SWUSH
WELL, YUN DOES COME FROM ICE HELL.
HE MUST FEEL RIGHT AT HOME ON THIS ICE.
SWUSH
HMM.
I GUESS WE'LL TRY FISHING HERE.
KRANK
TWZ TWZ
KRANK
YUN!
BRING THE BAIT, PLEASE!
!
YUN YUN!
SRT SRT
POP
THANKS. THESE TASTY WORMS WILL MAKE GREAT BAIT.
TMP TMP TMP
YUN!
YUUUN!
SWUSH
AGH.
HE'S GOOFING AROUND TOO MUCH!

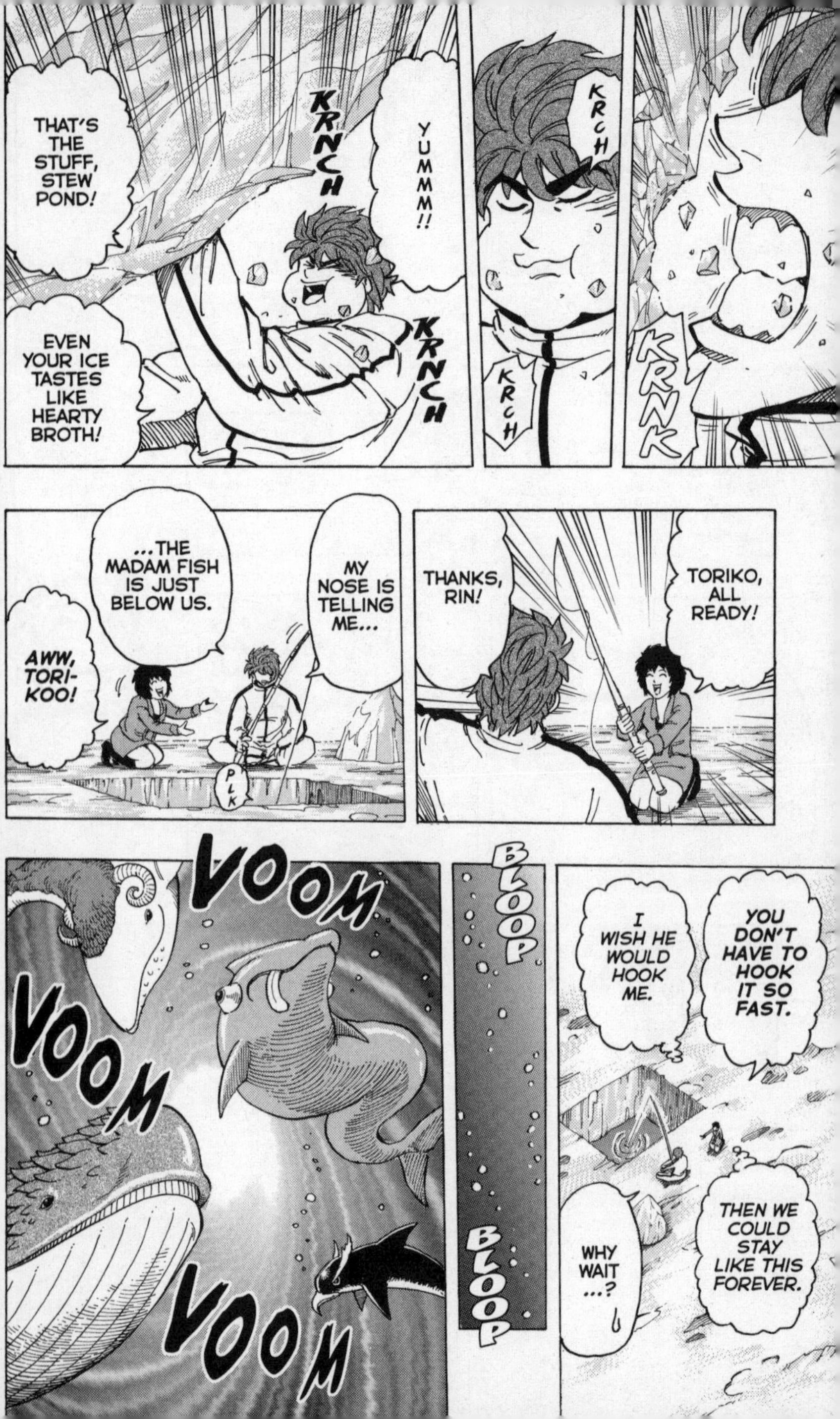
KRNK
KRCH
KRCH
YUMMM!!
KRNCH
THAT'S THE STUFF, STEW POND!
EVEN YOUR ICE TASTES LIKE HEARTY BROTH!
KRNCH
TORIKO, ALL READY!
THANKS, RIN!
MY NOSE IS TELLING ME...
...THE MADAM FISH IS JUST BELOW US.
AWW, TORI-KOO!
PLK
YOU DON'T HAVE TO HOOK IT SO FAST.
I WISH HE WOULD HOOK ME.
THEN WE COULD STAY LIKE THIS FOREVER.
WHY WAIT...?
BLOOP
BLOOP
VOOM
VOOM
VOOM

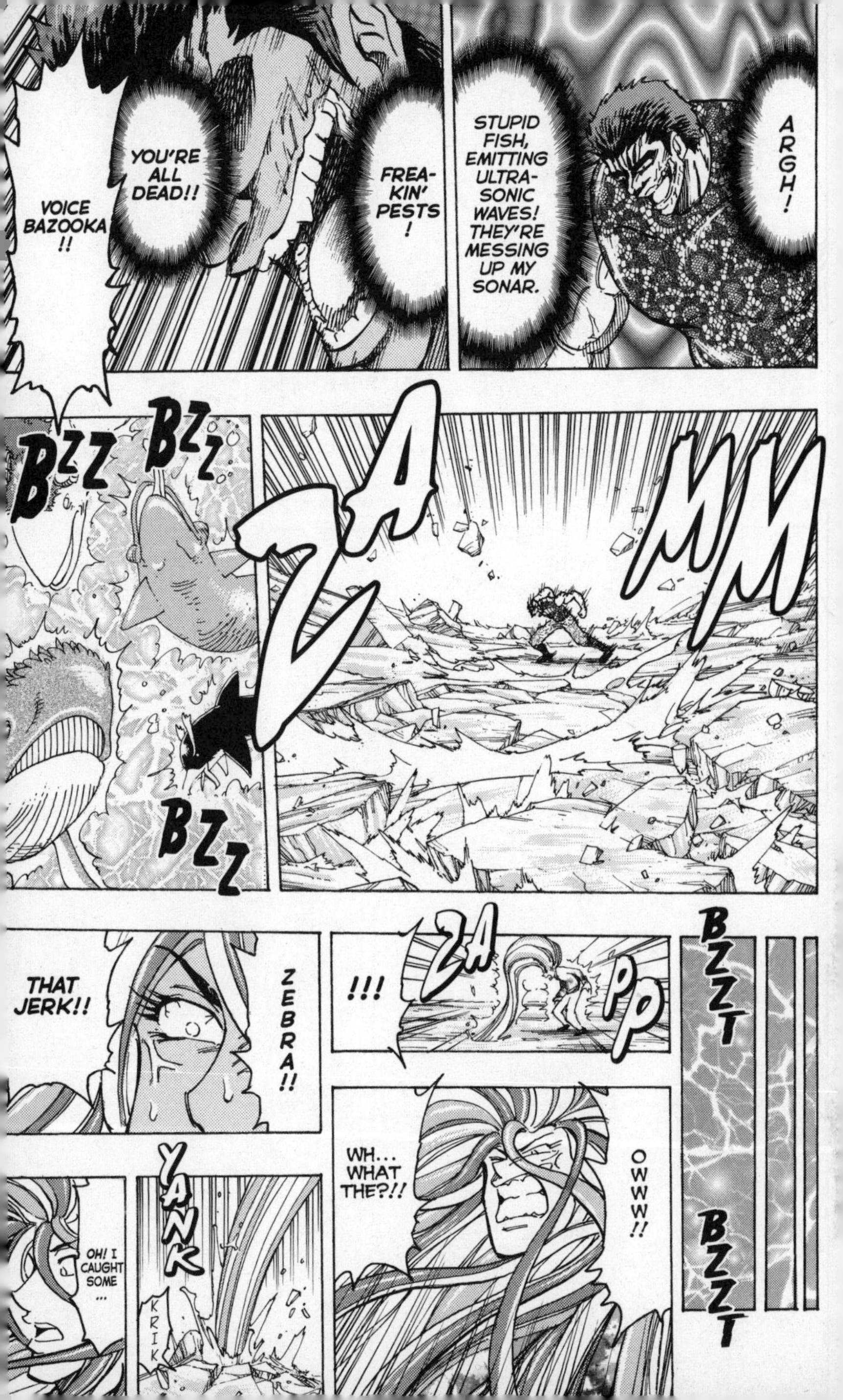

ARGH!
STUPID FISH, EMITTING ULTRA-SONIC WAVES! THEY'RE MESSING UP MY SONAR.
FREA-KIN' PESTS!
YOU'RE ALL DEAD!!
VOICE BAZOOKA!!
ZAMM
BZZ
BZZ
BZZ
BZZT
BZZT
ZAPP
!!!
ZEBRA!!
THAT JERK!!
OWWW!!
WH... WHAT THE?!!
YANK
KRIK
OH! I CAUGHT SOME ...

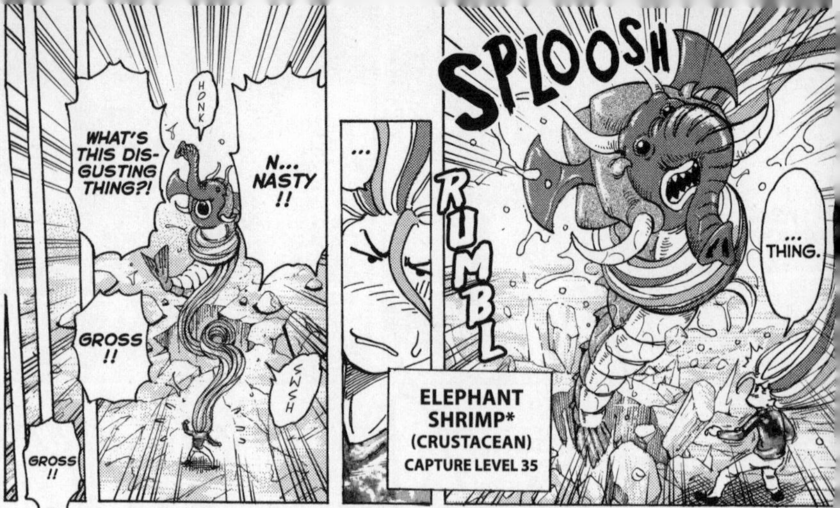
SPLOOSH
RUMBL
...THING.
ELEPHANT SHRIMP* (CRUSTACEAN) CAPTURE LEVEL 35
...
HONK
N... NASTY!!
WHAT'S THIS DISGUSTING THING?!
SWSH
GROSS!!
GROSS!!

*ELEPHANT SHRIMP SUBMITTED BY KOJI SAKO FROM GIFU!

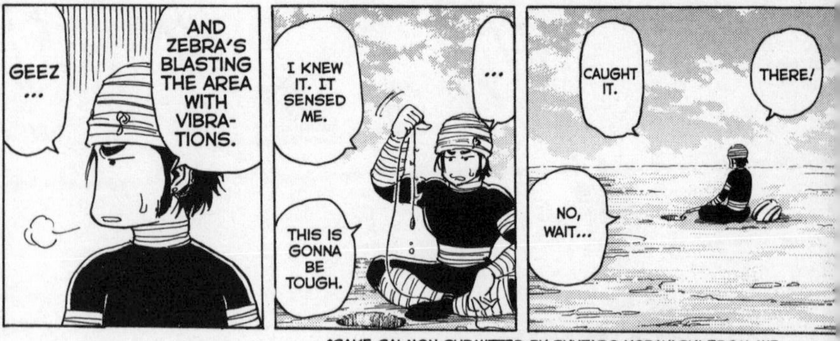
THERE!
CAUGHT IT.
NO, WAIT...
...
I KNEW IT. IT SENSED ME.
THIS IS GONNA BE TOUGH.
AND ZEBRA'S BLASTING THE AREA WITH VIBRATIONS.
GEEZ...

*SAKE SALMON SUBMITTED BY RYUTARO KOBAYASHI FROM MIE; BUTTERFLY EEL SUBMITTED BY ETTSUN FROM GIFU!

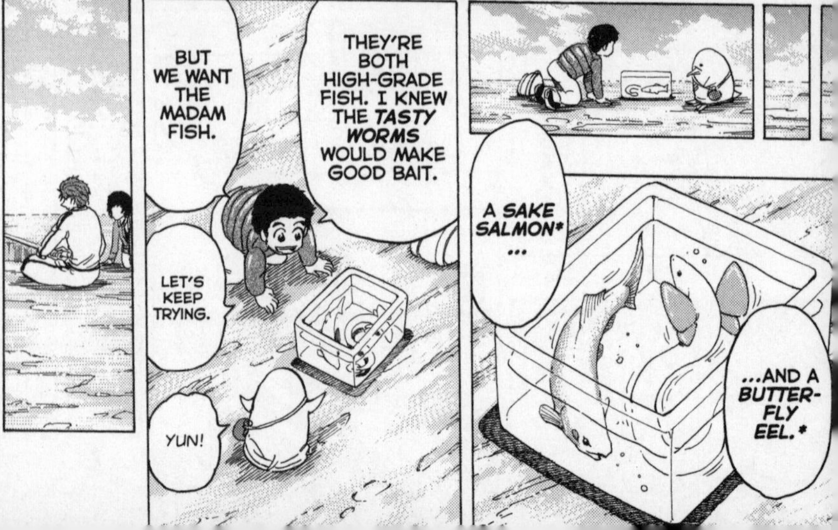
A SAKE SALMON*...
...AND A BUTTERFLY EEL.*
THEY'RE BOTH HIGH-GRADE FISH. I KNEW THE TASTY WORMS WOULD MAKE GOOD BAIT.
BUT WE WANT THE MADAM FISH.
LET'S KEEP TRYING.
YUN!

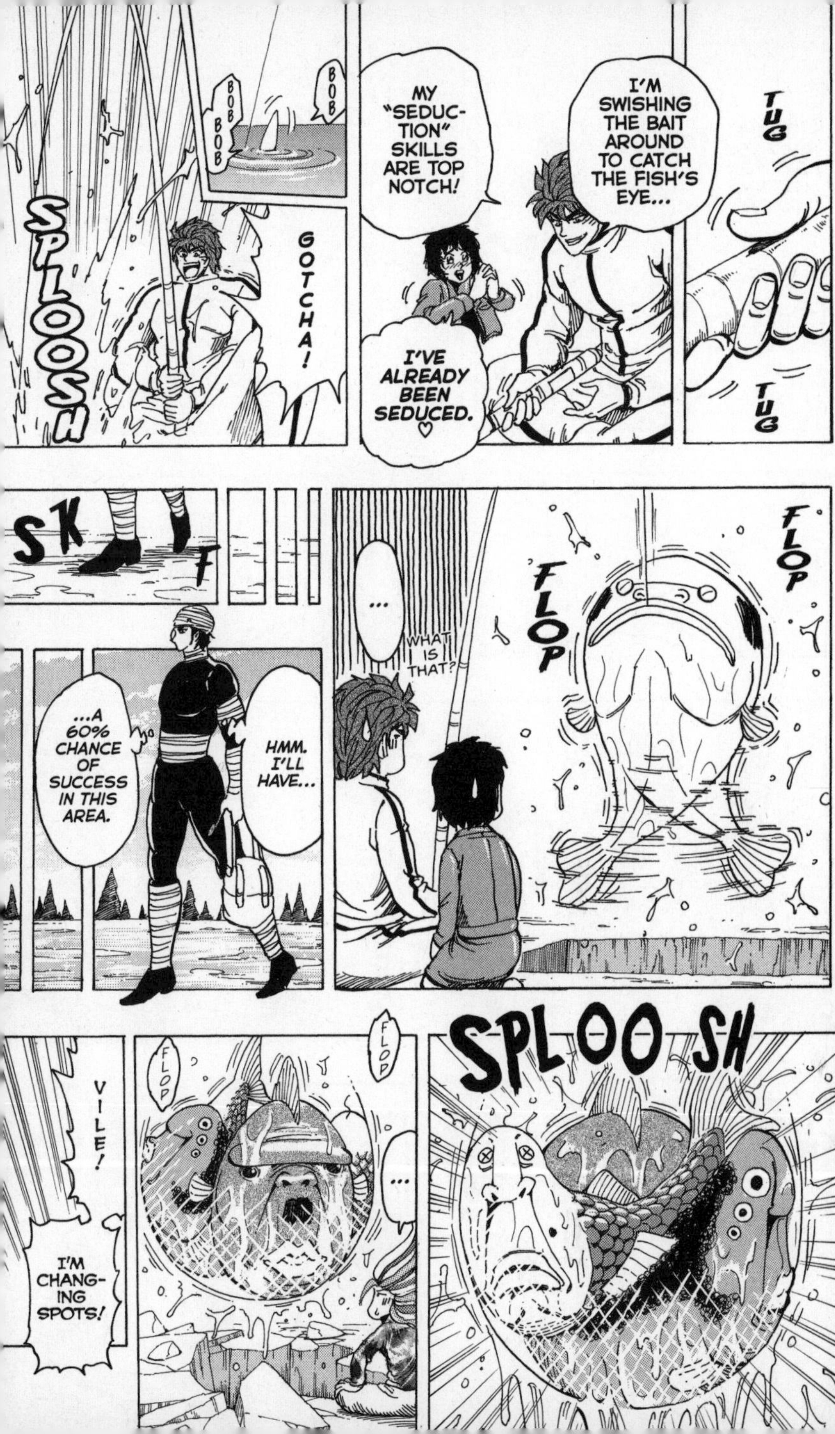
TUG
TUG
I'M SWISHING THE BAIT AROUND TO CATCH THE FISH'S EYE...
MY "SEDUCTION" SKILLS ARE TOP NOTCH!
I'VE ALREADY BEEN SEDUCED. ♡
BOB BOB
BOB BOB
GOTCHA!
SPLOOSH
FLOP
FLOP
...
WHAT IS THAT?
SK
F
HMM. I'LL HAVE...
...A 60% CHANCE OF SUCCESS IN THIS AREA.
SPLOOSH
FLOP
FLOP
...
VILE!
I'M CHANGING SPOTS!

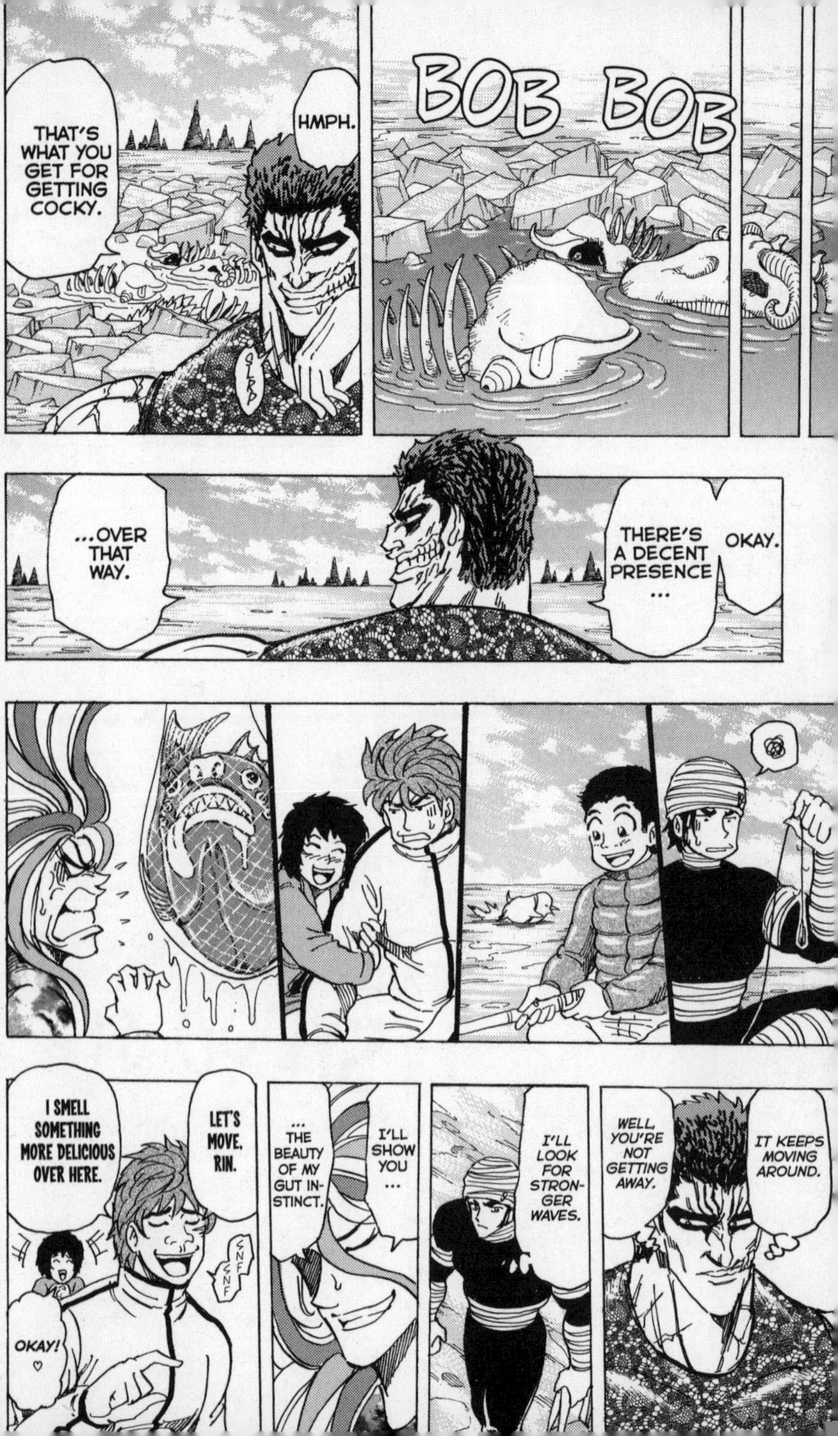
BOB BOB
HMPH.
THAT'S WHAT YOU GET FOR GETTING COCKY.
SLRP
OKAY.
THERE'S A DECENT PRESENCE ...
...OVER THAT WAY.
IT KEEPS MOVING AROUND.
WELL, YOU'RE NOT GETTING AWAY.
I'LL LOOK FOR STRONGER WAVES.
I'LL SHOW YOU ...
... THE BEAUTY OF MY GUT INSTINCT.
LET'S MOVE, RIN.
I SMELL SOMETHING MORE DELICIOUS OVER HERE.
SNF SNF
OKAY! ♡

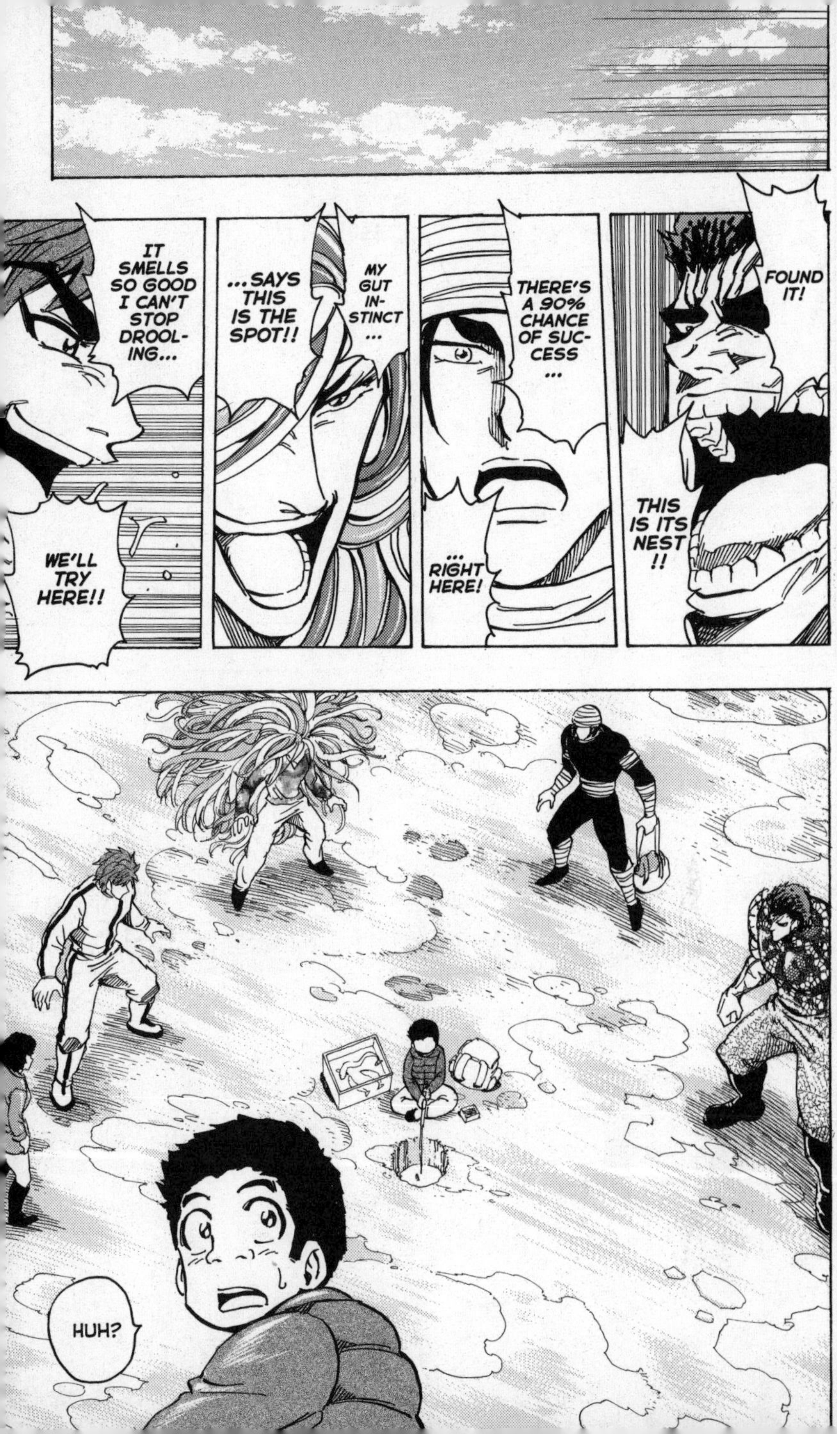
FOUND IT!
THIS IS ITS NEST!!
THERE'S A 90% CHANCE OF SUCCESS...
...RIGHT HERE!
MY GUT INSTINCT...
...SAYS THIS IS THE SPOT!!
IT SMELLS SO GOOD I CAN'T STOP DROOLING...
WE'LL TRY HERE!!
HUH?

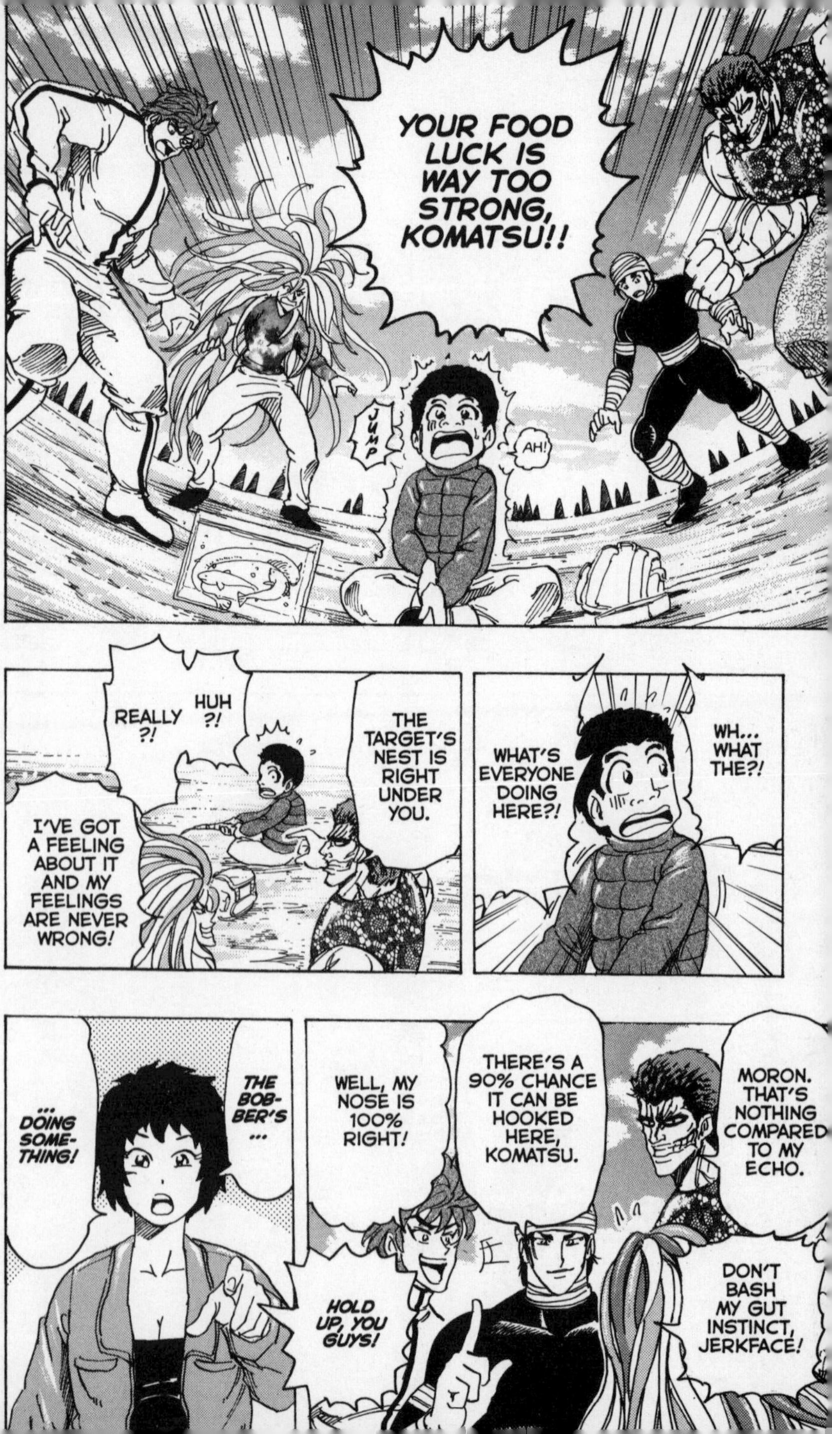
YOUR FOOD LUCK IS WAY TOO STRONG, KOMATSU!!
AH!
JUMP
WH... WHAT THE?!
WHAT'S EVERYONE DOING HERE?!
THE TARGET'S NEST IS RIGHT UNDER YOU.
HUH ?!
REALLY ?!
I'VE GOT A FEELING ABOUT IT AND MY FEELINGS ARE NEVER WRONG!
MORON. THAT'S NOTHING COMPARED TO MY ECHO.
THERE'S A 90% CHANCE IT CAN BE HOOKED HERE, KOMATSU.
WELL, MY NOSE IS 100% RIGHT!
DON'T BASH MY GUT INSTINCT, JERKFACE!
HOLD UP, YOU GUYS!
THE BOBBER'S ...
... DOING SOMETHING!

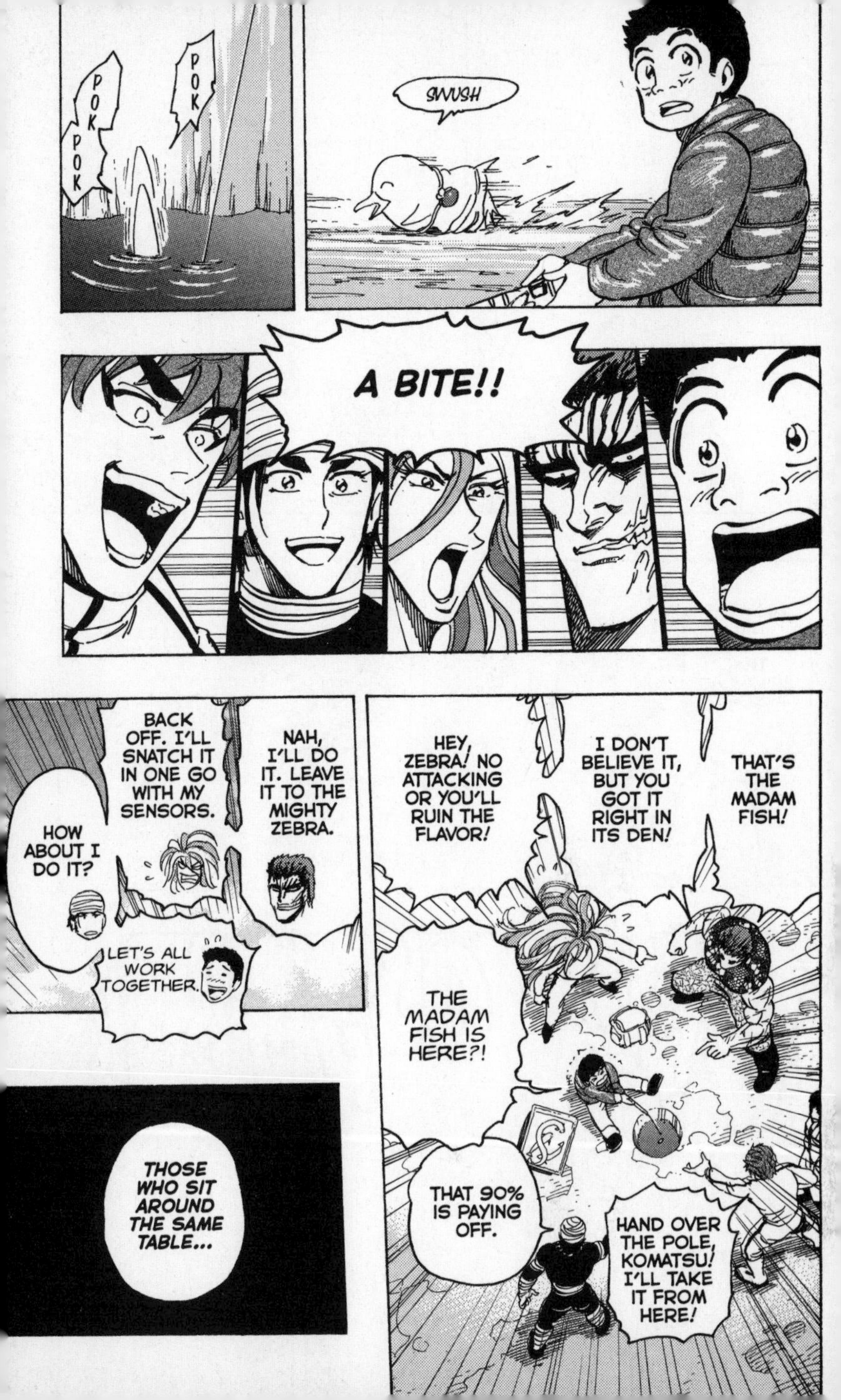
SWUSH
POK POK
POK POK
A BITE!!
THAT'S THE MADAM FISH!
I DON'T BELIEVE IT, BUT YOU GOT IT RIGHT IN ITS DEN!
HEY, ZEBRA! NO ATTACKING OR YOU'LL RUIN THE FLAVOR!
THE MADAM FISH IS HERE?!
HAND OVER THE POLE, KOMATSU! I'LL TAKE IT FROM HERE!
THAT 90% IS PAYING OFF.
NAH, I'LL DO IT. LEAVE IT TO THE MIGHTY ZEBRA.
BACK OFF. I'LL SNATCH IT IN ONE GO WITH MY SENSORS.
HOW ABOUT I DO IT?
LET'S ALL WORK TOGETHER.
THOSE WHO SIT AROUND THE SAME TABLE...

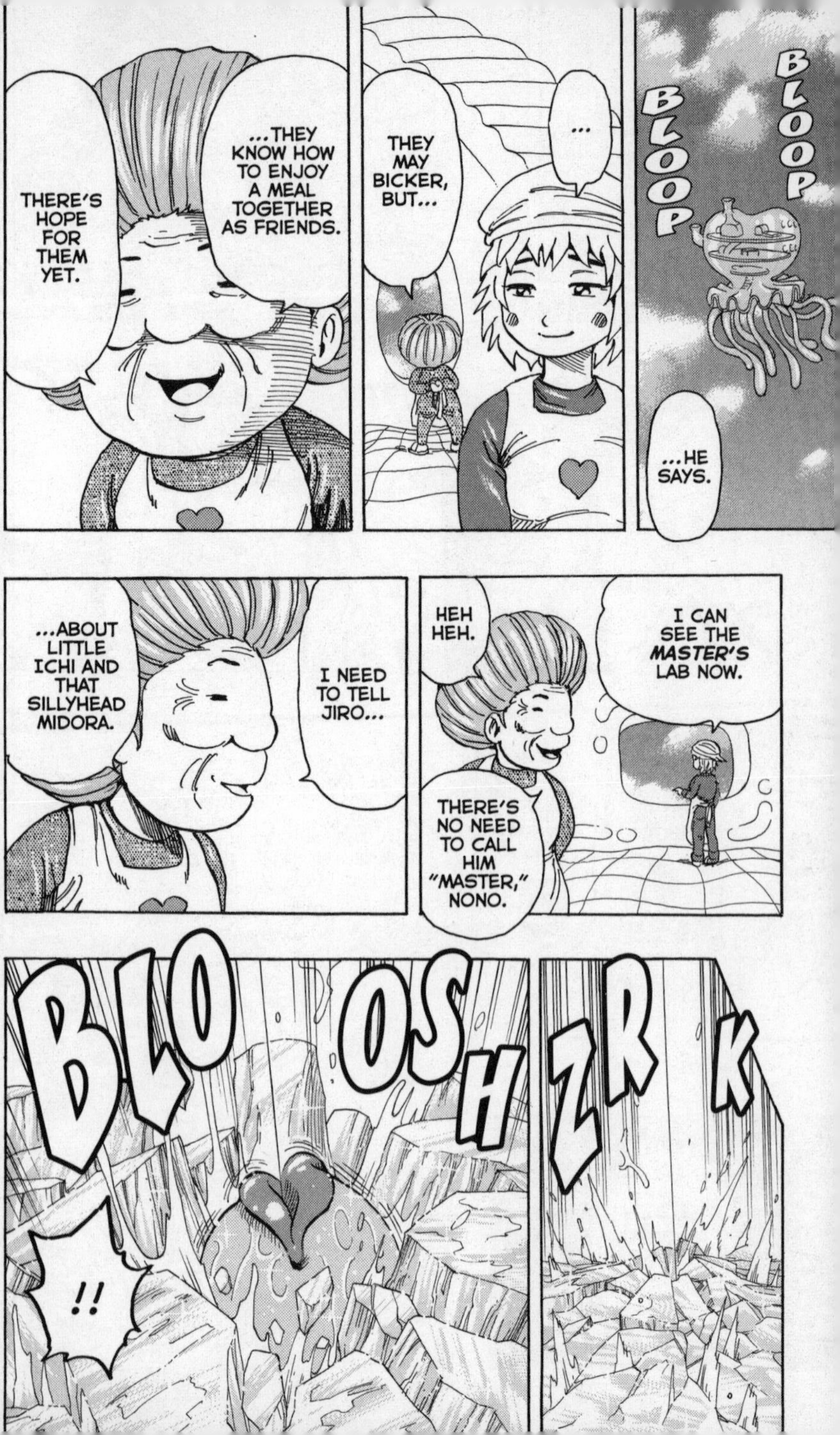
BLOOP
BLOOP
...HE SAYS.
...
THEY MAY BICKER, BUT...
...THEY KNOW HOW TO ENJOY A MEAL TOGETHER AS FRIENDS.
THERE'S HOPE FOR THEM YET.
I CAN SEE THE *MASTER'S* LAB NOW.
HEH HEH.
THERE'S NO NEED TO CALL HIM "MASTER," NONO.
I NEED TO TELL JIRO...
...ABOUT LITTLE ICHI AND THAT SILLYHEAD MIDORA.
ZRK
BLOOSH
!!

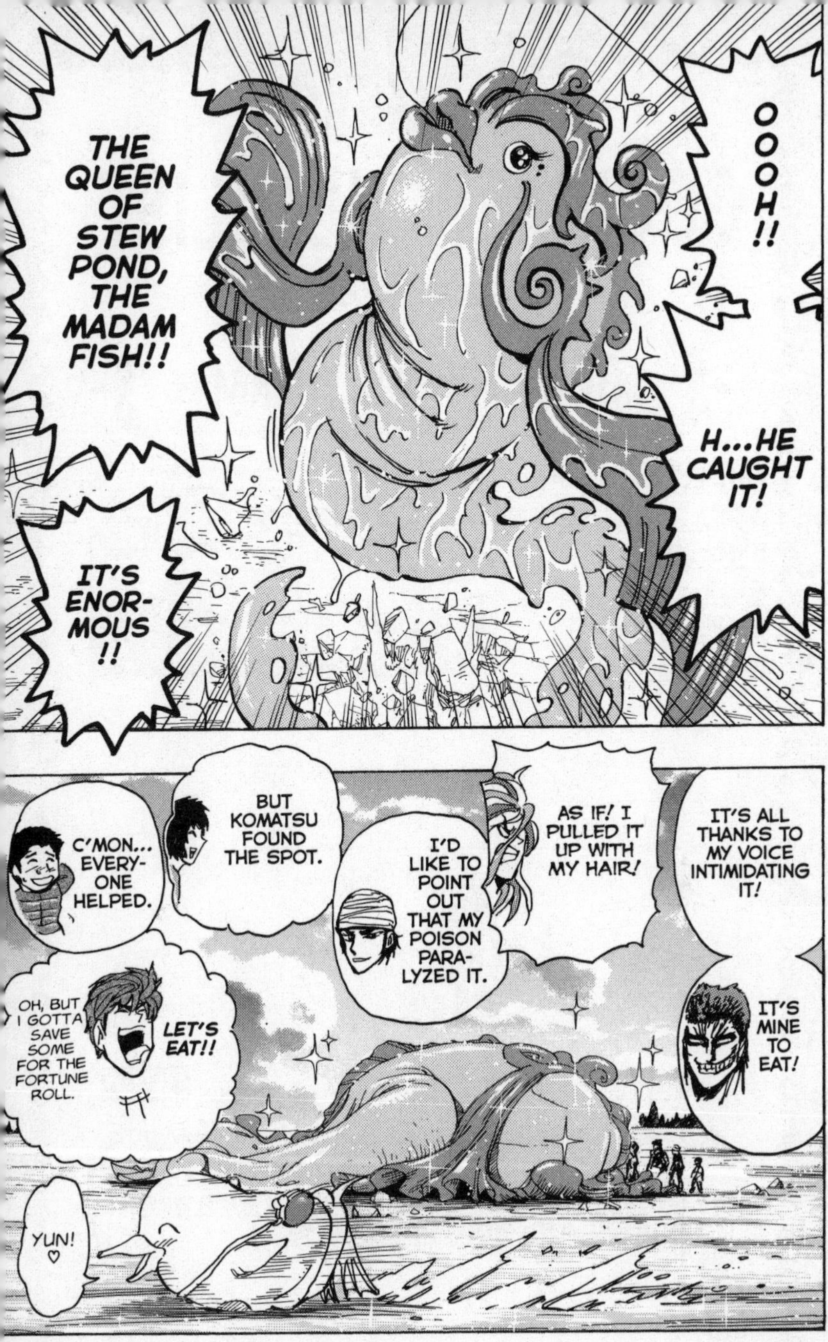
OOOOH!!
H...HE CAUGHT IT!
THE QUEEN OF STEW POND, THE MADAM FISH!!
IT'S ENORMOUS!!
IT'S ALL THANKS TO MY VOICE INTIMIDATING IT!
AS IF! I PULLED IT UP WITH MY HAIR!
I'D LIKE TO POINT OUT THAT MY POISON PARALYZED IT.
BUT KOMATSU FOUND THE SPOT.
C'MON... EVERYONE HELPED.
IT'S MINE TO EAT!
LET'S EAT!!
OH, BUT I GOTTA SAVE SOME FOR THE FORTUNE ROLL.
YUN! ♡

TORIKO

GOURMET CHECKLIST

Vol. 204

⟨ BEAN SPROUT WORM ⟩
(WORM)

CAPTURE LEVEL: LESS THAN 1
HABITAT: VIRTUALLY EVERYWHERE
LENGTH: 6 CM
HEIGHT: ---
WEIGHT: 1 GRAM
PRICE: 200 YEN PER BAG

STEP RIGHT UP, STEP RIGHT UP!

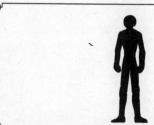

SCALE

A WORM THAT LIVES IN THE GROUND AND FEEDS ON HUMUS. ITS BODY IS LONG, SKINNY AND VERY SEGMENTED. THE FACT THAT IT'S SMALL MAKES IT LOOK A LOT LIKE A BEAN SPROUT. THE WORMS LOSE CONSCIOUSNESS AFTER BAGGING, SO IT IS COMMON PRACTICE TO FRY THEM UP AND EAT THEM RIGHT OUT IN THE FIELD WHERE THEY ARE CAPTURED.

GOURMET 176: KING VINEGAR!!

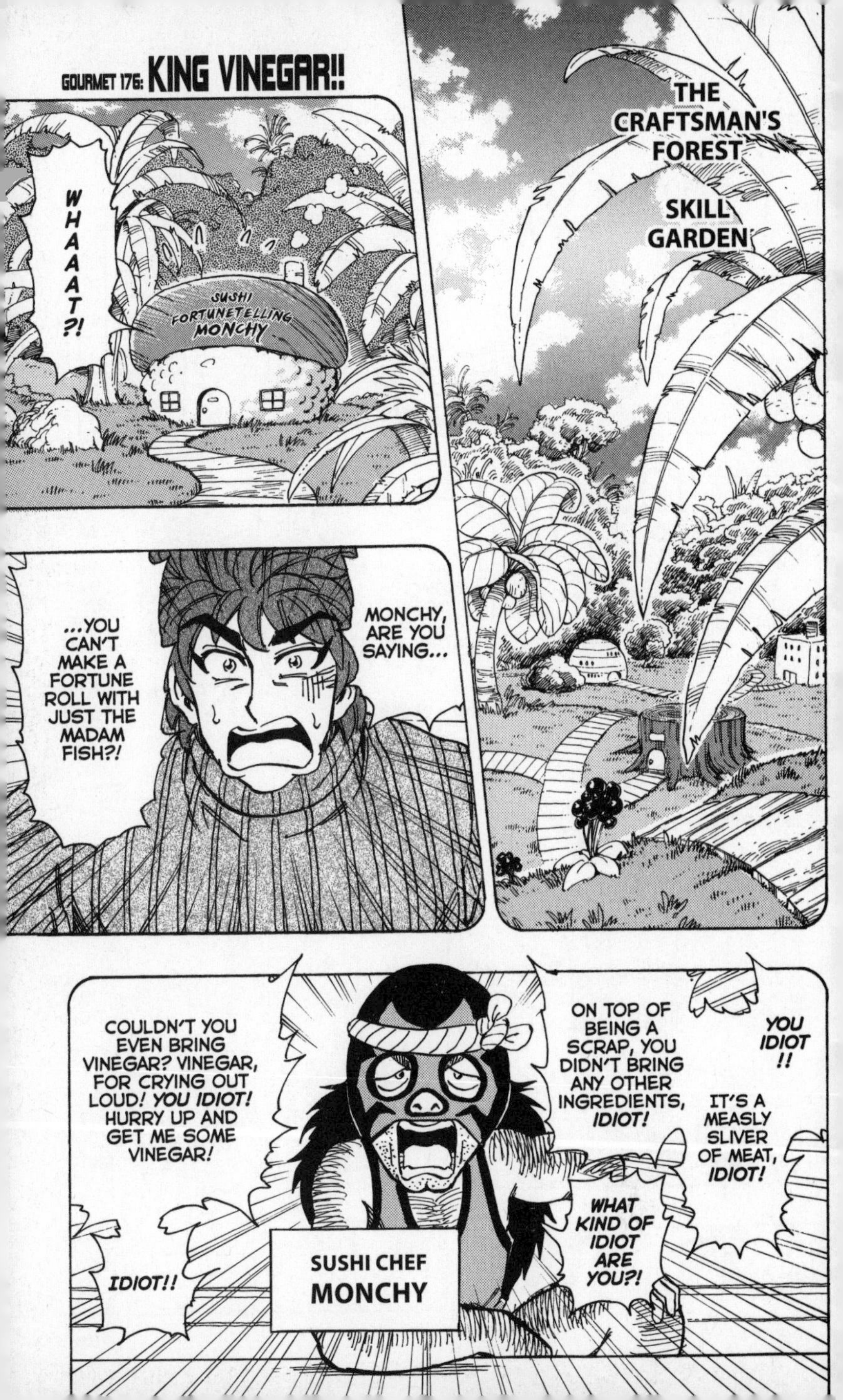
THE CRAFTSMAN'S FOREST
SKILL GARDEN
SUSHI FORTUNETELLING MONCHY
WHAAAAT?!
MONCHY, ARE YOU SAYING...
...YOU CAN'T MAKE A FORTUNE ROLL WITH JUST THE MADAM FISH?!
YOU IDIOT!!
ON TOP OF BEING A SCRAP, YOU DIDN'T BRING ANY OTHER INGREDIENTS, IDIOT!
IT'S A MEASLY SLIVER OF MEAT, IDIOT!
COULDN'T YOU EVEN BRING VINEGAR? VINEGAR, FOR CRYING OUT LOUD! YOU IDIOT! HURRY UP AND GET ME SOME VINEGAR!
WHAT KIND OF IDIOT ARE YOU?!
SUSHI CHEF MONCHY
IDIOT!!

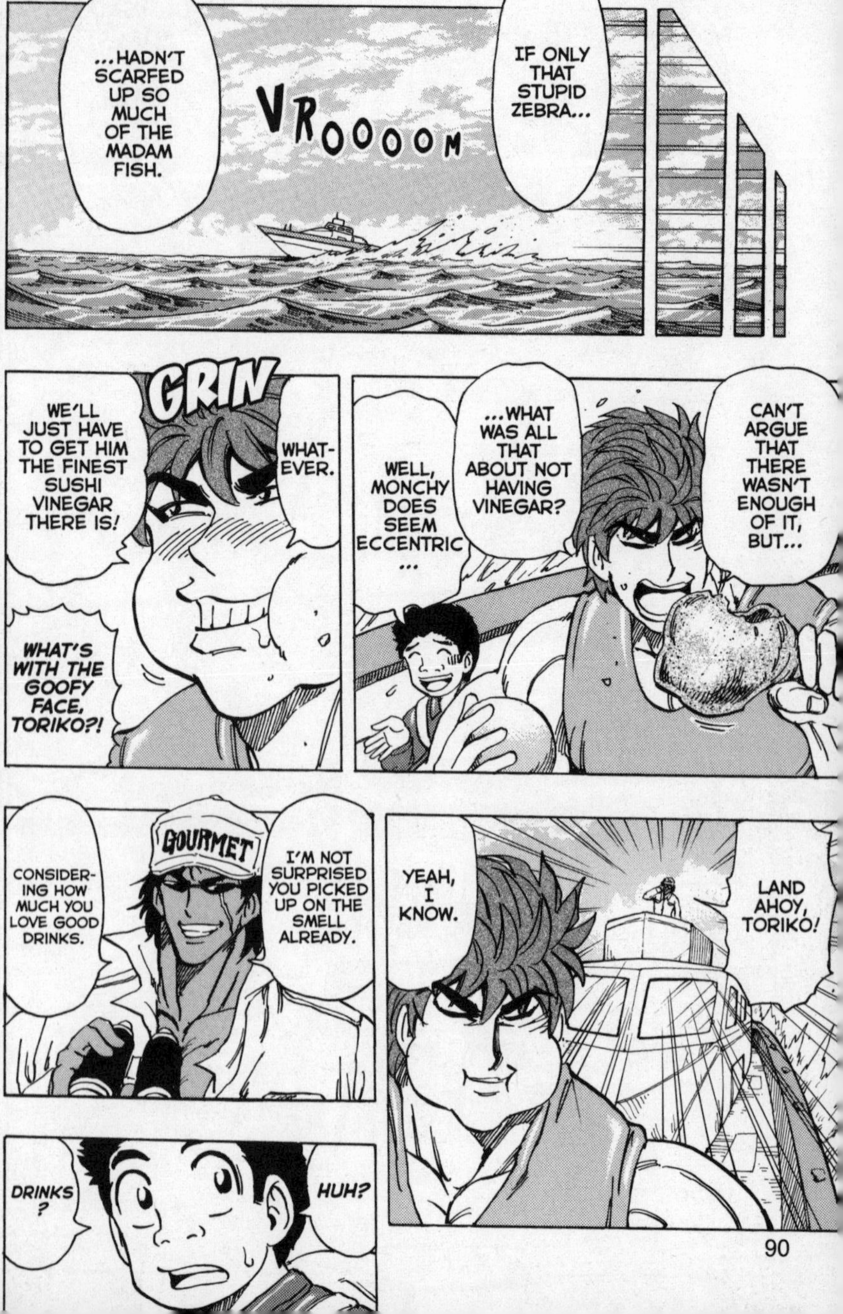
IF ONLY THAT STUPID ZEBRA...
VROOOOM
...HADN'T SCARFED UP SO MUCH OF THE MADAM FISH.
CAN'T ARGUE THAT THERE WASN'T ENOUGH OF IT, BUT...
...WHAT WAS ALL THAT ABOUT NOT HAVING VINEGAR?
WELL, MONCHY DOES SEEM ECCENTRIC...
WHAT-EVER.
GRIN
WE'LL JUST HAVE TO GET HIM THE FINEST SUSHI VINEGAR THERE IS!
WHAT'S WITH THE GOOFY FACE, TORIKO?!
LAND AHOY, TORIKO!
YEAH, I KNOW.
GOURMET
I'M NOT SURPRISED YOU PICKED UP ON THE SMELL ALREADY.
CONSIDER-ING HOW MUCH YOU LOVE GOOD DRINKS.
HUH?
DRINKS?

GOURMET 176: KING VINEGAR!!

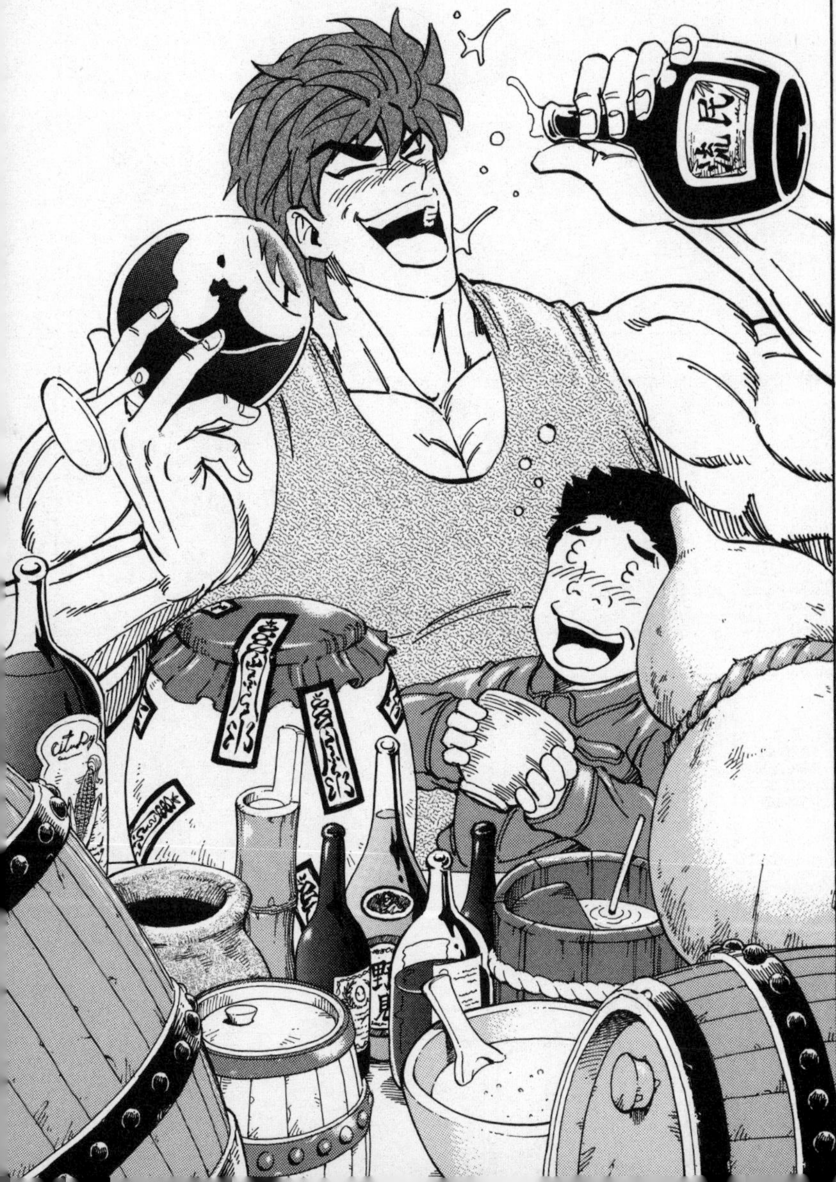

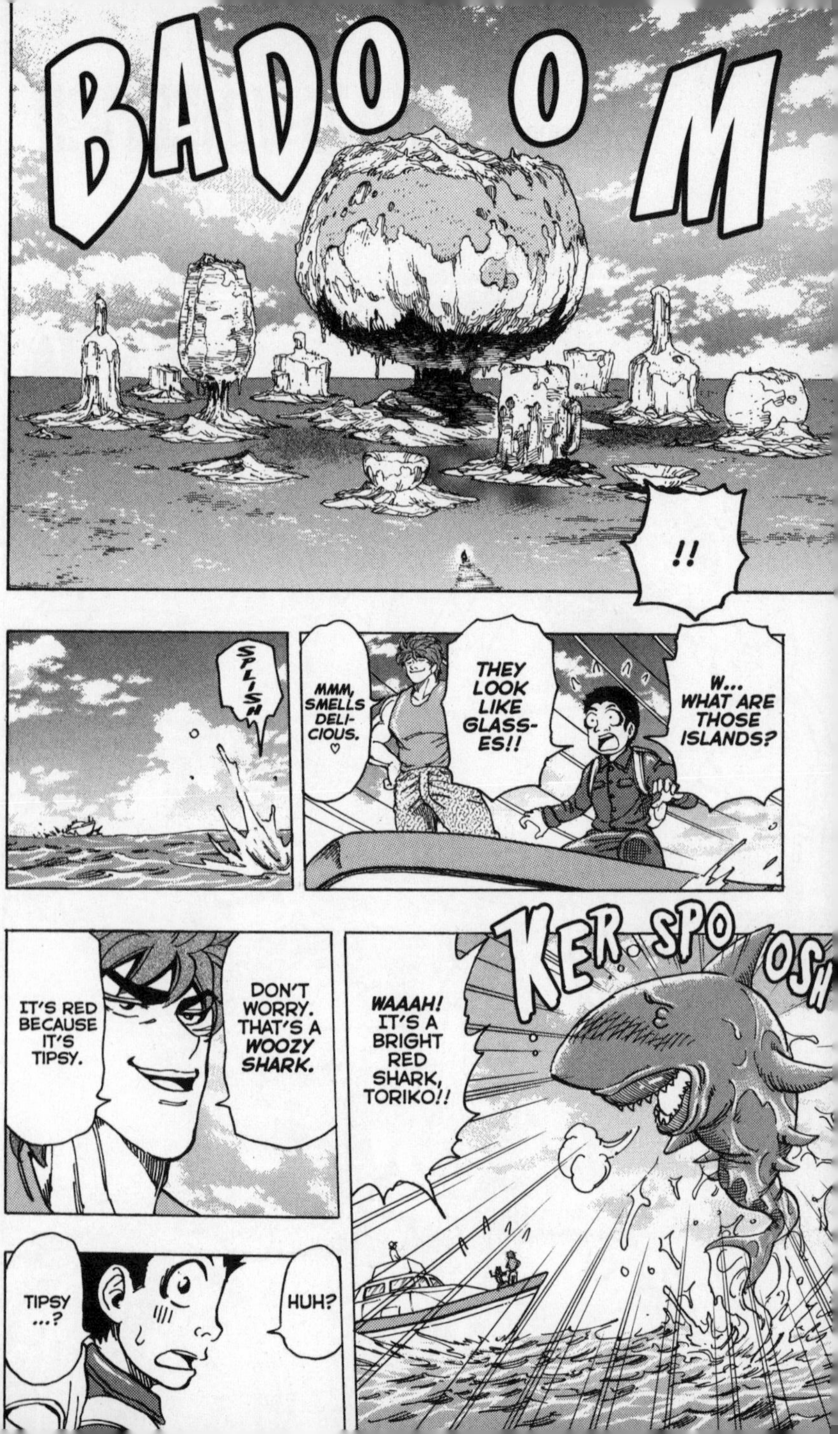
BADOOM
!!
W... WHAT ARE THOSE ISLANDS?
THEY LOOK LIKE GLASSES!!
MMM, SMELLS DELICIOUS. ♡
SPLISH
KER-SPOOSH
WAAAH! IT'S A BRIGHT RED SHARK, TORIKO!!
DON'T WORRY. THAT'S A *WOOZY SHARK.*
IT'S RED BECAUSE IT'S TIPSY.
HUH?
TIPSY ...?

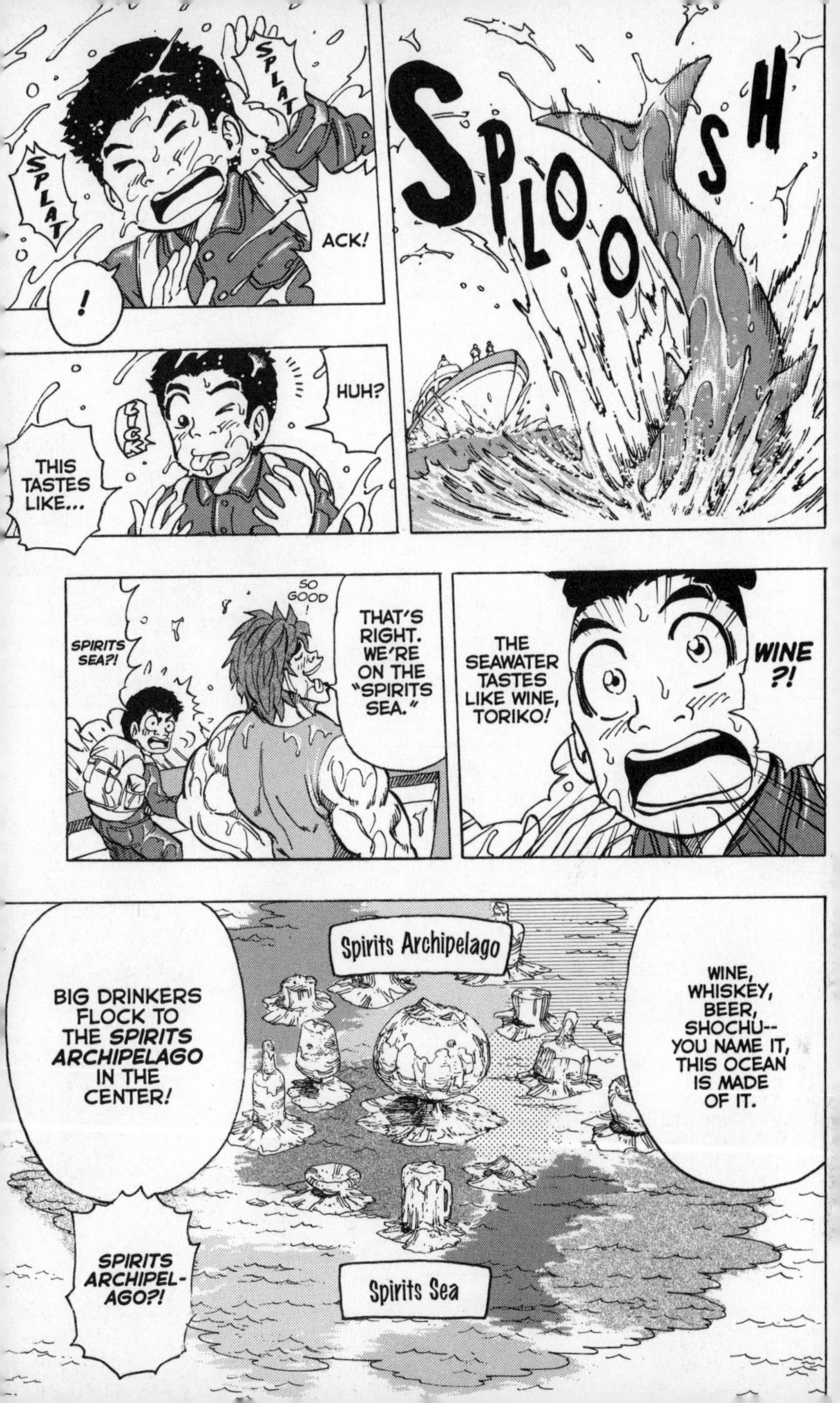
SPLOOOSH
SPLAT
ACK!
SPLAT
!
HUH?
LICK
THIS TASTES LIKE...
WINE ?!
THE SEAWATER TASTES LIKE WINE, TORIKO!
SO GOOD!
THAT'S RIGHT. WE'RE ON THE "SPIRITS SEA."
SPIRITS SEA?!
WINE, WHISKEY, BEER, SHOCHU-- YOU NAME IT, THIS OCEAN IS MADE OF IT.
Spirits Archipelago
BIG DRINKERS FLOCK TO THE *SPIRITS ARCHIPELAGO* IN THE CENTER!
Spirits Sea
SPIRITS ARCHIPEL-AGO?!

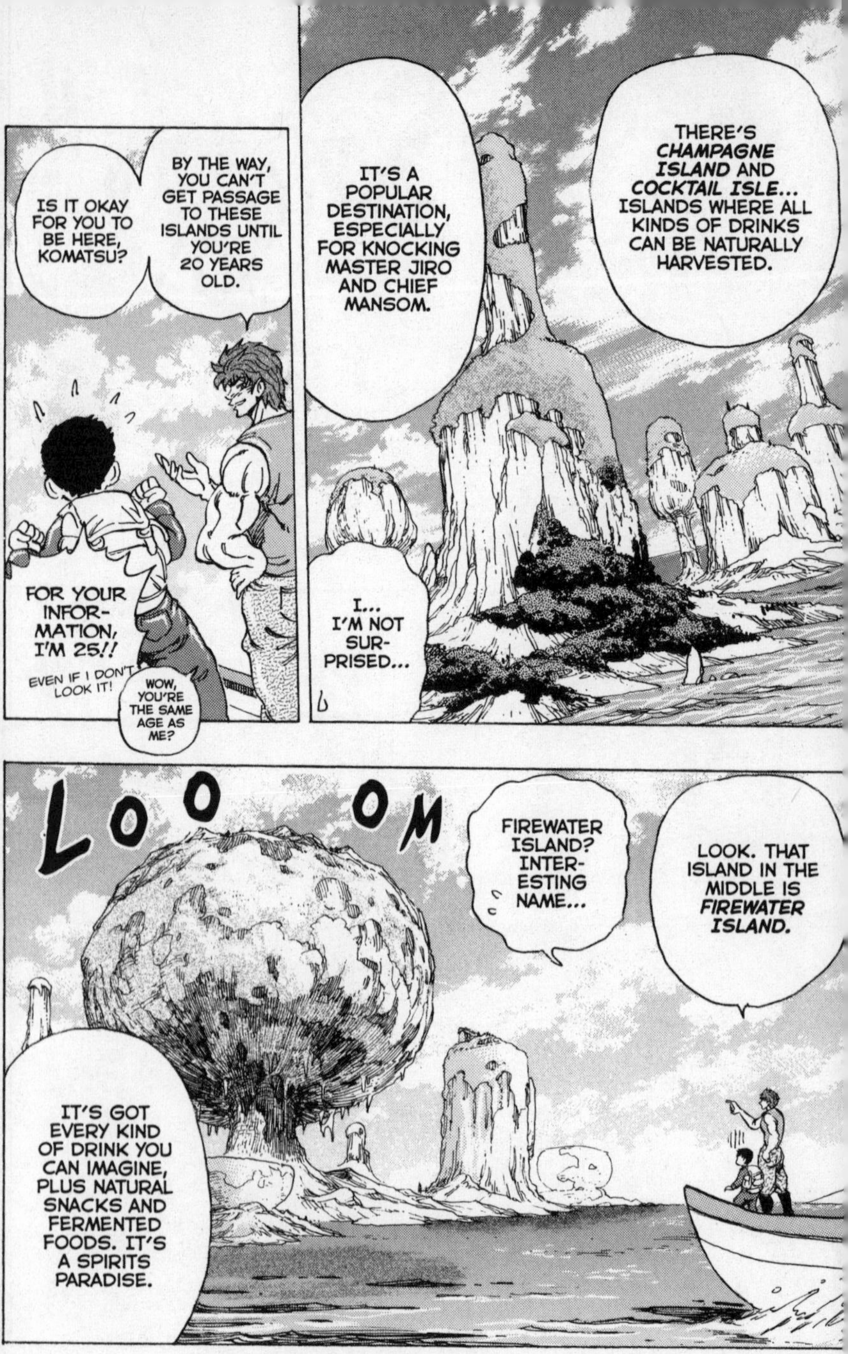
THERE'S CHAMPAGNE ISLAND AND COCKTAIL ISLE... ISLANDS WHERE ALL KINDS OF DRINKS CAN BE NATURALLY HARVESTED.
IT'S A POPULAR DESTINATION, ESPECIALLY FOR KNOCKING MASTER JIRO AND CHIEF MANSOM.
I... I'M NOT SURPRISED...
BY THE WAY, YOU CAN'T GET PASSAGE TO THESE ISLANDS UNTIL YOU'RE 20 YEARS OLD.
IS IT OKAY FOR YOU TO BE HERE, KOMATSU?
FOR YOUR INFORMATION, I'M 25!!
EVEN IF I DON'T LOOK IT!
WOW, YOU'RE THE SAME AGE AS ME?
LOOM
LOOK. THAT ISLAND IN THE MIDDLE IS FIREWATER ISLAND.
FIREWATER ISLAND? INTERESTING NAME...
IT'S GOT EVERY KIND OF DRINK YOU CAN IMAGINE, PLUS NATURAL SNACKS AND FERMENTED FOODS. IT'S A SPIRITS PARADISE.

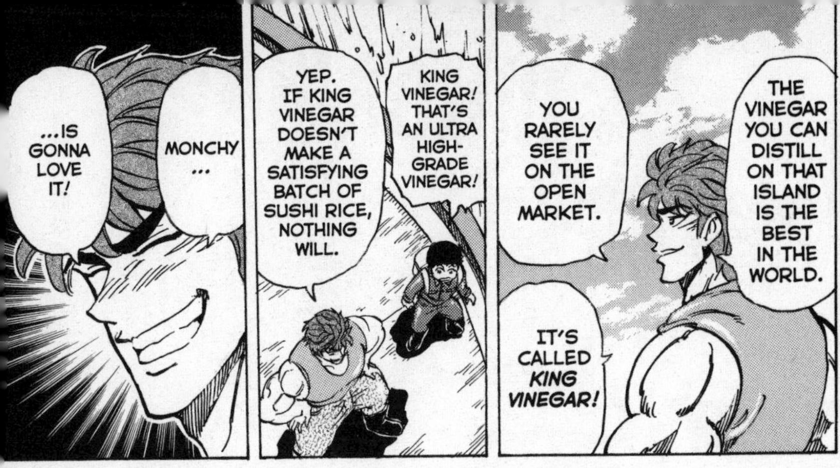
THE VINEGAR YOU CAN DISTILL ON THAT ISLAND IS THE BEST IN THE WORLD.
YOU RARELY SEE IT ON THE OPEN MARKET.
IT'S CALLED *KING VINEGAR!*
KING VINEGAR! THAT'S AN ULTRA HIGH-GRADE VINEGAR!
YEP. IF KING VINEGAR DOESN'T MAKE A SATISFYING BATCH OF SUSHI RICE, NOTHING WILL.
MONCHY ...
...IS GONNA LOVE IT!

Menu 15.

KING VINEGAR

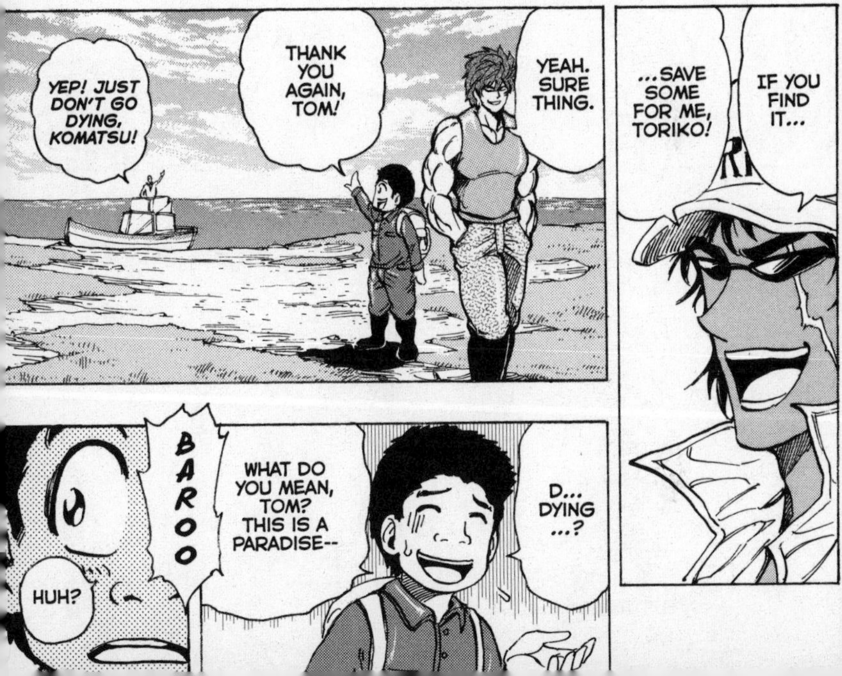
IF YOU FIND IT...
...SAVE SOME FOR ME, TORIKO!
YEAH. SURE THING.
THANK YOU AGAIN, TOM!
YEP! JUST DON'T GO DYING, KOMATSU!
D... DYING ...?
WHAT DO YOU MEAN, TOM? THIS IS A PARADISE--
BAROO
HUH?

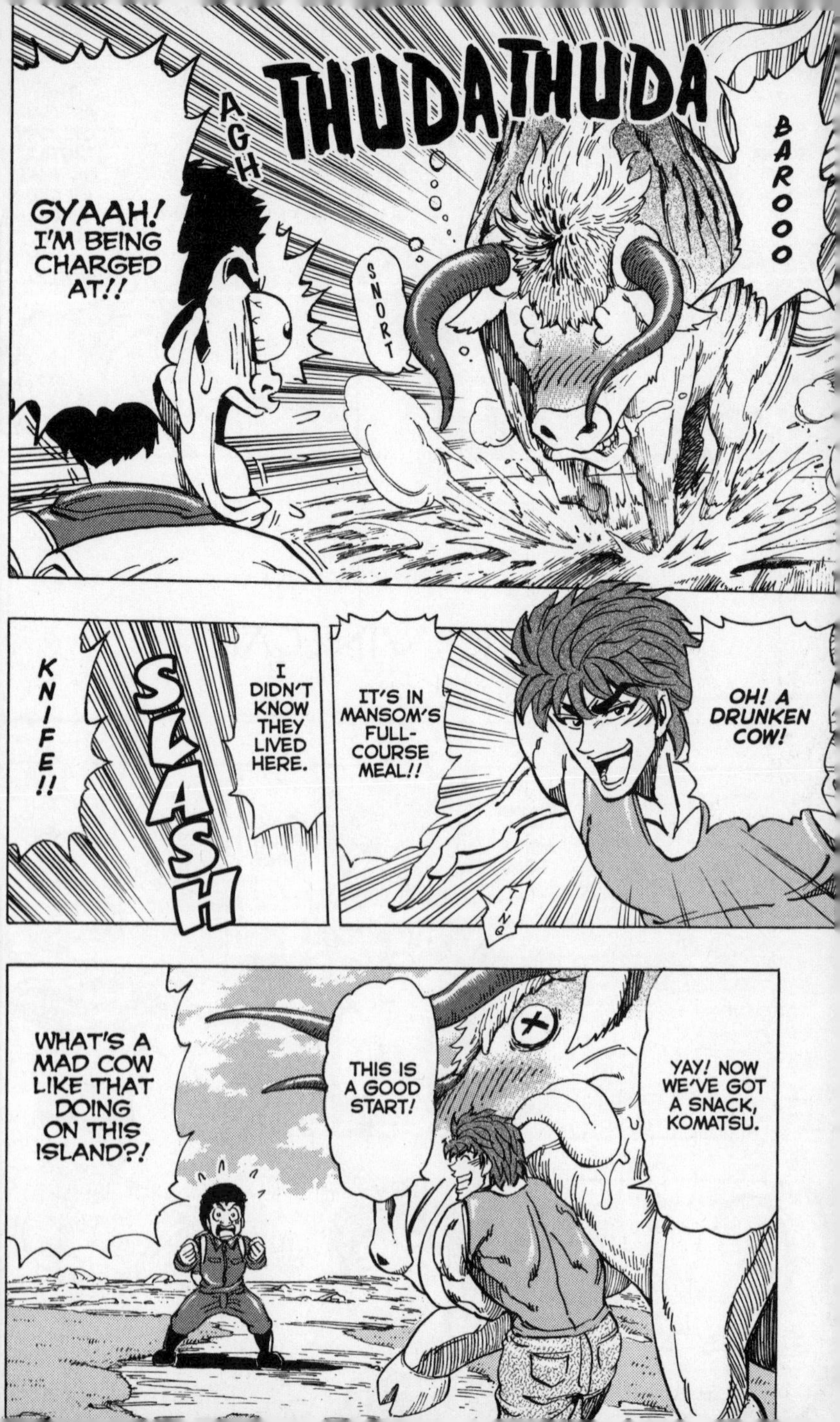
BAROOO
THUDATHUDA
SNORT
AGH
GYAAH! I'M BEING CHARGED AT!!
OH! A DRUNKEN COW!
IT'S IN MANSOM'S FULL-COURSE MEAL!!
TING
I DIDN'T KNOW THEY LIVED HERE.
SLASH
KNIFE!!
YAY! NOW WE'VE GOT A SNACK, KOMATSU.
THIS IS A GOOD START!
WHAT'S A MAD COW LIKE THAT DOING ON THIS ISLAND?!

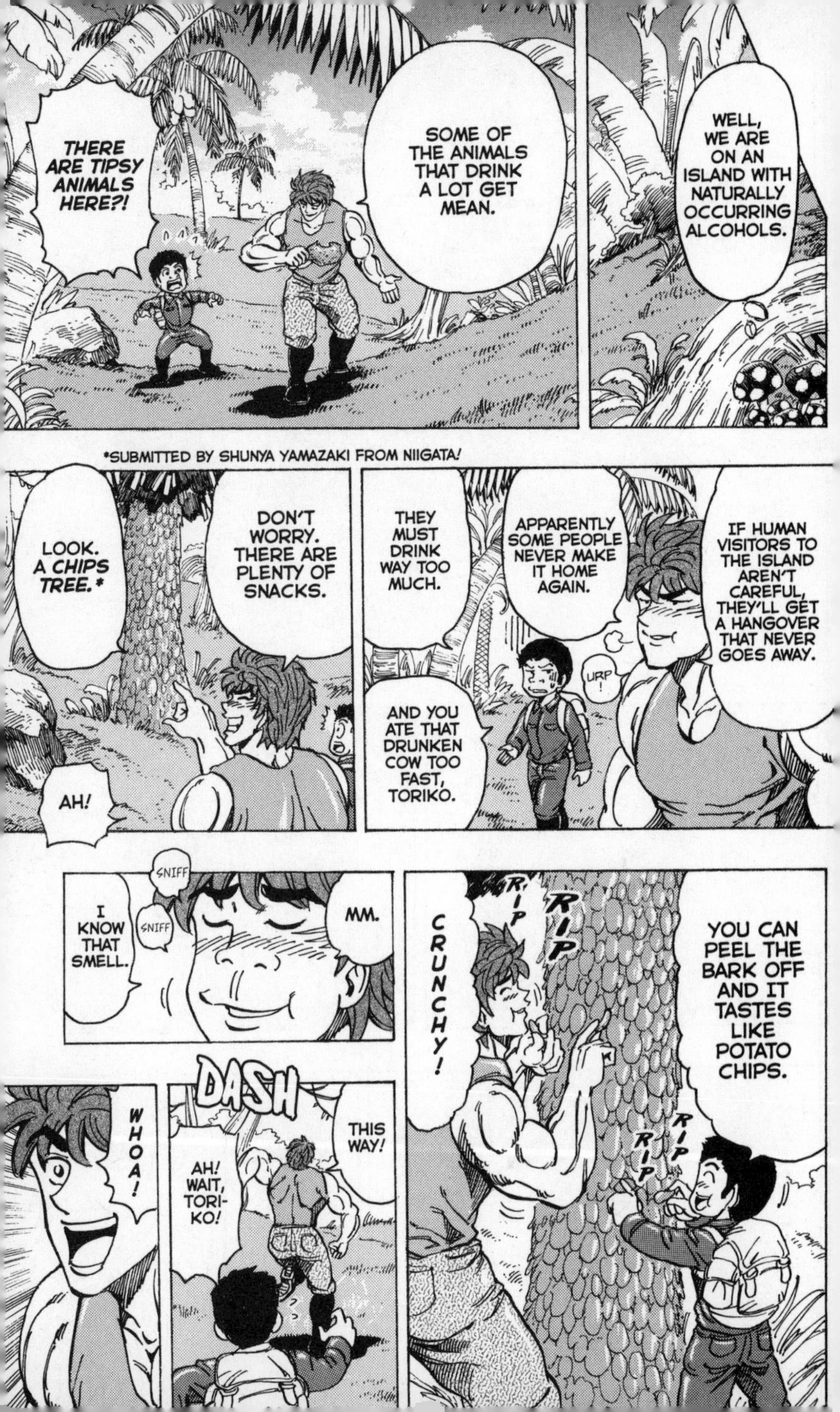
WELL, WE ARE ON AN ISLAND WITH NATURALLY OCCURRING ALCOHOLS.
SOME OF THE ANIMALS THAT DRINK A LOT GET MEAN.
THERE ARE TIPSY ANIMALS HERE?!
IF HUMAN VISITORS TO THE ISLAND AREN'T CAREFUL, THEY'LL GET A HANGOVER THAT NEVER GOES AWAY.
APPARENTLY SOME PEOPLE NEVER MAKE IT HOME AGAIN.
URP!
THEY MUST DRINK WAY TOO MUCH.
AND YOU ATE THAT DRUNKEN COW TOO FAST, TORIKO.
DON'T WORRY. THERE ARE PLENTY OF SNACKS.
LOOK. A CHIPS TREE.*
AH!
YOU CAN PEEL THE BARK OFF AND IT TASTES LIKE POTATO CHIPS.
RIP
RIP
CRUNCHY!
RIP
RIP
MM.
SNIFF
SNIFF
I KNOW THAT SMELL.
THIS WAY!
DASH
AH! WAIT, TORI-KO!
WHOA!
*SUBMITTED BY SHUNYA YAMAZAKI FROM NIIGATA!

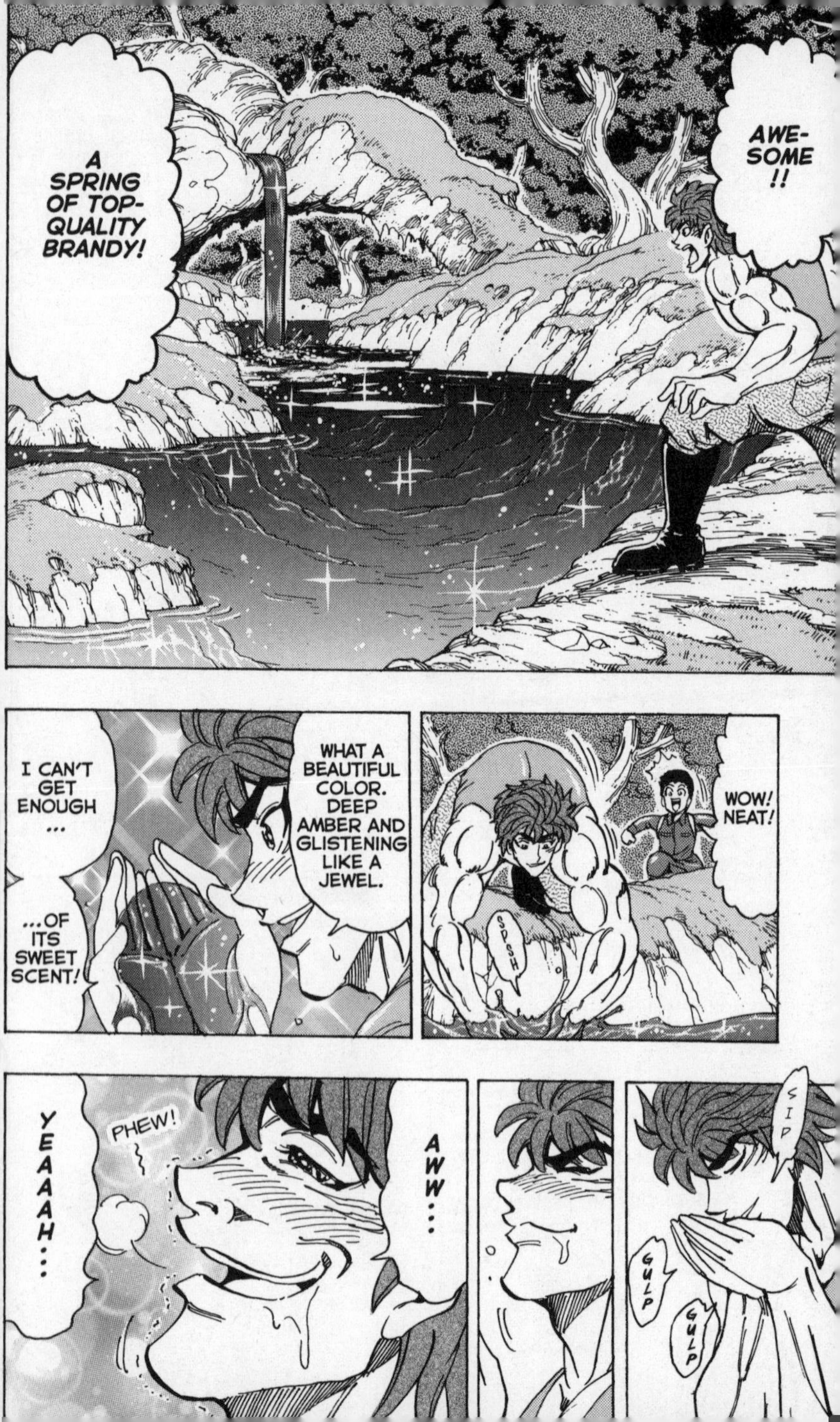
AWE-SOME!!
A SPRING OF TOP-QUALITY BRANDY!
WOW! NEAT!
SPSH
WHAT A BEAUTIFUL COLOR. DEEP AMBER AND GLISTENING LIKE A JEWEL.
I CAN'T GET ENOUGH...
...OF ITS SWEET SCENT!
SIP
GULP
GULP
AWW...
PHEW!
YEAAAAH...

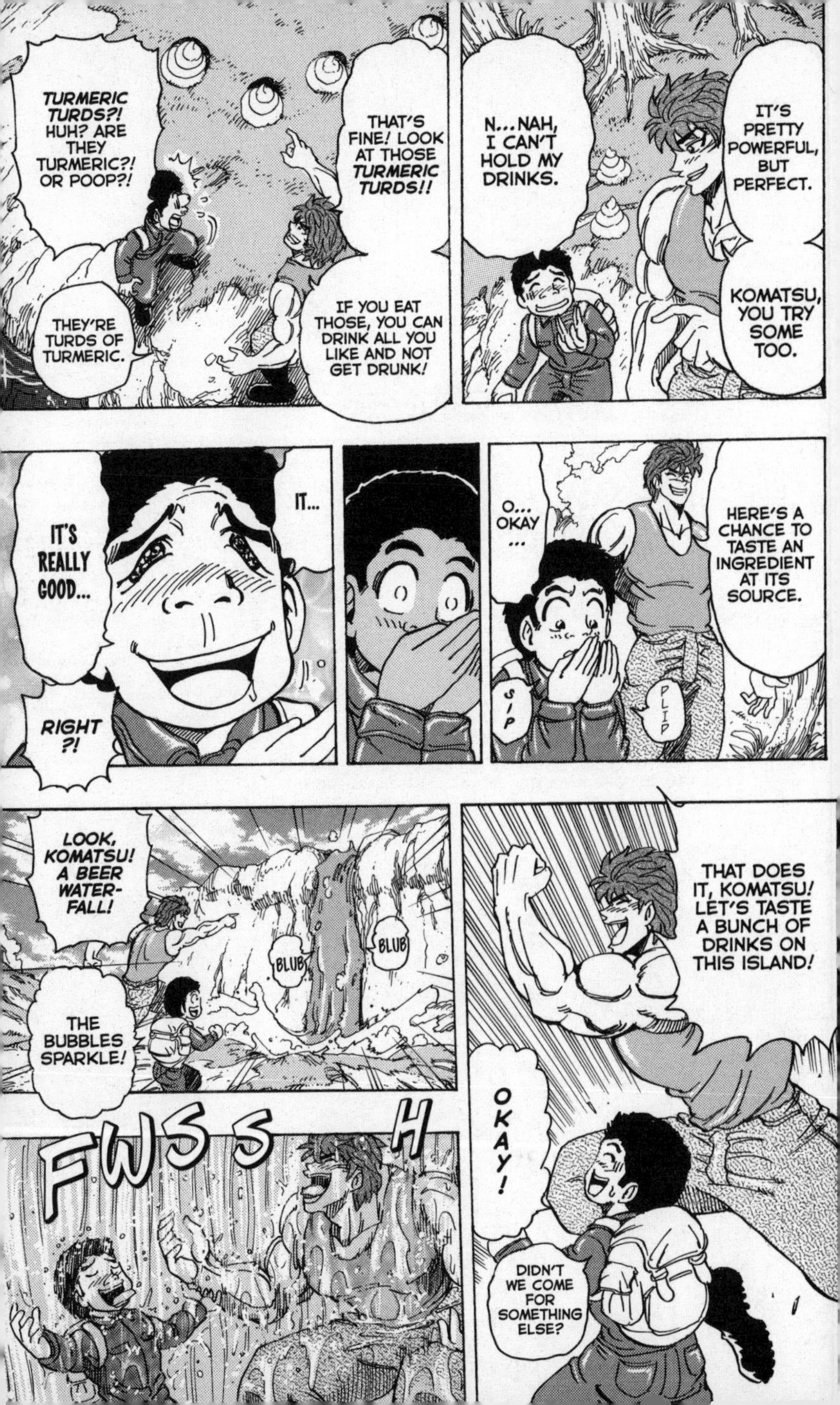

IT'S PRETTY POWERFUL, BUT PERFECT.
KOMATSU, YOU TRY SOME TOO.
N...NAH, I CAN'T HOLD MY DRINKS.
THAT'S FINE! LOOK AT THOSE *TURMERIC TURDS!!*
TURMERIC TURDS?! HUH? ARE THEY TURMERIC?! OR POOP?!
IF YOU EAT THOSE, YOU CAN DRINK ALL YOU LIKE AND NOT GET DRUNK!
THEY'RE TURDS OF TURMERIC.
HERE'S A CHANCE TO TASTE AN INGREDIENT AT ITS SOURCE.
O... OKAY ...
SIP
PLIP
IT...
IT'S REALLY GOOD...
RIGHT?!
THAT DOES IT, KOMATSU! LET'S TASTE A BUNCH OF DRINKS ON THIS ISLAND!
OKAY!
DIDN'T WE COME FOR SOMETHING ELSE?
LOOK, KOMATSU! A BEER WATER-FALL!
BLUB
BLUB
THE BUBBLES SPARKLE!
FWSSSH

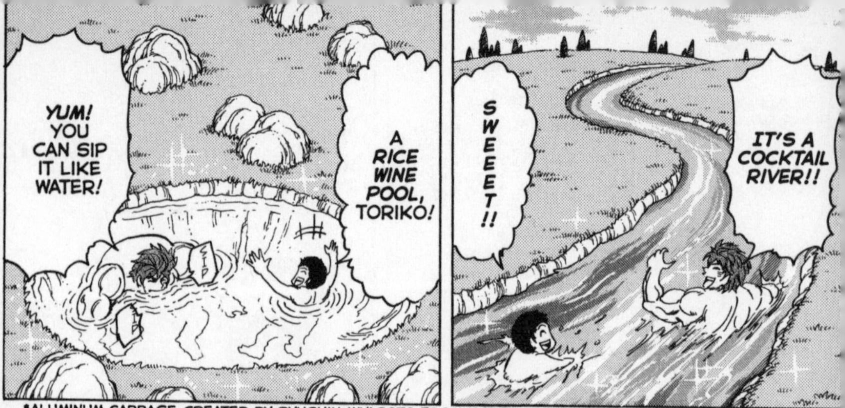
IT'S A COCKTAIL RIVER!!
SWEEEET!!
A RICE WINE POOL, TORIKO!
YUM! YOU CAN SIP IT LIKE WATER!
SIP

*ALUMINUM CABBAGE CREATED BY RYUSHIN MIYASOTO FROM HYOGO; ONION CHEESE CREATED BY FIRE MELON FROM KYOTO!

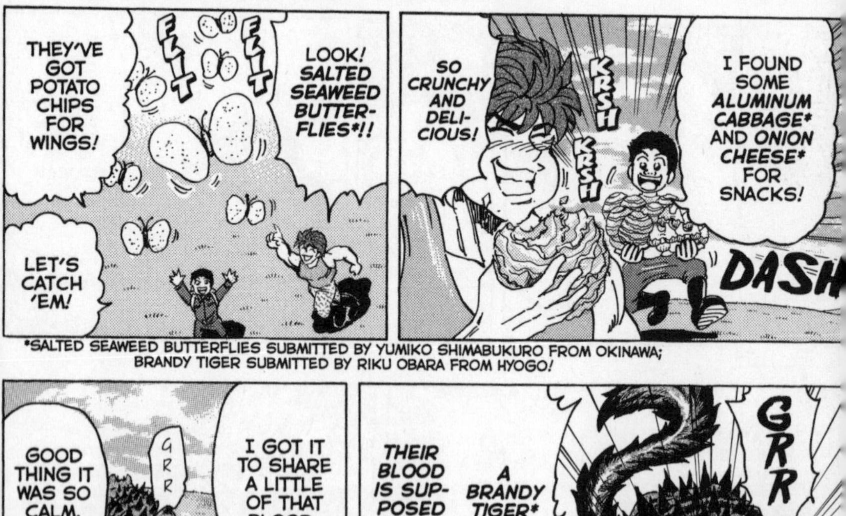
I FOUND SOME ALUMINUM CABBAGE* AND ONION CHEESE* FOR SNACKS!
DASH
KRSH
KRSH
SO CRUNCHY AND DELICIOUS!
LOOK! SALTED SEAWEED BUTTERFLIES*!!
FLIT
FLIT
THEY'VE GOT POTATO CHIPS FOR WINGS!
LET'S CATCH 'EM!

*SALTED SEAWEED BUTTERFLIES SUBMITTED BY YUMIKO SHIMABUKURO FROM OKINAWA; BRANDY TIGER SUBMITTED BY RIKU OBARA FROM HYOGO!

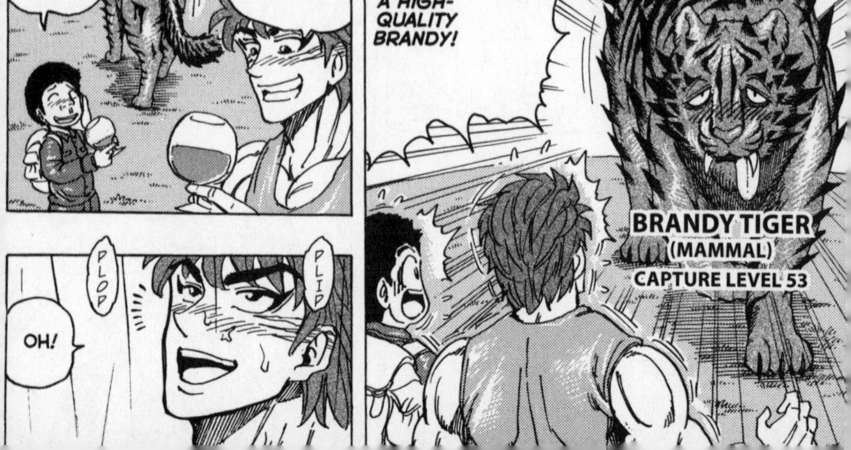
GRR
A BRANDY TIGER*!!
THEIR BLOOD IS SUPPOSED TO BE A HIGH-QUALITY BRANDY!
BRANDY TIGER
(MAMMAL)
CAPTURE LEVEL 53
I GOT IT TO SHARE A LITTLE OF THAT BLOOD.
GRR
GOOD THING IT WAS SO CALM.
PLIP
PLOP
OH!

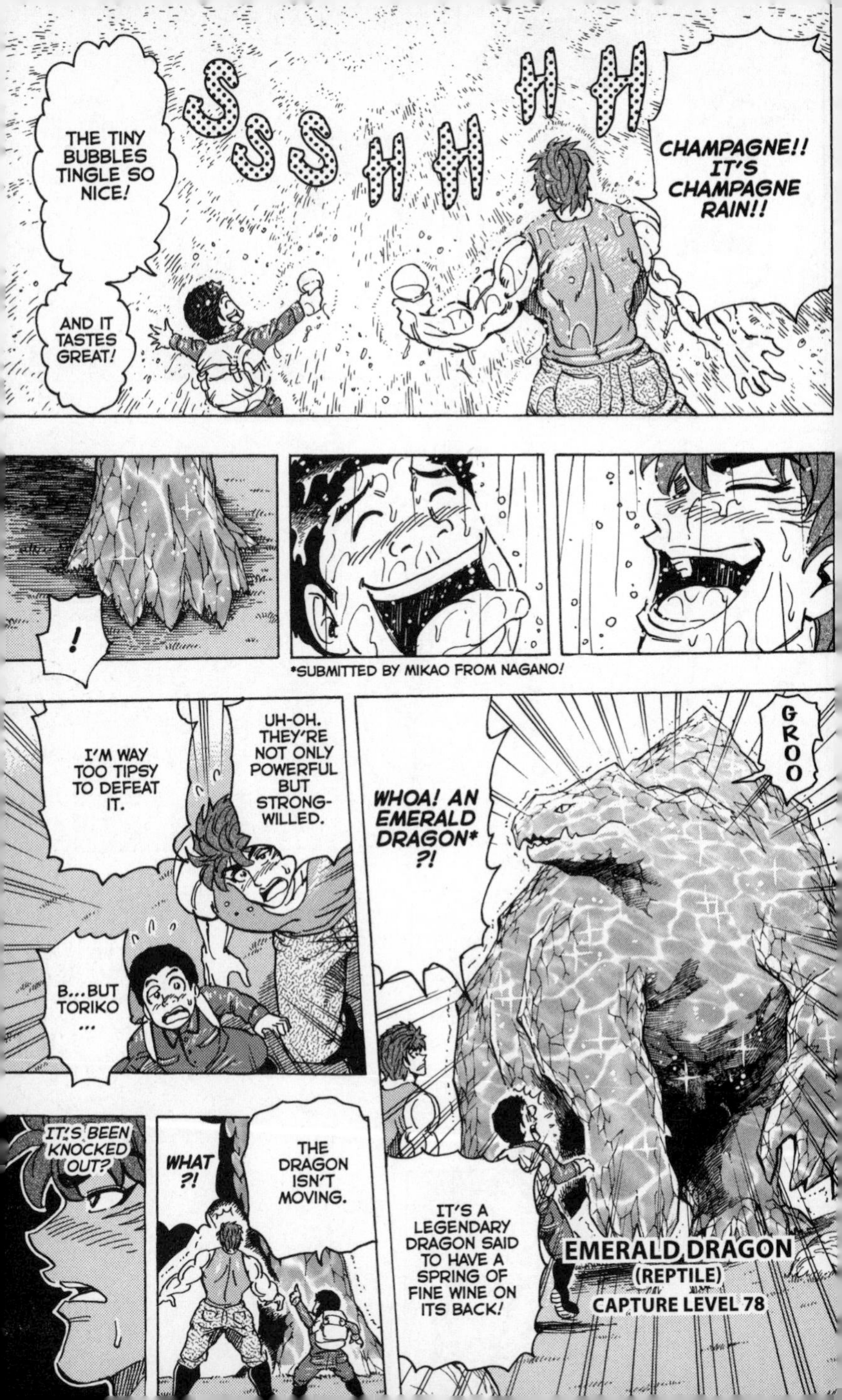
CHAMPAGNE!! IT'S CHAMPAGNE RAIN!!
SSSHHHH
THE TINY BUBBLES TINGLE SO NICE!
AND IT TASTES GREAT!
!
*SUBMITTED BY MIKAO FROM NAGANO!
GROO
WHOA! AN EMERALD DRAGON* ?!
IT'S A LEGENDARY DRAGON SAID TO HAVE A SPRING OF FINE WINE ON ITS BACK!
EMERALD DRAGON
(REPTILE)
CAPTURE LEVEL 78
UH-OH. THEY'RE NOT ONLY POWERFUL BUT STRONG-WILLED.
I'M WAY TOO TIPSY TO DEFEAT IT.
B...BUT TORIKO ...
THE DRAGON ISN'T MOVING.
WHAT ?!
IT'S BEEN KNOCKED OUT?

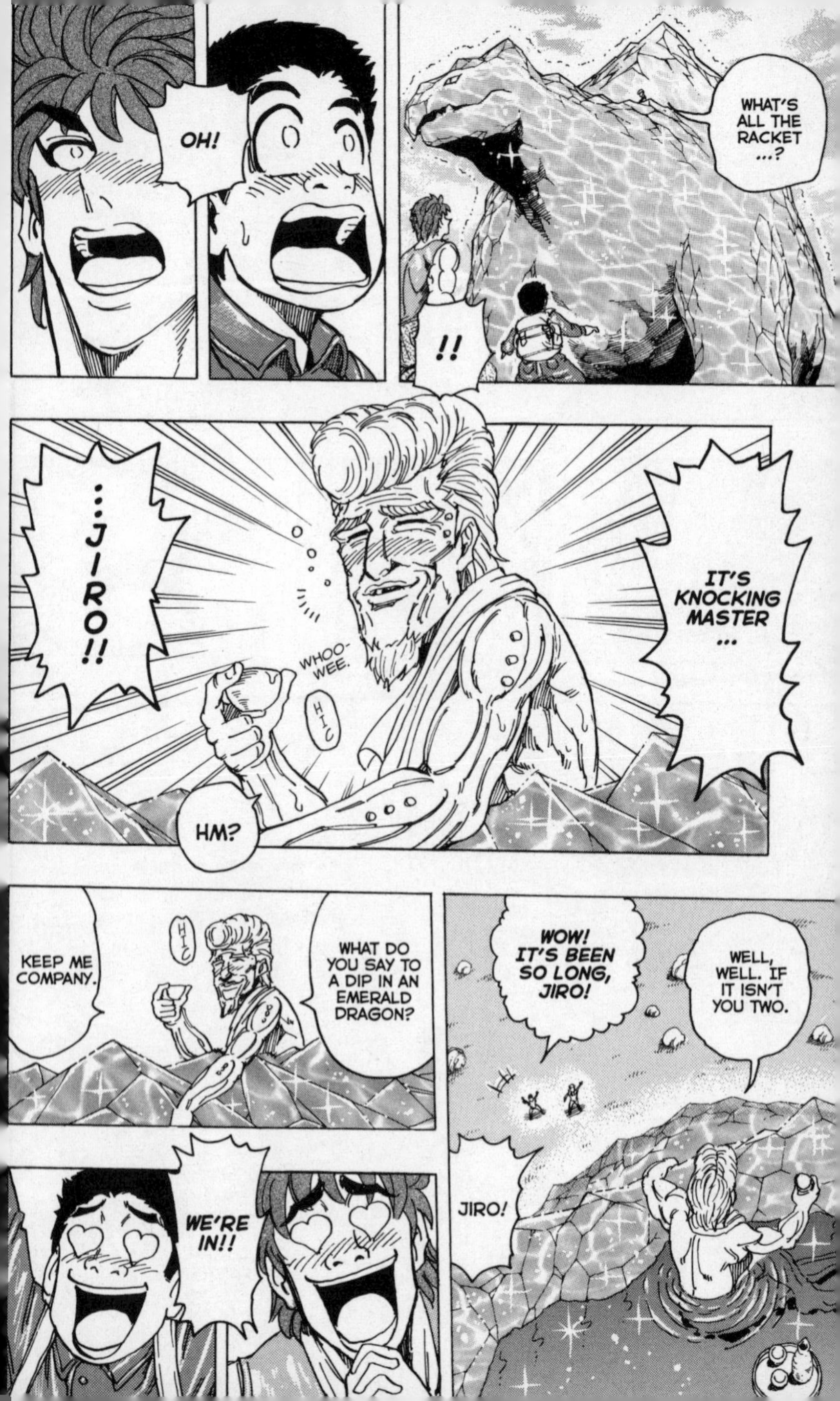
WHAT'S ALL THE RACKET ...?
!!
OH!
IT'S KNOCKING MASTER ...
WHOO-WEE.
HIC
HM?
...JIRO!!
WELL, WELL. IF IT ISN'T YOU TWO.
WOW! IT'S BEEN SO LONG, JIRO!
JIRO!
WHAT DO YOU SAY TO A DIP IN AN EMERALD DRAGON?
HIC
KEEP ME COMPANY.
WE'RE IN!!

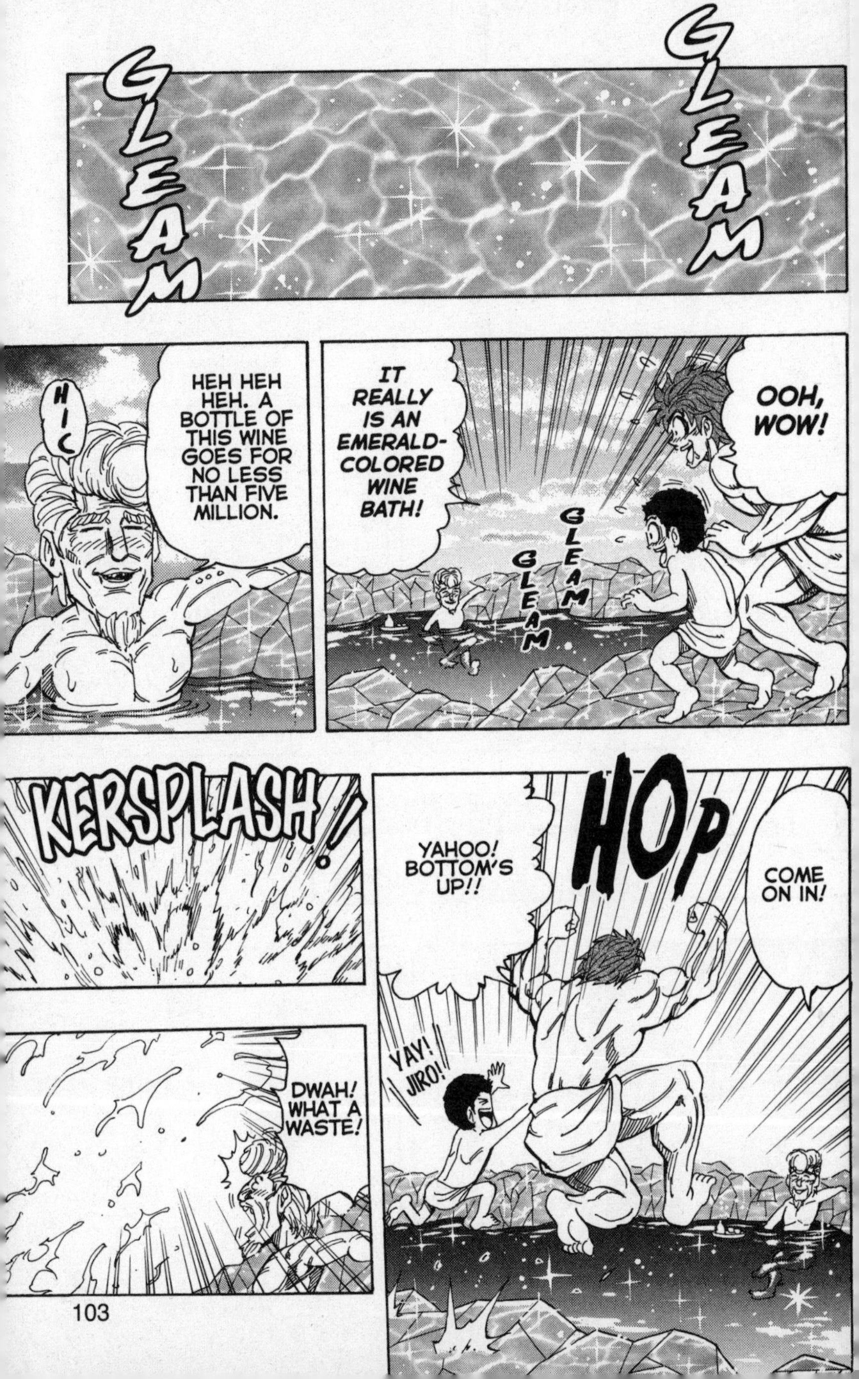
GLEAM
GLEAM
OOH, WOW!
IT REALLY IS AN EMERALD-COLORED WINE BATH!
GLEAM
GLEAM
HIC
HEH HEH HEH. A BOTTLE OF THIS WINE GOES FOR NO LESS THAN FIVE MILLION.
HOP
COME ON IN!
YAHOO! BOTTOM'S UP!!
YAY! JIRO!
KERSPLASH!
DWAH! WHAT A WASTE!

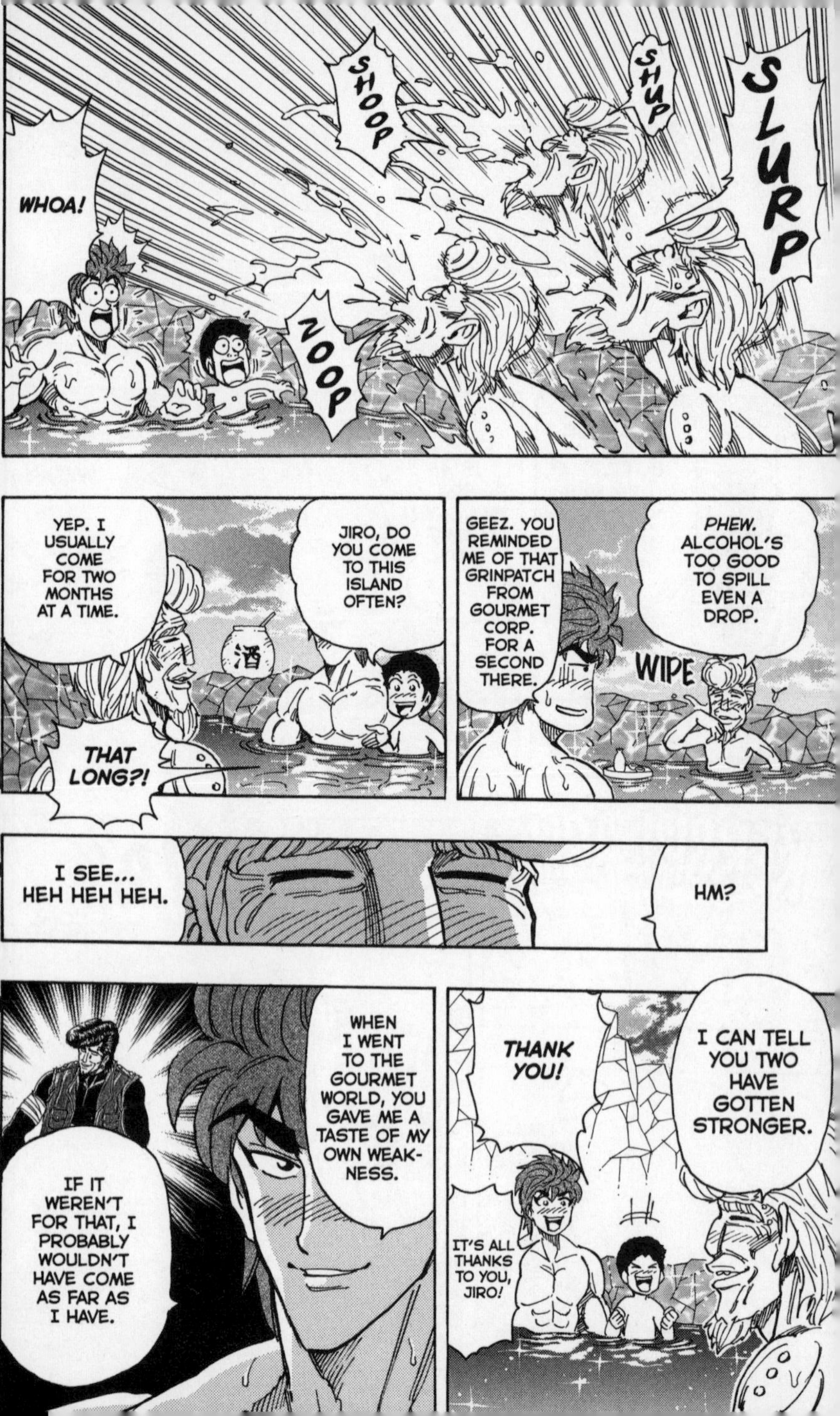
SLURP
SHUP
SHOOP
ZOOOP
WHOA!
PHEW. ALCOHOL'S TOO GOOD TO SPILL EVEN A DROP.
WIPE
GEEZ. YOU REMINDED ME OF THAT GRINPATCH FROM GOURMET CORP. FOR A SECOND THERE.
JIRO, DO YOU COME TO THIS ISLAND OFTEN?
YEP. I USUALLY COME FOR TWO MONTHS AT A TIME.
THAT LONG?!
HM?
I SEE... HEH HEH HEH.
I CAN TELL YOU TWO HAVE GOTTEN STRONGER.
THANK YOU!
IT'S ALL THANKS TO YOU, JIRO!
WHEN I WENT TO THE GOURMET WORLD, YOU GAVE ME A TASTE OF MY OWN WEAK-NESS.
IF IT WEREN'T FOR THAT, I PROBABLY WOULDN'T HAVE COME AS FAR AS I HAVE.

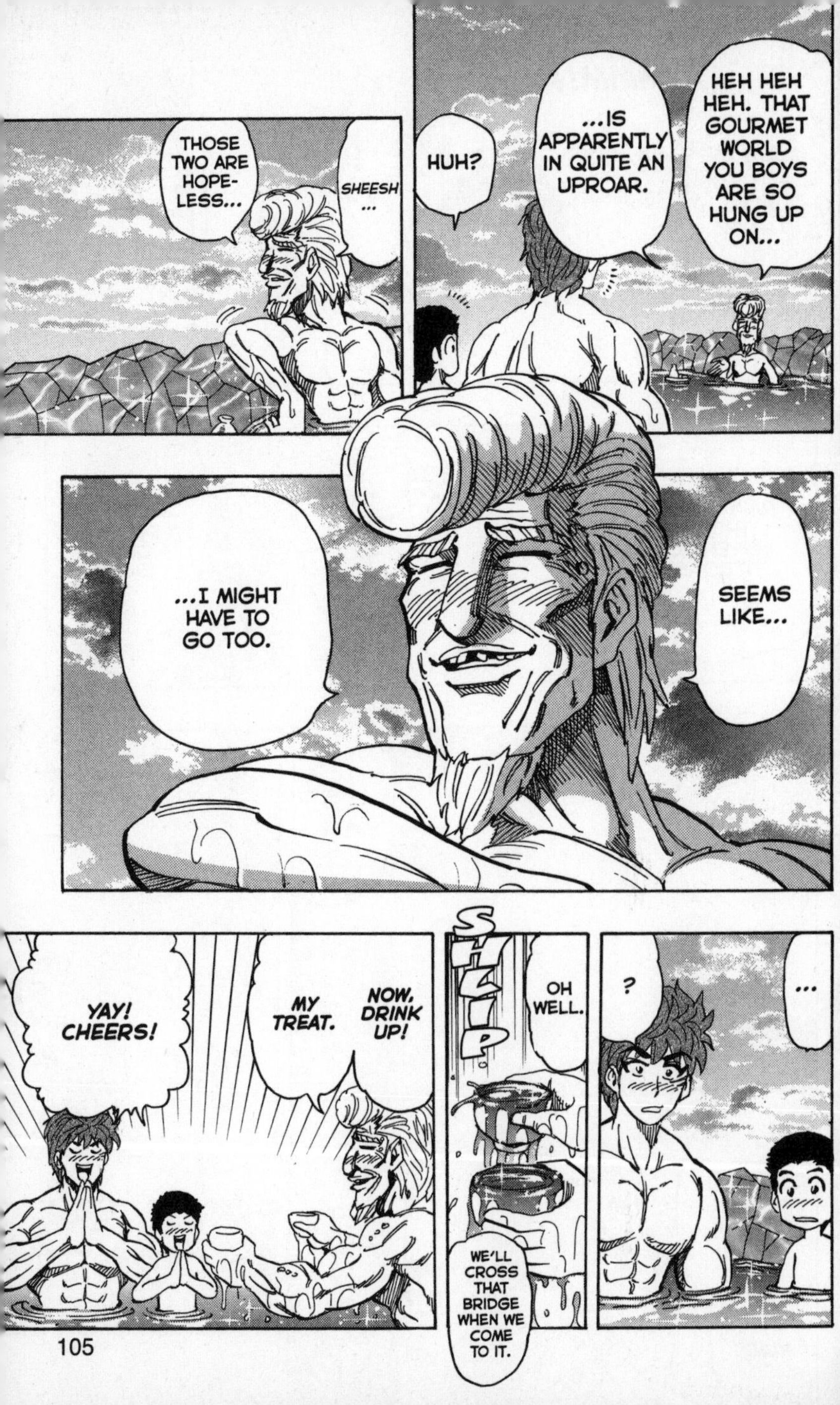
HEH HEH HEH. THAT GOURMET WORLD YOU BOYS ARE SO HUNG UP ON...
...IS APPARENTLY IN QUITE AN UPROAR.
HUH?
SHEESH...
THOSE TWO ARE HOPELESS...
SEEMS LIKE...
...I MIGHT HAVE TO GO TOO.
...
?
SHLIP
OH WELL.
WE'LL CROSS THAT BRIDGE WHEN WE COME TO IT.
NOW, DRINK UP!
MY TREAT.
YAY! CHEERS!

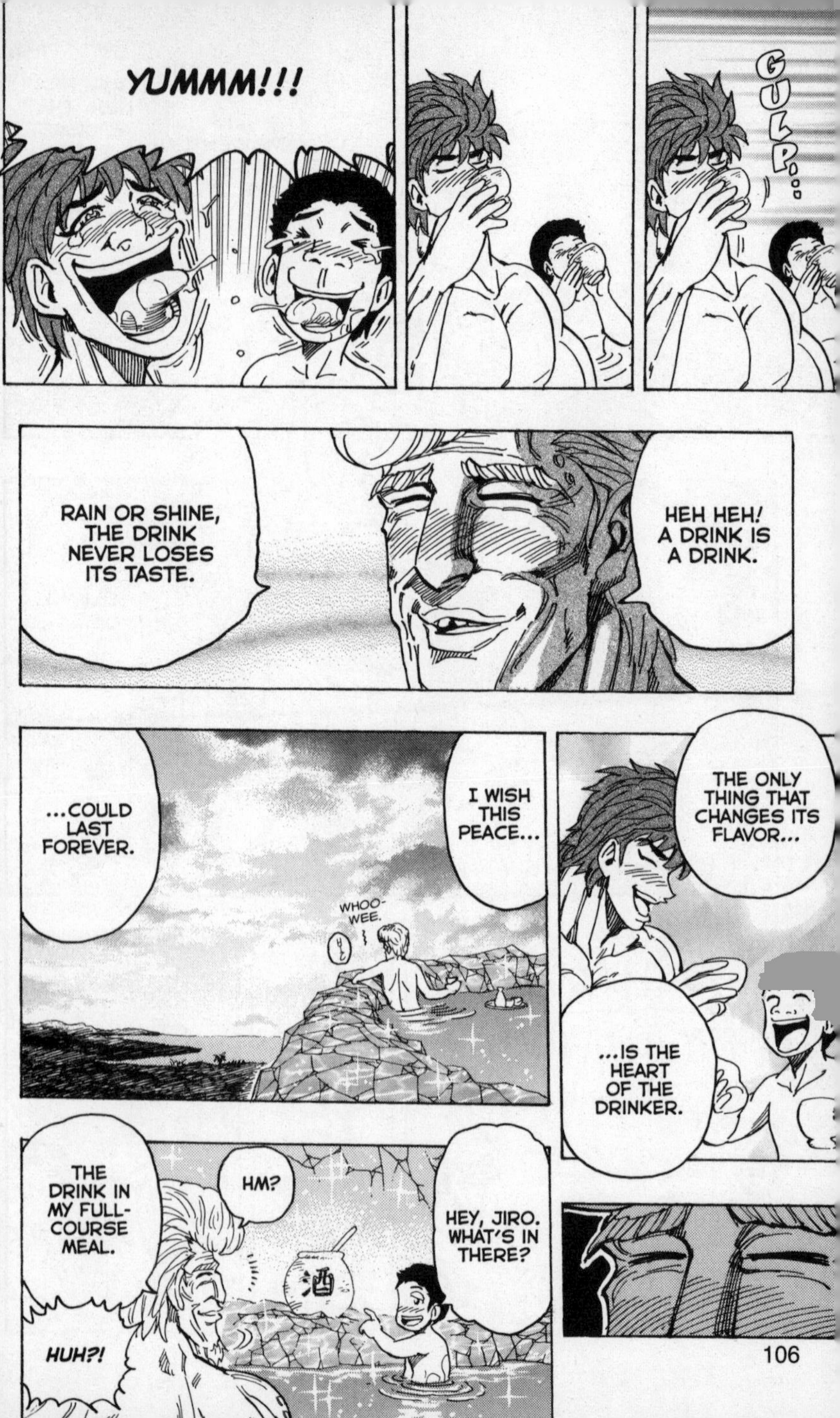
GULP...
YUMMM!!!
HEH HEH! A DRINK IS A DRINK.
RAIN OR SHINE, THE DRINK NEVER LOSES ITS TASTE.
THE ONLY THING THAT CHANGES ITS FLAVOR...
...IS THE HEART OF THE DRINKER.
I WISH THIS PEACE...
...COULD LAST FOREVER.
WHOO-WEE.
HEY, JIRO. WHAT'S IN THERE?
HM?
THE DRINK IN MY FULL-COURSE MEAL.
酒
HUH?!

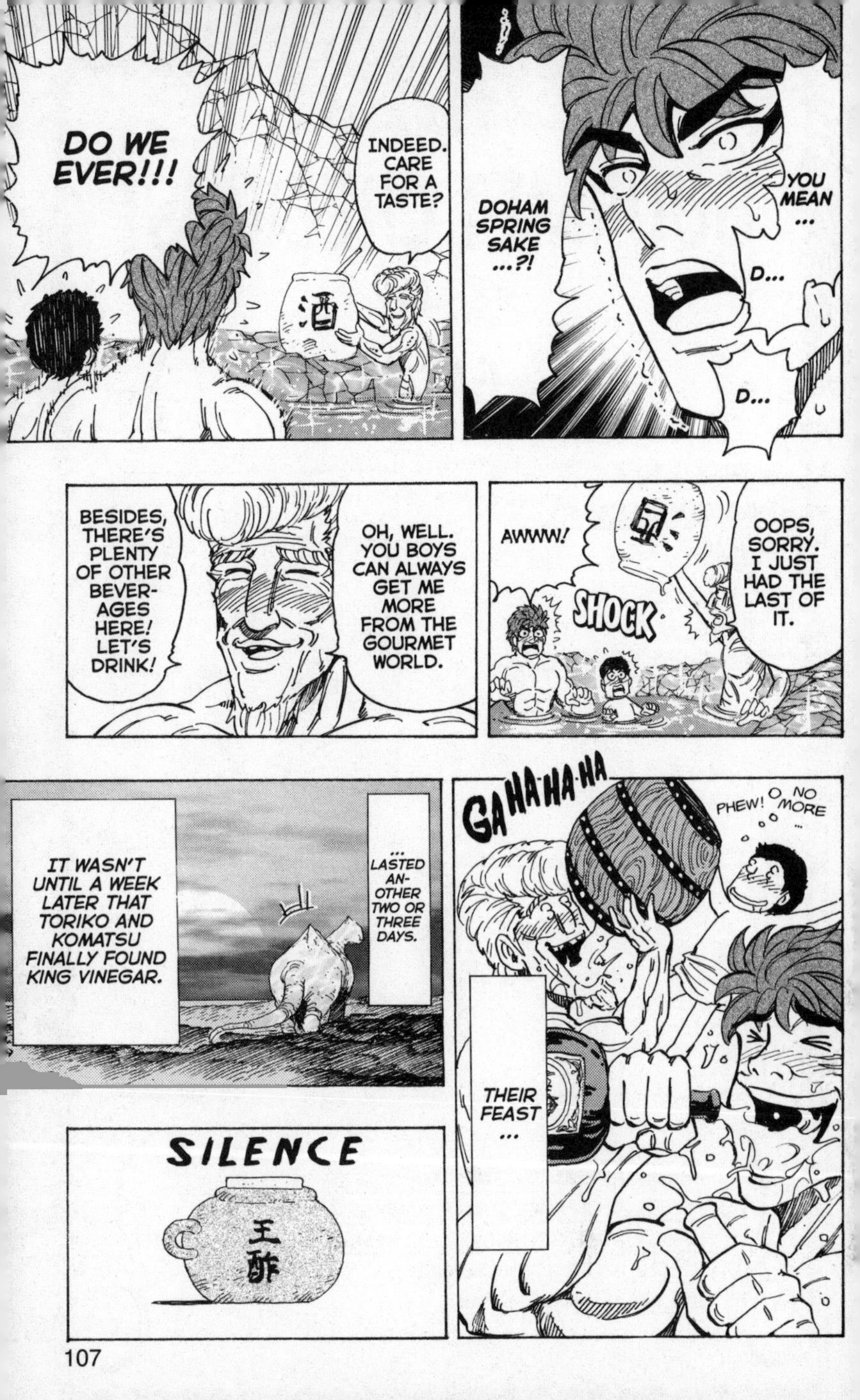

YOU MEAN ...
DOHAM SPRING SAKE ...?!
D...
D...
INDEED. CARE FOR A TASTE?
酒
DO WE EVER!!!
OOPS, SORRY. I JUST HAD THE LAST OF IT.
AWWW!
SHOCK
OH, WELL. YOU BOYS CAN ALWAYS GET ME MORE FROM THE GOURMET WORLD.
BESIDES, THERE'S PLENTY OF OTHER BEVERAGES HERE! LET'S DRINK!
GAHAHAHA
PHEW!
NO MORE ...
THEIR FEAST ...
... LASTED ANOTHER TWO OR THREE DAYS.
IT WASN'T UNTIL A WEEK LATER THAT TORIKO AND KOMATSU FINALLY FOUND KING VINEGAR.
SILENCE
王酢

TORIKO

GOURMET CHECKLIST

Vol. 205

GARLIP
(PLANT)

CAPTURE LEVEL: 16
HABITAT: ALPINE SUMMITS
LENGTH: ---
HEIGHT: 30 CM
WEIGHT: ---
PRICE: 5,000 YEN PER BLOSSOM

WOW! NATURAL GARLIPS*!!

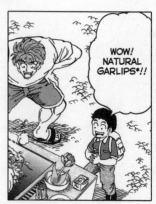

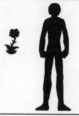

SCALE

A PERENNIAL PLANT FROM THE LILY FAMILY. THIS STRANGE PLANT SPROUTS GARLIC FROM THE CENTER OF A TULIP FLOWER. BECAUSE IT ONLY BLOSSOMS ON THE PEAKS OF TALL MOUNTAINS, IT HAS A PRETTY HIGH CAPTURE LEVEL FOR A PLANT. THE TASTE OF THE GARLIP DEPENDS ON THE COLOR OF THE FLOWER. RED GARLIPS ARE SAID TO HAVE A VERY SHARP TASTE, WHILE YELLOW GARLIPS ARE SWEET.

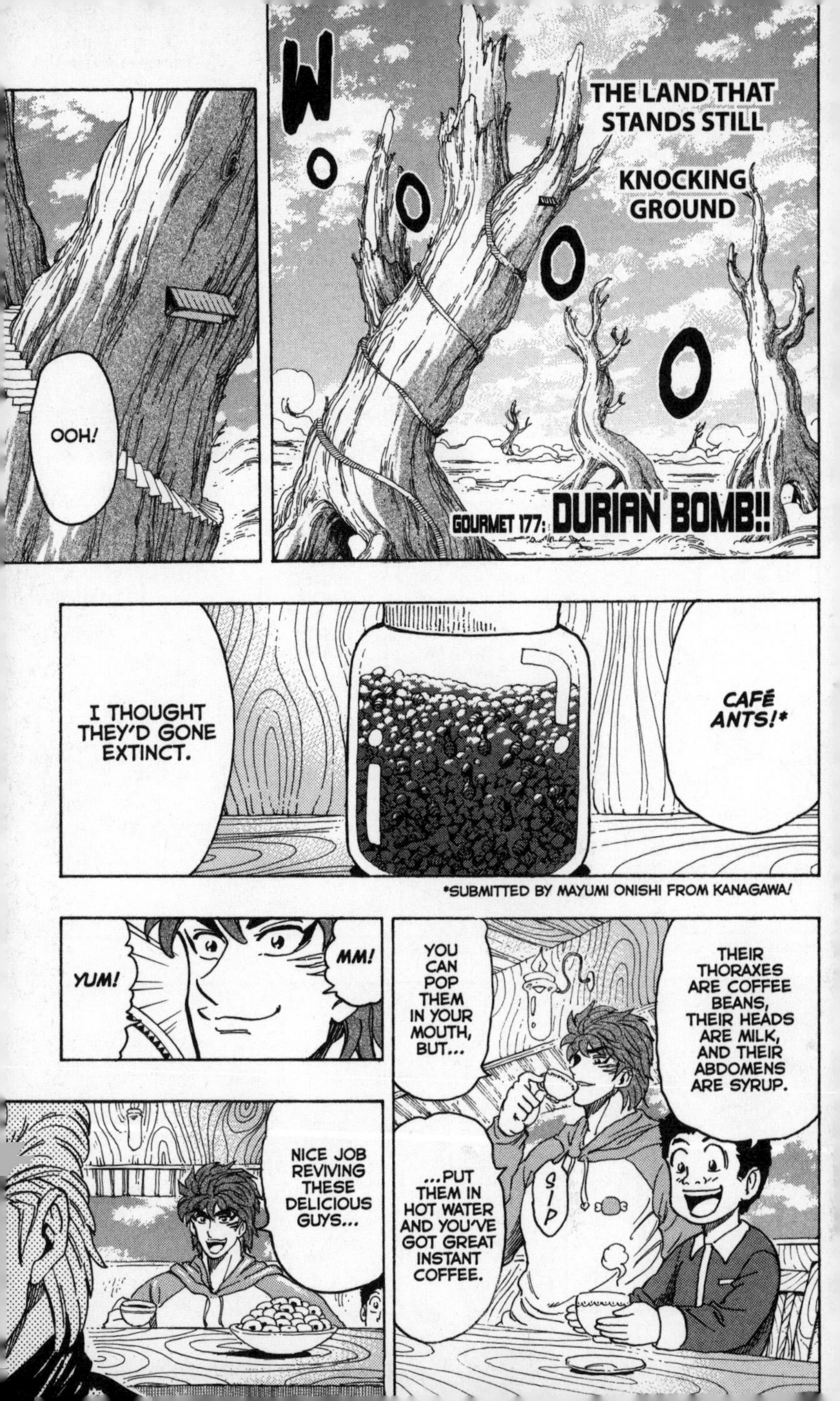
WOOOOO
THE LAND THAT STANDS STILL
KNOCKING GROUND
GOURMET 177: DURIAN BOMB!!
OOH!
CAFÉ ANTS!*
I THOUGHT THEY'D GONE EXTINCT.
*SUBMITTED BY MAYUMI ONISHI FROM KANAGAWA!
THEIR THORAXES ARE COFFEE BEANS, THEIR HEADS ARE MILK, AND THEIR ABDOMENS ARE SYRUP.
YOU CAN POP THEM IN YOUR MOUTH, BUT...
...PUT THEM IN HOT WATER AND YOU'VE GOT GREAT INSTANT COFFEE.
SIP
MM!
YUM!
NICE JOB REVIVING THESE DELICIOUS GUYS...

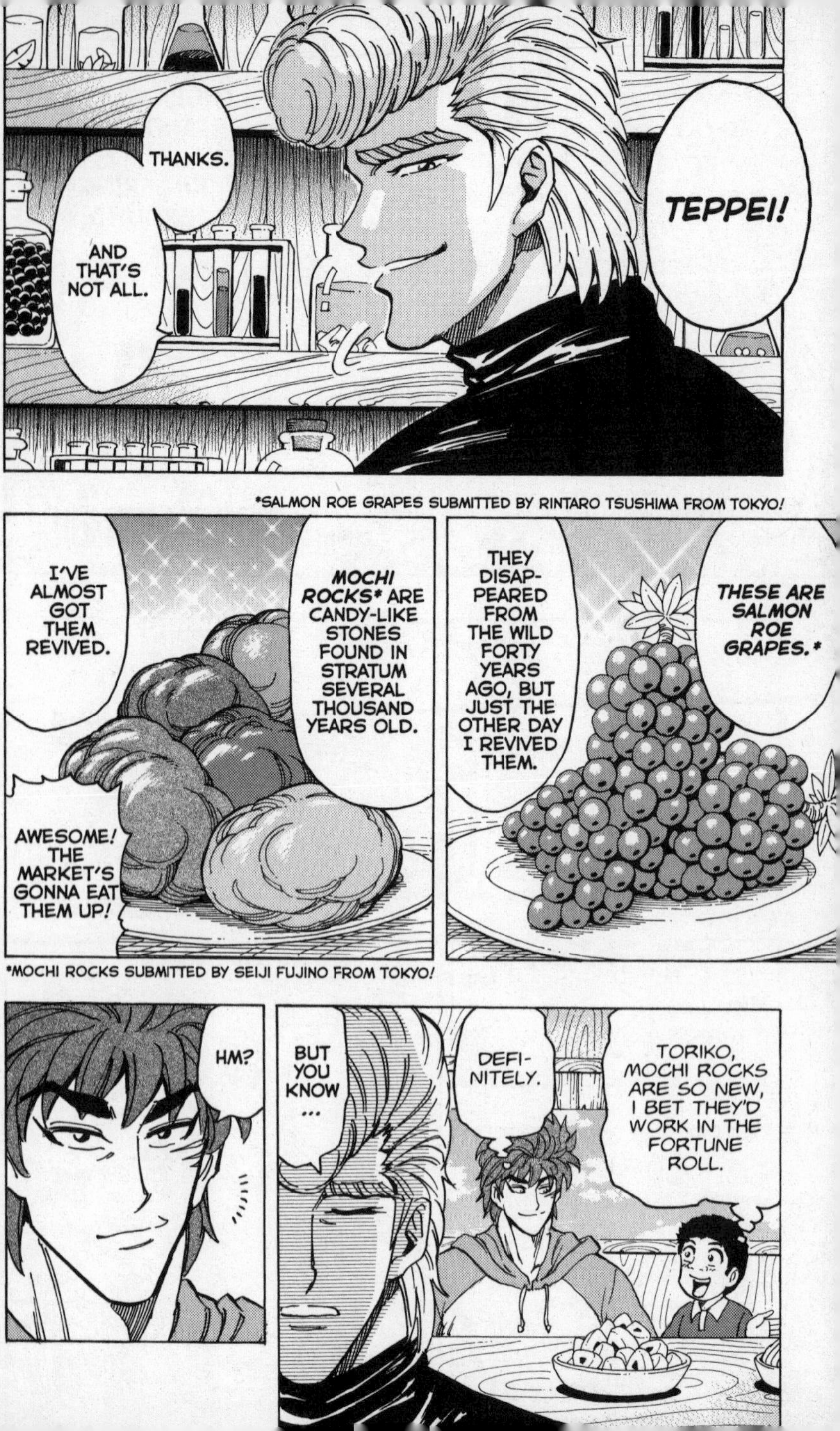
TEPPEI!
THANKS.
AND THAT'S NOT ALL.
*SALMON ROE GRAPES SUBMITTED BY RINTARO TSUSHIMA FROM TOKYO!
THESE ARE SALMON ROE GRAPES.*
THEY DISAPPEARED FROM THE WILD FORTY YEARS AGO, BUT JUST THE OTHER DAY I REVIVED THEM.
MOCHI ROCKS* ARE CANDY-LIKE STONES FOUND IN STRATUM SEVERAL THOUSAND YEARS OLD.
I'VE ALMOST GOT THEM REVIVED.
AWESOME! THE MARKET'S GONNA EAT THEM UP!
*MOCHI ROCKS SUBMITTED BY SEIJI FUJINO FROM TOKYO!
TORIKO, MOCHI ROCKS ARE SO NEW, I BET THEY'D WORK IN THE FORTUNE ROLL.
DEFINITELY.
BUT YOU KNOW ...
HM?

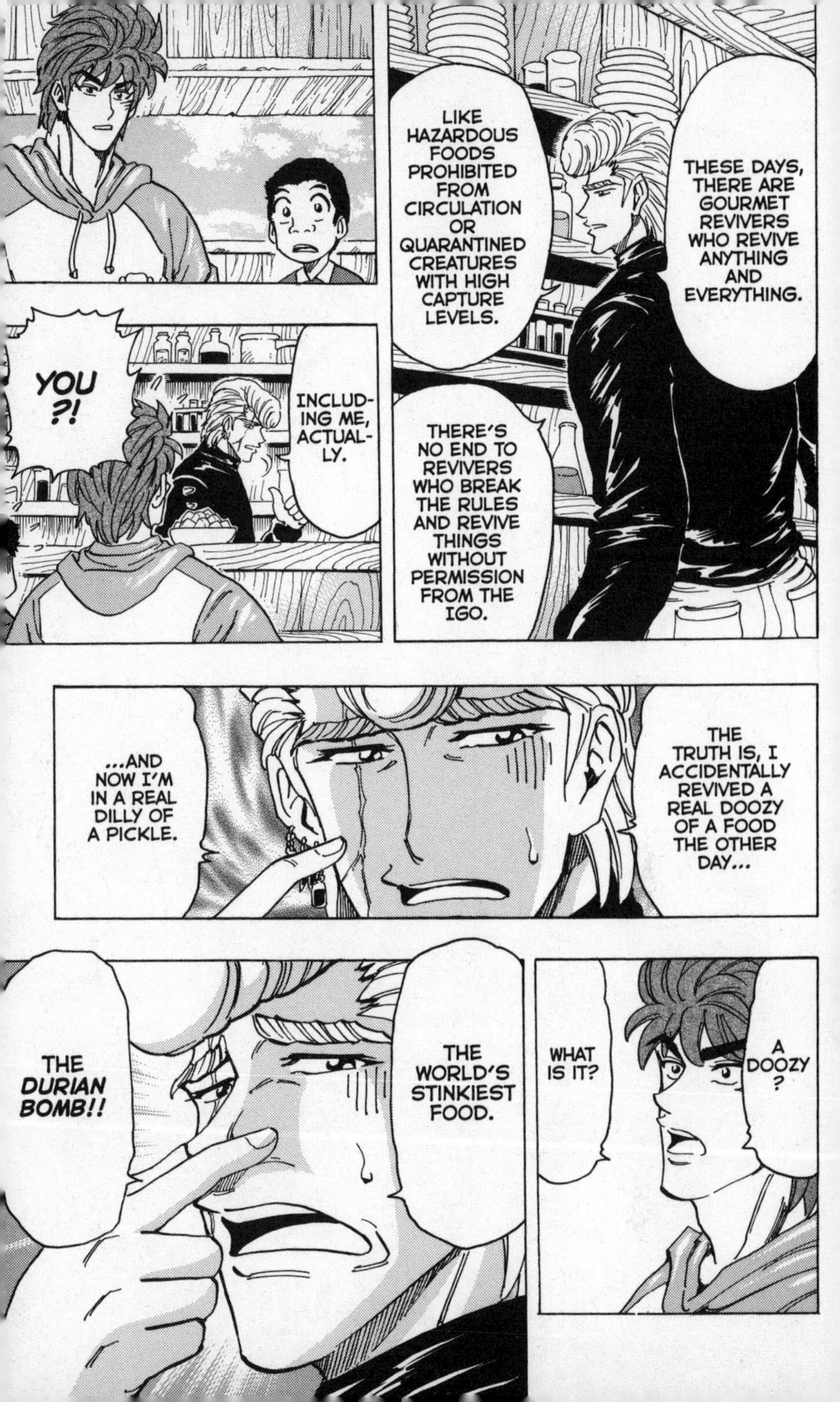
THESE DAYS, THERE ARE GOURMET REVIVERS WHO REVIVE ANYTHING AND EVERYTHING.
LIKE HAZARDOUS FOODS PROHIBITED FROM CIRCULATION OR QUARANTINED CREATURES WITH HIGH CAPTURE LEVELS.
THERE'S NO END TO REVIVERS WHO BREAK THE RULES AND REVIVE THINGS WITHOUT PERMISSION FROM THE IGO.
INCLUD-ING ME, ACTUAL-LY.
YOU?!
THE TRUTH IS, I ACCIDENTALLY REVIVED A REAL DOOZY OF A FOOD THE OTHER DAY...
...AND NOW I'M IN A REAL DILLY OF A PICKLE.
A DOOZY?
WHAT IS IT?
THE WORLD'S STINKIEST FOOD.
THE DURIAN BOMB!!

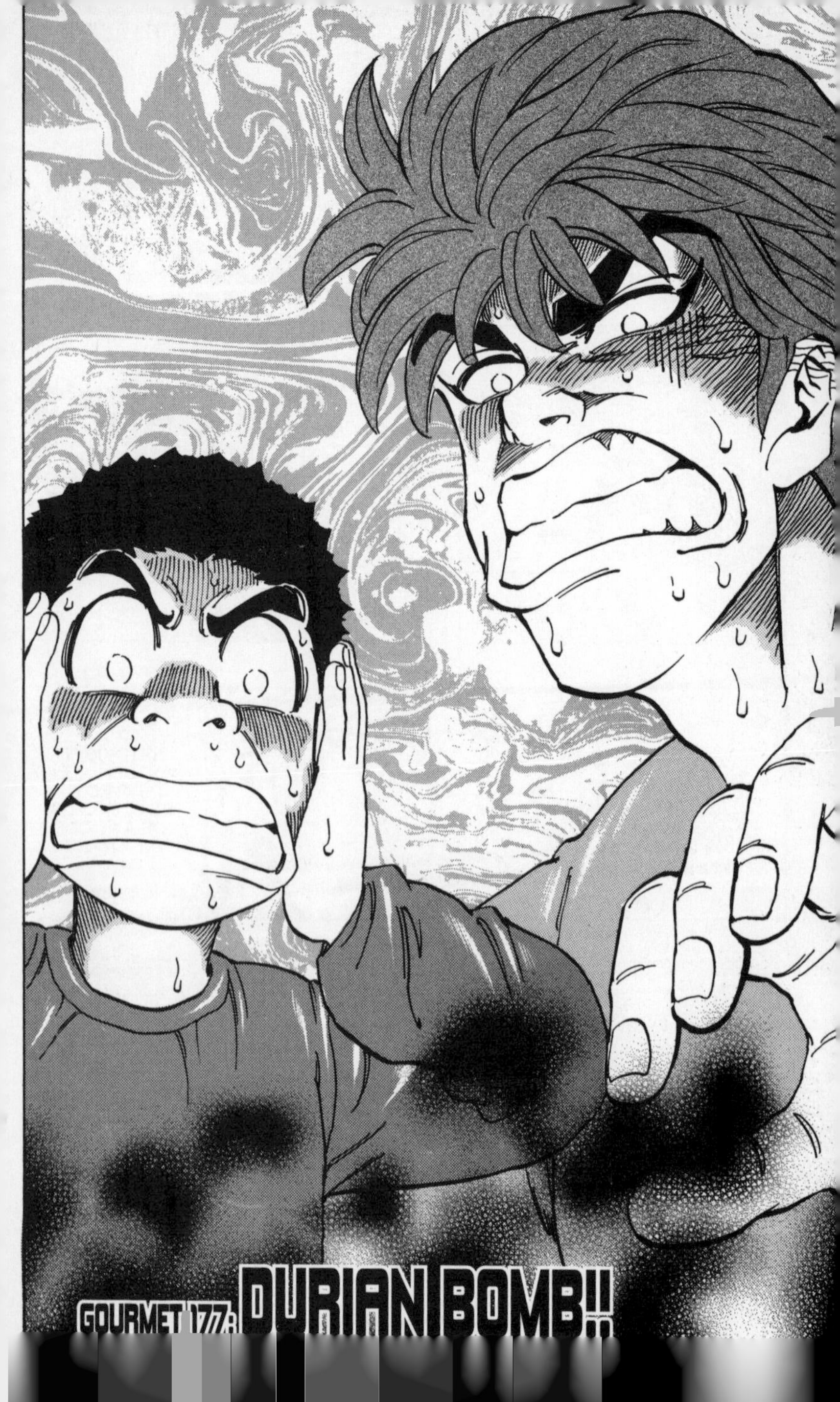
GOURMET 177: DURIAN BOMB!!

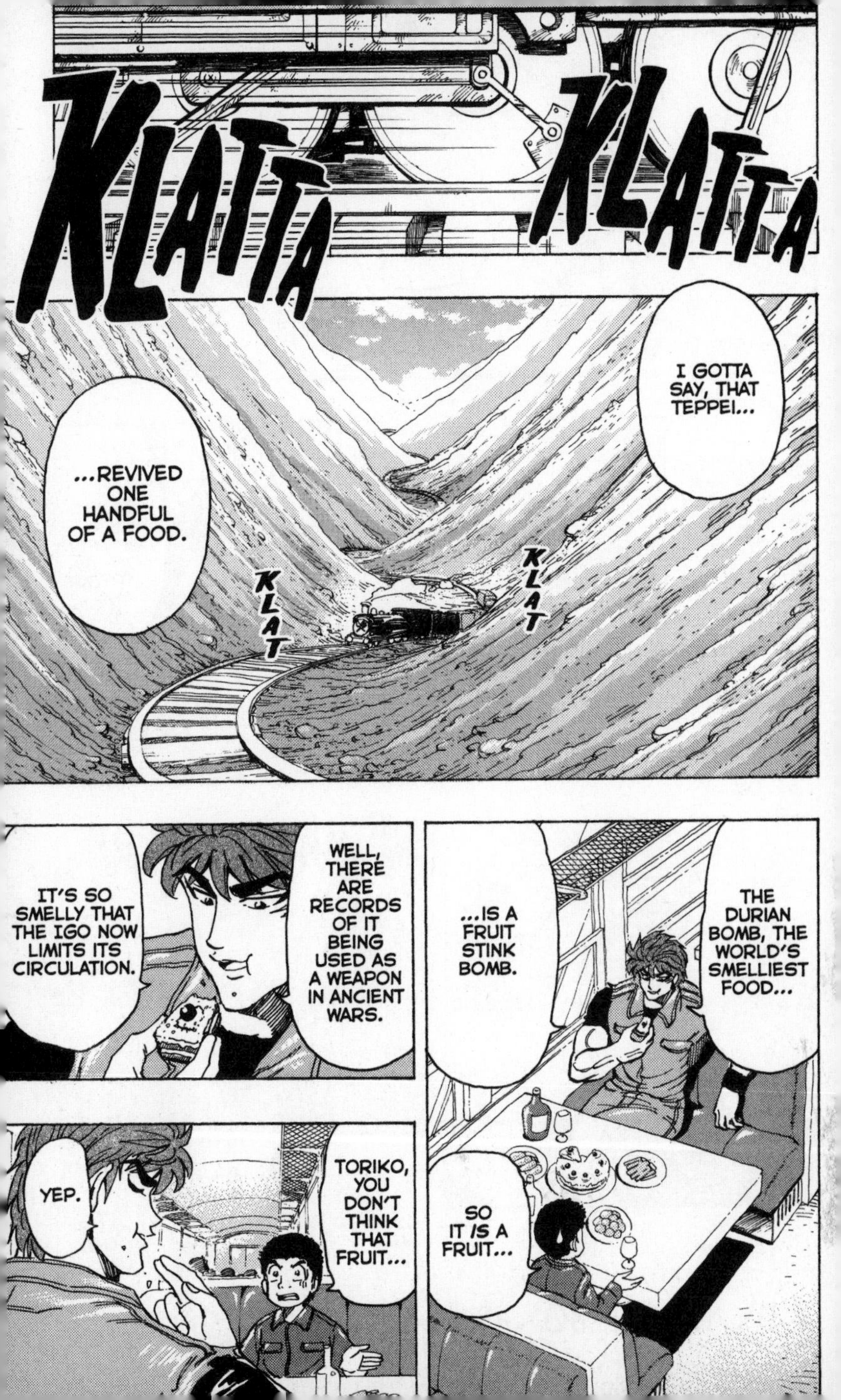
KLATTA
KLATTA
I GOTTA SAY, THAT TEPPEI...
KLAT
...REVIVED ONE HANDFUL OF A FOOD.
KLAT
THE DURIAN BOMB, THE WORLD'S SMELLIEST FOOD...
...IS A FRUIT STINK BOMB.
SO IT IS A FRUIT...
WELL, THERE ARE RECORDS OF IT BEING USED AS A WEAPON IN ANCIENT WARS.
IT'S SO SMELLY THAT THE IGO NOW LIMITS ITS CIRCULATION.
TORIKO, YOU DON'T THINK THAT FRUIT...
YEP.

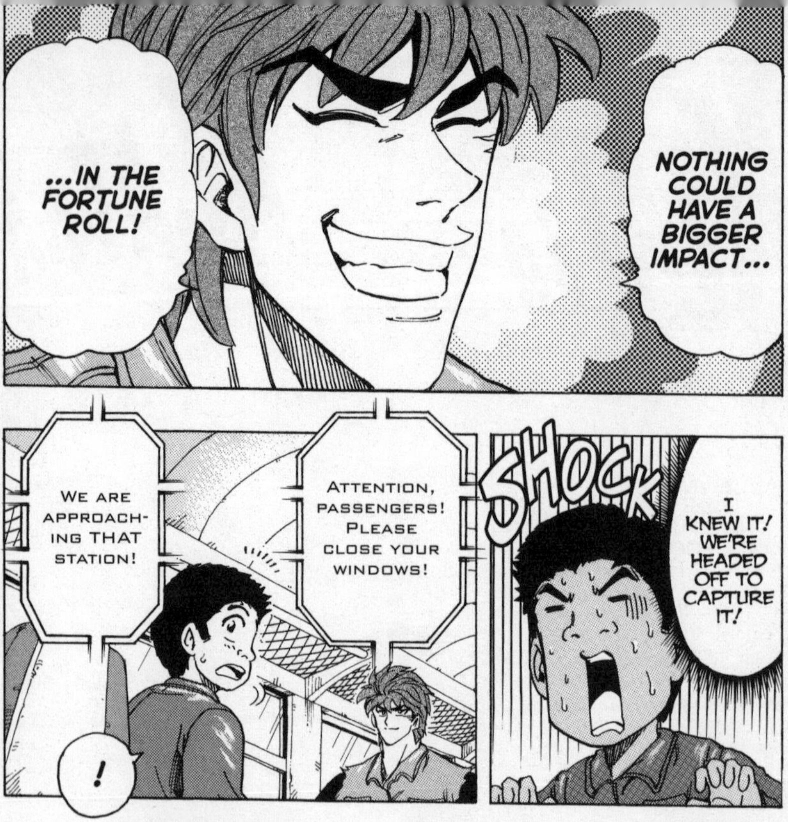
NOTHING COULD HAVE A BIGGER IMPACT...
...IN THE FORTUNE ROLL!
SHOCK
I KNEW IT! WE'RE HEADED OFF TO CAPTURE IT!
ATTENTION, PASSENGERS! PLEASE CLOSE YOUR WINDOWS!
WE ARE APPROACH-ING THAT STATION!
!
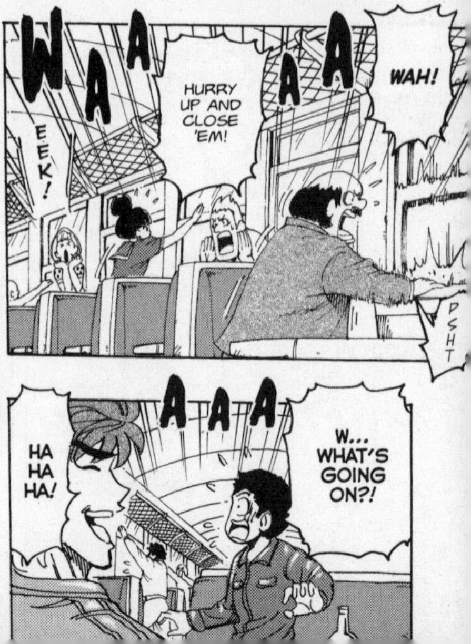
WAH!
WAAAAA
HURRY UP AND CLOSE 'EM!
EEK!
PSHT
AAA
W... WHAT'S GOING ON?!
HA HA HA!
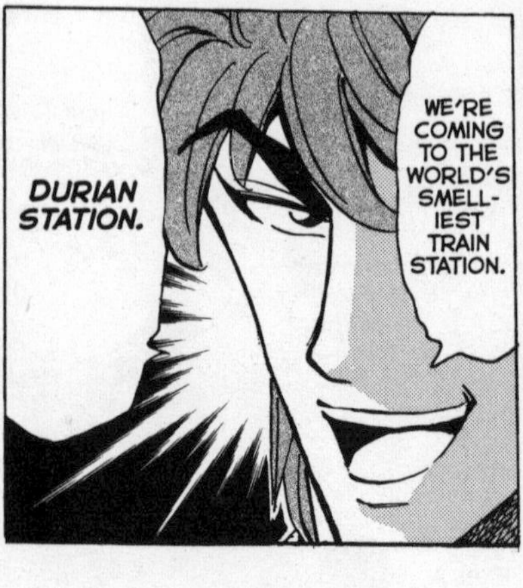
WE'RE COMING TO THE WORLD'S SMELL-IEST TRAIN STATION.
DURIAN STATION.

Menu 16.

DURIAN BOMB

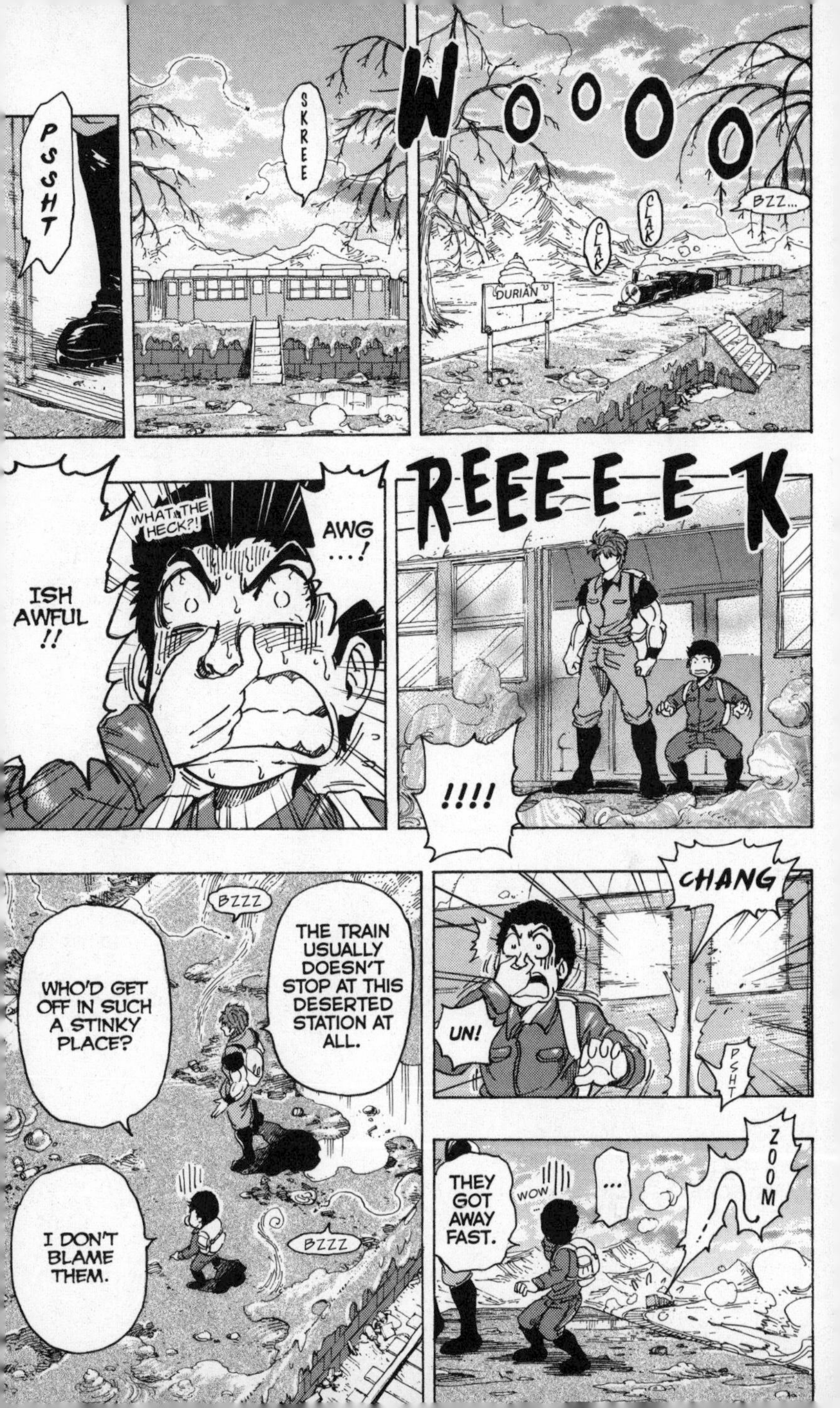
WOOOO
BZZ...
CLAK
CLAK
DURIAN
SKREE
PSSHT
REEEEEK
!!!!
AWG...!
WHAT THE HECK?!
ISH AWFUL!!
CHANG
UN!
PSHT
ZOOM
...
WOW...
THEY GOT AWAY FAST.
BZZZ
THE TRAIN USUALLY DOESN'T STOP AT THIS DESERTED STATION AT ALL.
WHO'D GET OFF IN SUCH A STINKY PLACE?
BZZZ
I DON'T BLAME THEM.

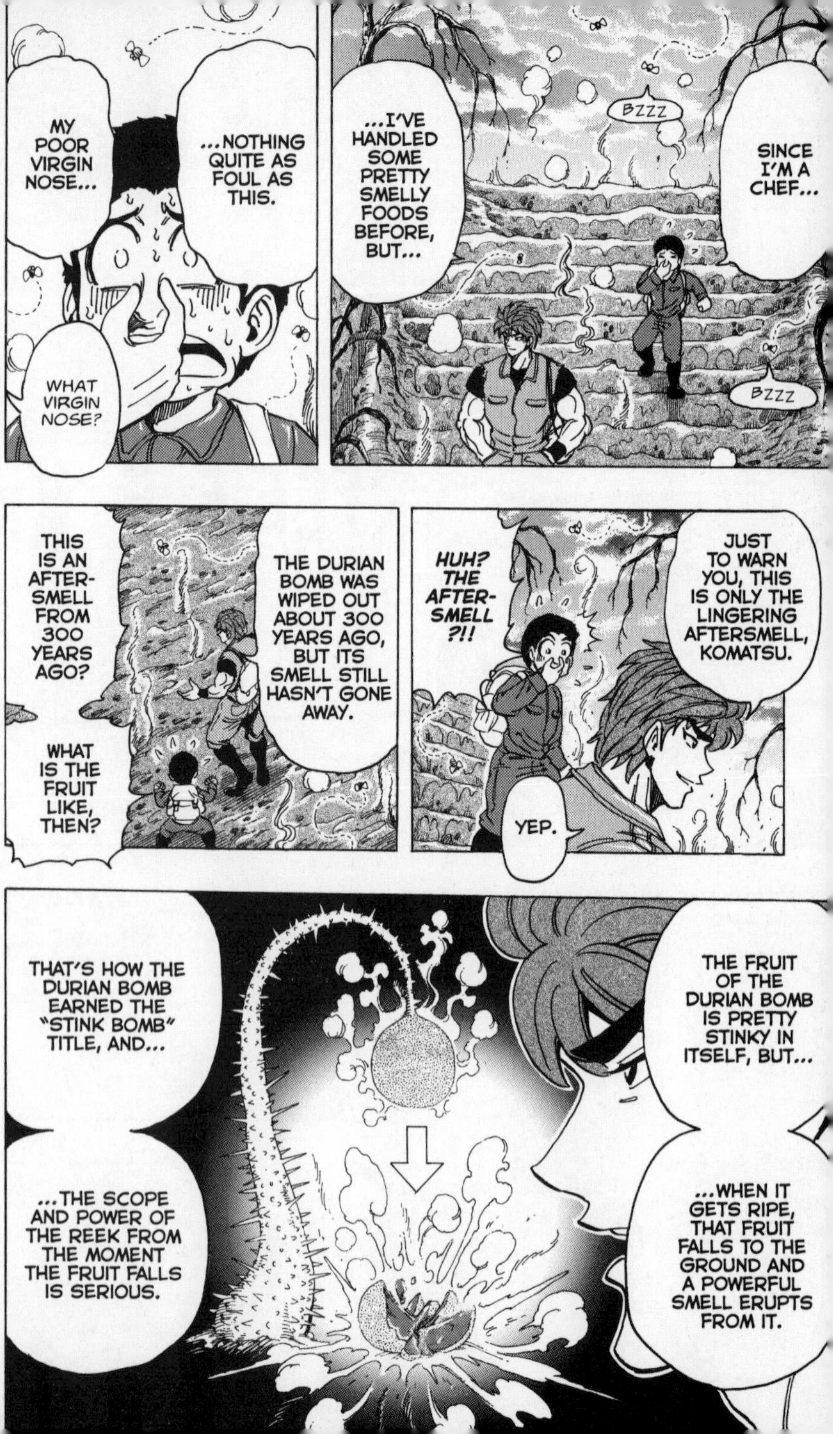
SINCE I'M A CHEF...
BZZZ
...I'VE HANDLED SOME PRETTY SMELLY FOODS BEFORE, BUT...
BZZZ
...NOTHING QUITE AS FOUL AS THIS.
MY POOR VIRGIN NOSE...
WHAT VIRGIN NOSE?
JUST TO WARN YOU, THIS IS ONLY THE LINGERING AFTERSMELL, KOMATSU.
HUH? THE AFTER-SMELL?!!
YEP.
THE DURIAN BOMB WAS WIPED OUT ABOUT 300 YEARS AGO, BUT ITS SMELL STILL HASN'T GONE AWAY.
THIS IS AN AFTER-SMELL FROM 300 YEARS AGO?
WHAT IS THE FRUIT LIKE, THEN?
THE FRUIT OF THE DURIAN BOMB IS PRETTY STINKY IN ITSELF, BUT...
...WHEN IT GETS RIPE, THAT FRUIT FALLS TO THE GROUND AND A POWERFUL SMELL ERUPTS FROM IT.
THAT'S HOW THE DURIAN BOMB EARNED THE "STINK BOMB" TITLE, AND...
...THE SCOPE AND POWER OF THE REEK FROM THE MOMENT THE FRUIT FALLS IS SERIOUS.

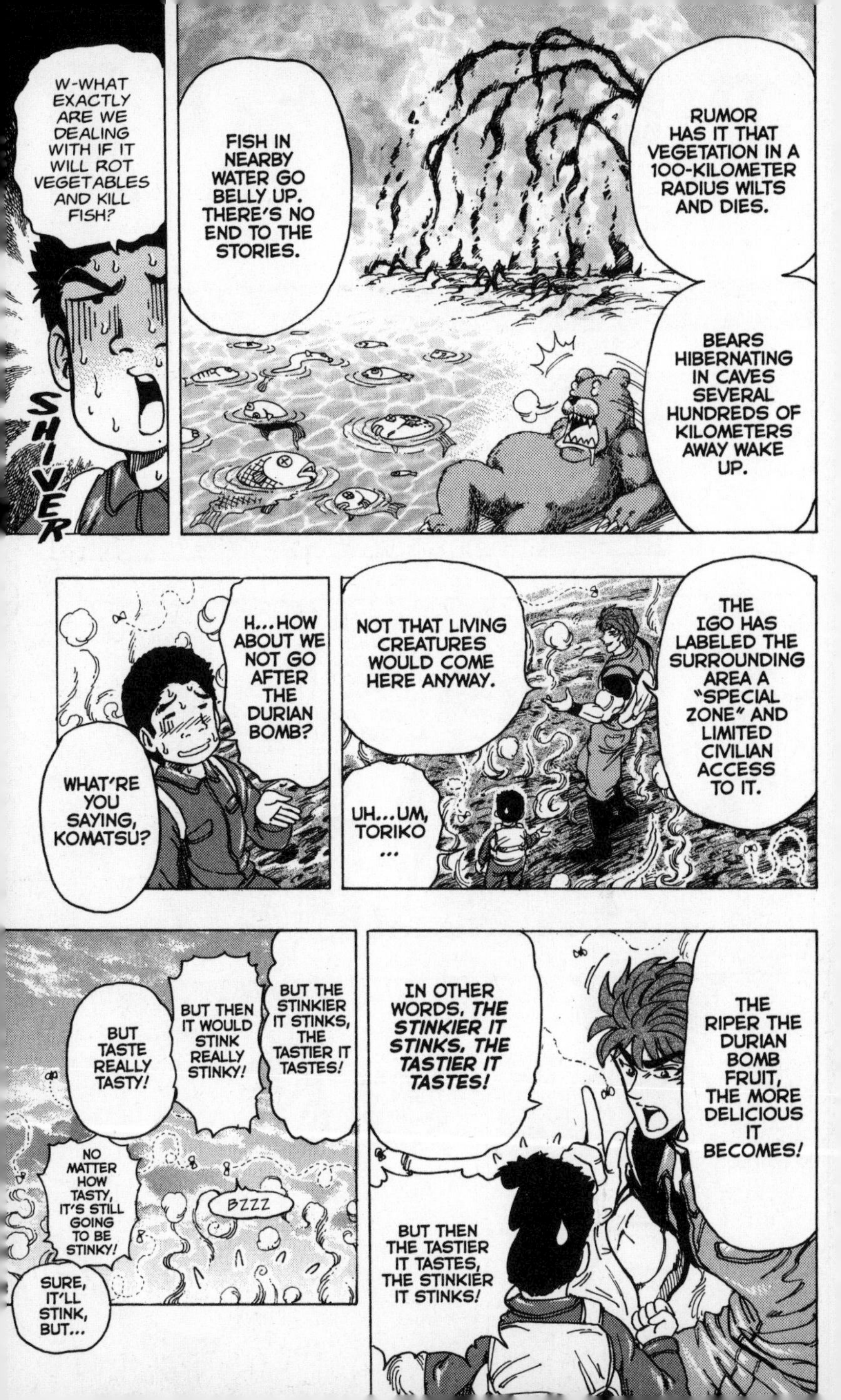
RUMOR HAS IT THAT VEGETATION IN A 100-KILOMETER RADIUS WILTS AND DIES.
FISH IN NEARBY WATER GO BELLY UP. THERE'S NO END TO THE STORIES.
BEARS HIBERNATING IN CAVES SEVERAL HUNDREDS OF KILOMETERS AWAY WAKE UP.
W-WHAT EXACTLY ARE WE DEALING WITH IF IT WILL ROT VEGETABLES AND KILL FISH?
SHIVER
THE IGO HAS LABELED THE SURROUNDING AREA A "SPECIAL ZONE" AND LIMITED CIVILIAN ACCESS TO IT.
NOT THAT LIVING CREATURES WOULD COME HERE ANYWAY.
UH...UM, TORIKO...
H...HOW ABOUT WE NOT GO AFTER THE DURIAN BOMB?
WHAT'RE YOU SAYING, KOMATSU?
THE RIPER THE DURIAN BOMB FRUIT, THE MORE DELICIOUS IT BECOMES!
IN OTHER WORDS, *THE STINKIER IT STINKS, THE TASTIER IT TASTES!*
BUT THEN THE TASTIER IT TASTES, THE STINKIER IT STINKS!
BUT THE STINKIER IT STINKS, THE TASTIER IT TASTES!
BUT THEN IT WOULD STINK REALLY STINKY!
BUT TASTE REALLY TASTY!
NO MATTER HOW TASTY, IT'S STILL GOING TO BE STINKY!
BZZZ
SURE, IT'LL STINK, BUT...

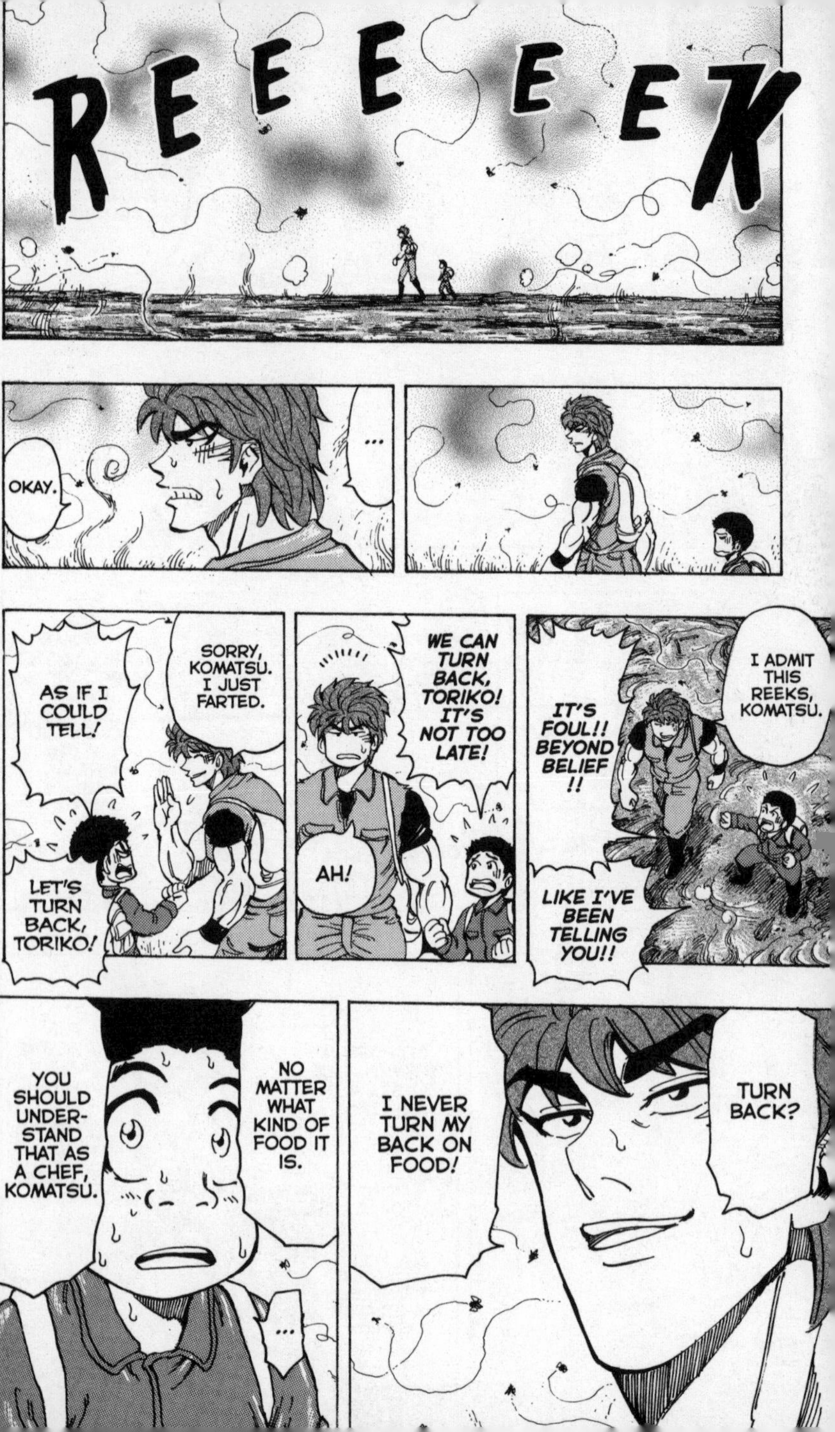
REEEEEK
...
OKAY.
I ADMIT THIS REEKS, KOMATSU.
IT'S FOUL!! BEYOND BELIEF!!
LIKE I'VE BEEN TELLING YOU!!
WE CAN TURN BACK, TORIKO! IT'S NOT TOO LATE!
AH!
SORRY, KOMATSU. I JUST FARTED.
AS IF I COULD TELL!
LET'S TURN BACK, TORIKO!
TURN BACK?
I NEVER TURN MY BACK ON FOOD!
NO MATTER WHAT KIND OF FOOD IT IS.
YOU SHOULD UNDER-STAND THAT AS A CHEF, KOMATSU.
...

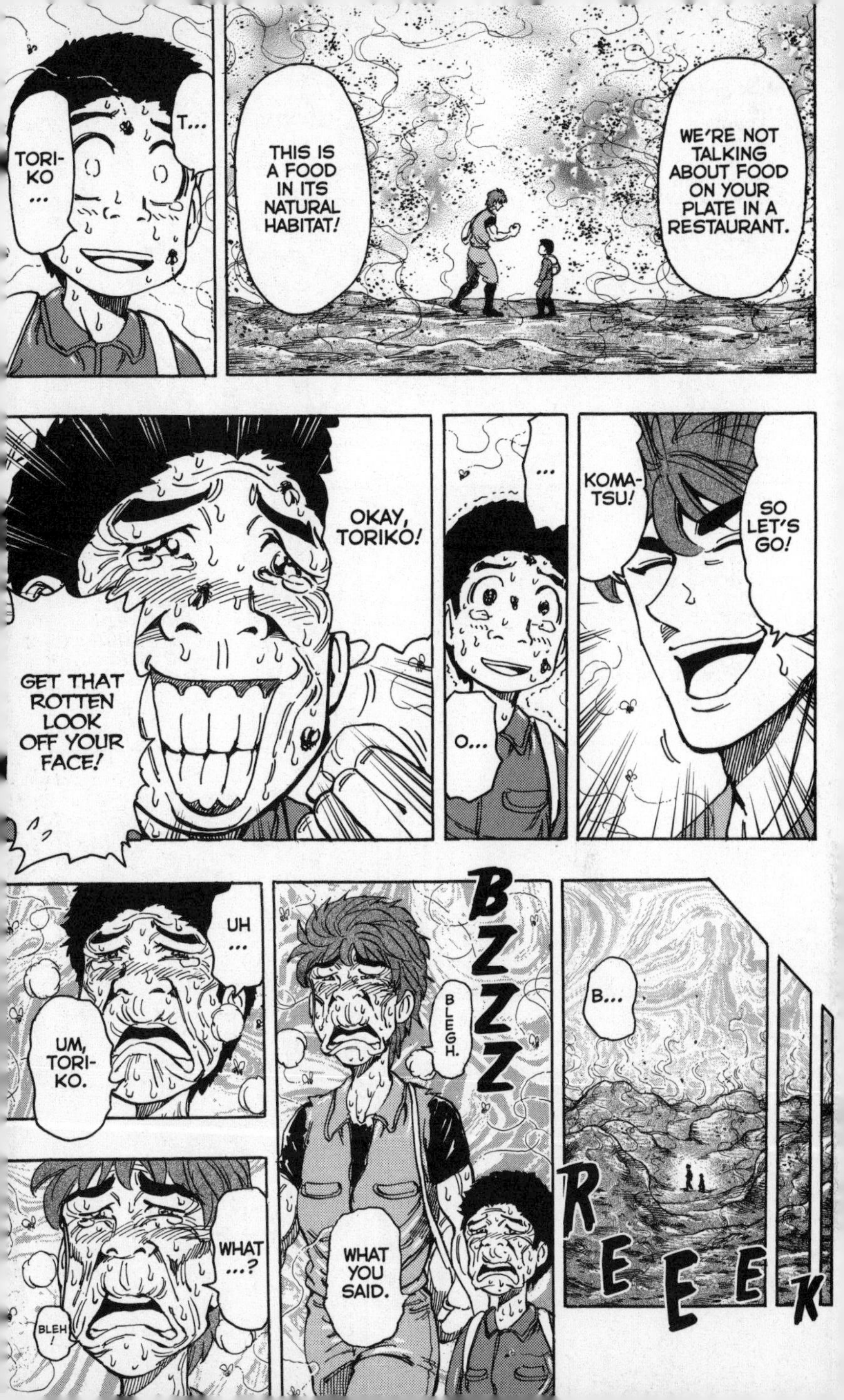
WE'RE NOT TALKING ABOUT FOOD ON YOUR PLATE IN A RESTAURANT.
THIS IS A FOOD IN ITS NATURAL HABITAT!
T...
TORIKO...
SO LET'S GO!
KOMATSU!
...
O...
OKAY, TORIKO!
GET THAT ROTTEN LOOK OFF YOUR FACE!
B...
REEEEK
BZZZ
BLEGH.
WHAT YOU SAID.
UH...
UM, TORIKO.
WHAT...?
BLEH!

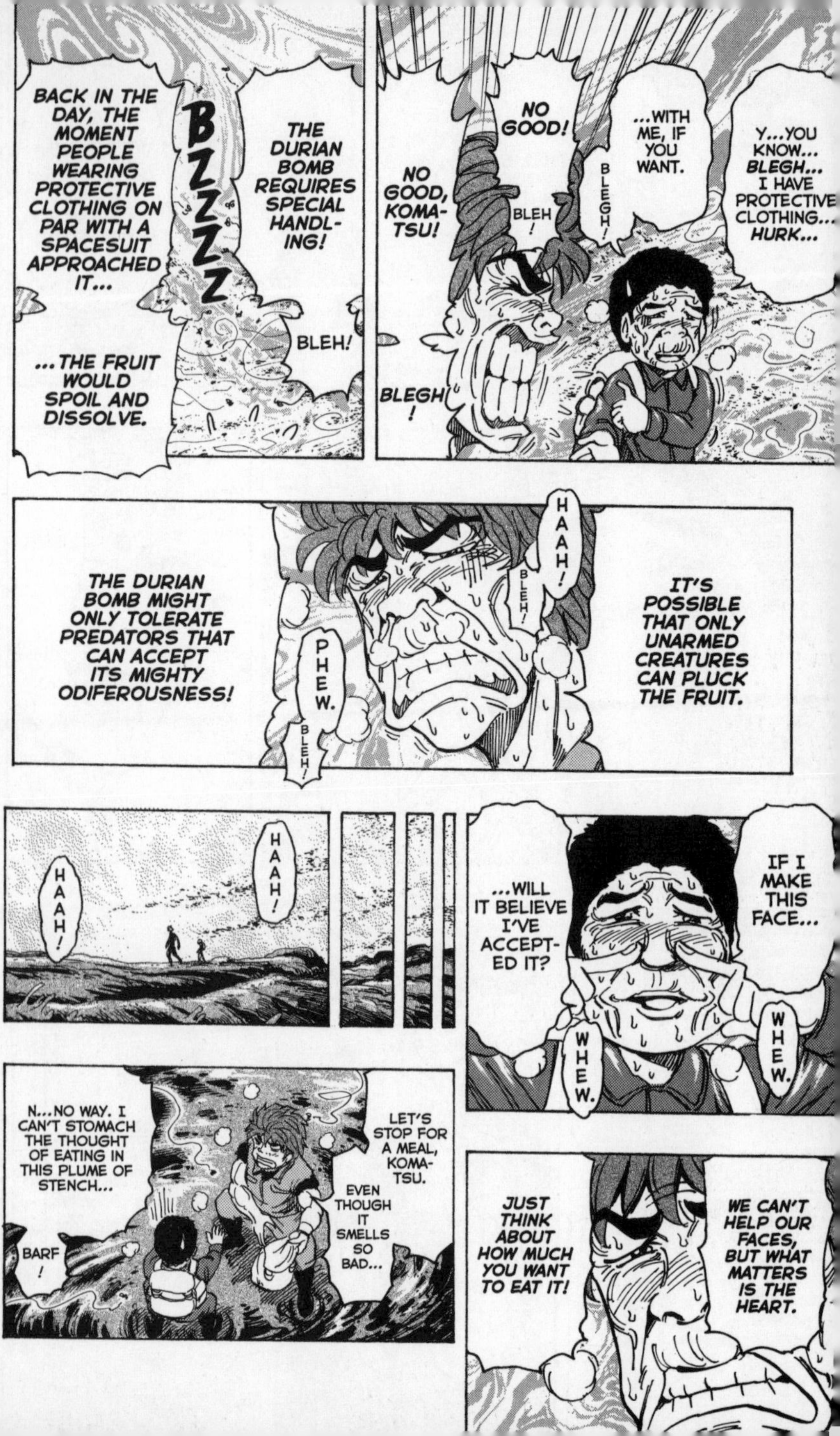

Y...YOU KNOW... BLEGH... I HAVE PROTECTIVE CLOTHING... HURK...
...WITH ME, IF YOU WANT.
BLEGH!
NO GOOD!
NO GOOD, KOMATSU!
BLEH!
BLEGH!
THE DURIAN BOMB REQUIRES SPECIAL HANDLING!
BZZZZ
BACK IN THE DAY, THE MOMENT PEOPLE WEARING PROTECTIVE CLOTHING ON PAR WITH A SPACESUIT APPROACHED IT...
BLEH!
...THE FRUIT WOULD SPOIL AND DISSOLVE.
IT'S POSSIBLE THAT ONLY UNARMED CREATURES CAN PLUCK THE FRUIT.
HAAH!
BLEH!
PHEW.
BLEH!
THE DURIAN BOMB MIGHT ONLY TOLERATE PREDATORS THAT CAN ACCEPT ITS MIGHTY ODIFEROUSNESS!
IF I MAKE THIS FACE...
...WILL IT BELIEVE I'VE ACCEPTED IT?
WHEW.
WHEW.
WE CAN'T HELP OUR FACES, BUT WHAT MATTERS IS THE HEART.
JUST THINK ABOUT HOW MUCH YOU WANT TO EAT IT!
HAAH!
HAAH!
LET'S STOP FOR A MEAL, KOMATSU.
EVEN THOUGH IT SMELLS SO BAD...
N...NO WAY. I CAN'T STOMACH THE THOUGHT OF EATING IN THIS PLUME OF STENCH...
BARF!

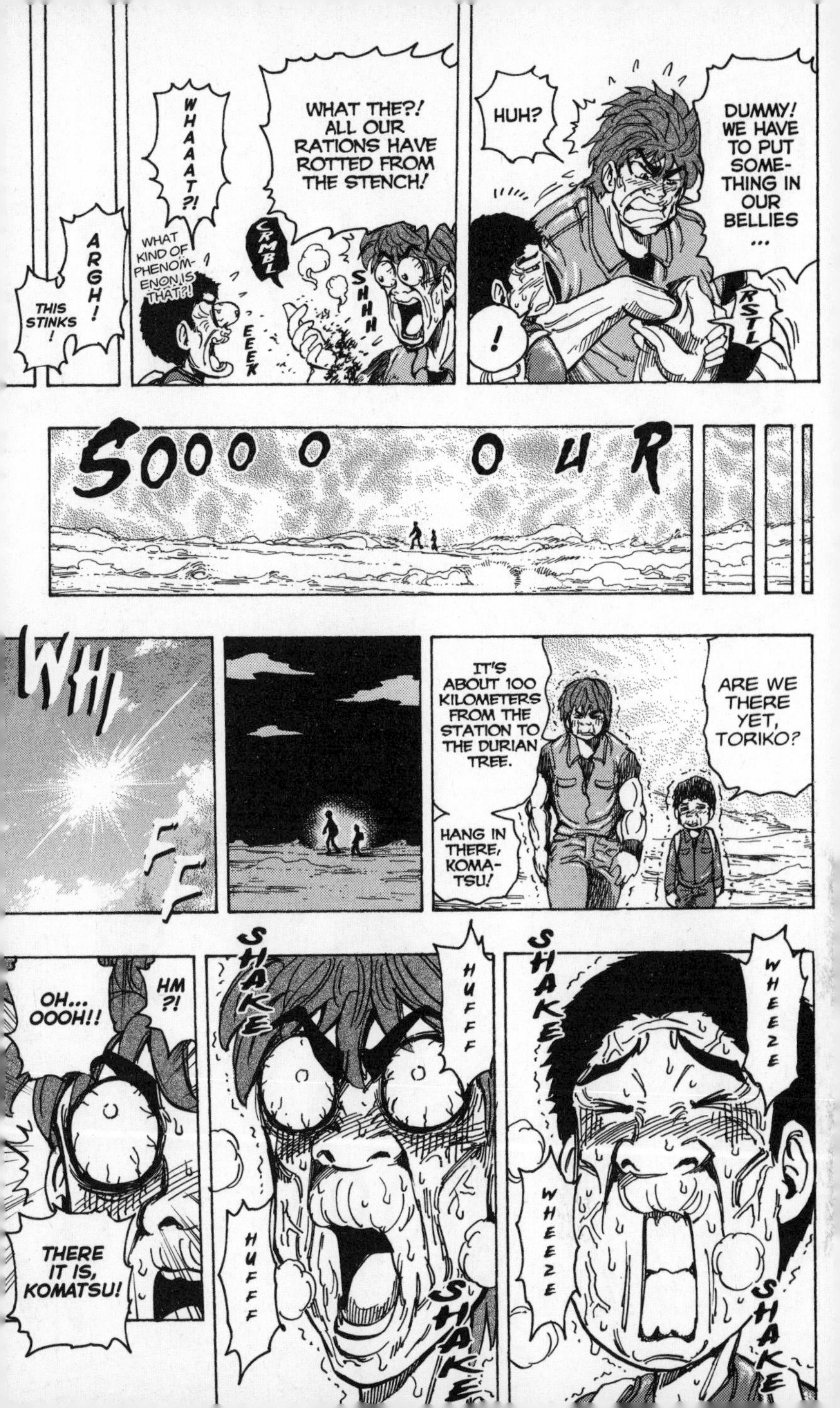
DUMMY! WE HAVE TO PUT SOMETHING IN OUR BELLIES...
HUH?
RSTL
!
WHAT THE?! ALL OUR RATIONS HAVE ROTTED FROM THE STENCH!
CRMBL
SHHH
WHAAAAT?!
WHAT KIND OF PHENOMENON IS THAT?!
EEEK
ARGH!
THIS STINKS!
SOOOO O OUR
ARE WE THERE YET, TORIKO?
IT'S ABOUT 100 KILOMETERS FROM THE STATION TO THE DURIAN TREE.
HANG IN THERE, KOMATSU!
WH
FF
WHEEZE
SHAKE
WHEEZE
SHAKE
HUFFF
SHAKE
HUFFF
SHAKE
HM?!
OH... OOOH!!
THERE IT IS, KOMATSU!

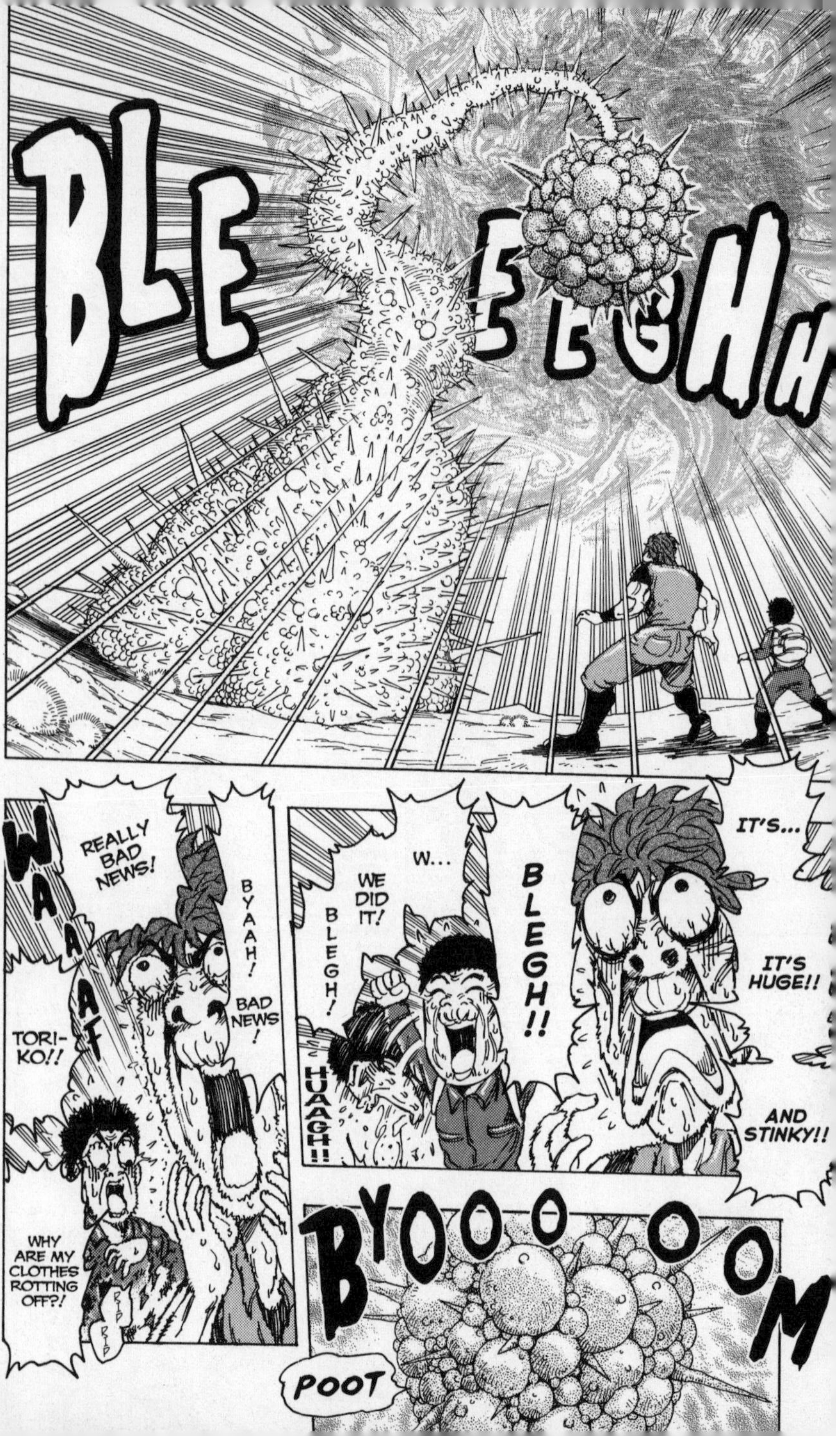

BLEEEGHH
IT'S...
BLEGH!!
W...
WE DID IT!
BLEGH!
IT'S HUGE!!
AND STINKY!!
HUAAAGH!!
BYOOOOOM
POOT
REALLY BAD NEWS!
BYAAH!
BAD NEWS!
WAAAAF
TORI-KO!!
WHY ARE MY CLOTHES ROTTING OFF?!
RIP
RIP

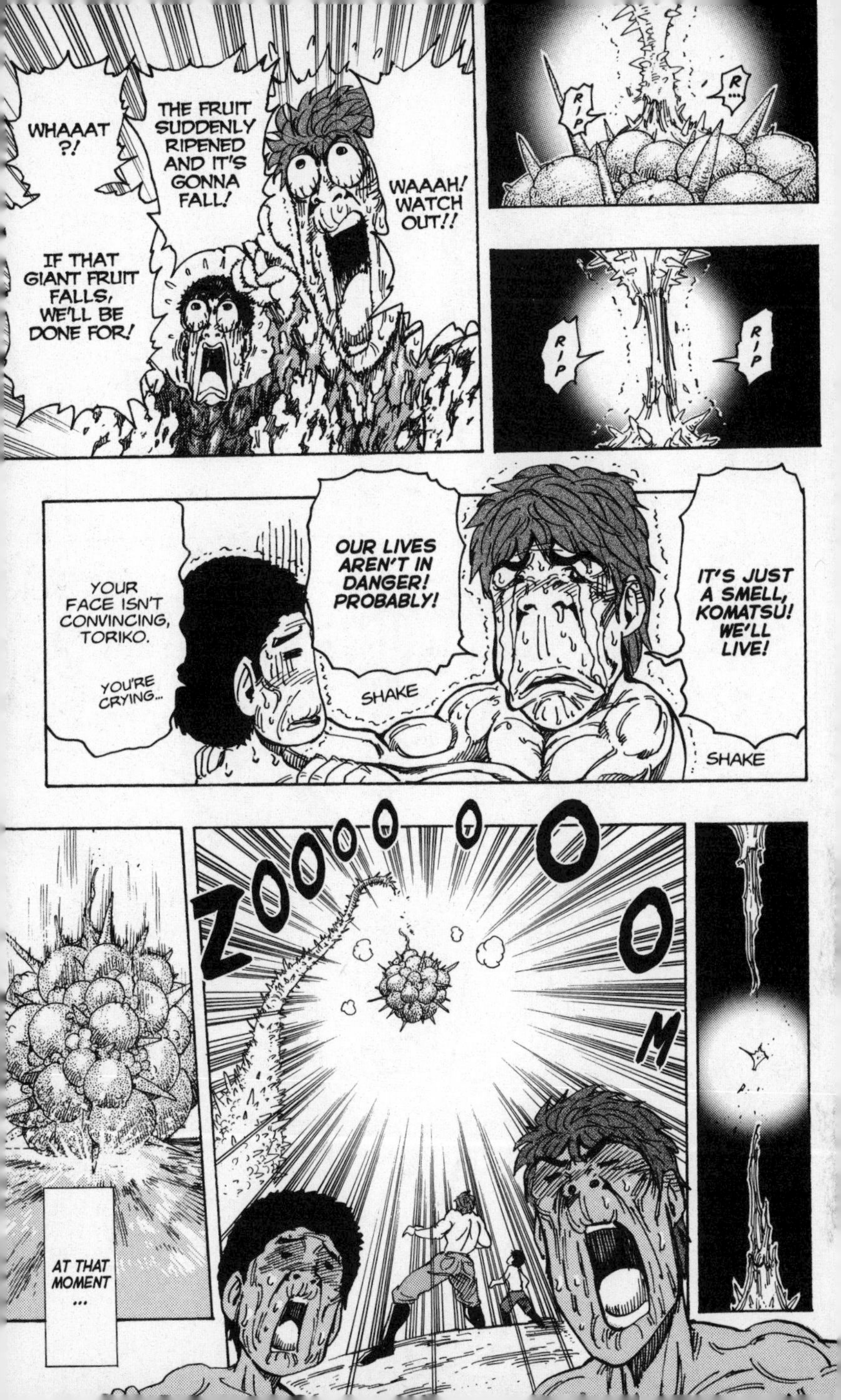

R...
RIP
RIP
RIP
WAAAH! WATCH OUT!!
THE FRUIT SUDDENLY RIPENED AND IT'S GONNA FALL!
WHAAAT?!
IF THAT GIANT FRUIT FALLS, WE'LL BE DONE FOR!
IT'S JUST A SMELL, KOMATSU! WE'LL LIVE!
OUR LIVES AREN'T IN DANGER! PROBABLY!
SHAKE
SHAKE
YOUR FACE ISN'T CONVINCING, TORIKO.
YOU'RE CRYING...
ZOOOOOOOOM
AT THAT MOMENT...

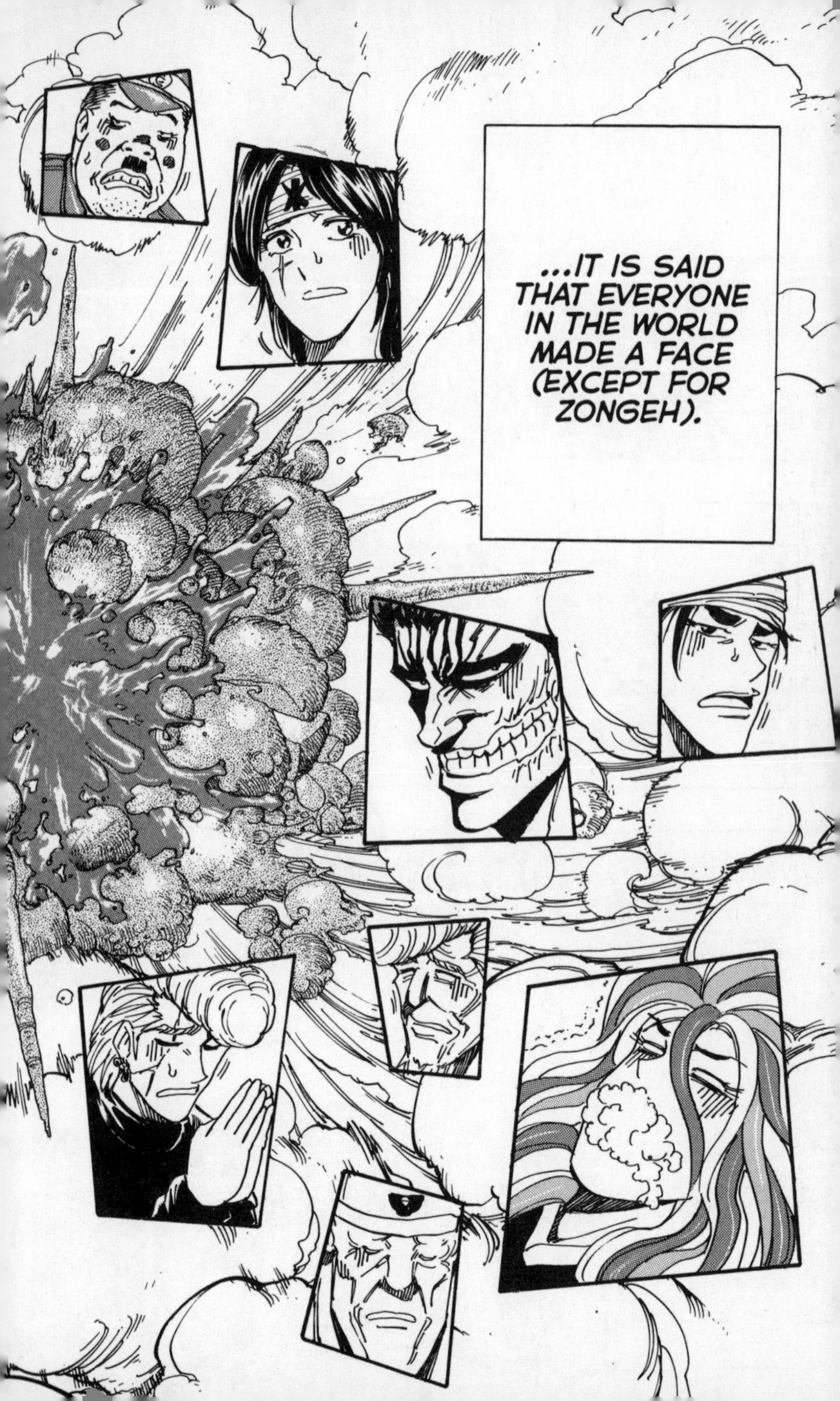
...IT IS SAID THAT EVERYONE IN THE WORLD MADE A FACE (EXCEPT FOR ZONGEH).

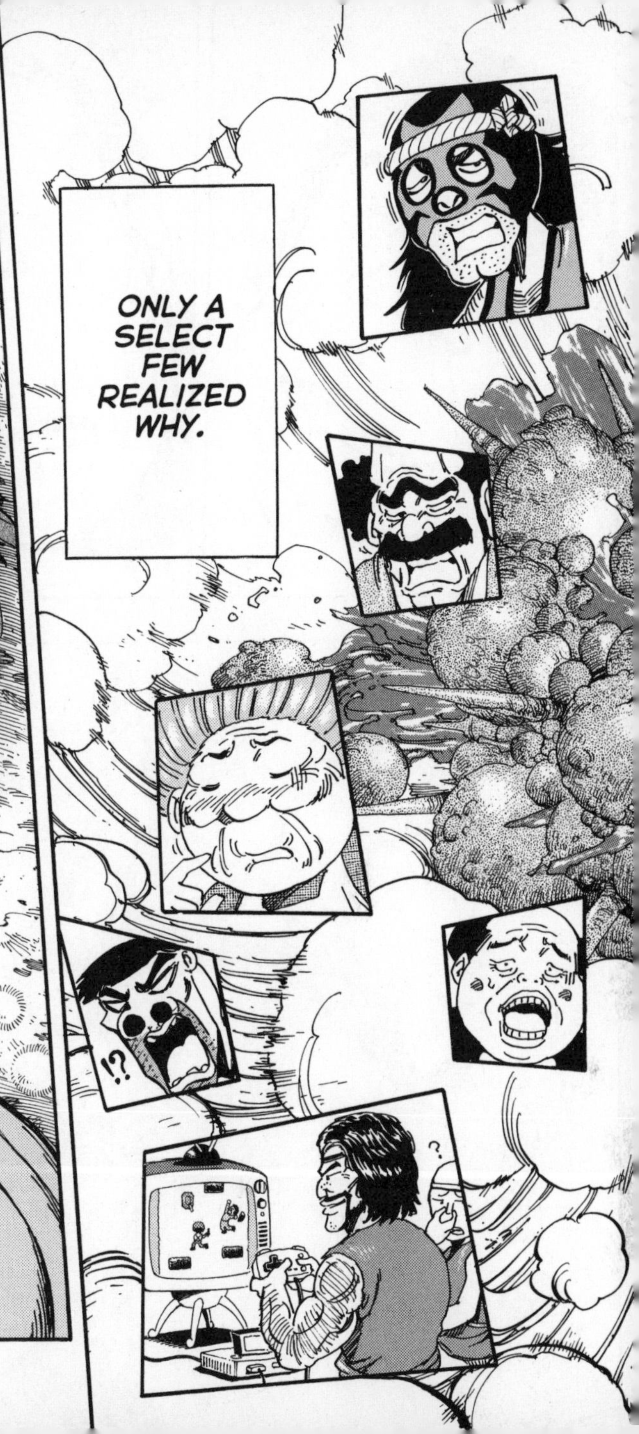
ONLY A SELECT FEW REALIZED WHY.
!?
?
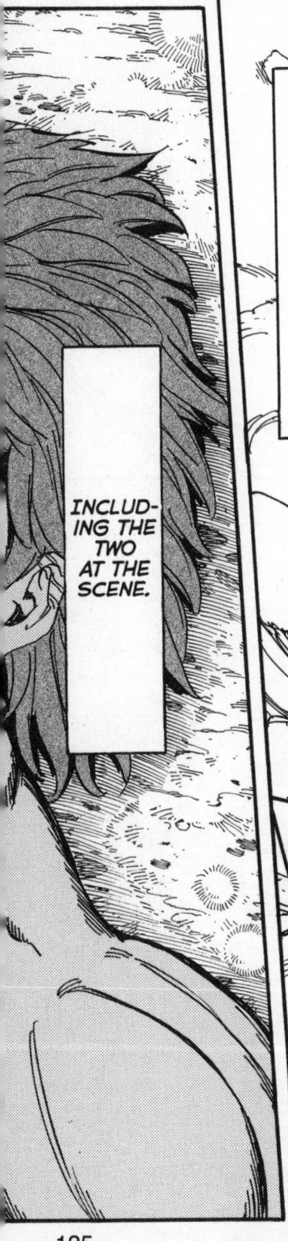
INCLUDING THE TWO AT THE SCENE.

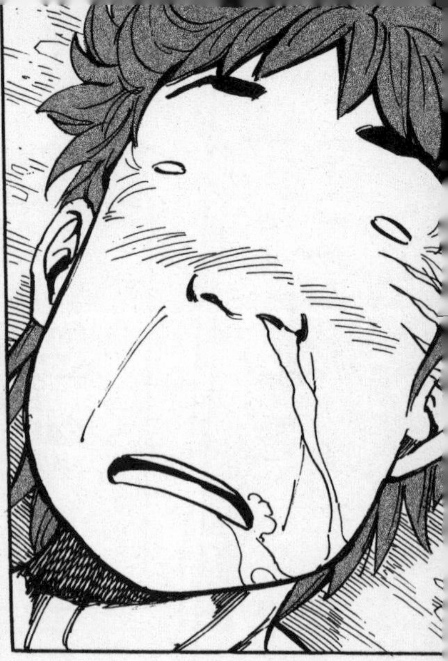
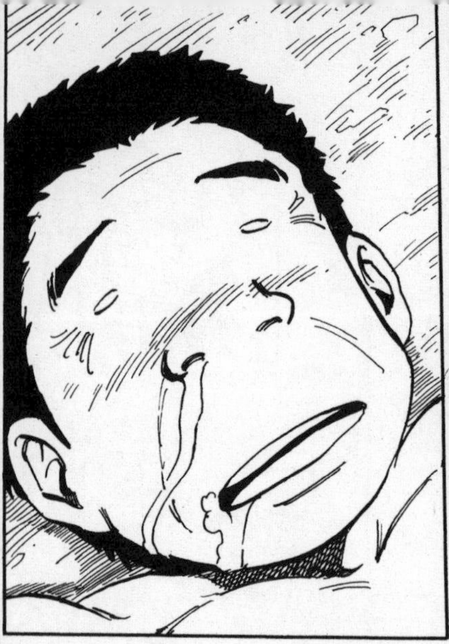
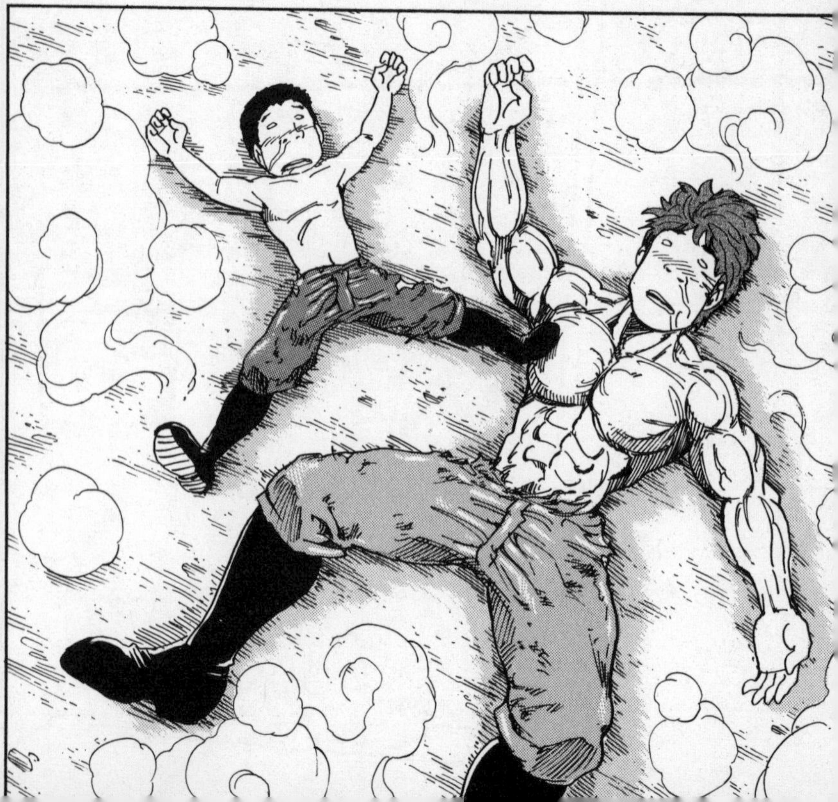

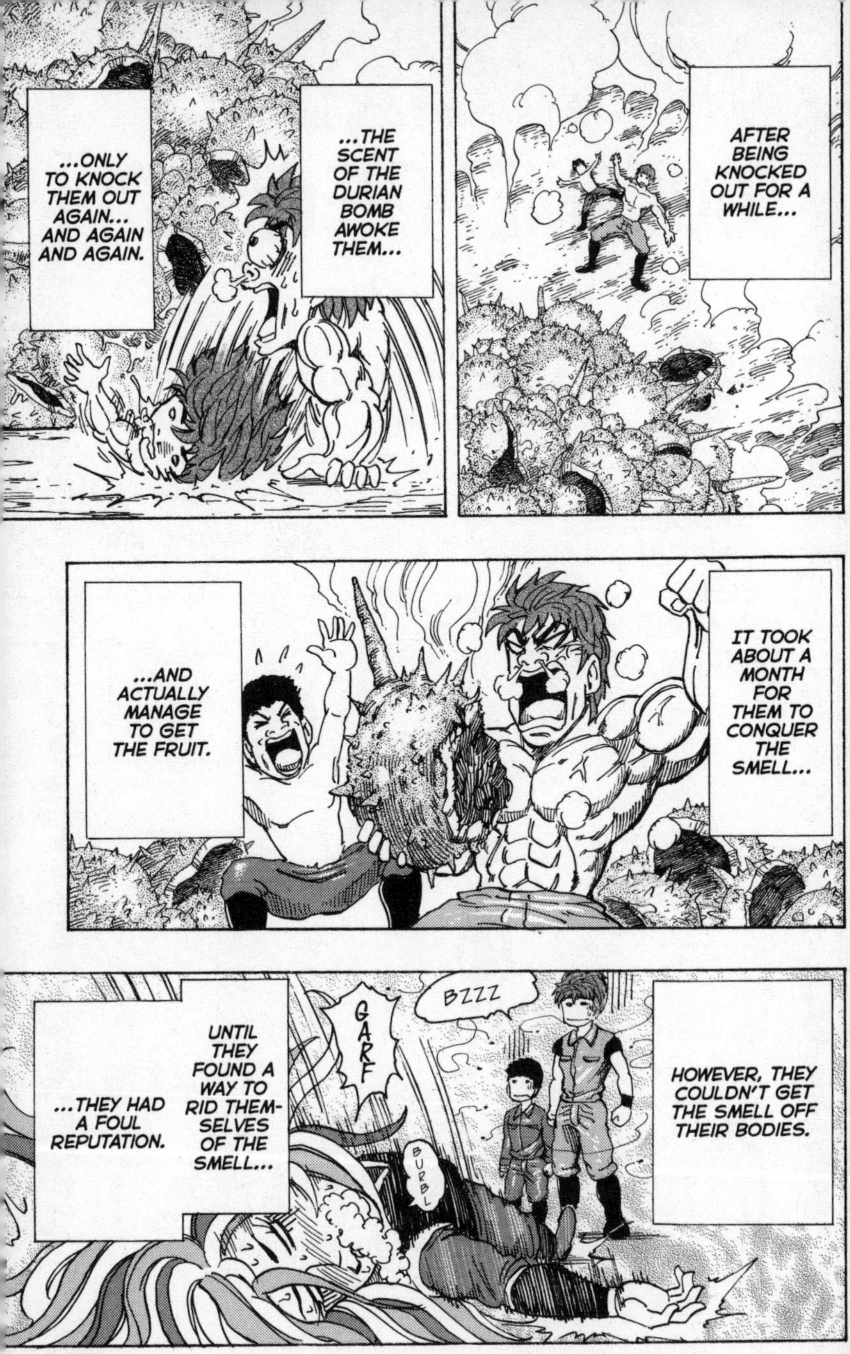
AFTER BEING KNOCKED OUT FOR A WHILE...
...THE SCENT OF THE DURIAN BOMB AWOKE THEM...
...ONLY TO KNOCK THEM OUT AGAIN... AND AGAIN AND AGAIN.
IT TOOK ABOUT A MONTH FOR THEM TO CONQUER THE SMELL...
...AND ACTUALLY MANAGE TO GET THE FRUIT.
HOWEVER, THEY COULDN'T GET THE SMELL OFF THEIR BODIES.
BZZZ
UNTIL THEY FOUND A WAY TO RID THEM-SELVES OF THE SMELL...
GARF
BURBL
...THEY HAD A FOUL REPUTATION.

TORIKO

GOURMET CHECKLIST

Vol. 206

 MOAI POTATO
(VEGETABLE)

CAPTURE LEVEL: 10
HABITAT: MOUNTAINS
LENGTH: 25 CM
HEIGHT: ---
WEIGHT: 300 G
PRICE: 1,000 YEN PER POTATO

POFF
POFF
PHEW!

MMMM. FRESHLY ROASTED *MOAI POTATO*! IT'S SO RICH.

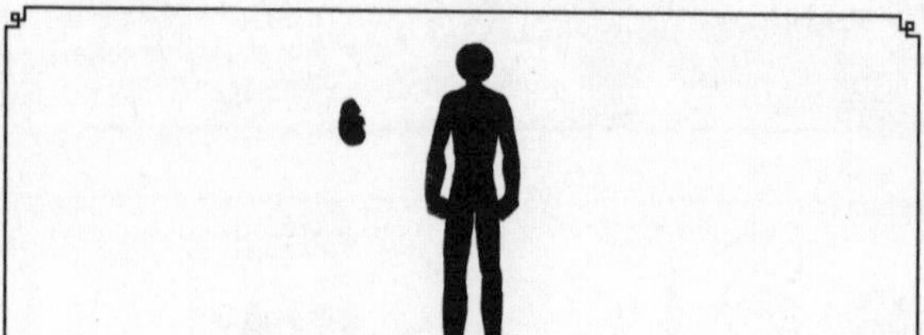

SCALE

A PERENNIAL PLANT IN THE CONVOLVULUS FAMILY (SAME AS THE MORNING GLORY). MOAI POTATO GROWS ON PRECIPITOUS MOUNTAIN CLIFFS. ITS STEM IS TWINED AND CREEPS ALONG THE GROUND. IT HAS HEART-SHAPED LEAVES AND ITS POTATOES RESEMBLES MOAI STATUES. MOAI POTATO IS STARCHY AND SWEET AND CAN ALSO SERVE AS A BASE FOR ALCOHOL. THEY'RE TASTY BAKED WHOLE, BUT GIVE SOME PEOPLE GAS.

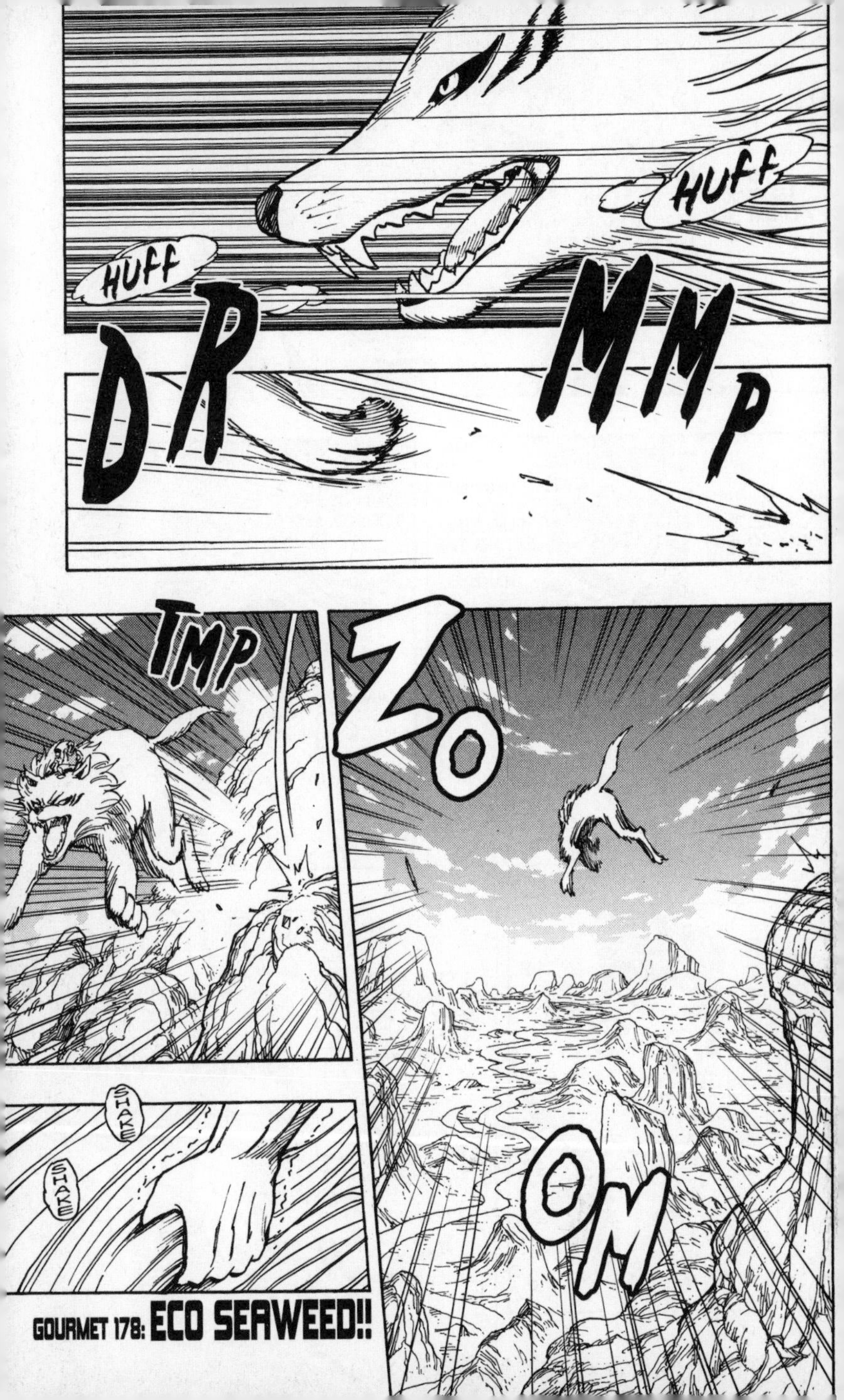
HUFF
HUFF
DRMMP
ZOOOM
TMP
SHAKE
SHAKE

GOURMET 178: ECO SEAWEED!!

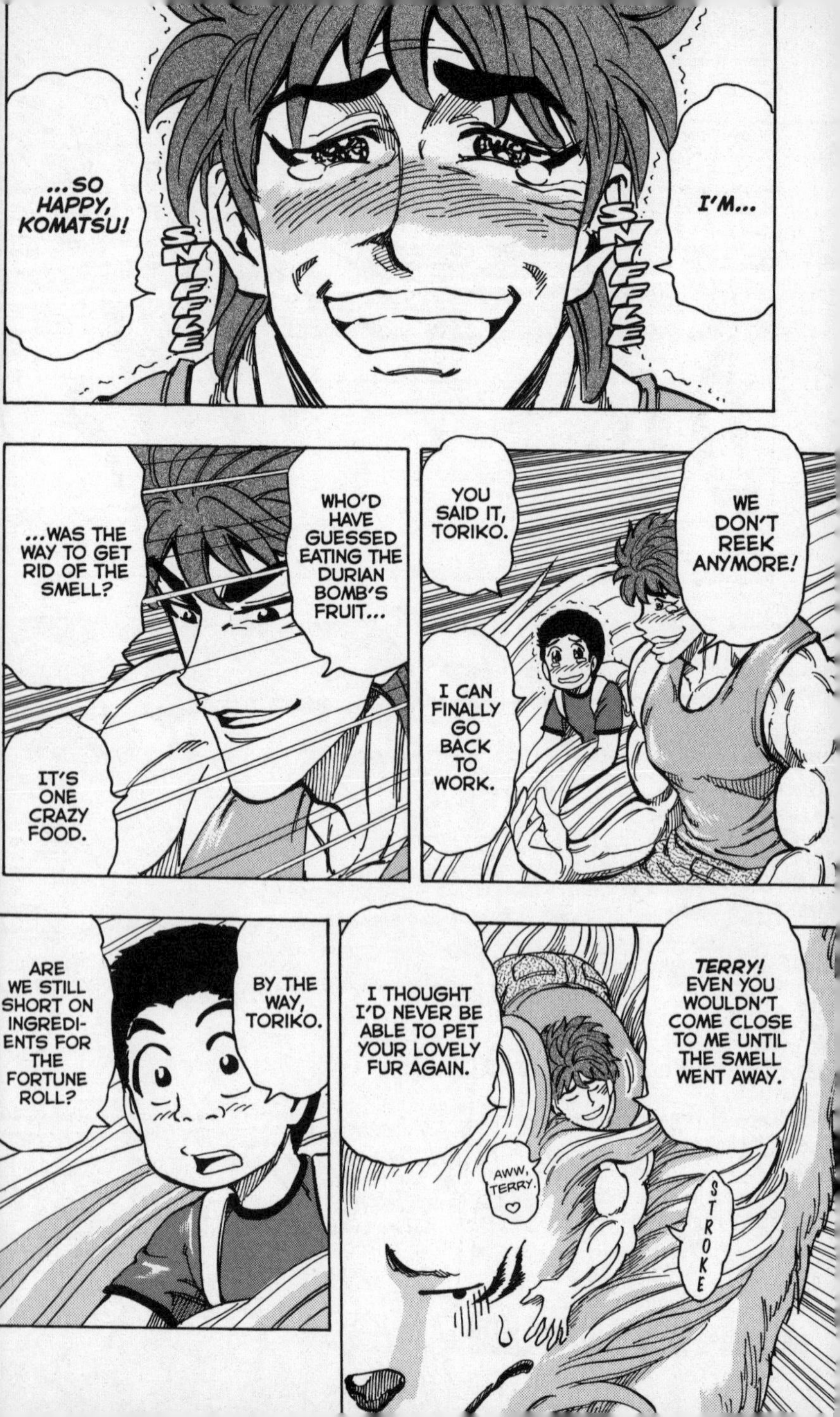
I'M...
SNIFFLE
SNIFFLE
...SO HAPPY, KOMATSU!
WE DON'T REEK ANYMORE!
YOU SAID IT, TORIKO.
I CAN FINALLY GO BACK TO WORK.
WHO'D HAVE GUESSED EATING THE DURIAN BOMB'S FRUIT...
...WAS THE WAY TO GET RID OF THE SMELL?
IT'S ONE CRAZY FOOD.
TERRY! EVEN YOU WOULDN'T COME CLOSE TO ME UNTIL THE SMELL WENT AWAY.
I THOUGHT I'D NEVER BE ABLE TO PET YOUR LOVELY FUR AGAIN.
STROKE
AWW, TERRY. ♡
BY THE WAY, TORIKO.
ARE WE STILL SHORT ON INGREDIENTS FOR THE FORTUNE ROLL?

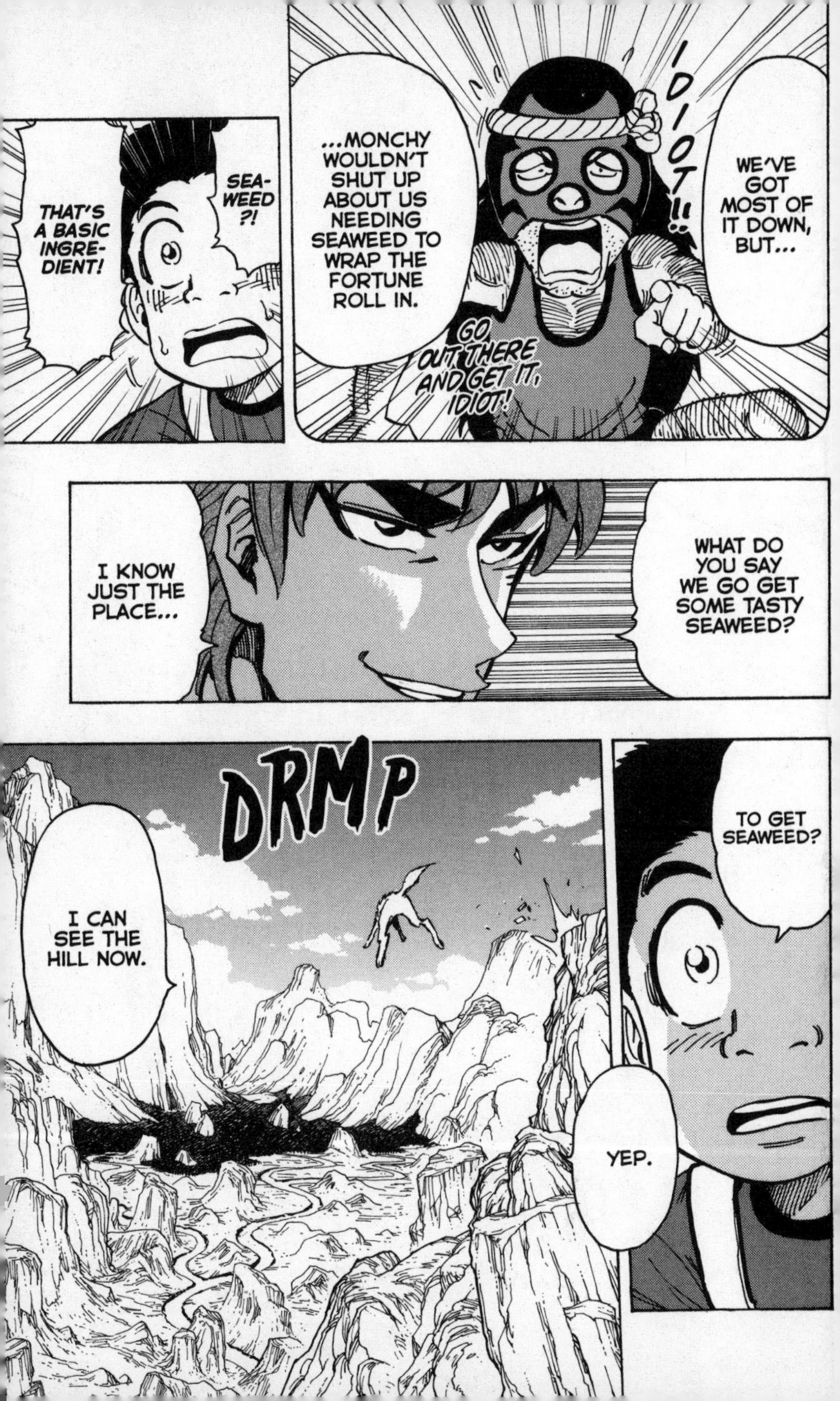

WE'VE GOT MOST OF IT DOWN, BUT...
IDIOT!!
...MONCHY WOULDN'T SHUT UP ABOUT US NEEDING SEAWEED TO WRAP THE FORTUNE ROLL IN.
GO OUT THERE AND GET IT, IDIOT!
SEA-WEED?!
THAT'S A BASIC INGRE-DIENT!
WHAT DO YOU SAY WE GO GET SOME TASTY SEAWEED?
I KNOW JUST THE PLACE...
TO GET SEAWEED?
YEP.
DRMP
I CAN SEE THE HILL NOW.

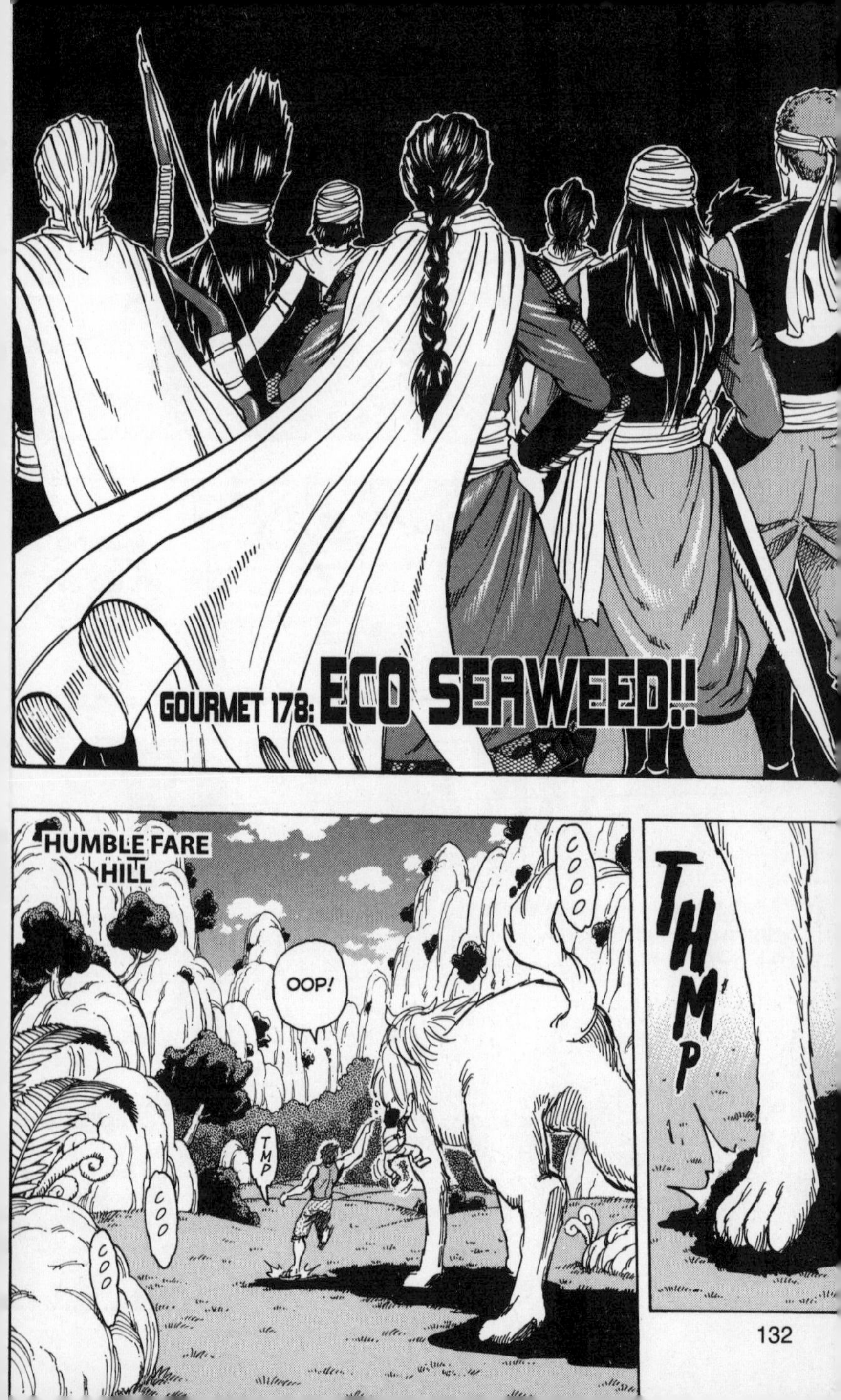
GOURMET 178: ECO SEAWEED!!
THMP
COOO
HUMBLE FARE HILL
OOP!
TMP
COO
COO

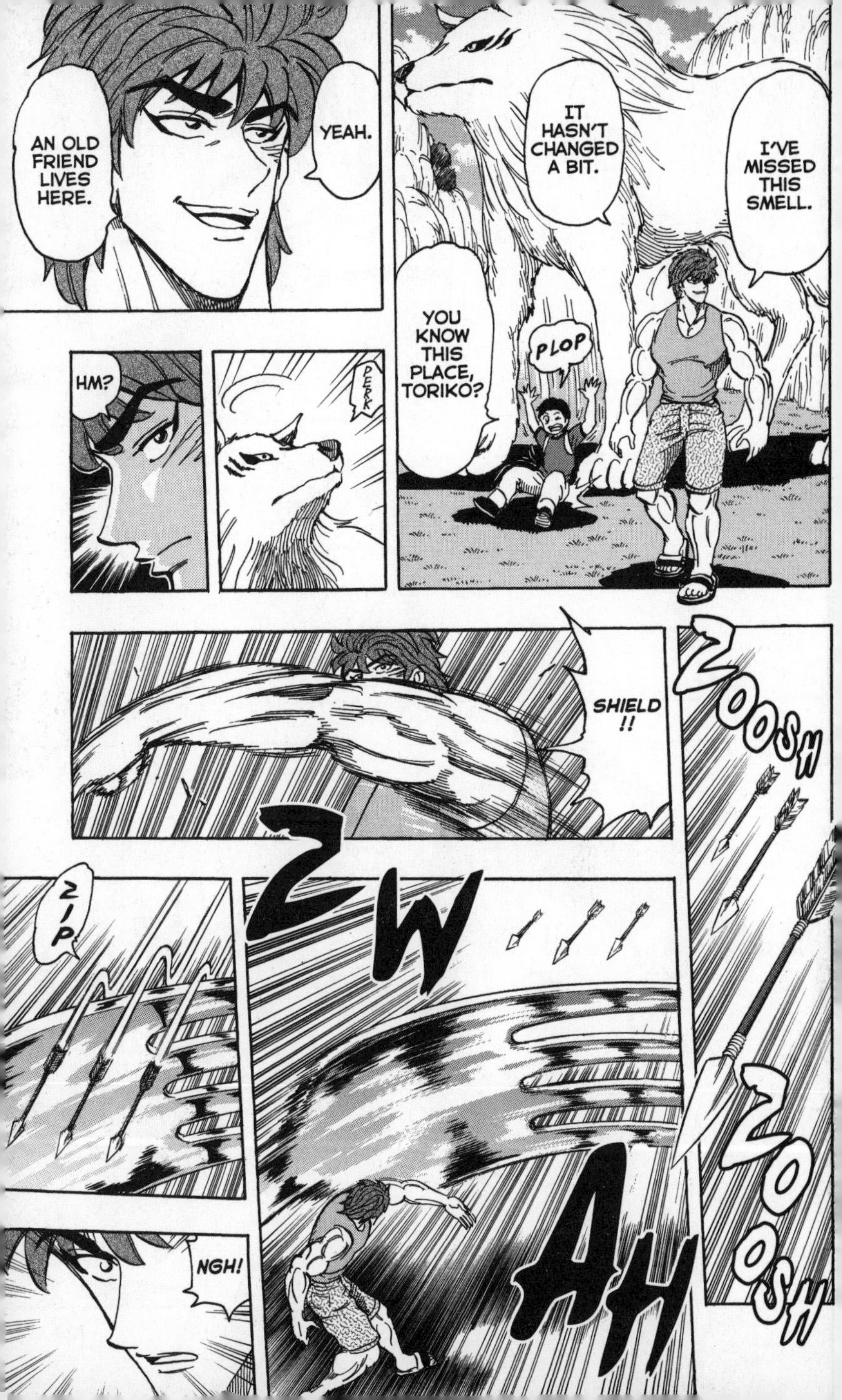
I'VE MISSED THIS SMELL.
IT HASN'T CHANGED A BIT.
YOU KNOW THIS PLACE, TORIKO?
PLOP
YEAH.
AN OLD FRIEND LIVES HERE.
PERK
HM?
ZOOSH
ZOOSH
SHIELD !!
ZWAH
ZIP
NGH!

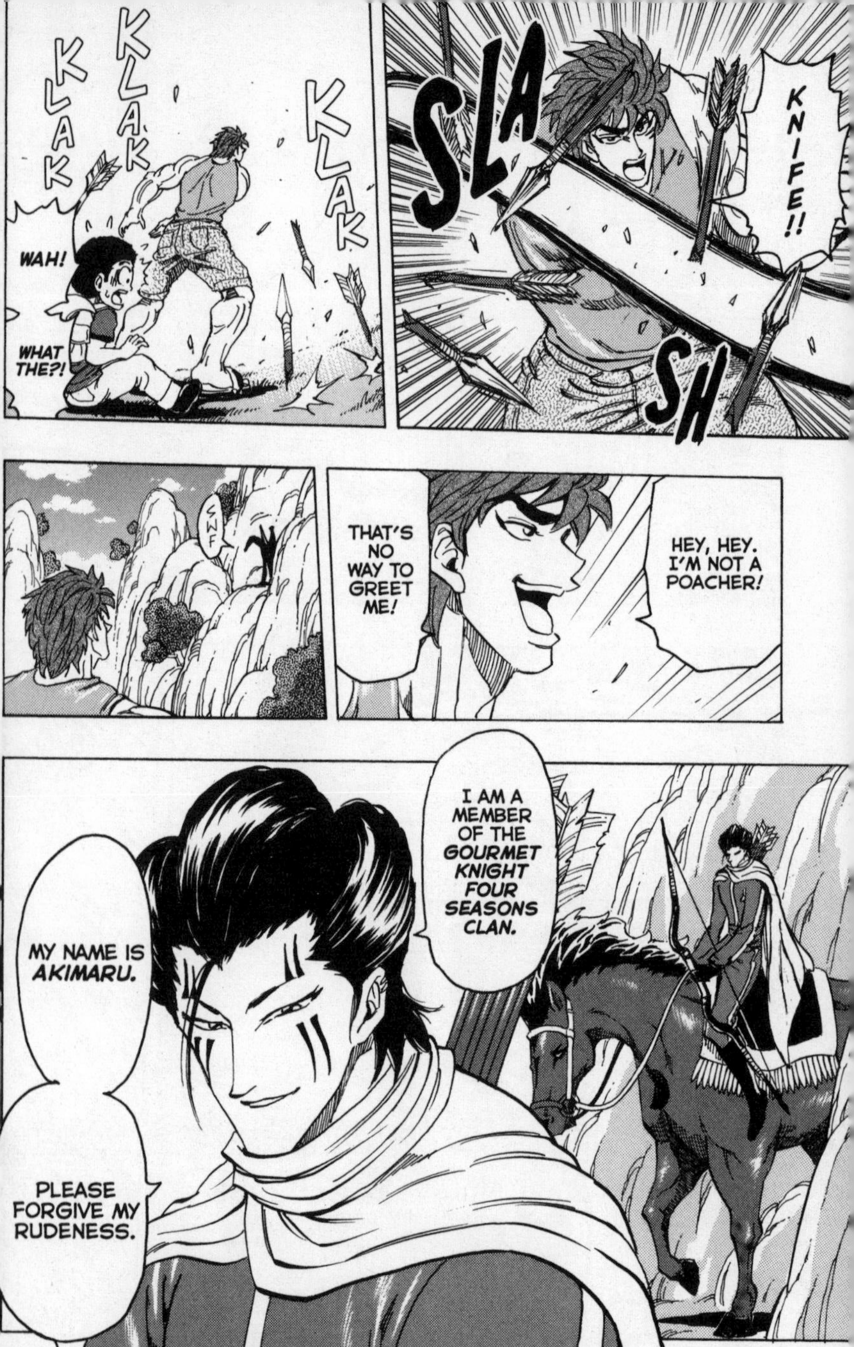
SLA
SH
KNIFE!!
KLAK
KLAK
KLAK
WAH!
WHAT THE?!
HEY, HEY. I'M NOT A POACHER!
THAT'S NO WAY TO GREET ME!
SNF
I AM A MEMBER OF THE GOURMET KNIGHT FOUR SEASONS CLAN.
MY NAME IS AKIMARU.
PLEASE FORGIVE MY RUDENESS.

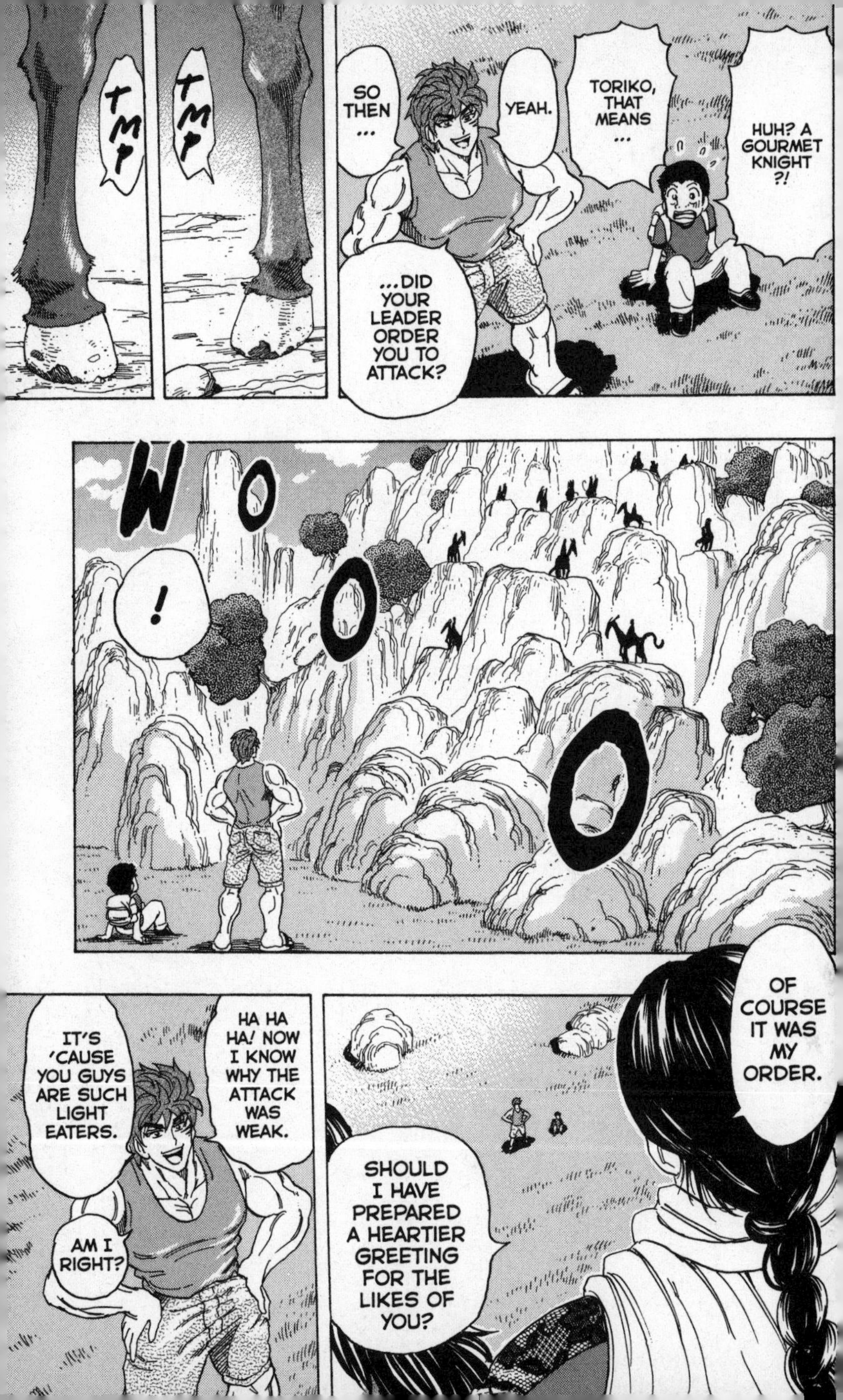

HUH? A GOURMET KNIGHT ?!
TORIKO, THAT MEANS ...
YEAH.
SO THEN ...
...DID YOUR LEADER ORDER YOU TO ATTACK?
TMP
TMP
WOOO
!
OF COURSE IT WAS MY ORDER.
SHOULD I HAVE PREPARED A HEARTIER GREETING FOR THE LIKES OF YOU?
HA HA HA! NOW I KNOW WHY THE ATTACK WAS WEAK.
IT'S 'CAUSE YOU GUYS ARE SUCH LIGHT EATERS.
AM I RIGHT?

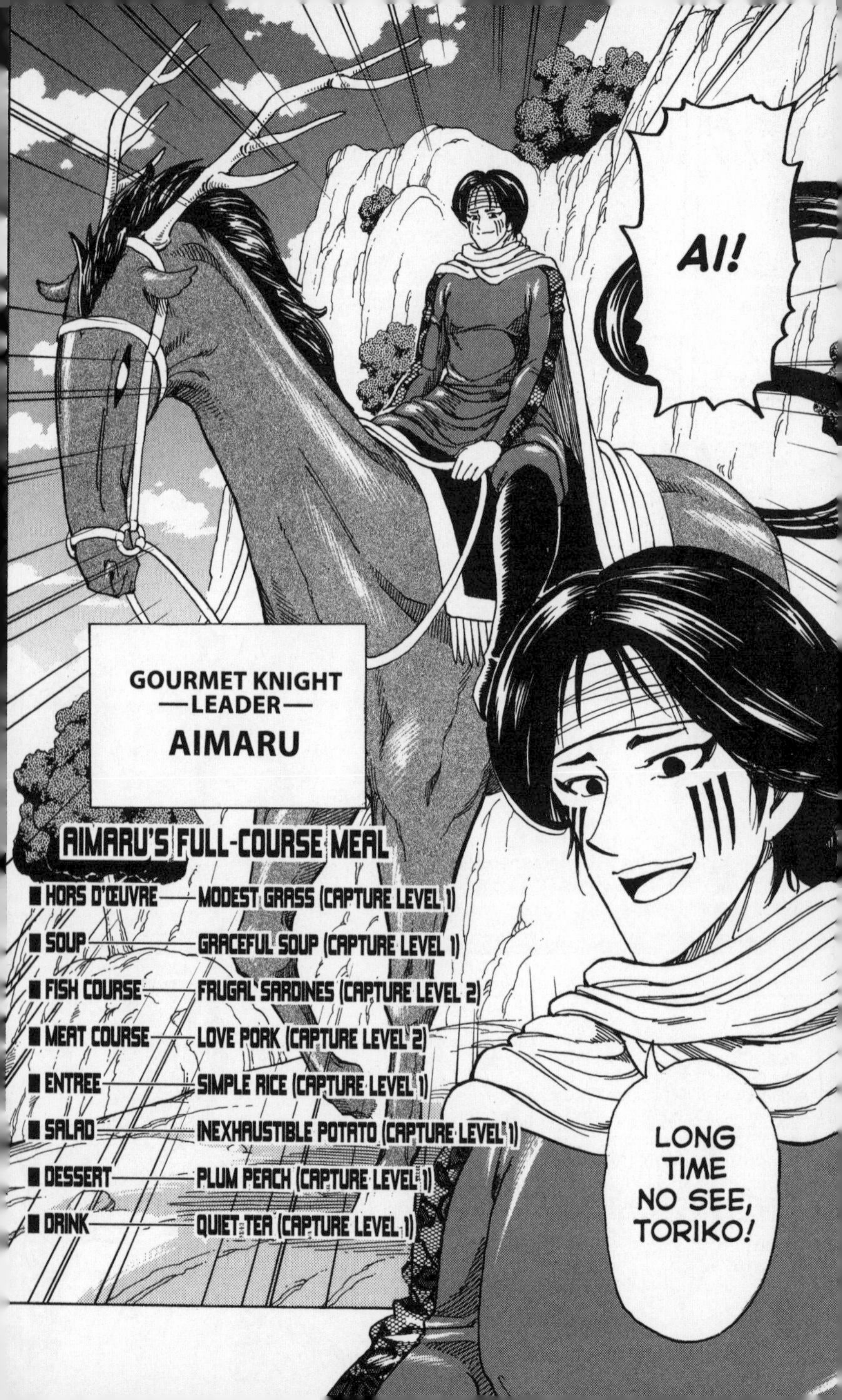
AI!
GOURMET KNIGHT
—LEADER—
AIMARU
AIMARU'S FULL-COURSE MEAL
■ HORS D'ŒUVRE—MODEST GRASS (CAPTURE LEVEL 1)
■ SOUP—GRACEFUL SOUP (CAPTURE LEVEL 1)
■ FISH COURSE—FRUGAL SARDINES (CAPTURE LEVEL 2)
■ MEAT COURSE—LOVE PORK (CAPTURE LEVEL 2)
■ ENTREE—SIMPLE RICE (CAPTURE LEVEL 1)
■ SALAD—INEXHAUSTIBLE POTATO (CAPTURE LEVEL 1)
■ DESSERT—PLUM PEACH (CAPTURE LEVEL 1)
■ DRINK—QUIET TEA (CAPTURE LEVEL 1)
LONG TIME NO SEE, TORIKO!

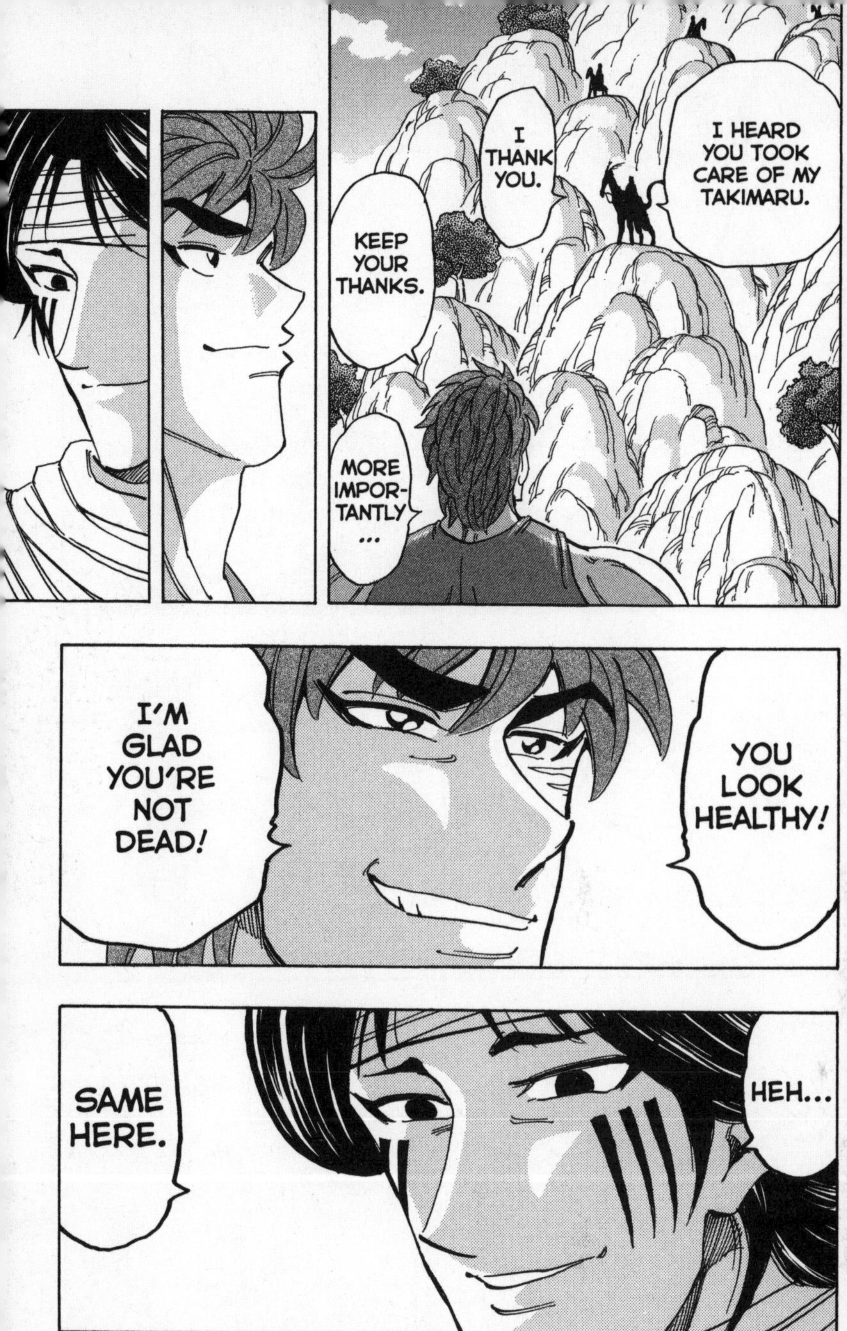
I HEARD YOU TOOK CARE OF MY TAKIMARU.
I THANK YOU.
KEEP YOUR THANKS.
MORE IMPOR-TANTLY...
YOU LOOK HEALTHY!
I'M GLAD YOU'RE NOT DEAD!
HEH...
SAME HERE.

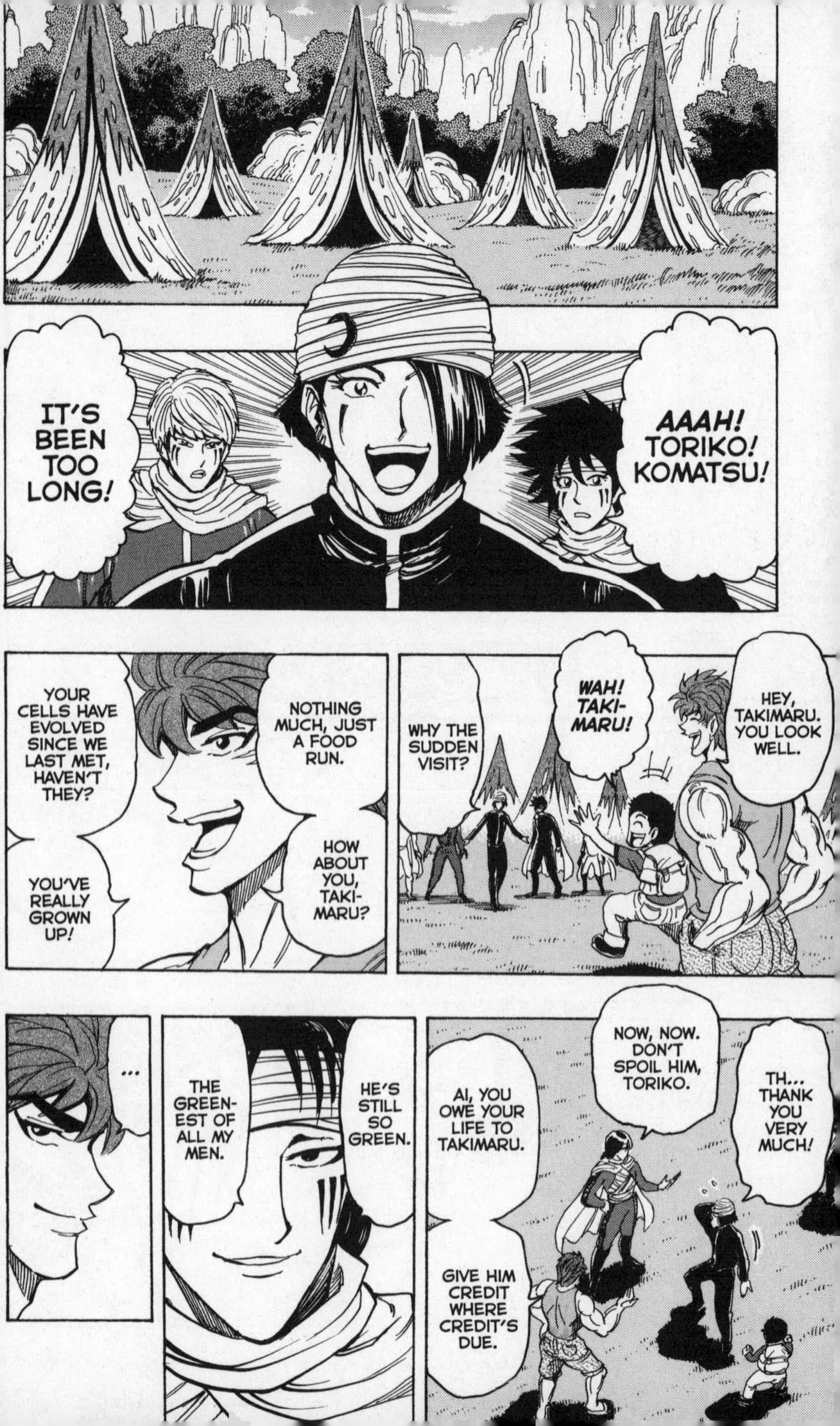
AAAH! TORIKO! KOMATSU!
IT'S BEEN TOO LONG!
HEY, TAKIMARU. YOU LOOK WELL.
WAH! TAKI-MARU!
WHY THE SUDDEN VISIT?
NOTHING MUCH, JUST A FOOD RUN.
HOW ABOUT YOU, TAKI-MARU?
YOUR CELLS HAVE EVOLVED SINCE WE LAST MET, HAVEN'T THEY?
YOU'VE REALLY GROWN UP!
TH... THANK YOU VERY MUCH!
NOW, NOW. DON'T SPOIL HIM, TORIKO.
AI, YOU OWE YOUR LIFE TO TAKIMARU.
GIVE HIM CREDIT WHERE CREDIT'S DUE.
HE'S STILL SO GREEN.
THE GREEN-EST OF ALL MY MEN.
...

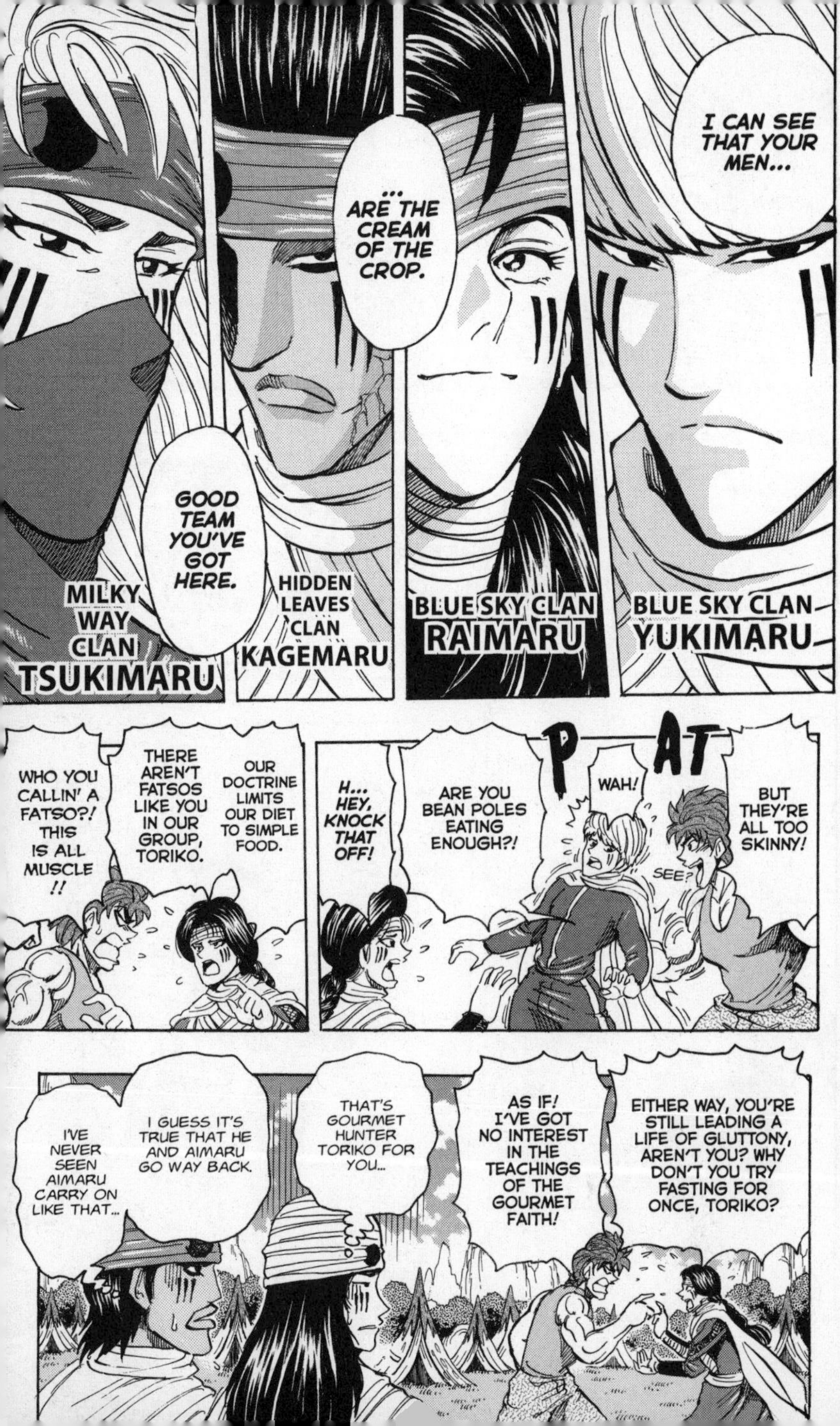
I CAN SEE THAT YOUR MEN...
BLUE SKY CLAN YUKIMARU
...ARE THE CREAM OF THE CROP.
BLUE SKY CLAN RAIMARU
HIDDEN LEAVES CLAN KAGEMARU
GOOD TEAM YOU'VE GOT HERE.
MILKY WAY CLAN TSUKIMARU
BUT THEY'RE ALL TOO SKINNY!
PAT
WAH!
SEE?
ARE YOU BEAN POLES EATING ENOUGH?!
H... HEY, KNOCK THAT OFF!
OUR DOCTRINE LIMITS OUR DIET TO SIMPLE FOOD.
THERE AREN'T FATSOS LIKE YOU IN OUR GROUP, TORIKO.
WHO YOU CALLIN' A FATSO?! THIS IS ALL MUSCLE!!
EITHER WAY, YOU'RE STILL LEADING A LIFE OF GLUTTONY, AREN'T YOU? WHY DON'T YOU TRY FASTING FOR ONCE, TORIKO?
AS IF! I'VE GOT NO INTEREST IN THE TEACHINGS OF THE GOURMET FAITH!
THAT'S GOURMET HUNTER TORIKO FOR YOU...
I GUESS IT'S TRUE THAT HE AND AIMARU GO WAY BACK.
I'VE NEVER SEEN AIMARU CARRY ON LIKE THAT...

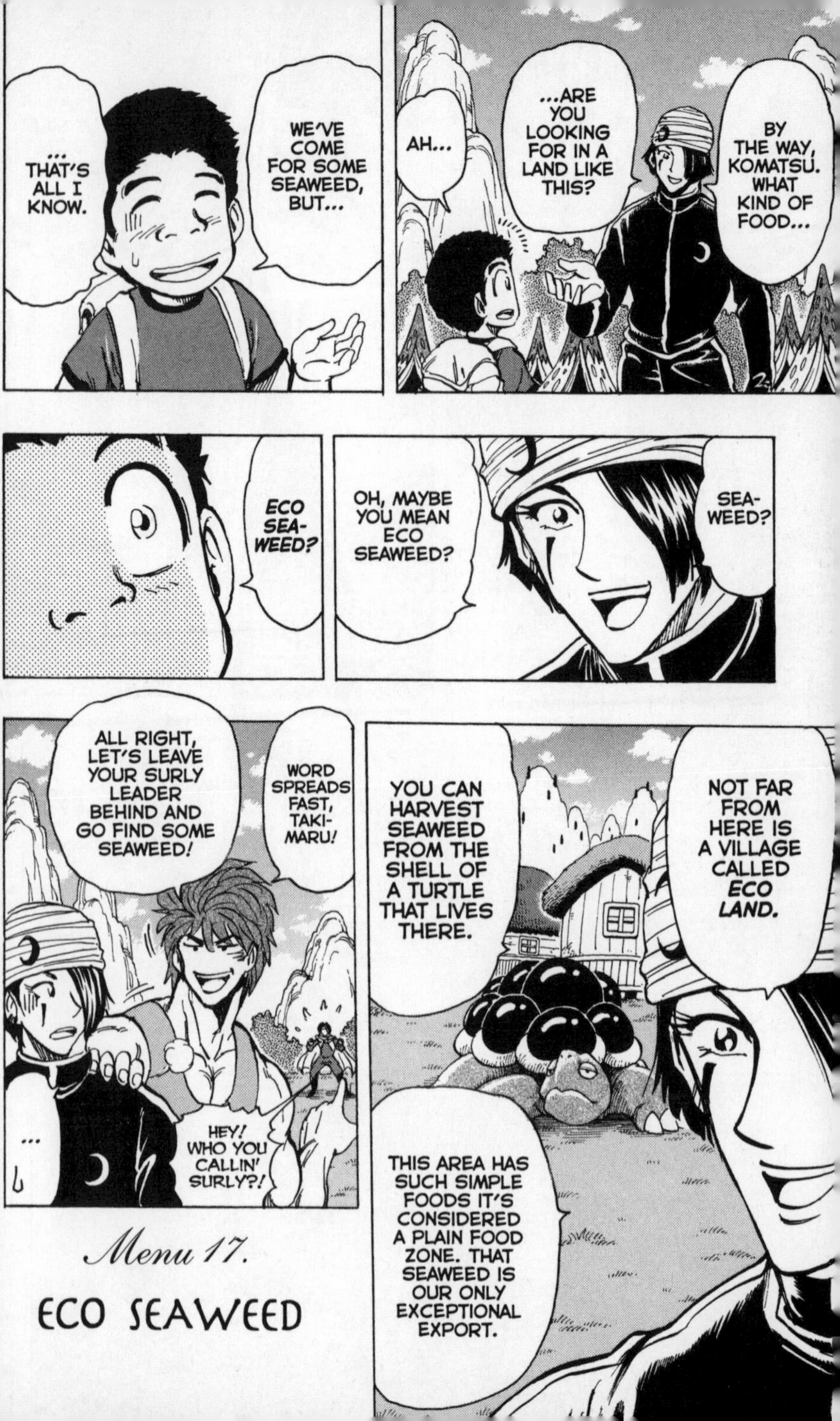
BY THE WAY, KOMATSU. WHAT KIND OF FOOD...
...ARE YOU LOOKING FOR IN A LAND LIKE THIS?
AH...
WE'VE COME FOR SOME SEAWEED, BUT...
...THAT'S ALL I KNOW.
SEA-WEED?
OH, MAYBE YOU MEAN ECO SEAWEED?
ECO SEA-WEED?
NOT FAR FROM HERE IS A VILLAGE CALLED *ECO LAND.*
YOU CAN HARVEST SEAWEED FROM THE SHELL OF A TURTLE THAT LIVES THERE.
THIS AREA HAS SUCH SIMPLE FOODS IT'S CONSIDERED A PLAIN FOOD ZONE. THAT SEAWEED IS OUR ONLY EXCEPTIONAL EXPORT.
WORD SPREADS FAST, TAKI-MARU!
ALL RIGHT, LET'S LEAVE YOUR SURLY LEADER BEHIND AND GO FIND SOME SEAWEED!
HEY! WHO YOU CALLIN' SURLY?!
...

Menu 17.

ECO SEAWEED

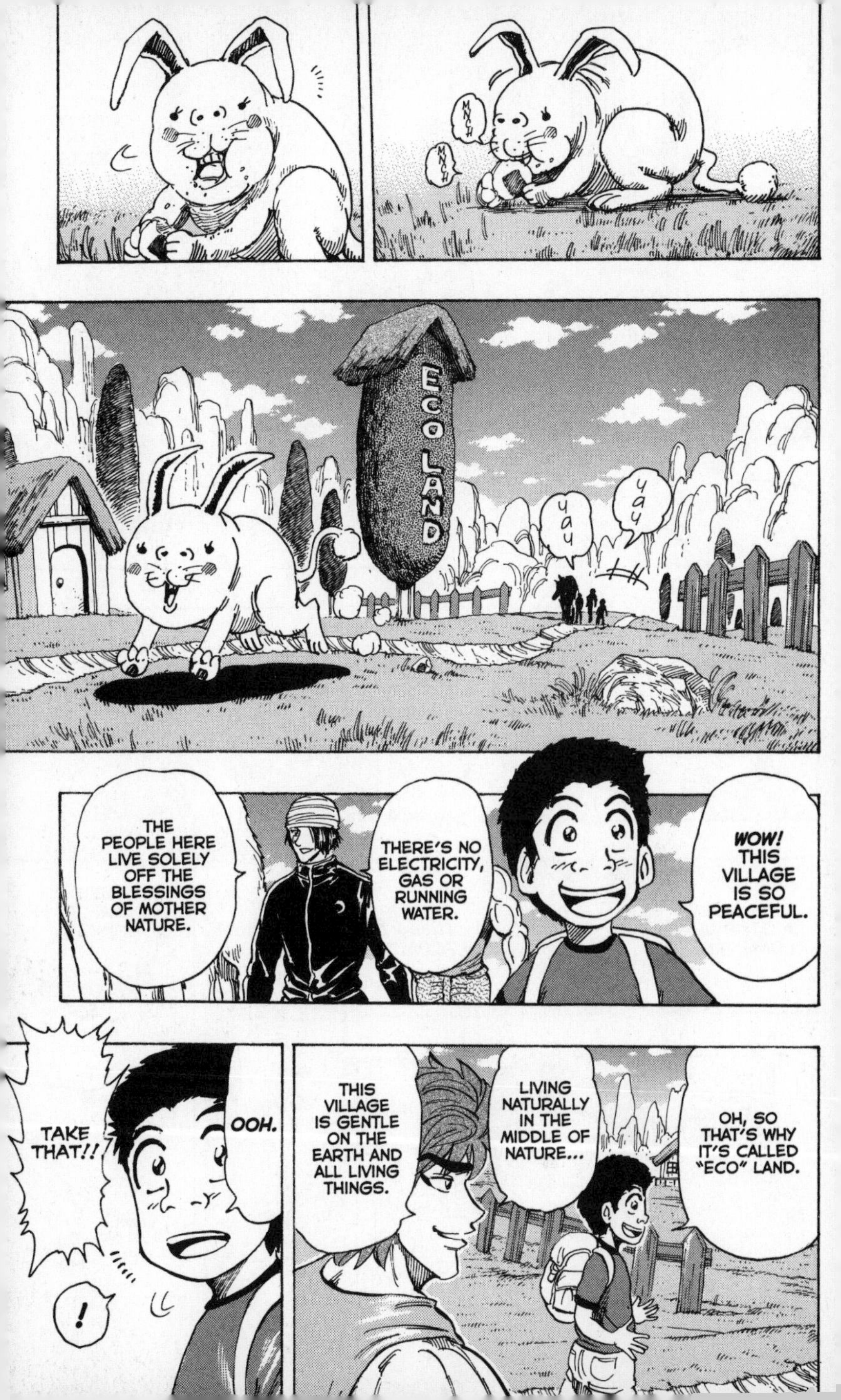
MNCH
MNCH
ECO LAND
yay
yay
WOW! THIS VILLAGE IS SO PEACEFUL.
THERE'S NO ELECTRICITY, GAS OR RUNNING WATER.
THE PEOPLE HERE LIVE SOLELY OFF THE BLESSINGS OF MOTHER NATURE.
OH, SO THAT'S WHY IT'S CALLED "ECO" LAND.
LIVING NATURALLY IN THE MIDDLE OF NATURE...
THIS VILLAGE IS GENTLE ON THE EARTH AND ALL LIVING THINGS.
OOH.
TAKE THAT!!
!

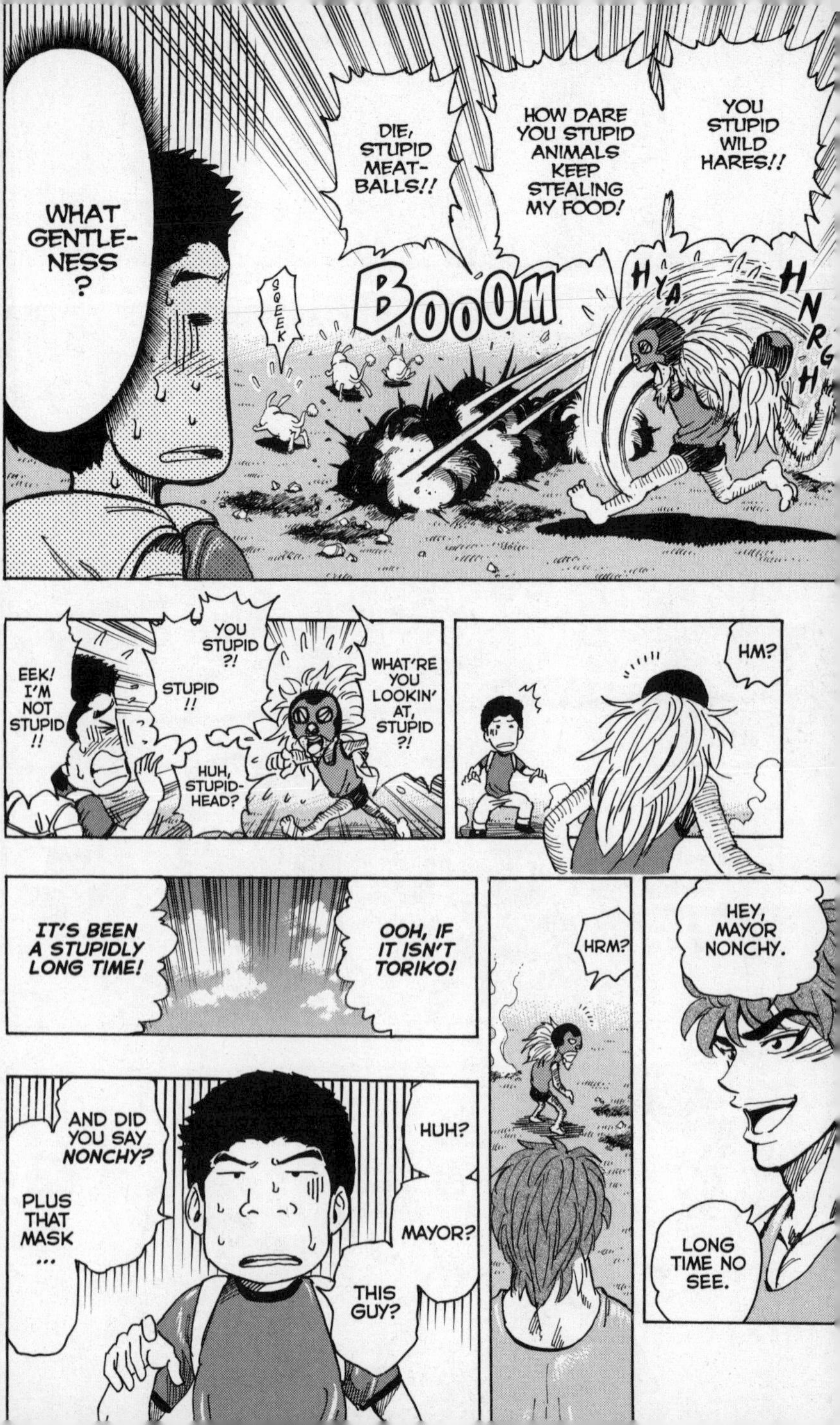

YOU STUPID WILD HARES!!
HNRGH
HYA
HOW DARE YOU STUPID ANIMALS KEEP STEALING MY FOOD!
DIE, STUPID MEAT-BALLS!!
BOOOM
SQEEK
WHAT GENTLE-NESS?
HM?
WHAT'RE YOU LOOKIN' AT, STUPID?!
YOU STUPID?!
HUH, STUPID-HEAD?
STUPID!!
EEK! I'M NOT STUPID!!
HEY, MAYOR NONCHY.
LONG TIME NO SEE.
HRM?
OOH, IF IT ISN'T TORIKO!
IT'S BEEN A STUPIDLY LONG TIME!
HUH?
MAYOR?
THIS GUY?
AND DID YOU SAY NONCHY?
PLUS THAT MASK...

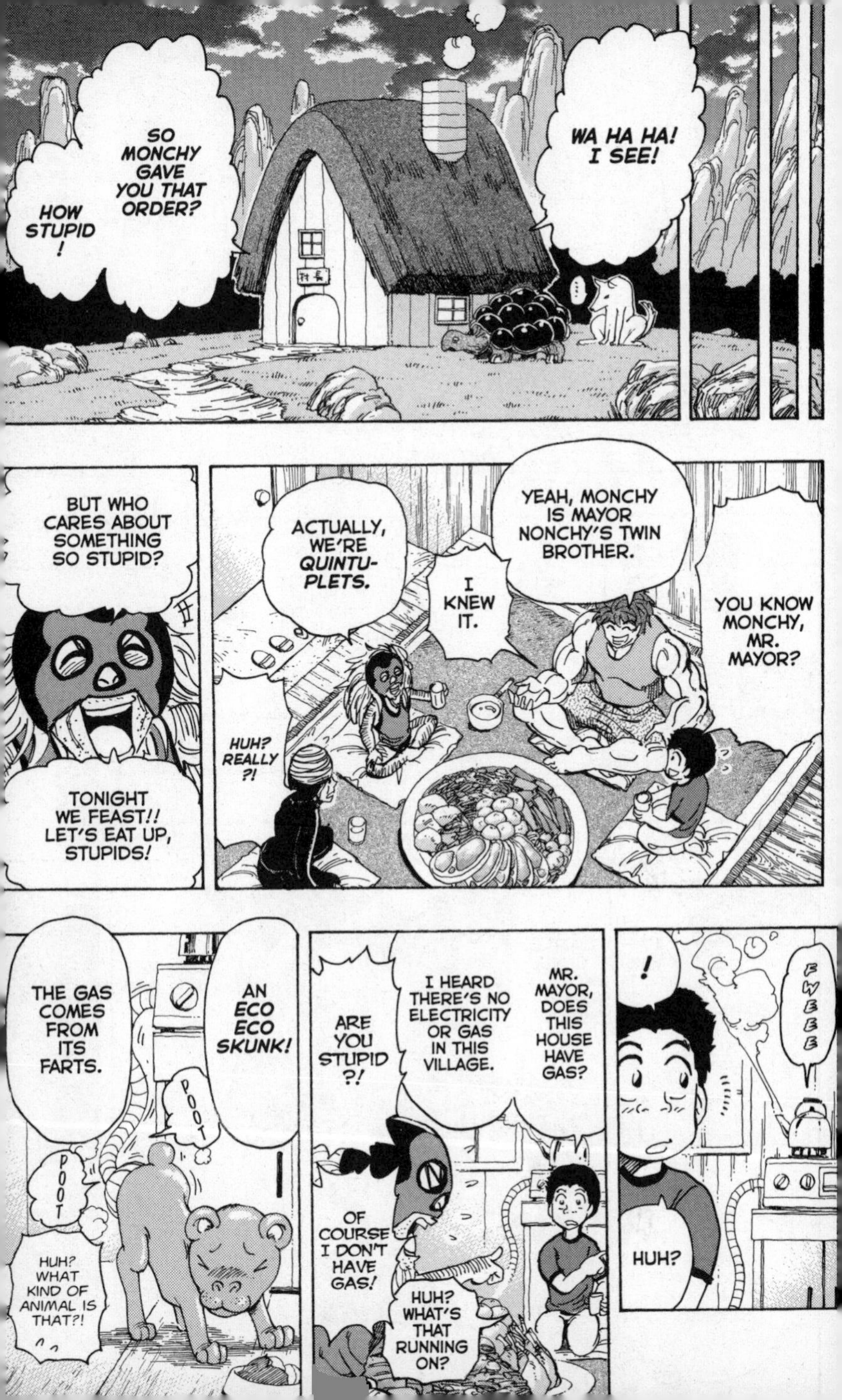
WA HA HA! I SEE!
SO MONCHY GAVE YOU THAT ORDER?
HOW STUPID!
YOU KNOW MONCHY, MR. MAYOR?
YEAH, MONCHY IS MAYOR NONCHY'S TWIN BROTHER.
I KNEW IT.
ACTUALLY, WE'RE *QUINTUPLETS.*
HUH? REALLY?!
BUT WHO CARES ABOUT SOMETHING SO STUPID?
TONIGHT WE FEAST!! LET'S EAT UP, STUPIDS!
FWEEE
!
HUH?
MR. MAYOR, DOES THIS HOUSE HAVE GAS?
I HEARD THERE'S NO ELECTRICITY OR GAS IN THIS VILLAGE.
ARE YOU STUPID?!
OF COURSE I DON'T HAVE GAS!
HUH? WHAT'S THAT RUNNING ON?
AN ECO ECO SKUNK!
THE GAS COMES FROM ITS FARTS.
POOT
POOT
HUH? WHAT KIND OF ANIMAL IS THAT?!

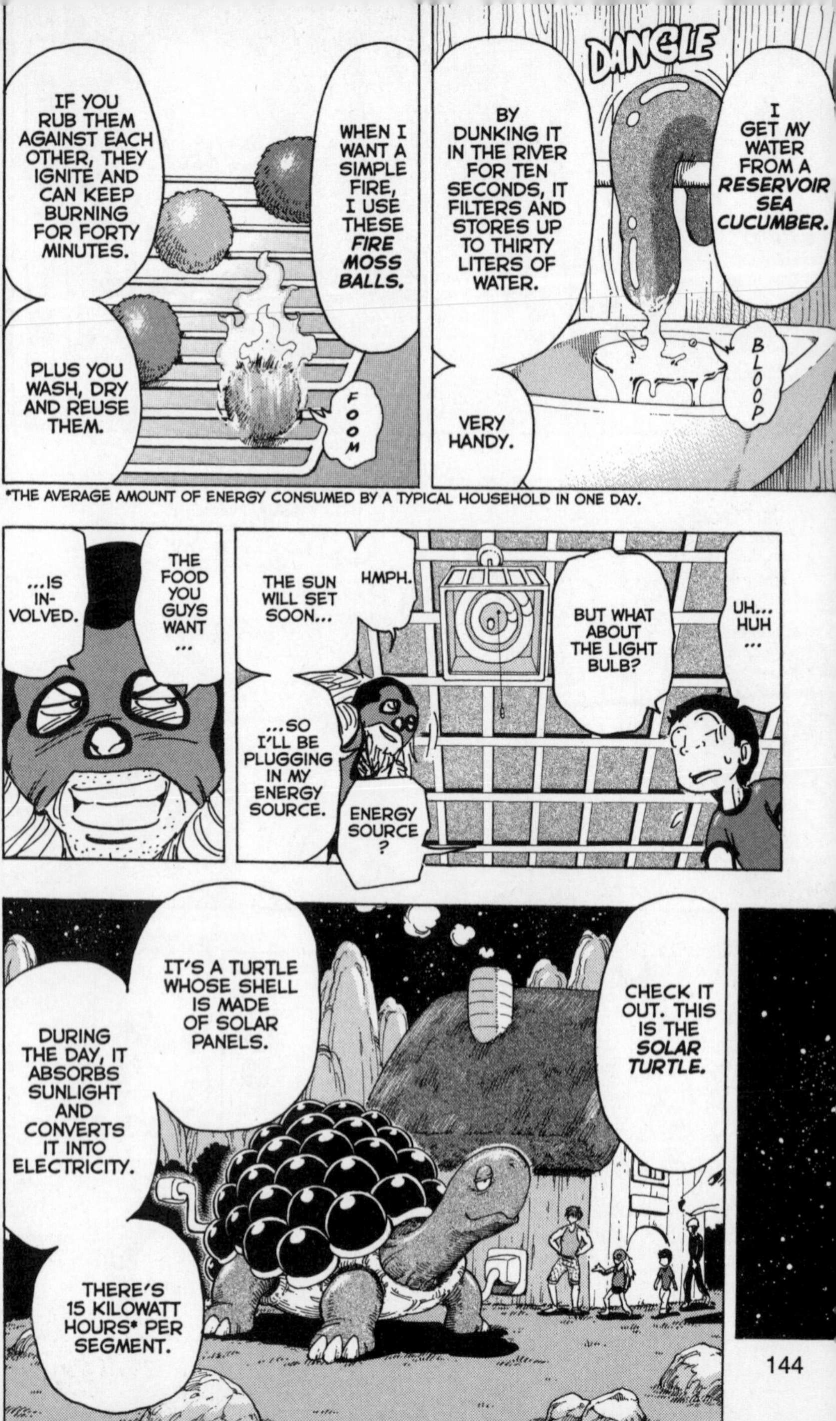
DANGLE
I GET MY WATER FROM A *RESERVOIR SEA CUCUMBER.*
BY DUNKING IT IN THE RIVER FOR TEN SECONDS, IT FILTERS AND STORES UP TO THIRTY LITERS OF WATER.
BLOOP
VERY HANDY.
WHEN I WANT A SIMPLE FIRE, I USE THESE *FIRE MOSS BALLS.*
IF YOU RUB THEM AGAINST EACH OTHER, THEY IGNITE AND CAN KEEP BURNING FOR FORTY MINUTES.
FOOM
PLUS YOU WASH, DRY AND REUSE THEM.
UH... HUH...
BUT WHAT ABOUT THE LIGHT BULB?
HMPH.
THE SUN WILL SET SOON...
...SO I'LL BE PLUGGING IN MY ENERGY SOURCE.
ENERGY SOURCE?
THE FOOD YOU GUYS WANT...
...IS IN-VOLVED.
CHECK IT OUT. THIS IS THE *SOLAR TURTLE.*
IT'S A TURTLE WHOSE SHELL IS MADE OF SOLAR PANELS.
DURING THE DAY, IT ABSORBS SUNLIGHT AND CONVERTS IT INTO ELECTRICITY.
THERE'S 15 KILOWATT HOURS* PER SEGMENT.

*THE AVERAGE AMOUNT OF ENERGY CONSUMED BY A TYPICAL HOUSEHOLD IN ONE DAY.

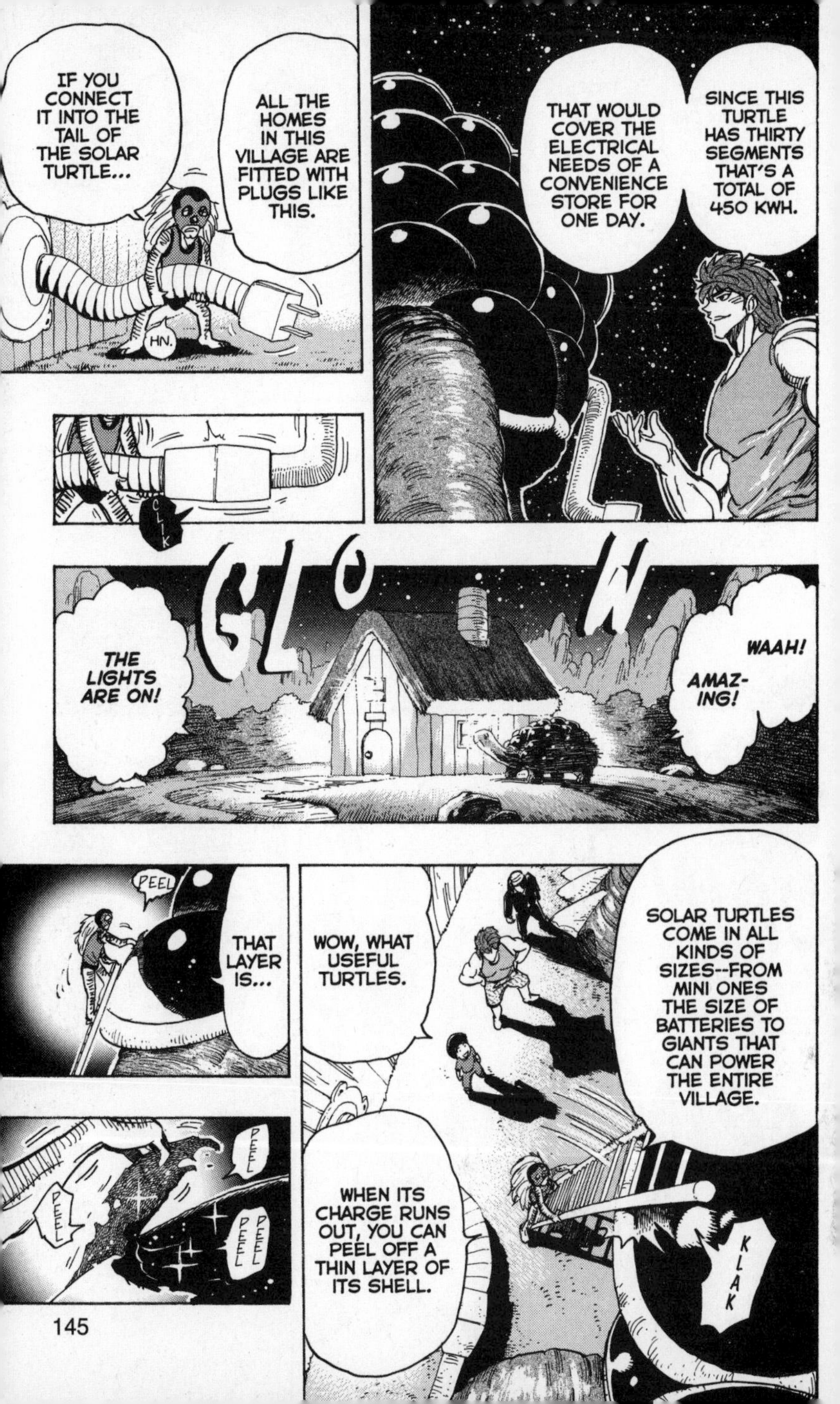
SINCE THIS TURTLE HAS THIRTY SEGMENTS THAT'S A TOTAL OF 450 KWH.
THAT WOULD COVER THE ELECTRICAL NEEDS OF A CONVENIENCE STORE FOR ONE DAY.
ALL THE HOMES IN THIS VILLAGE ARE FITTED WITH PLUGS LIKE THIS.
IF YOU CONNECT IT INTO THE TAIL OF THE SOLAR TURTLE...
HN.
CLIK
GLOW
WAAH!
AMAZ-ING!
THE LIGHTS ARE ON!
SOLAR TURTLES COME IN ALL KINDS OF SIZES--FROM MINI ONES THE SIZE OF BATTERIES TO GIANTS THAT CAN POWER THE ENTIRE VILLAGE.
WOW, WHAT USEFUL TURTLES.
KLAK
WHEN ITS CHARGE RUNS OUT, YOU CAN PEEL OFF A THIN LAYER OF ITS SHELL.
THAT LAYER IS...
PEEL
PEEL
PEEL
PEEL
PEEL

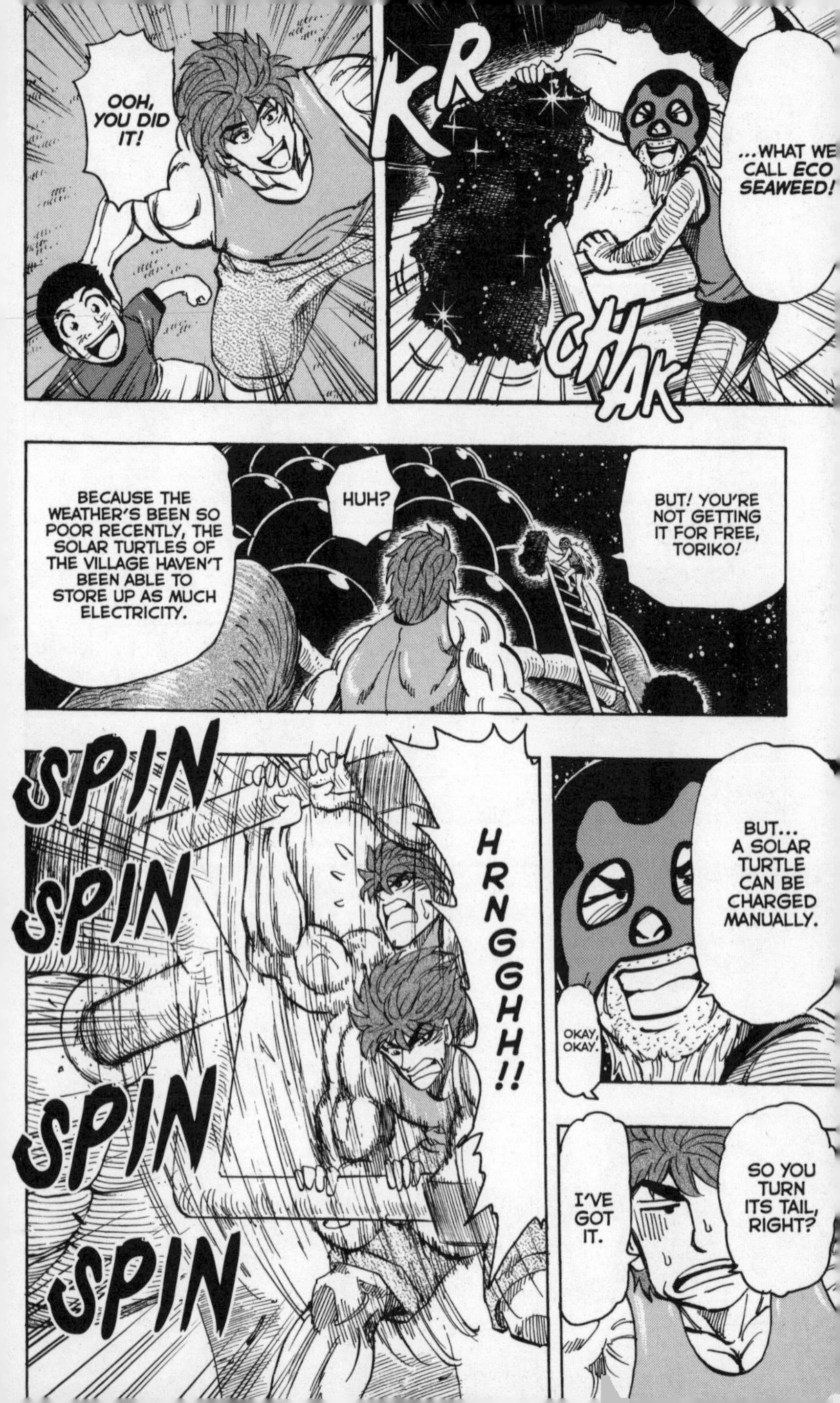
KR
...WHAT WE CALL ECO SEAWEED!
CHAK
OOH, YOU DID IT!
BUT! YOU'RE NOT GETTING IT FOR FREE, TORIKO!
HUH?
BECAUSE THE WEATHER'S BEEN SO POOR RECENTLY, THE SOLAR TURTLES OF THE VILLAGE HAVEN'T BEEN ABLE TO STORE UP AS MUCH ELECTRICITY.
BUT... A SOLAR TURTLE CAN BE CHARGED MANUALLY.
OKAY, OKAY.
SO YOU TURN ITS TAIL, RIGHT?
I'VE GOT IT.
HRNGGHH!!
SPIN
SPIN
SPIN
SPIN

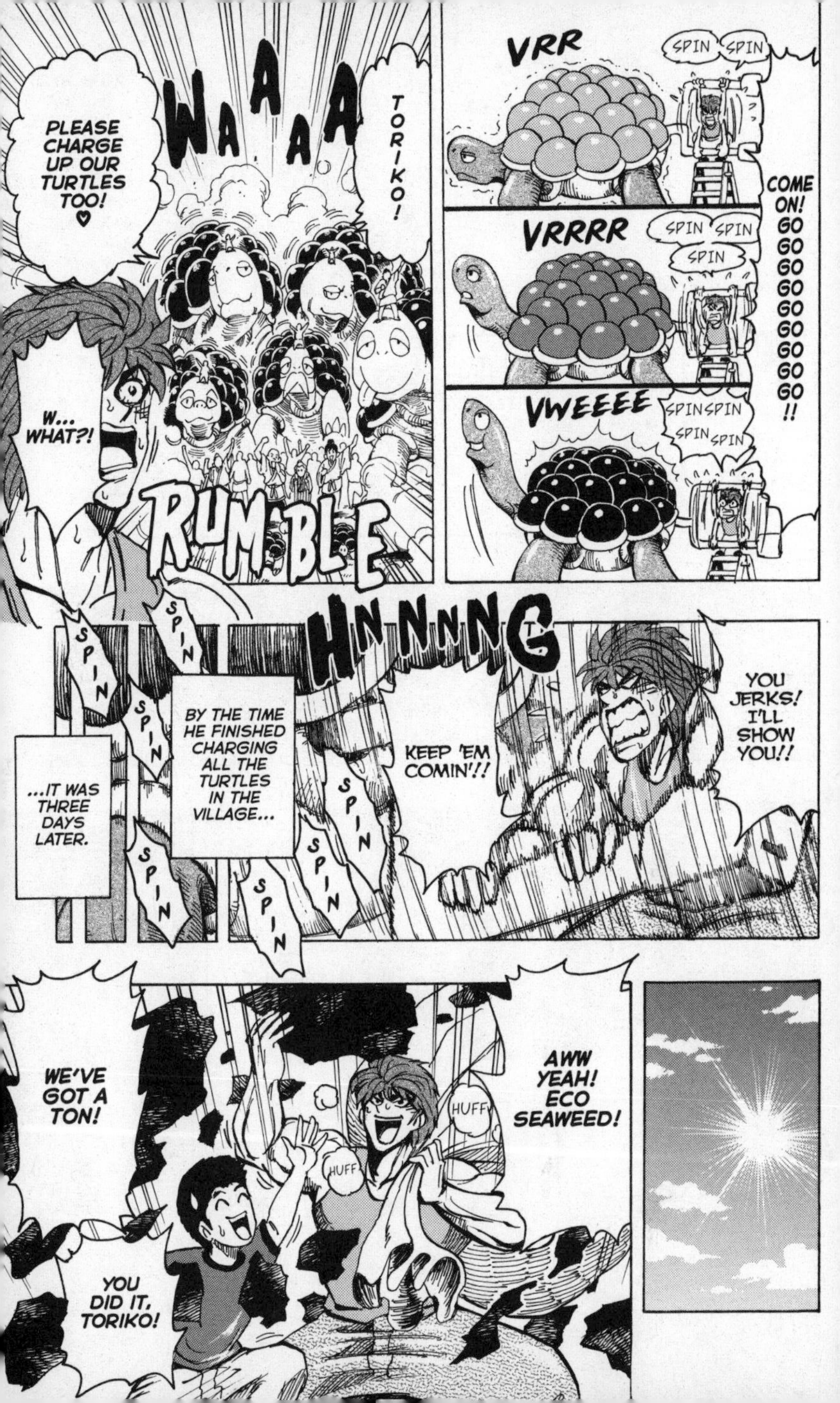
VRR
SPIN SPIN
COME ON! GO GO GO GO GO GO GO GO GO GO GO!!
VRRRR
SPIN SPIN
SPIN
VWEEEE
SPINSPIN
SPIN SPIN
TORIKO!
WAAAA
PLEASE CHARGE UP OUR TURTLES TOO! ♥
W... WHAT?!
RUMBLE
HNNNNG
YOU JERKS! I'LL SHOW YOU!!
KEEP 'EM COMIN'!!
SPIN
SPIN
SPIN
SPIN
BY THE TIME HE FINISHED CHARGING ALL THE TURTLES IN THE VILLAGE...
SPIN
SPIN
SPIN
...IT WAS THREE DAYS LATER.
AWW YEAH! ECO SEAWEED!
HUFF
HUFF
WE'VE GOT A TON!
YOU DID IT, TORIKO!

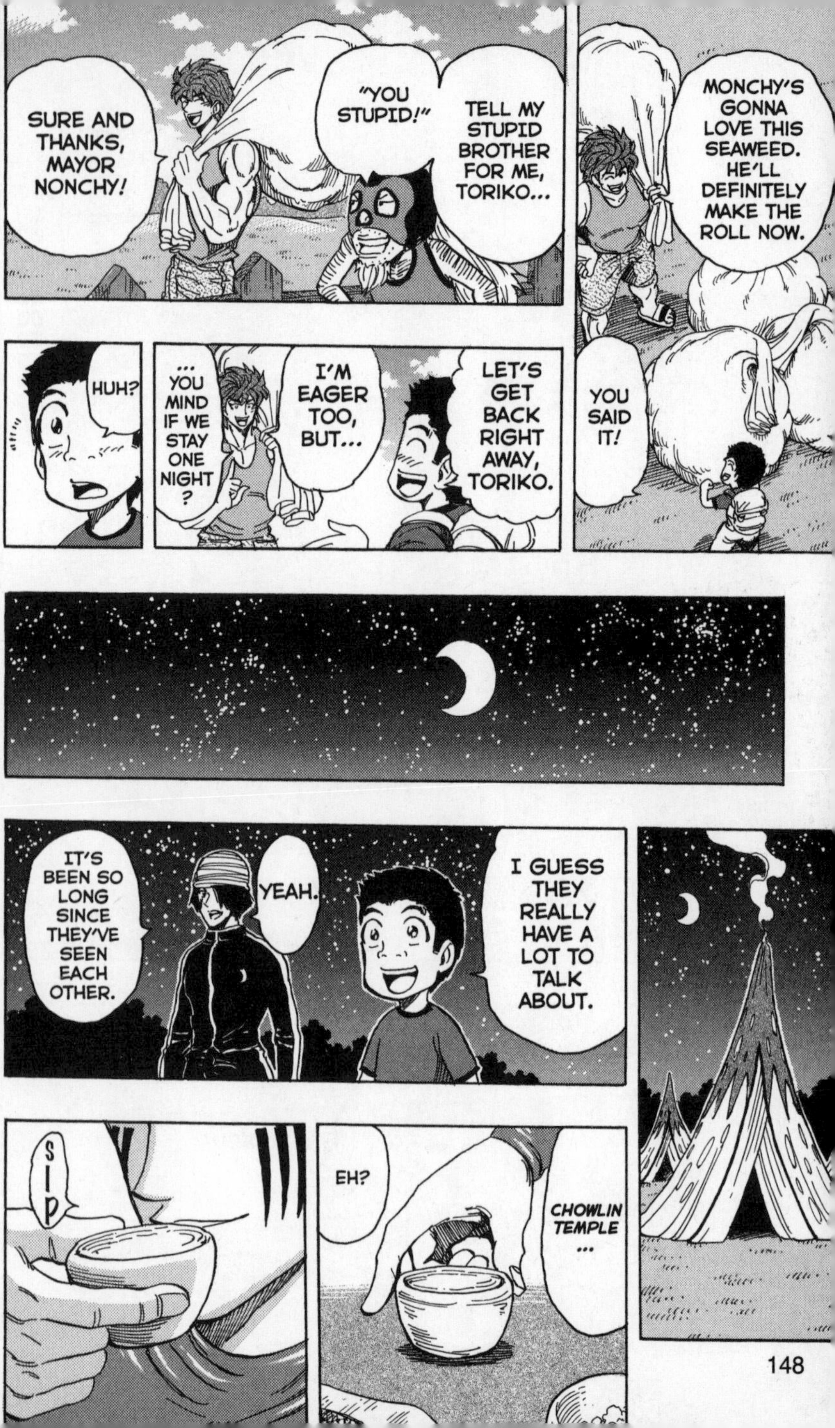
MONCHY'S GONNA LOVE THIS SEAWEED. HE'LL DEFINITELY MAKE THE ROLL NOW.
YOU SAID IT!
TELL MY STUPID BROTHER FOR ME, TORIKO...
"YOU STUPID!"
SURE AND THANKS, MAYOR NONCHY!
LET'S GET BACK RIGHT AWAY, TORIKO.
I'M EAGER TOO, BUT...
...YOU MIND IF WE STAY ONE NIGHT?
HUH?
I GUESS THEY REALLY HAVE A LOT TO TALK ABOUT.
YEAH.
IT'S BEEN SO LONG SINCE THEY'VE SEEN EACH OTHER.
EH?
CHOWLIN TEMPLE...
SIP

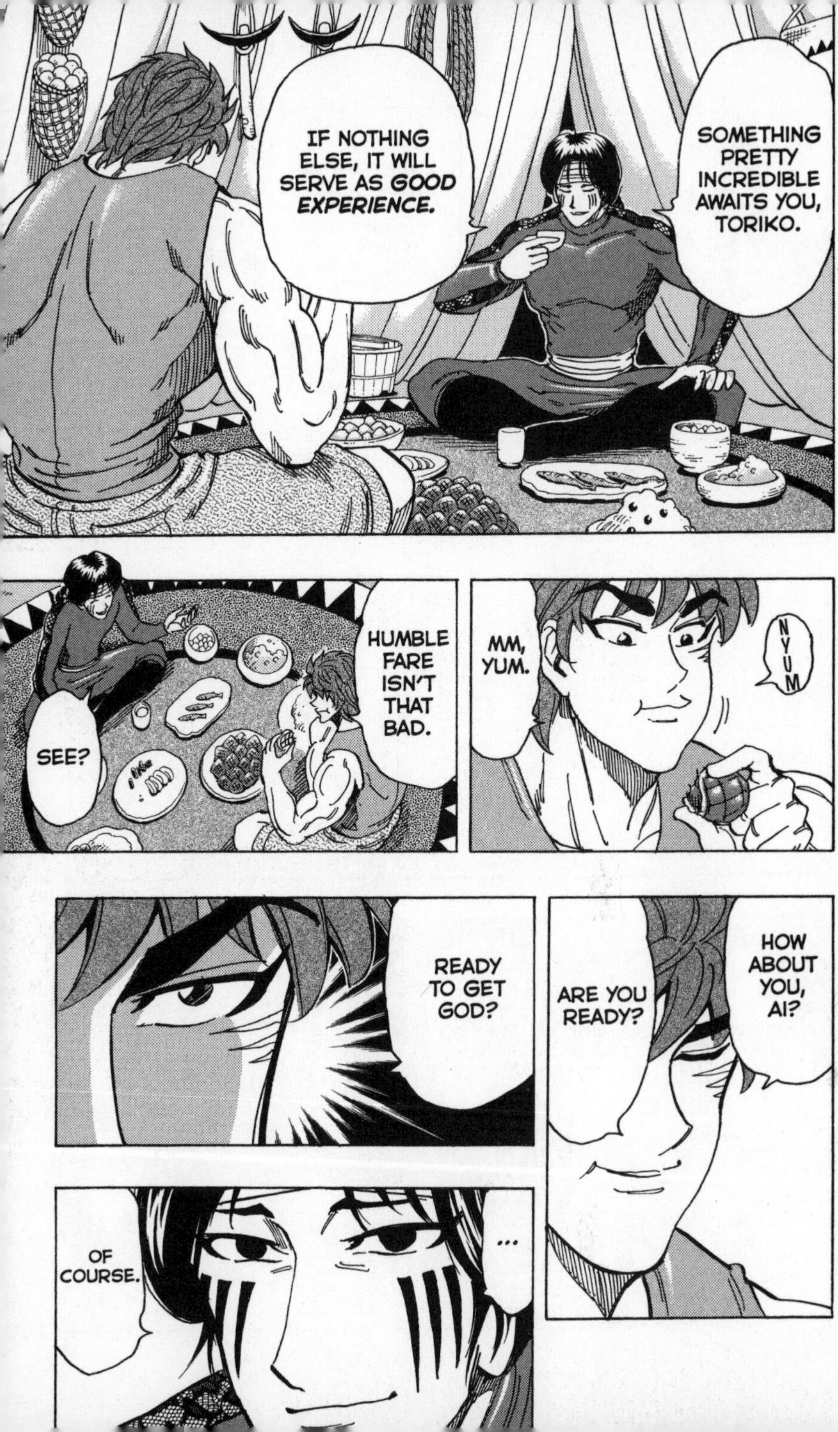
SOMETHING PRETTY INCREDIBLE AWAITS YOU, TORIKO.
IF NOTHING ELSE, IT WILL SERVE AS *GOOD EXPERIENCE.*
NYUM
MM, YUM.
HUMBLE FARE ISN'T THAT BAD.
SEE?
HOW ABOUT YOU, AI?
ARE YOU READY?
READY TO GET GOD?
...
OF COURSE.

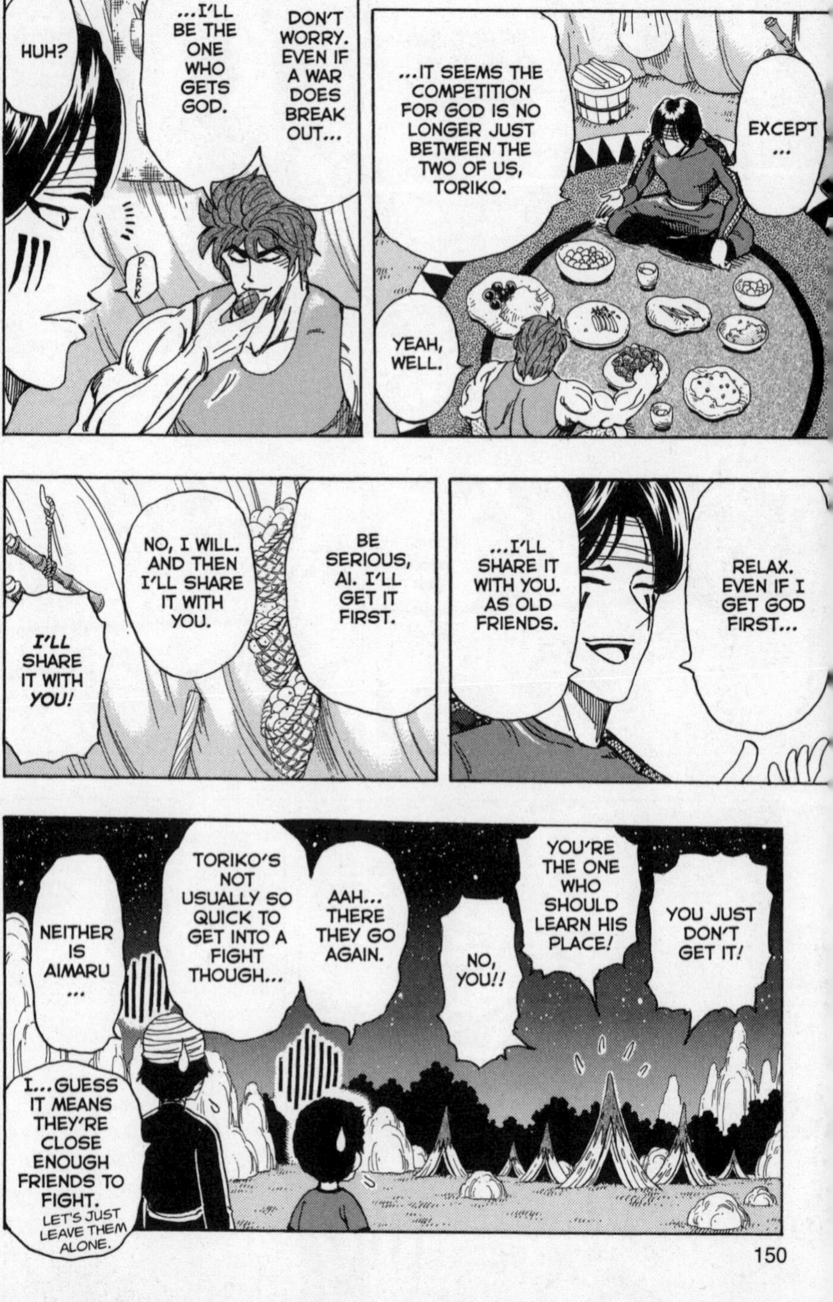
EXCEPT...
...IT SEEMS THE COMPETITION FOR GOD IS NO LONGER JUST BETWEEN THE TWO OF US, TORIKO.
YEAH, WELL.
DON'T WORRY. EVEN IF A WAR DOES BREAK OUT...
...I'LL BE THE ONE WHO GETS GOD.
PERK
HUH?
RELAX. EVEN IF I GET GOD FIRST...
...I'LL SHARE IT WITH YOU. AS OLD FRIENDS.
BE SERIOUS, AI. I'LL GET IT FIRST.
NO, I WILL. AND THEN I'LL SHARE IT WITH YOU.
I'LL SHARE IT WITH *YOU!*
YOU JUST DON'T GET IT!
YOU'RE THE ONE WHO SHOULD LEARN HIS PLACE!
NO, YOU!!
AAH... THERE THEY GO AGAIN.
TORIKO'S NOT USUALLY SO QUICK TO GET INTO A FIGHT THOUGH...
NEITHER IS AIMARU...
I...GUESS IT MEANS THEY'RE CLOSE ENOUGH FRIENDS TO FIGHT.
LET'S JUST LEAVE THEM ALONE.

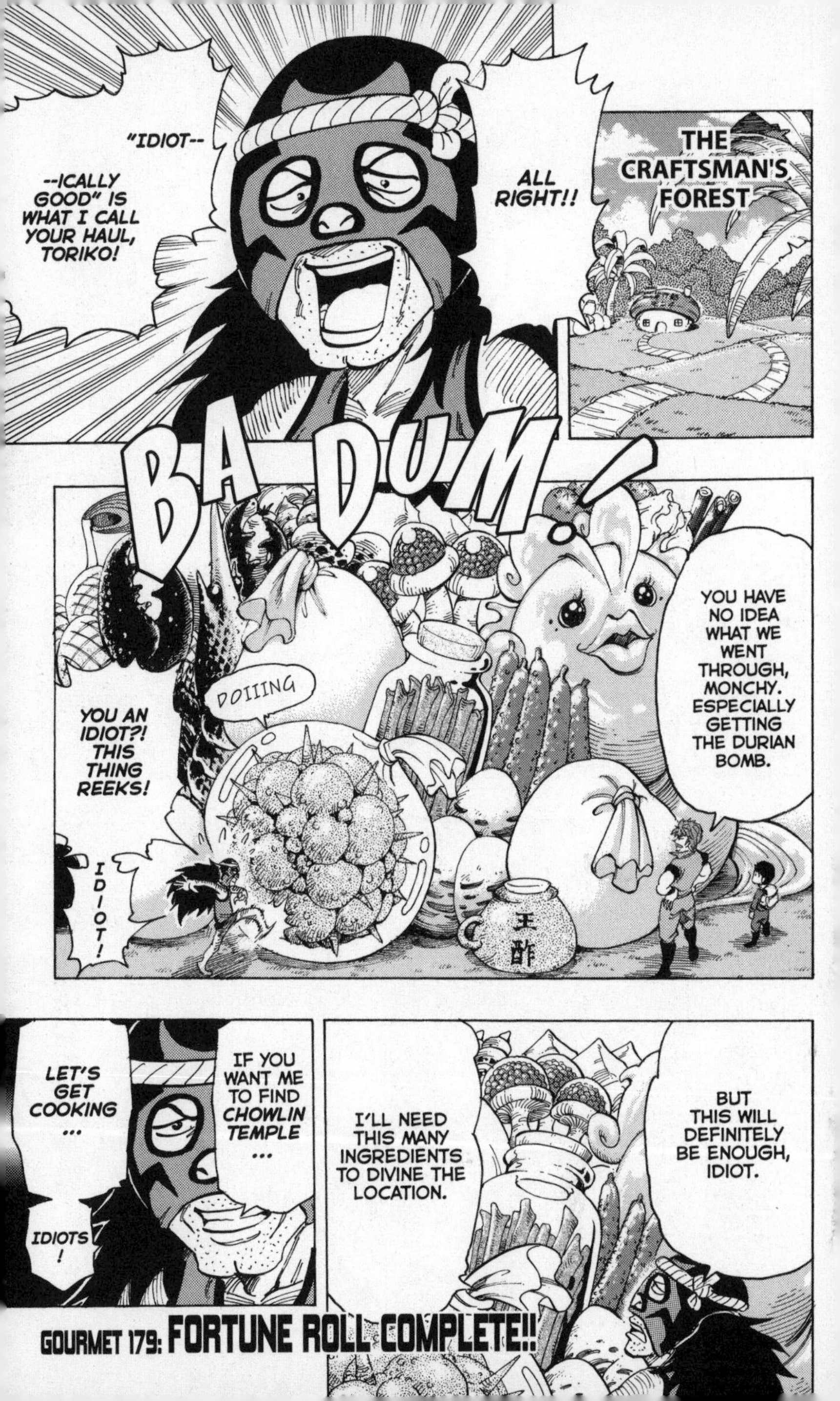
THE CRAFTSMAN'S FOREST
ALL RIGHT!!
"IDIOT--
--ICALLY GOOD" IS WHAT I CALL YOUR HAUL, TORIKO!
BA DUM!
YOU HAVE NO IDEA WHAT WE WENT THROUGH, MONCHY. ESPECIALLY GETTING THE DURIAN BOMB.
DOIIING
YOU AN IDIOT?! THIS THING REEKS!
IDIOT!
王酢
BUT THIS WILL DEFINITELY BE ENOUGH, IDIOT.
I'LL NEED THIS MANY INGREDIENTS TO DIVINE THE LOCATION.
IF YOU WANT ME TO FIND CHOWLIN TEMPLE ...
LET'S GET COOKING ...
IDIOTS!

GOURMET 179: FORTUNE ROLL COMPLETE!!

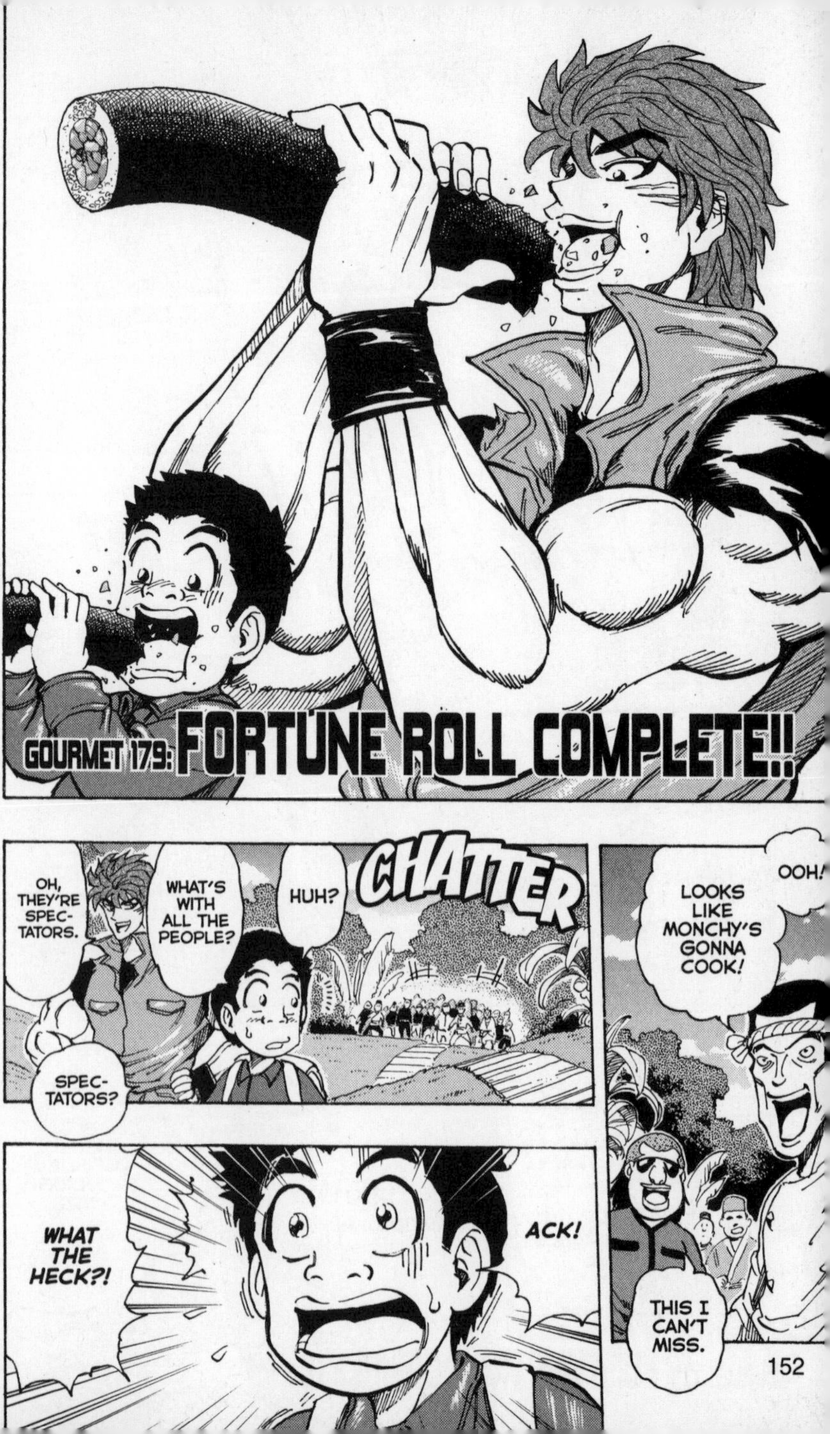
GOURMET 179: FORTUNE ROLL COMPLETE!!
OOH!
LOOKS LIKE MONCHY'S GONNA COOK!
THIS I CAN'T MISS.
CHATTER
HUH?
WHAT'S WITH ALL THE PEOPLE?
OH, THEY'RE SPEC-TATORS.
SPEC-TATORS?
ACK!
WHAT THE HECK?!

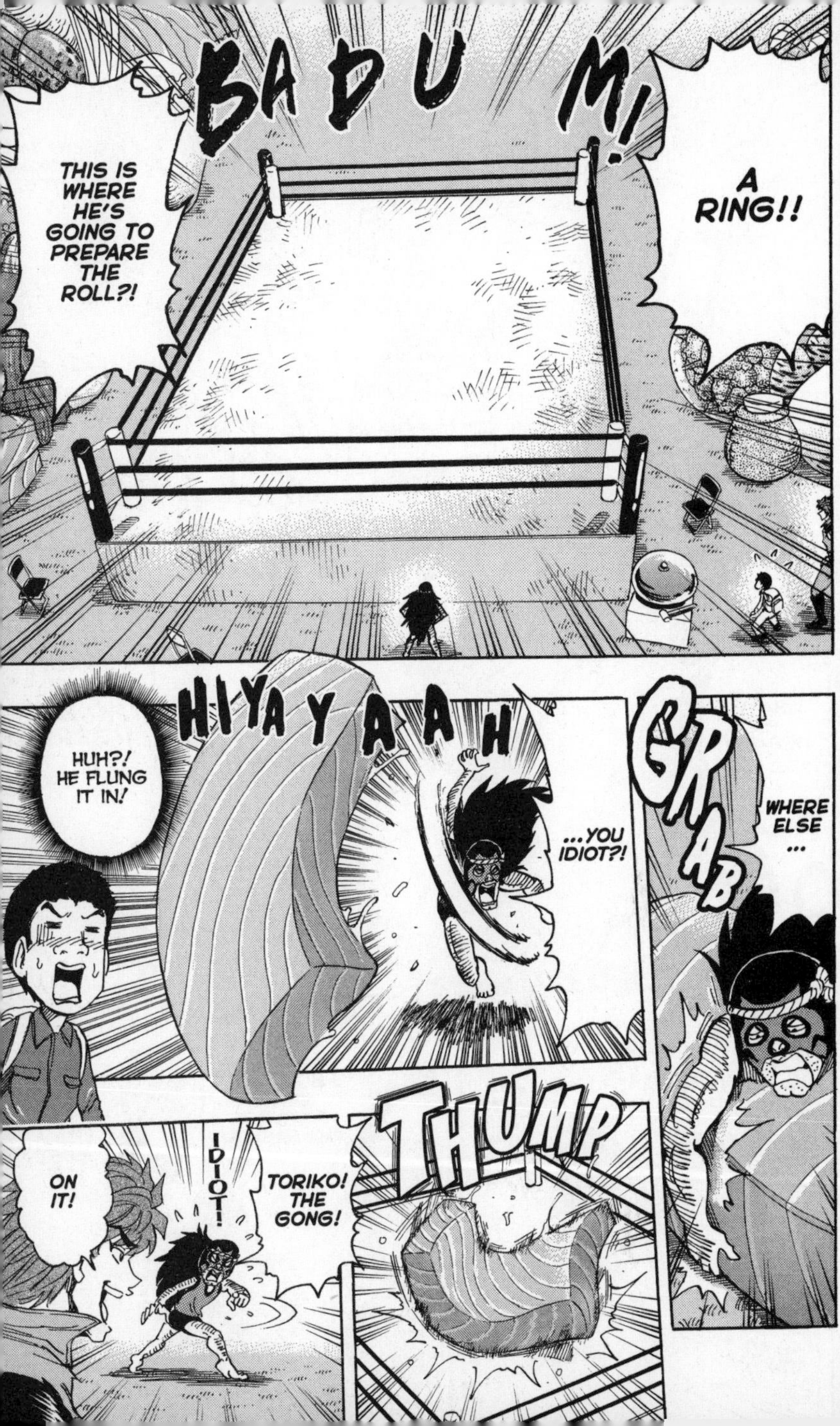
BADUM!
A RING!!
THIS IS WHERE HE'S GOING TO PREPARE THE ROLL?!
GRAB
WHERE ELSE ...
HIYAYAAH
...YOU IDIOT?!
HUH?! HE FLUNG IT IN!
THUMP
TORIKO! THE GONG!
IDIOT!
ON IT!

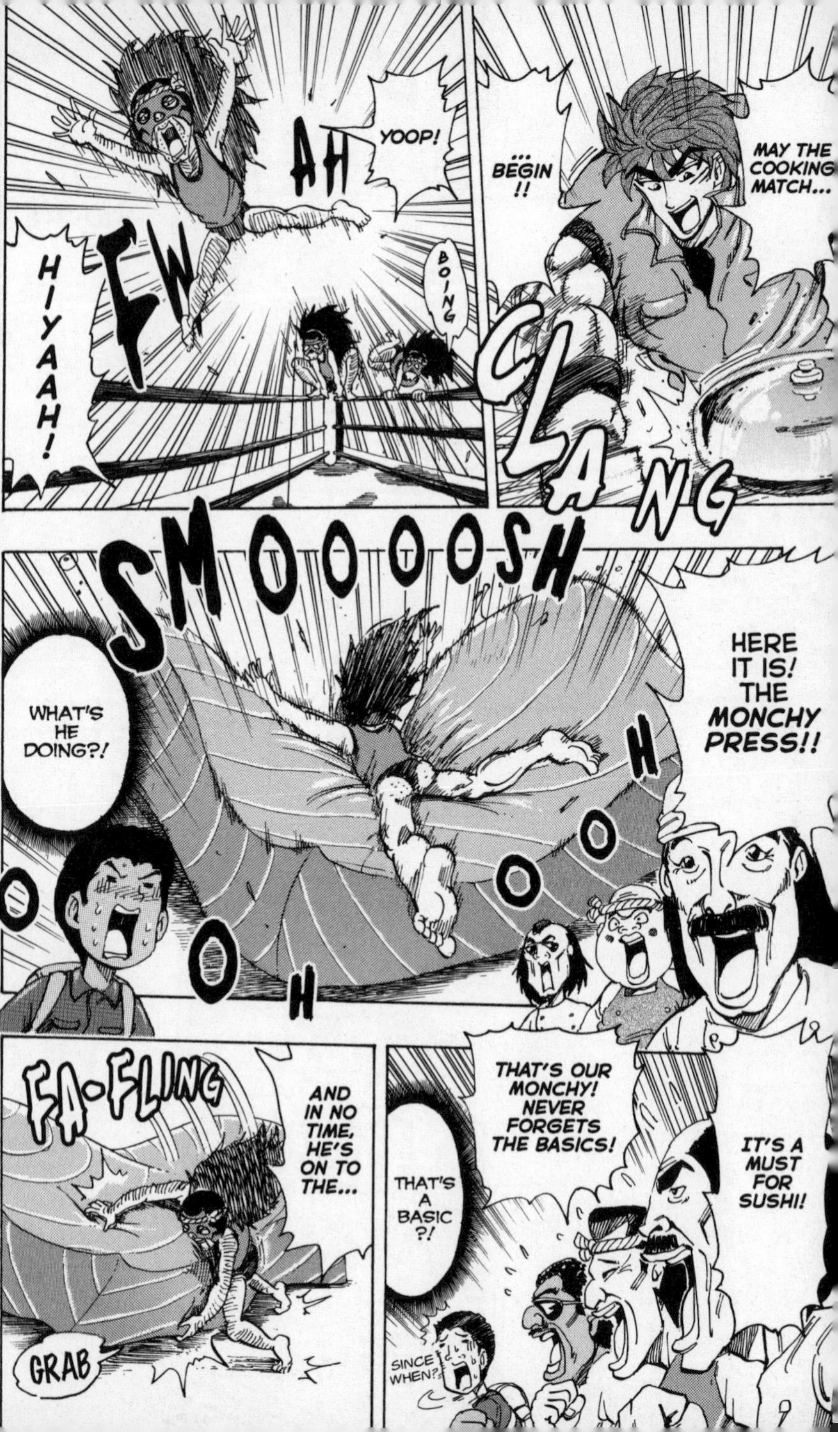
MAY THE COOKING MATCH...
...BEGIN!!
CLANG
YOOP!
AH
FW
HIYAAAH!
BOING
SMOOOOSH
HERE IT IS! THE MONCHY PRESS!!
OOOOH
WHAT'S HE DOING?!
THAT'S OUR MONCHY! NEVER FORGETS THE BASICS!
IT'S A MUST FOR SUSHI!
THAT'S A BASIC?!
SINCE WHEN?!
FA-FLING
AND IN NO TIME, HE'S ON TO THE...
GRAB

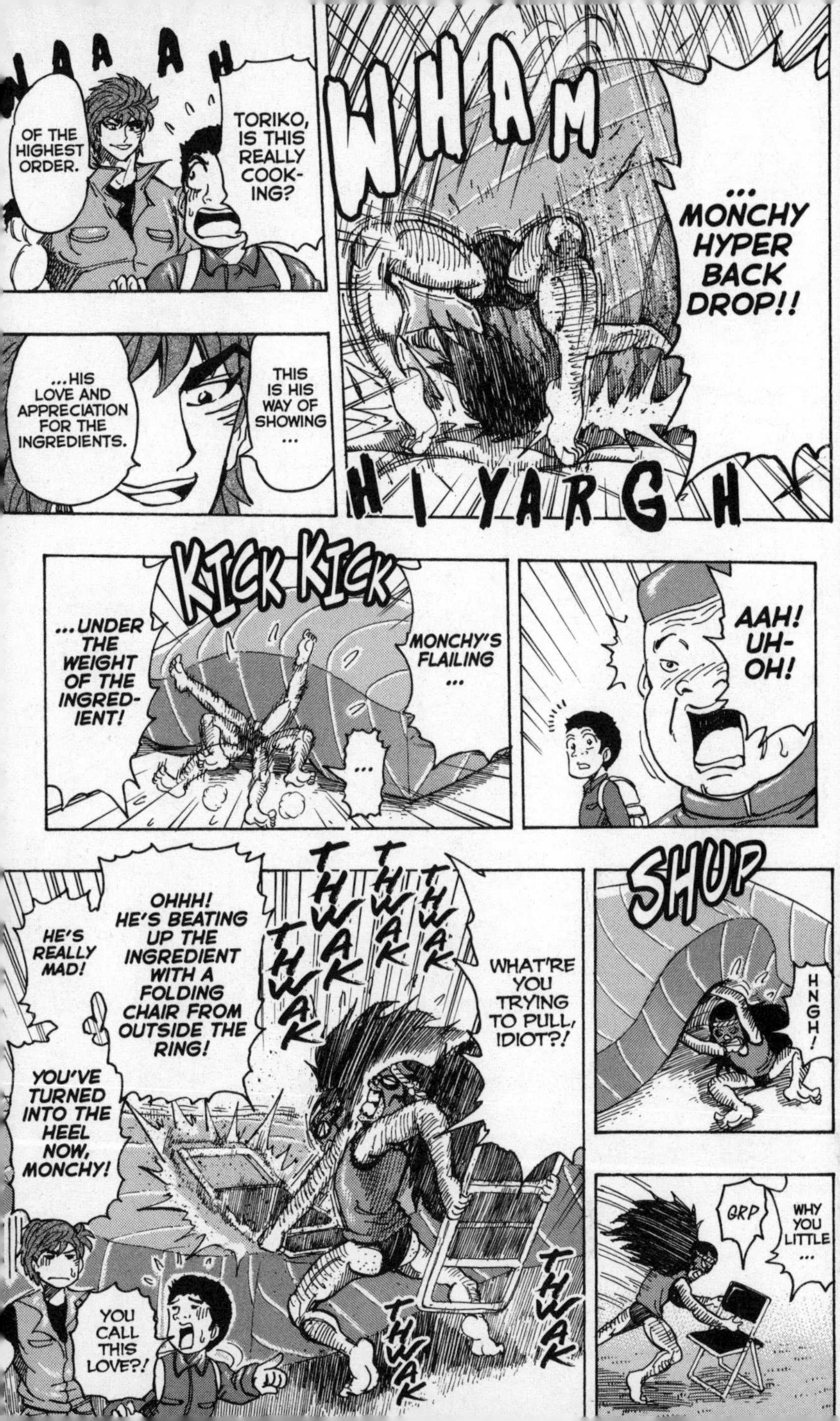
WHAM
...MONCHY HYPER BACK DROP!!
HIYARGH
NAAAAH
TORIKO, IS THIS REALLY COOKING?
OF THE HIGHEST ORDER.
THIS IS HIS WAY OF SHOWING...
...HIS LOVE AND APPRECIATION FOR THE INGREDIENTS.
AAH! UH-OH!
KICK KICK
MONCHY'S FLAILING...
...UNDER THE WEIGHT OF THE INGREDIENT!
...
SHUP
HNGH!
WHY YOU LITTLE...
GRP
THWAK THWAK THWAK THWAK
WHAT'RE YOU TRYING TO PULL, IDIOT?!
OHHH! HE'S BEATING UP THE INGREDIENT WITH A FOLDING CHAIR FROM OUTSIDE THE RING!
HE'S REALLY MAD!
YOU'VE TURNED INTO THE HEEL NOW, MONCHY!
YOU CALL THIS LOVE?!
THWAK
THWAK

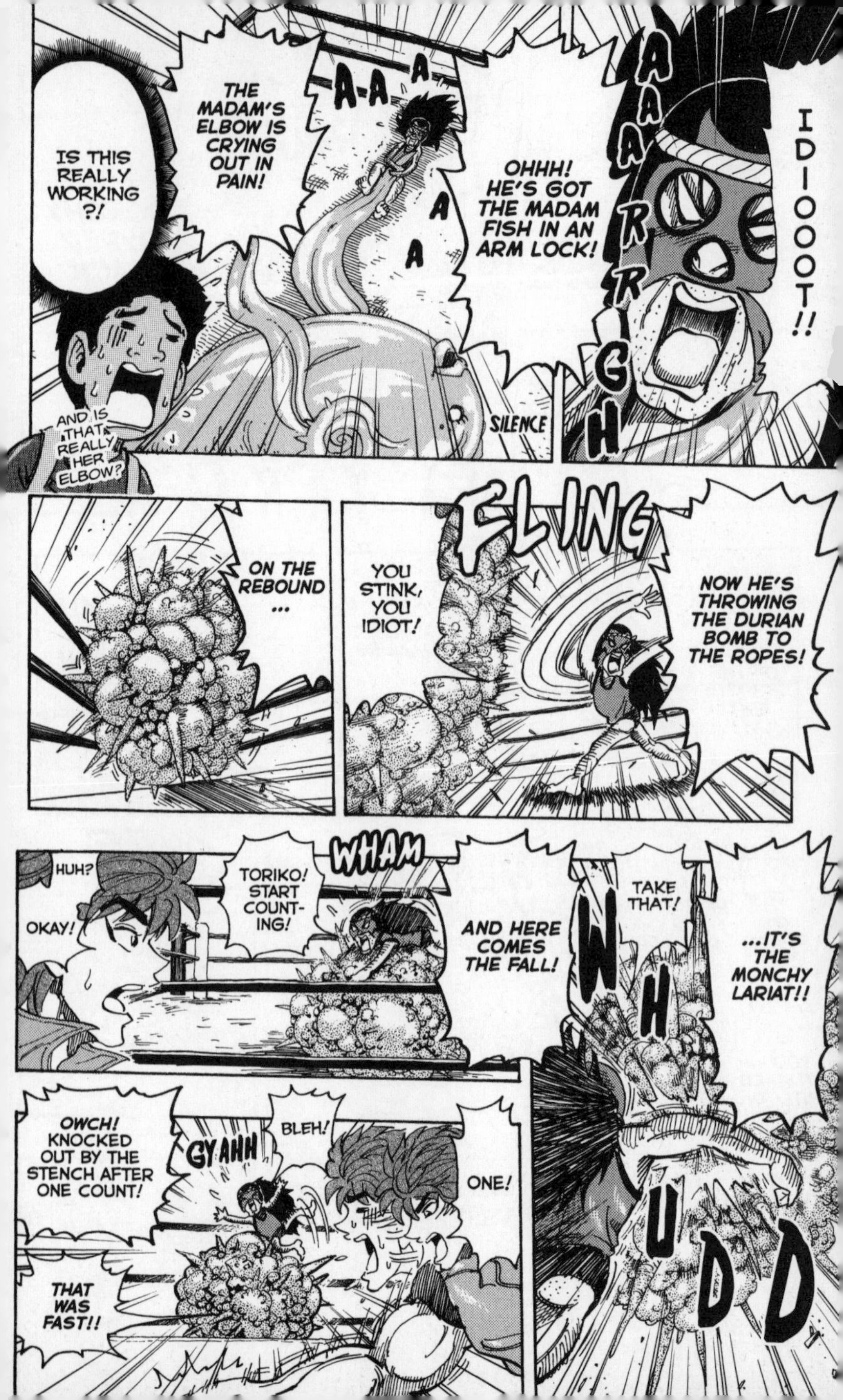
IDIOOOT!!
AAARRGH
OHHH! HE'S GOT THE MADAM FISH IN AN ARM LOCK!
THE MADAM'S ELBOW IS CRYING OUT IN PAIN!
A-A-A-A-A-A
SILENCE
IS THIS REALLY WORKING ?!
AND IS THAT REALLY HER ELBOW?
FLING
NOW HE'S THROWING THE DURIAN BOMB TO THE ROPES!
YOU STINK, YOU IDIOT!
ON THE REBOUND ...
...IT'S THE MONCHY LARIAT!!
TAKE THAT!
WHUDD
WHAM
AND HERE COMES THE FALL!
TORIKO! START COUNTING!
HUH?
OKAY!
ONE!
BLEH!
GYAHH
OWCH! KNOCKED OUT BY THE STENCH AFTER ONE COUNT!
THAT WAS FAST!!

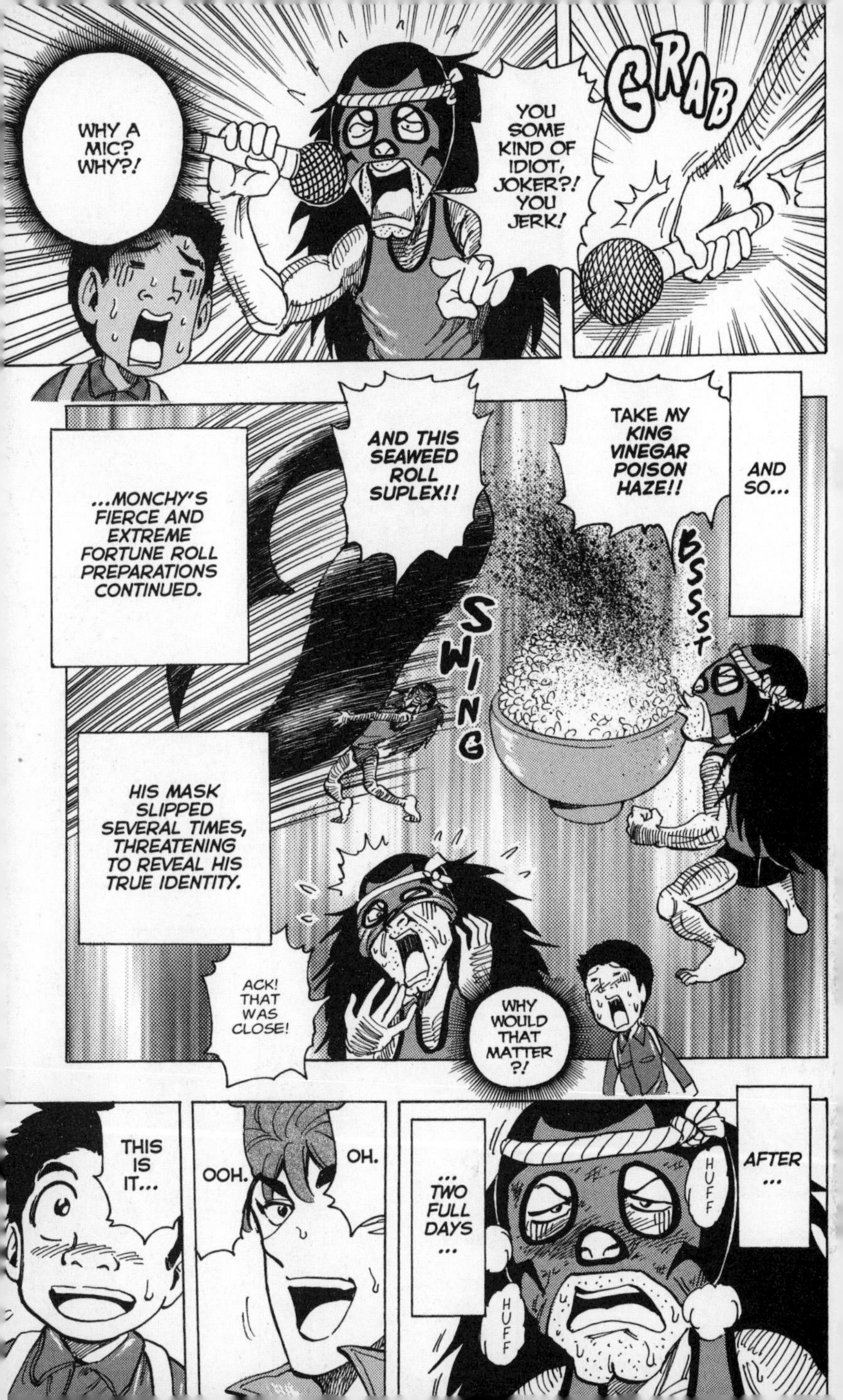
GRAB
YOU SOME KIND OF IDIOT, JOKER?! YOU JERK!
WHY A MIC? WHY?!
AND SO...
TAKE MY KING VINEGAR POISON HAZE!!
BSSST
AND THIS SEAWEED ROLL SUPLEX!!
SWING
...MONCHY'S FIERCE AND EXTREME FORTUNE ROLL PREPARATIONS CONTINUED.
HIS MASK SLIPPED SEVERAL TIMES, THREATENING TO REVEAL HIS TRUE IDENTITY.
ACK! THAT WAS CLOSE!
WHY WOULD THAT MATTER?!
AFTER...
HUFF
HUFF
...TWO FULL DAYS...
OH.
OOH.
THIS IS IT...

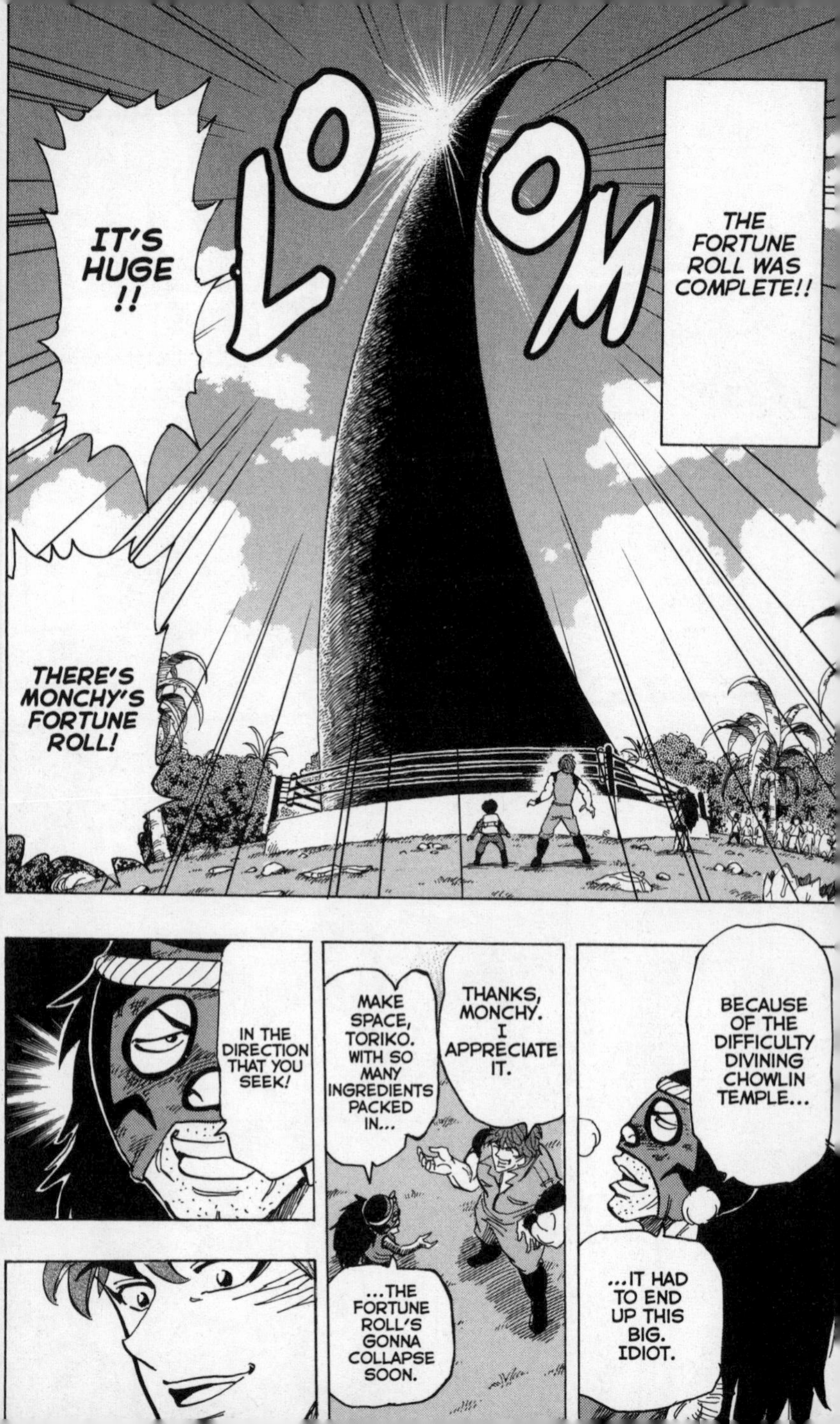
THE FORTUNE ROLL WAS COMPLETE!!
LOOM
IT'S HUGE!!
THERE'S MONCHY'S FORTUNE ROLL!
BECAUSE OF THE DIFFICULTY DIVINING CHOWLIN TEMPLE...
...IT HAD TO END UP THIS BIG. IDIOT.
THANKS, MONCHY. I APPRECIATE IT.
MAKE SPACE, TORIKO. WITH SO MANY INGREDIENTS PACKED IN...
...THE FORTUNE ROLL'S GONNA COLLAPSE SOON.
IN THE DIRECTION THAT YOU SEEK!

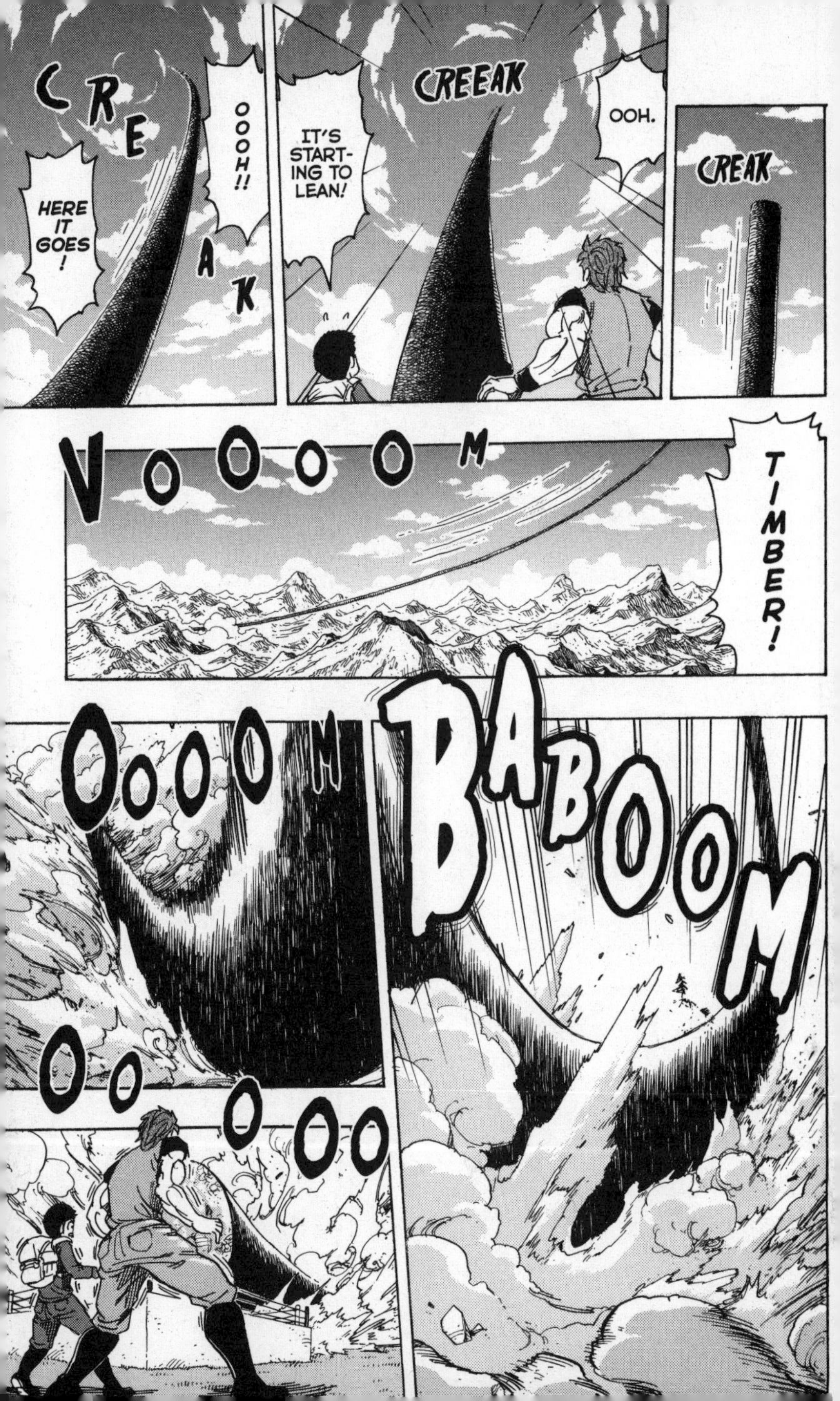
CREAK
OOH.
CREEAK
IT'S STARTING TO LEAN!
OOOOH!!
CREAK
HERE IT GOES!
TIMBER!
VOOOOM
BABOOOM
OOOOM
OOOOOO

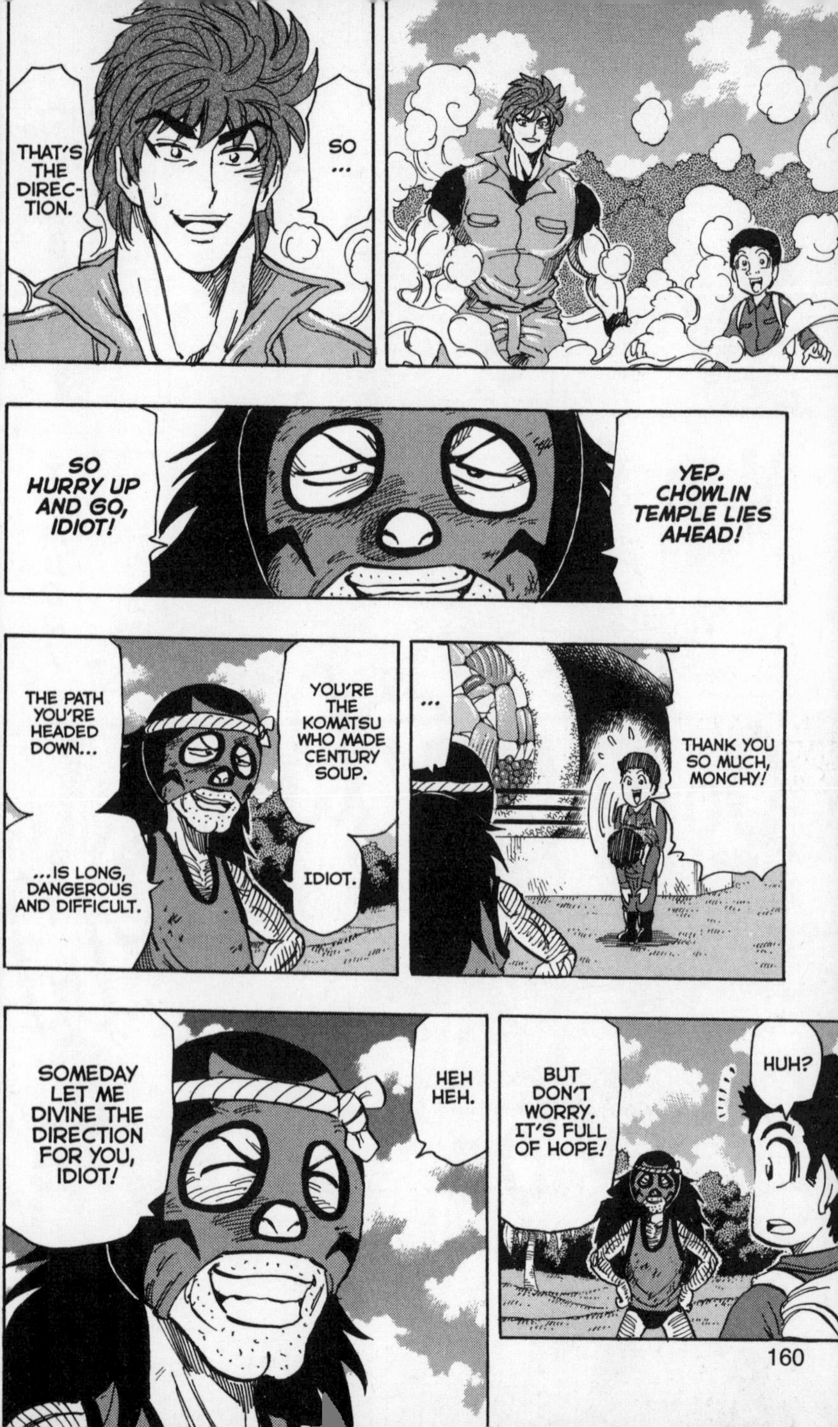
SO ...
THAT'S THE DIREC- TION.
YEP. CHOWLIN TEMPLE LIES AHEAD!
SO HURRY UP AND GO, IDIOT!
THANK YOU SO MUCH, MONCHY!
...
YOU'RE THE KOMATSU WHO MADE CENTURY SOUP.
IDIOT.
THE PATH YOU'RE HEADED DOWN...
...IS LONG, DANGEROUS AND DIFFICULT.
HUH?
BUT DON'T WORRY. IT'S FULL OF HOPE!
HEH HEH.
SOMEDAY LET ME DIVINE THE DIRECTION FOR YOU, IDIOT!

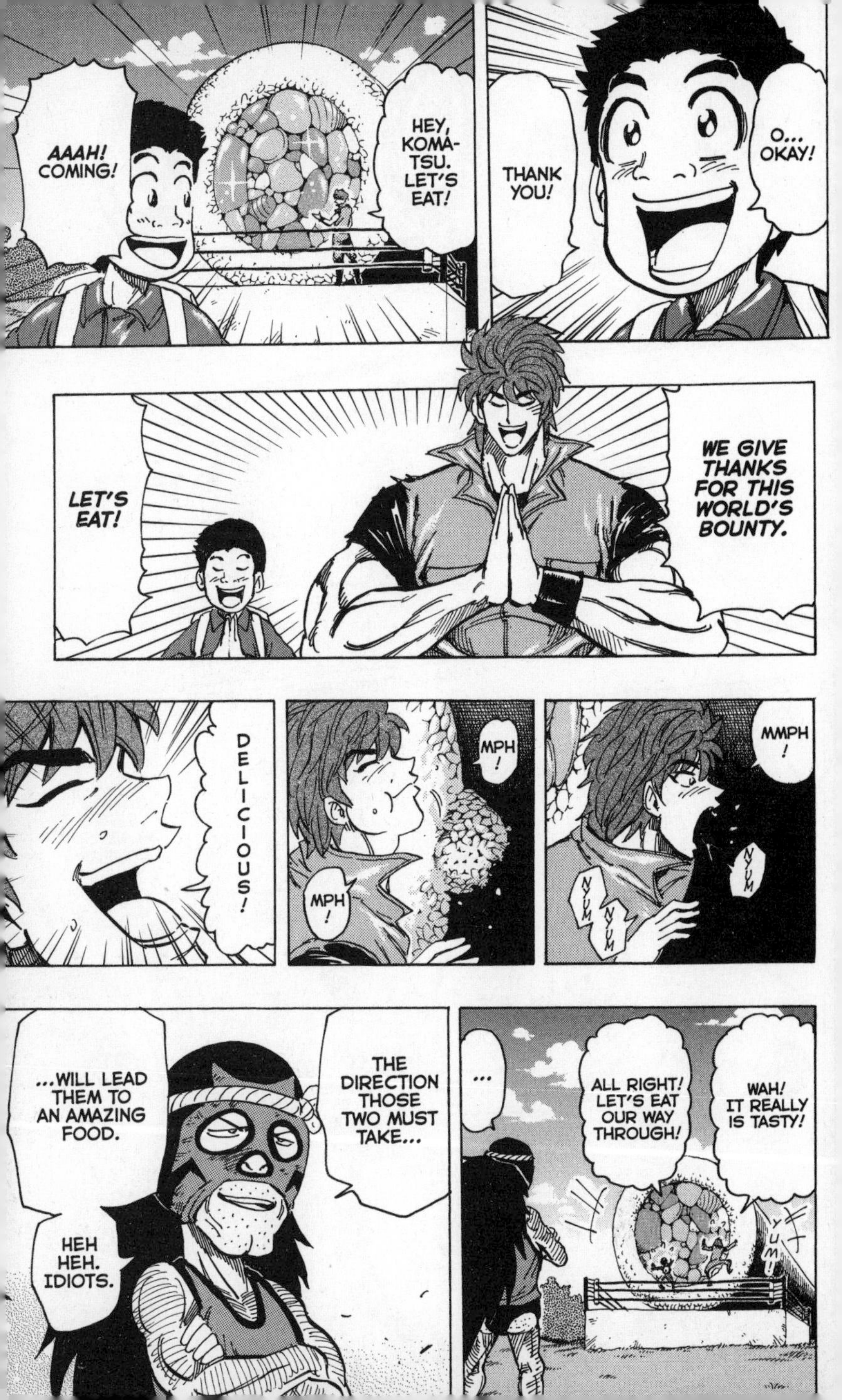
O... OKAY!
THANK YOU!
HEY, KOMATSU. LET'S EAT!
AAAH! COMING!
WE GIVE THANKS FOR THIS WORLD'S BOUNTY.
LET'S EAT!
MMPH!
NYUM
NYUM NYUM
MPH!
MPH!
DELICIOUS!
WAH! IT REALLY IS TASTY!
YUM!
ALL RIGHT! LET'S EAT OUR WAY THROUGH!
...
THE DIRECTION THOSE TWO MUST TAKE...
...WILL LEAD THEM TO AN AMAZING FOOD.
HEH HEH. IDIOTS.

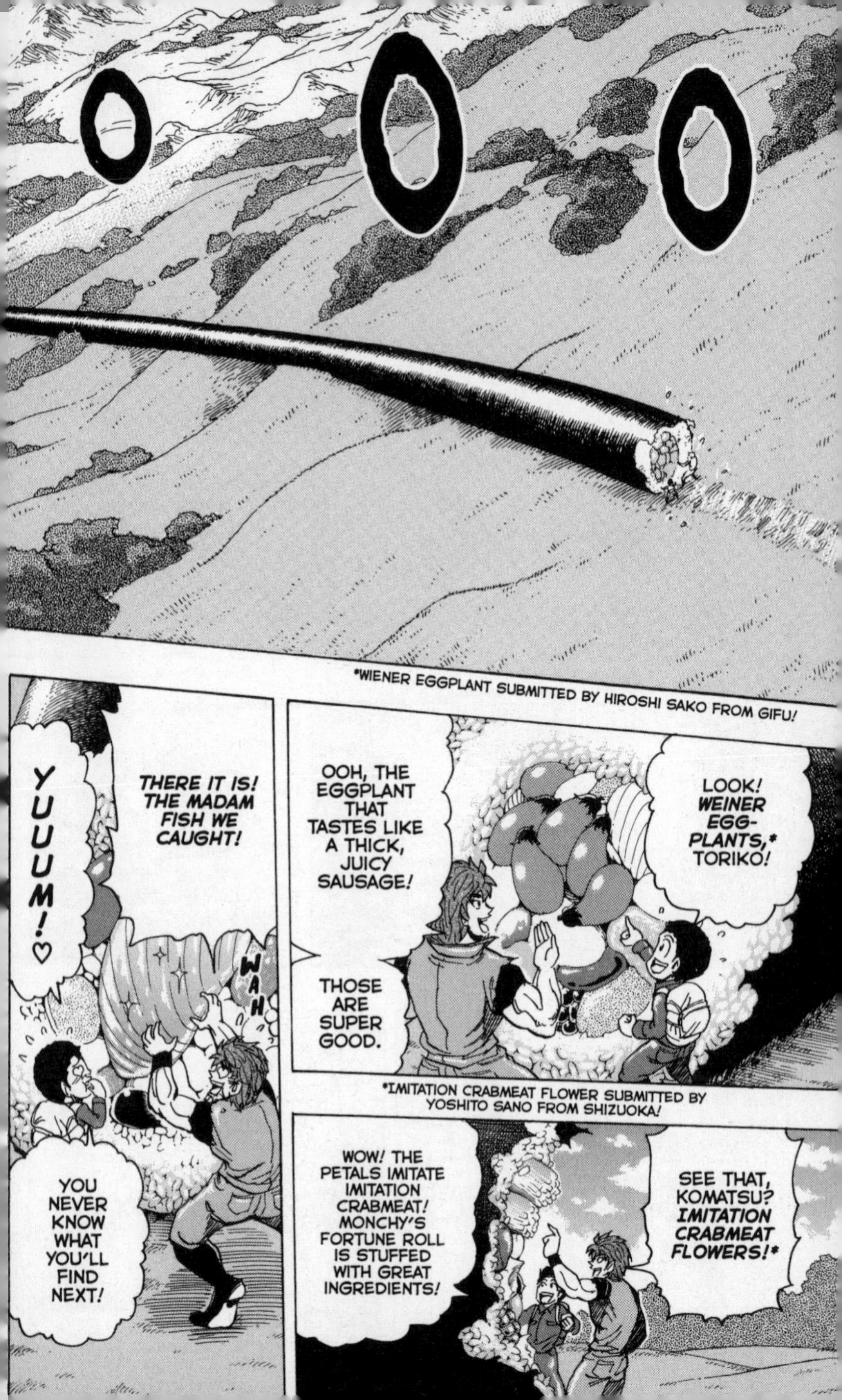
*WIENER EGGPLANT SUBMITTED BY HIROSHI SAKO FROM GIFU!
LOOK! WEINER EGG-PLANTS,* TORIKO!
OOH, THE EGGPLANT THAT TASTES LIKE A THICK, JUICY SAUSAGE!
THOSE ARE SUPER GOOD.
*IMITATION CRABMEAT FLOWER SUBMITTED BY YOSHITO SANO FROM SHIZUOKA!
SEE THAT, KOMATSU? IMITATION CRABMEAT FLOWERS!*
WOW! THE PETALS IMITATE IMITATION CRABMEAT! MONCHY'S FORTUNE ROLL IS STUFFED WITH GREAT INGREDIENTS!
THERE IT IS! THE MADAM FISH WE CAUGHT!
YUUUUM!♡
WAH
YOU NEVER KNOW WHAT YOU'LL FIND NEXT!

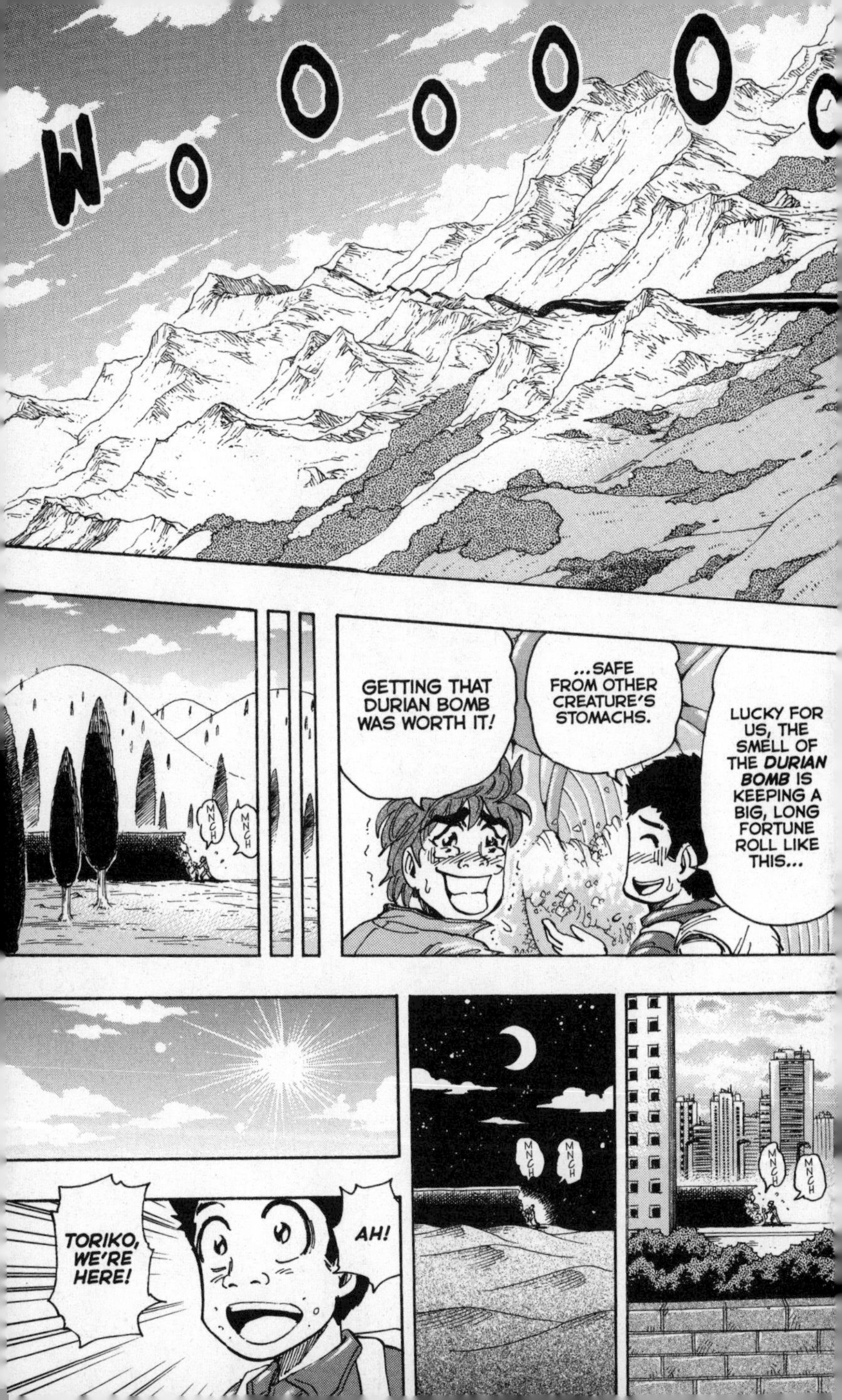
WOOOOOO
LUCKY FOR US, THE SMELL OF THE *DURIAN BOMB* IS KEEPING A BIG, LONG FORTUNE ROLL LIKE THIS...
...SAFE FROM OTHER CREATURE'S STOMACHS.
GETTING THAT DURIAN BOMB WAS WORTH IT!
MNCH
MNCH
MNCH
MNCH
MNCH
MNCH
AH!
TORIKO, WE'RE HERE!

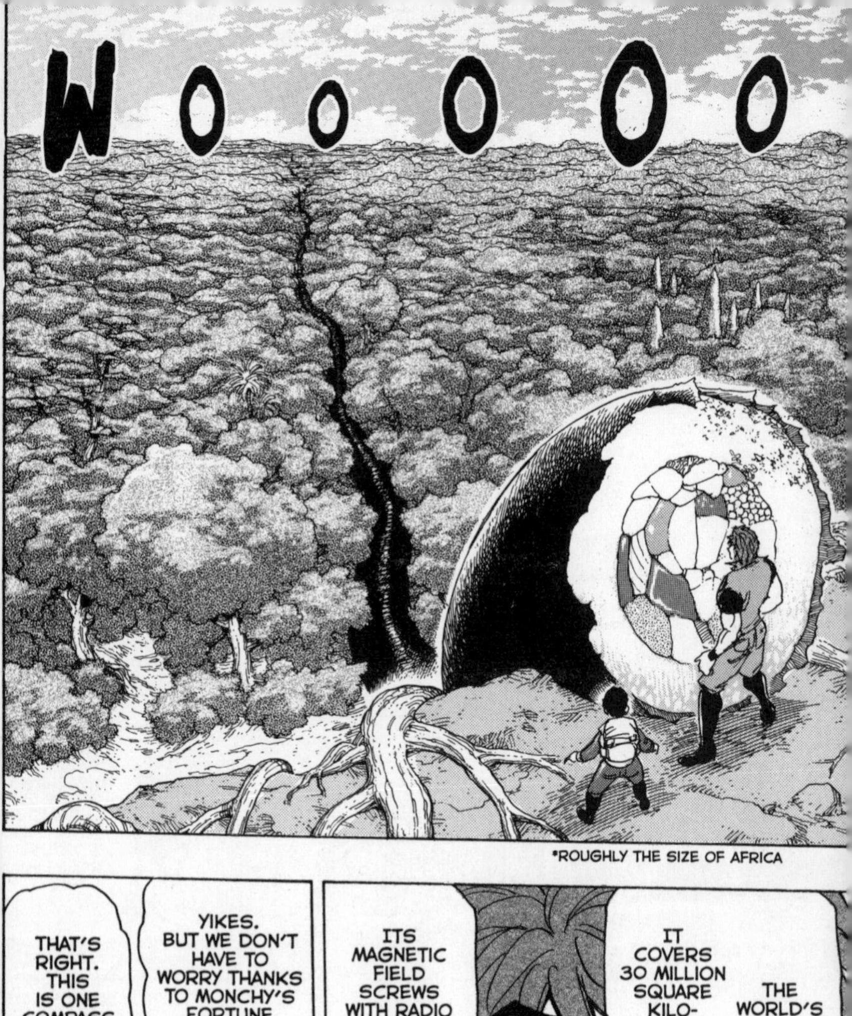
WOOOOO

*ROUGHLY THE SIZE OF AFRICA

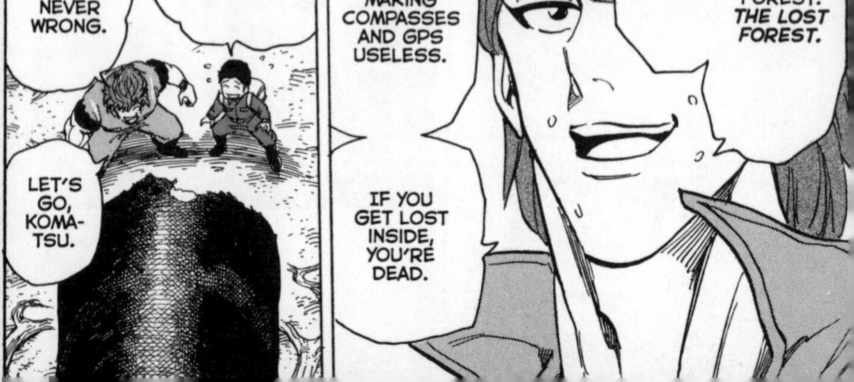
THE WORLD'S BIGGEST FOREST. *THE LOST FOREST.*
IT COVERS 30 MILLION SQUARE KILO-METERS.*
ITS MAGNETIC FIELD SCREWS WITH RADIO WAVES, MAKING COMPASSES AND GPS USELESS.
IF YOU GET LOST INSIDE, YOU'RE DEAD.
YIKES. BUT WE DON'T HAVE TO WORRY THANKS TO MONCHY'S FORTUNE ROLL.
THAT'S RIGHT. THIS IS ONE COMPASS THAT'S NEVER WRONG.
LET'S GO, KOMATSU.

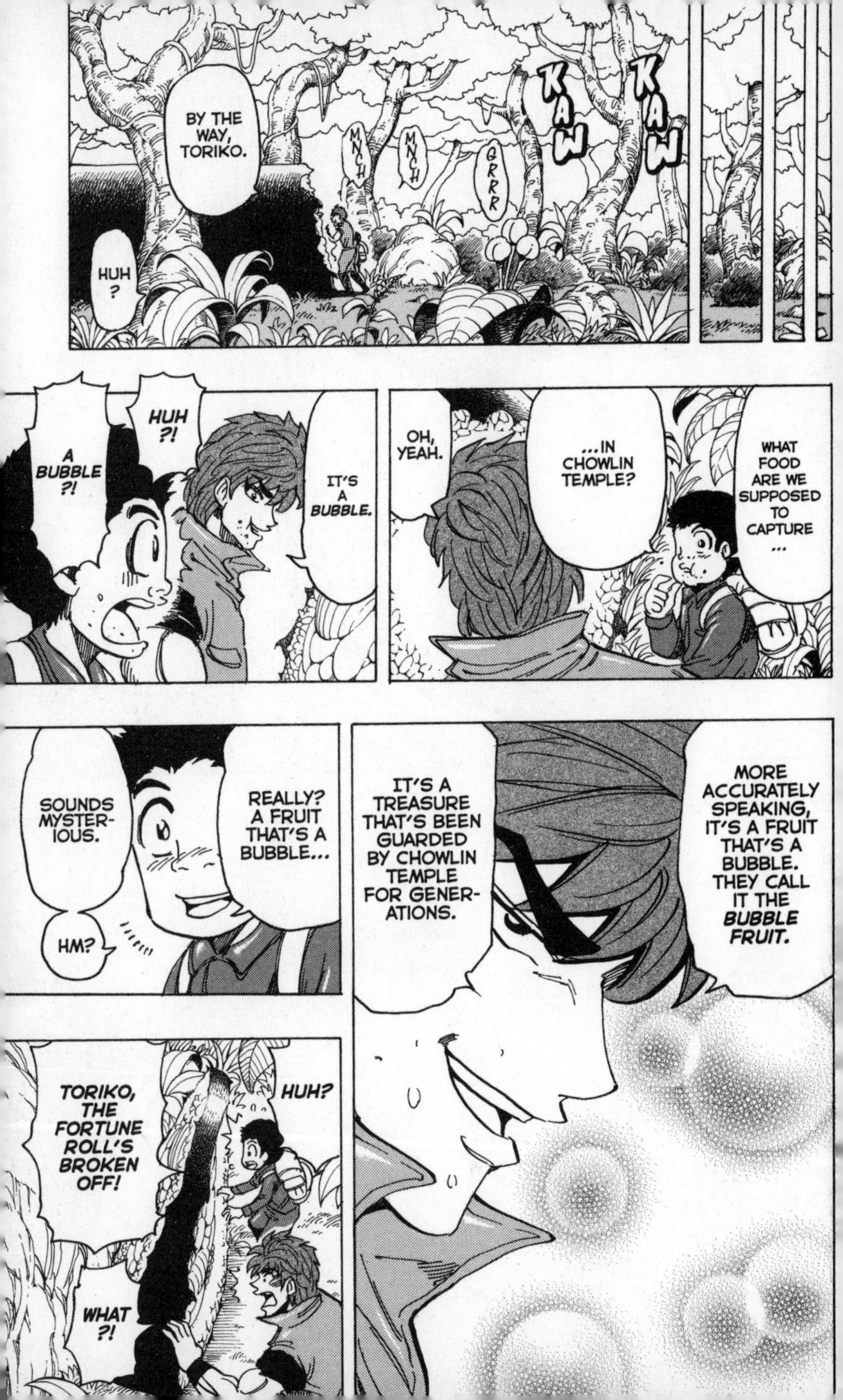
KAW
KAW
GRRR
MNCH
MNCH
BY THE WAY, TORIKO.
HUH?
WHAT FOOD ARE WE SUPPOSED TO CAPTURE...
...IN CHOWLIN TEMPLE?
OH, YEAH.
IT'S A *BUBBLE.*
HUH?!
A *BUBBLE*?!
MORE ACCURATELY SPEAKING, IT'S A FRUIT THAT'S A BUBBLE. THEY CALL IT THE *BUBBLE FRUIT.*
IT'S A TREASURE THAT'S BEEN GUARDED BY CHOWLIN TEMPLE FOR GENERATIONS.
REALLY? A FRUIT THAT'S A BUBBLE...
SOUNDS MYSTERIOUS.
HM?
HUH?
TORIKO, THE FORTUNE ROLL'S BROKEN OFF!
WHAT?!

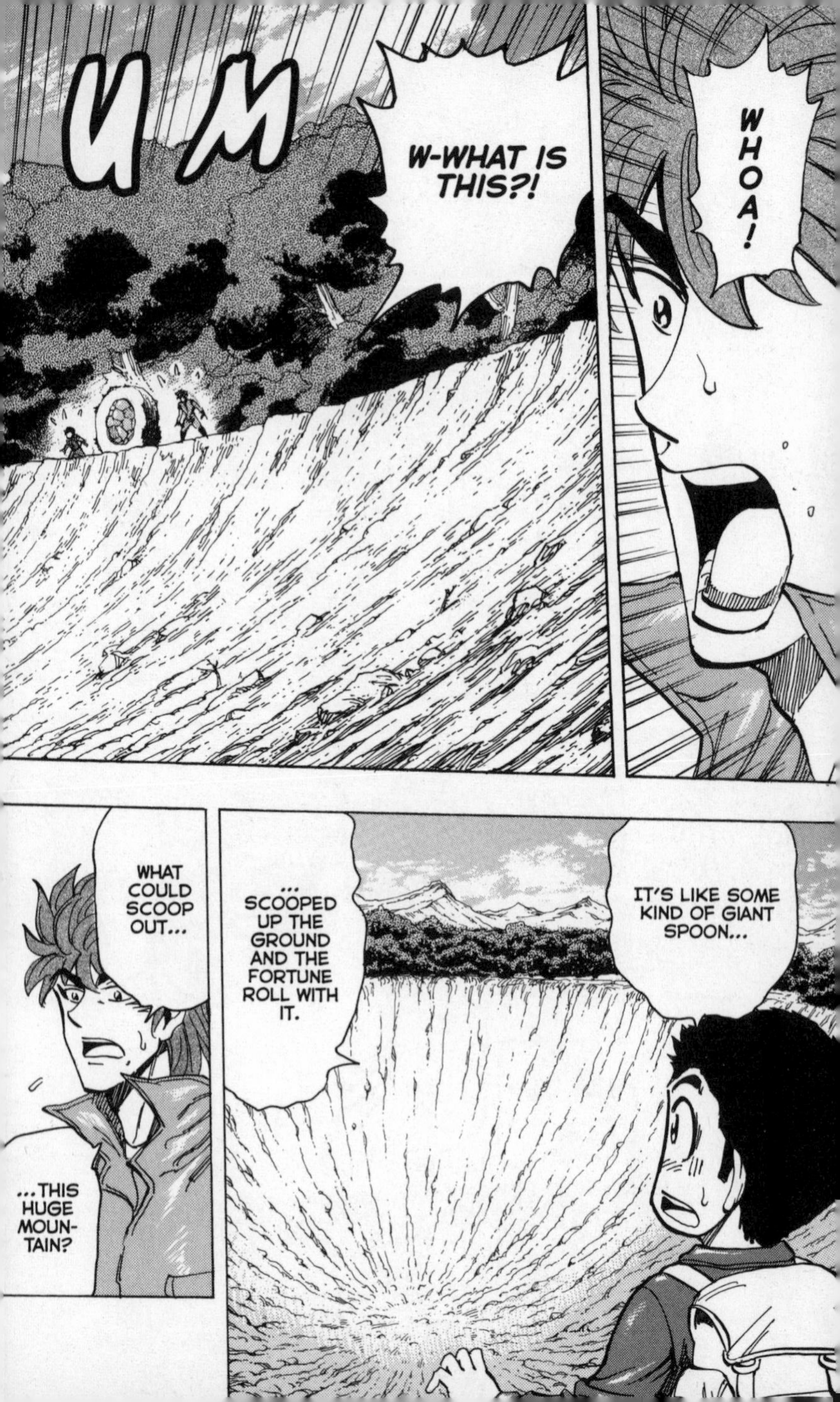
WHOA!
W-WHAT IS THIS?!
U M
IT'S LIKE SOME KIND OF GIANT SPOON...
...SCOOPED UP THE GROUND AND THE FORTUNE ROLL WITH IT.
WHAT COULD SCOOP OUT...
...THIS HUGE MOUNTAIN?

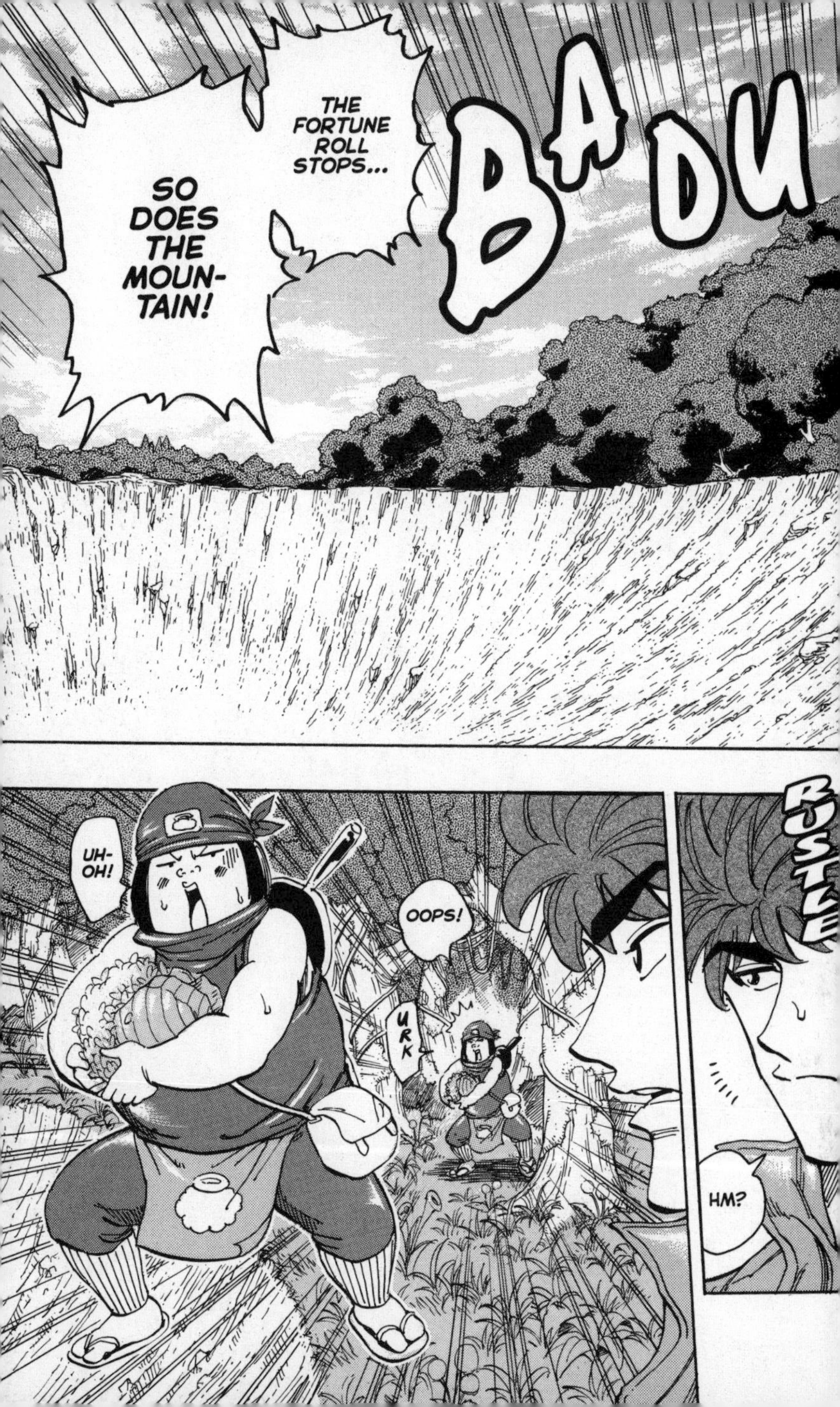
BADU
THE FORTUNE ROLL STOPS...
SO DOES THE MOUN-TAIN!
RUSTLE
HM?
OOPS!
URK
UH-OH!

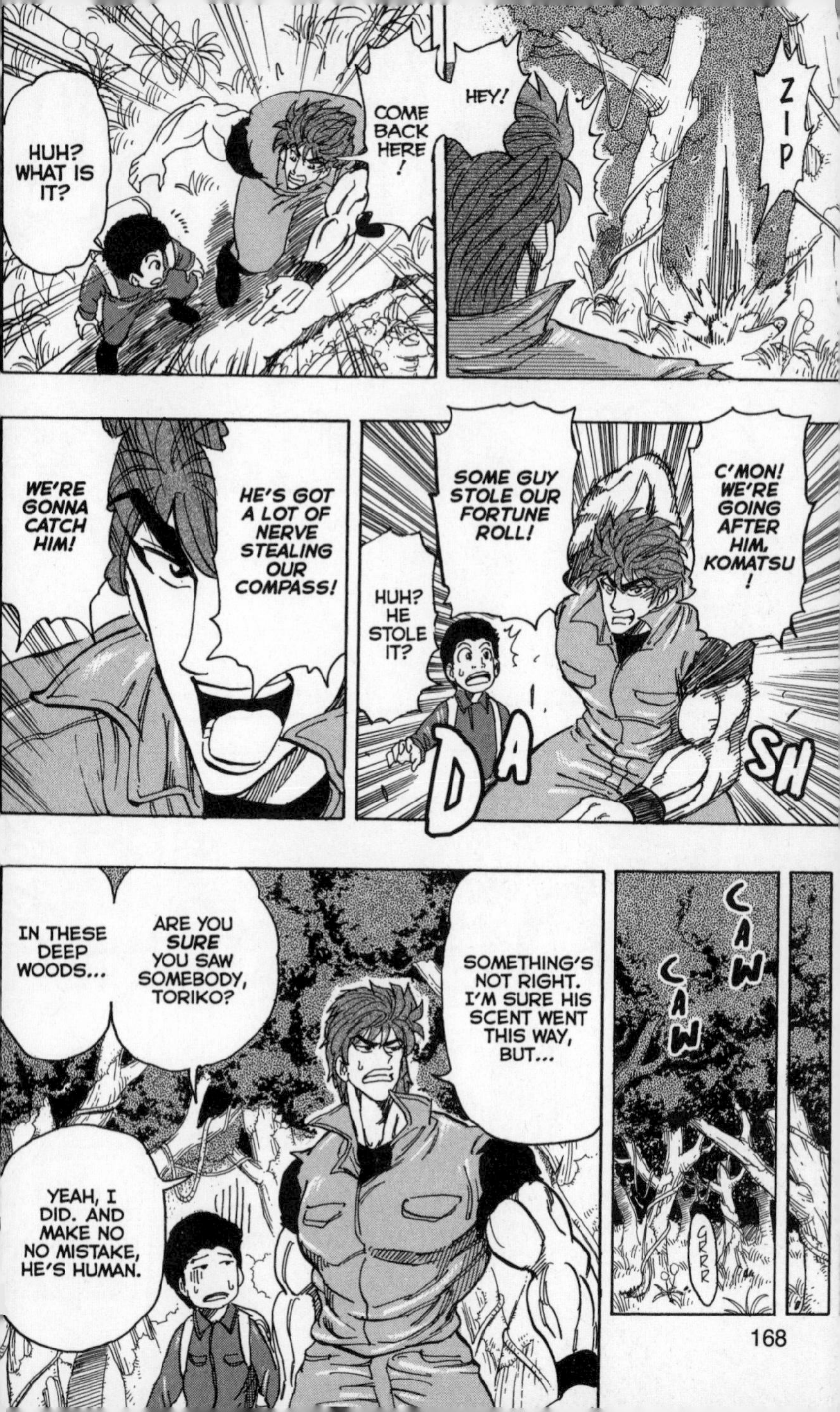
ZIP
HEY!
COME BACK HERE!
HUH? WHAT IS IT?
C'MON! WE'RE GOING AFTER HIM, KOMATSU!
SOME GUY STOLE OUR FORTUNE ROLL!
HUH? HE STOLE IT?
DASH
HE'S GOT A LOT OF NERVE STEALING OUR COMPASS!
WE'RE GONNA CATCH HIM!
CAW
CAW
GRRR
SOMETHING'S NOT RIGHT. I'M SURE HIS SCENT WENT THIS WAY, BUT...
ARE YOU *SURE* YOU SAW SOMEBODY, TORIKO?
IN THESE DEEP WOODS...
YEAH, I DID. AND MAKE NO NO MISTAKE, HE'S HUMAN.

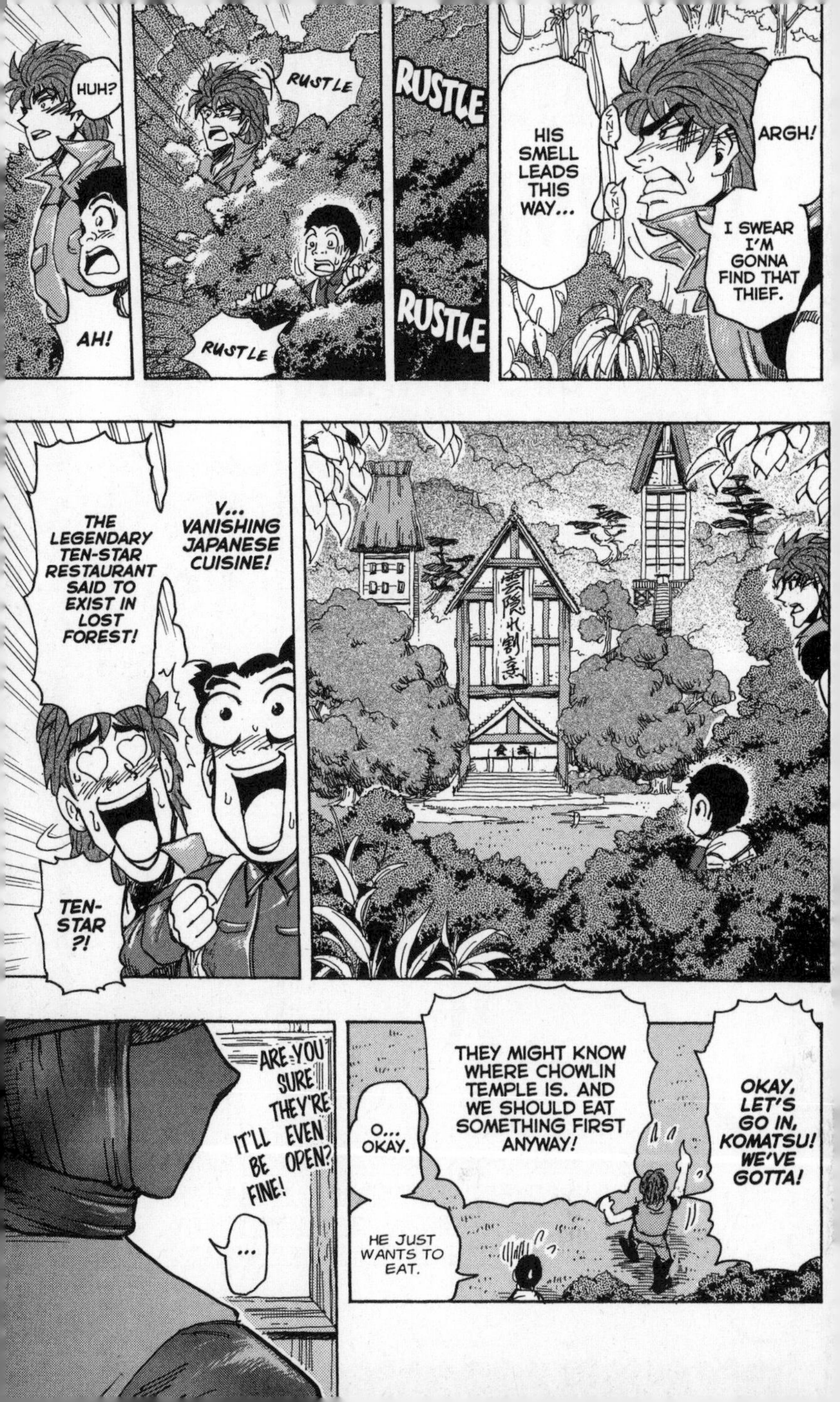
ARGH!
I SWEAR I'M GONNA FIND THAT THIEF.
SNF
SNF
HIS SMELL LEADS THIS WAY...
RUSTLE
RUSTLE
RUSTLE
RUSTLE
HUH?
AH!
THE LEGENDARY TEN-STAR RESTAURANT SAID TO EXIST IN LOST FOREST!
V... VANISHING JAPANESE CUISINE!
TEN-STAR?!
OKAY, LET'S GO IN, KOMATSU! WE'VE GOTTA!
THEY MIGHT KNOW WHERE CHOWLIN TEMPLE IS. AND WE SHOULD EAT SOMETHING FIRST ANYWAY!
O... OKAY.
HE JUST WANTS TO EAT.
ARE YOU SURE THEY'RE IT'LL EVEN BE OPEN? FINE!
...

TORIKO

GOURMET CHECKLIST
Vol. 207

DREAM WALNUT
(PLANT)

CAPTURE LEVEL: 4 (IN THE WILD)

HABITAT: SHEER CLIFF FACES
DEEP IN THE MOUNTAINS
(CAN ALSO BE
ARTIFICIALLY
CULTIVATED)

LENGTH: 4 CM

HEIGHT: ---

WEIGHT: 35 G

PRICE: 150 YEN PER NUT

OH, SHE'S GOT ROASTED *DREAM CHESTNUTS** TOO! GIMME TEN, LADY!!

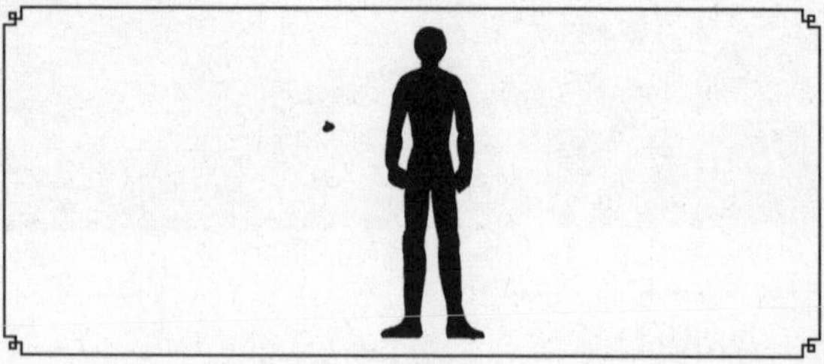

SCALE

A DECIDUOUS TREE RELATED TO THE BEECH. IT HAS LONG, ALTERNATING ELLIPTICAL LEAVES. ITS FLOWERS ARE A PALE YELLOW AND IN AUTUMN THEY'RE COVERED IN BURRS THAT BEAR A CREAMY-TASTING FRUIT. THEY'RE SWEET WHEN LIGHTLY ROASTED, BUT WHEN WHIPPED UP INTO A MONT BLANC BY A SKILLED PASTIER, DREAM WALNUTS BECOME AS DREAMY AS THEIR NAME SUGGESTS.

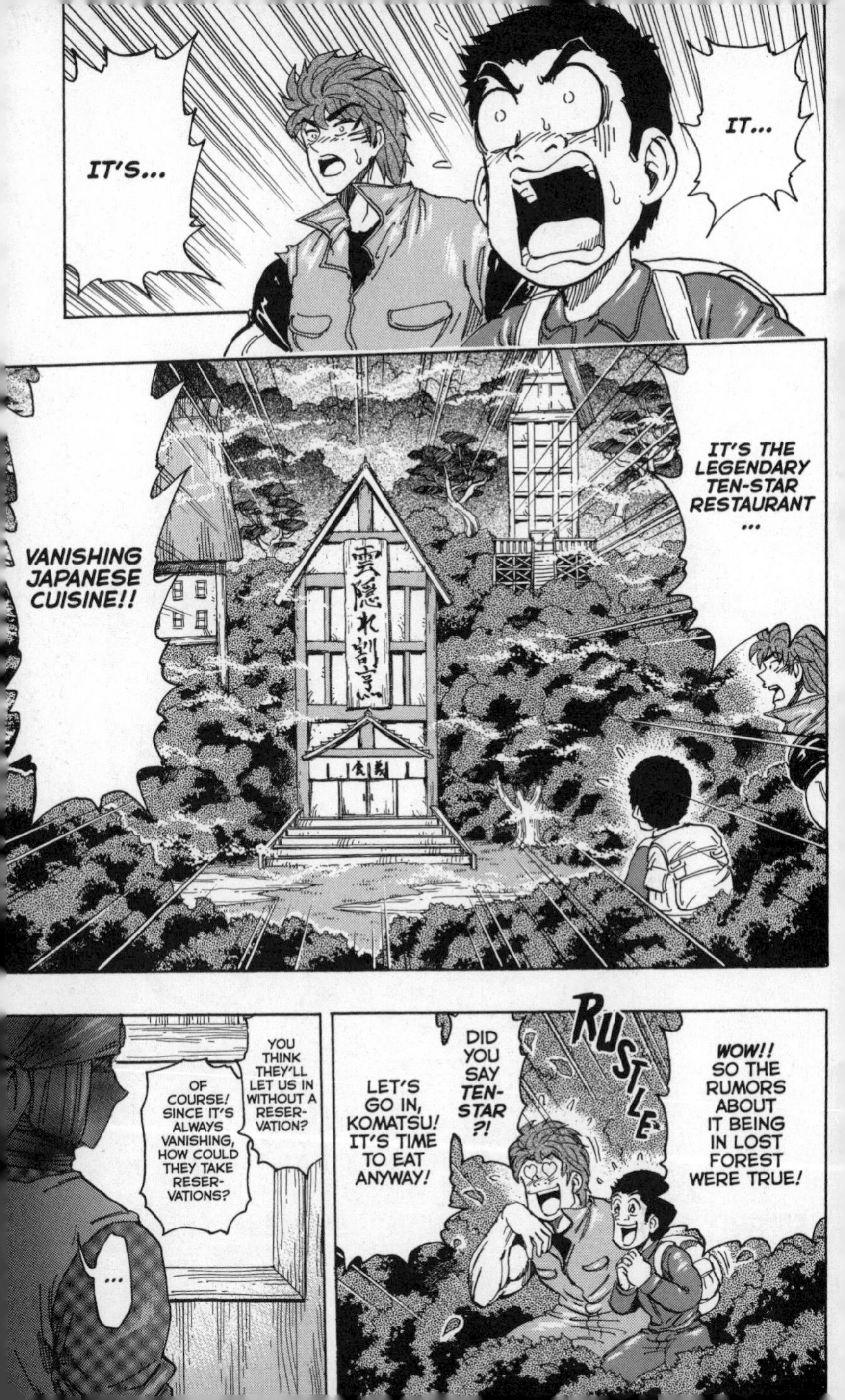
IT...
IT'S...
IT'S THE LEGENDARY TEN-STAR RESTAURANT...
VANISHING JAPANESE CUISINE!!
雲隠れ割烹
WOW!! SO THE RUMORS ABOUT IT BEING IN LOST FOREST WERE TRUE!
RUSTLE
DID YOU SAY TEN-STAR?!
LET'S GO IN, KOMATSU! IT'S TIME TO EAT ANYWAY!
YOU THINK THEY'LL LET US IN WITHOUT A RESERVATION?
OF COURSE! SINCE IT'S ALWAYS VANISHING, HOW COULD THEY TAKE RESERVATIONS?
...

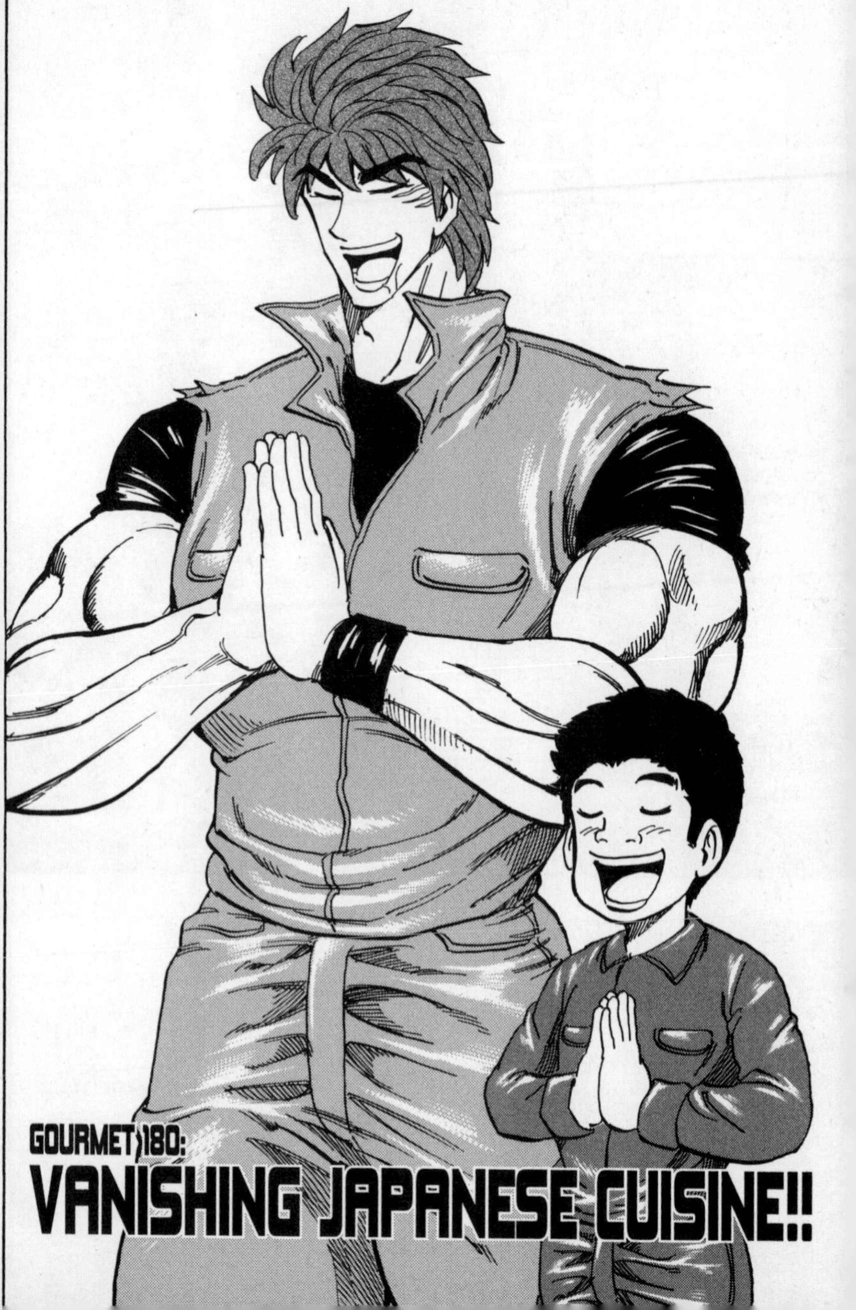
GOURMET 180:
VANISHING JAPANESE CUISINE!!

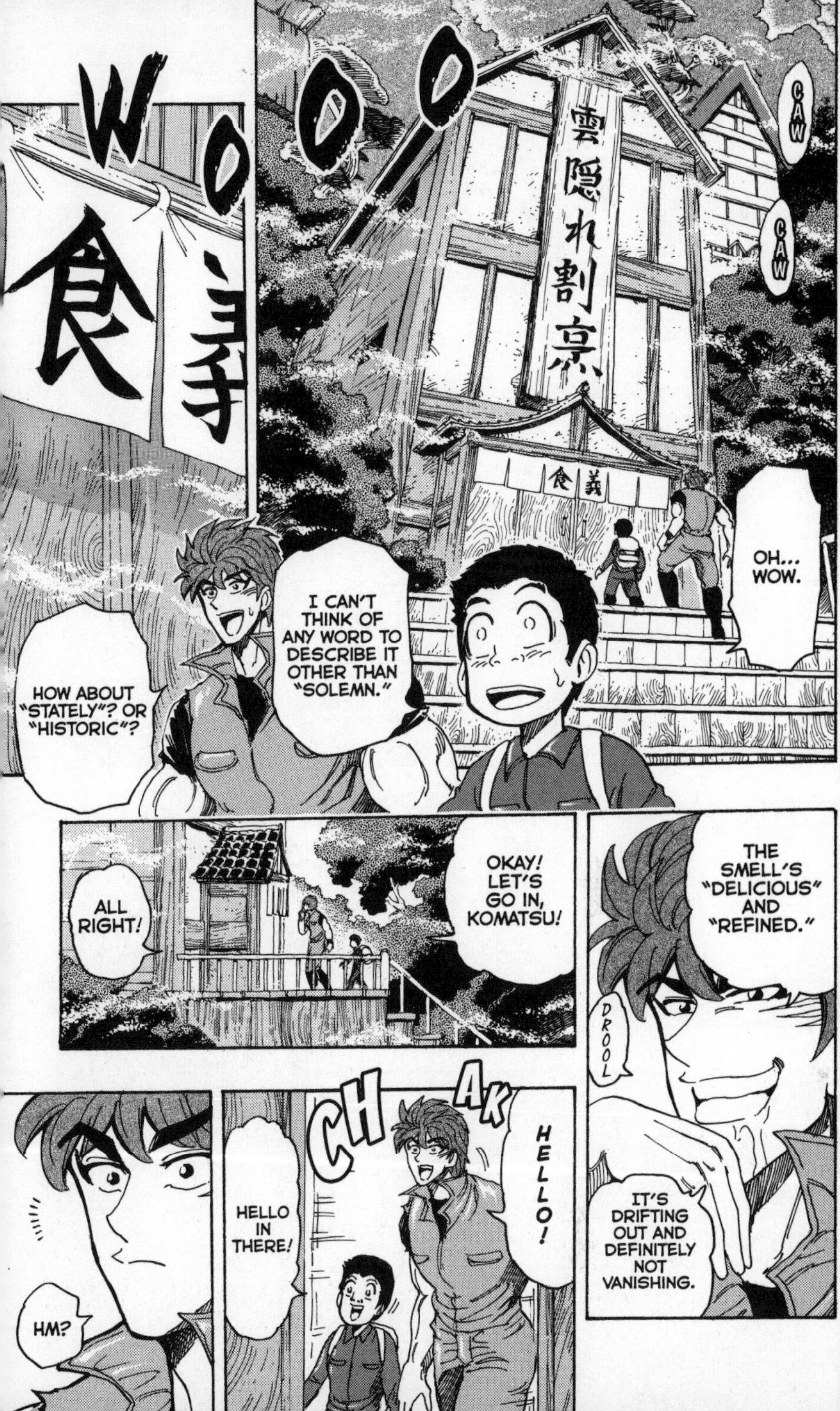
WOOO
雲隠れ割烹
食義
CAW
CAW
OH... WOW.
I CAN'T THINK OF ANY WORD TO DESCRIBE IT OTHER THAN "SOLEMN."
HOW ABOUT "STATELY"? OR "HISTORIC"?
THE SMELL'S "DELICIOUS" AND "REFINED."
DROOL
IT'S DRIFTING OUT AND DEFINITELY NOT VANISHING.
OKAY! LET'S GO IN, KOMATSU!
ALL RIGHT!
CHAK
HELLO!
HELLO IN THERE!
HM?

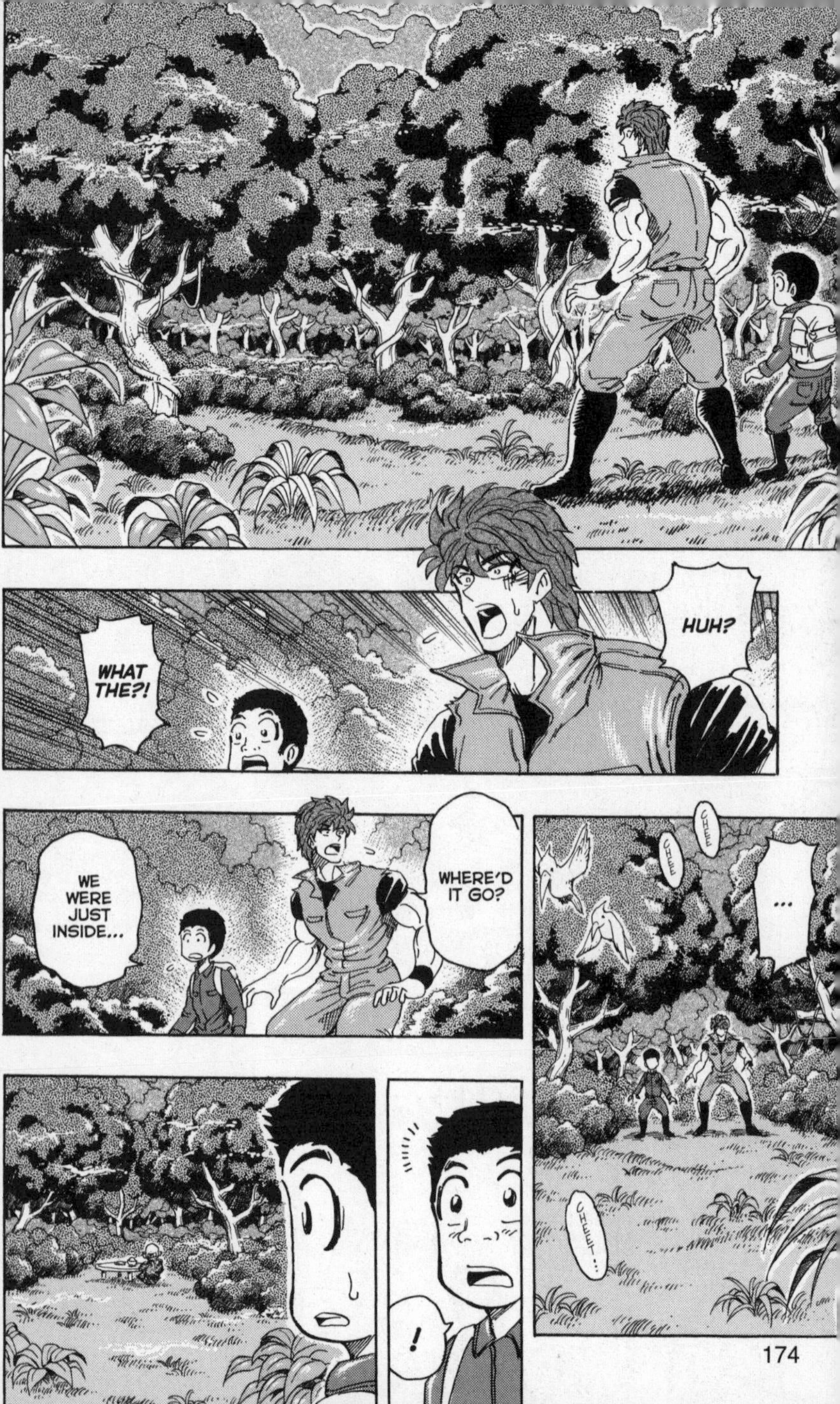
HUH?
WHAT THE?!
CHEE
CHEE
...
CHEEET...
WHERE'D IT GO?
WE WERE JUST INSIDE...
!

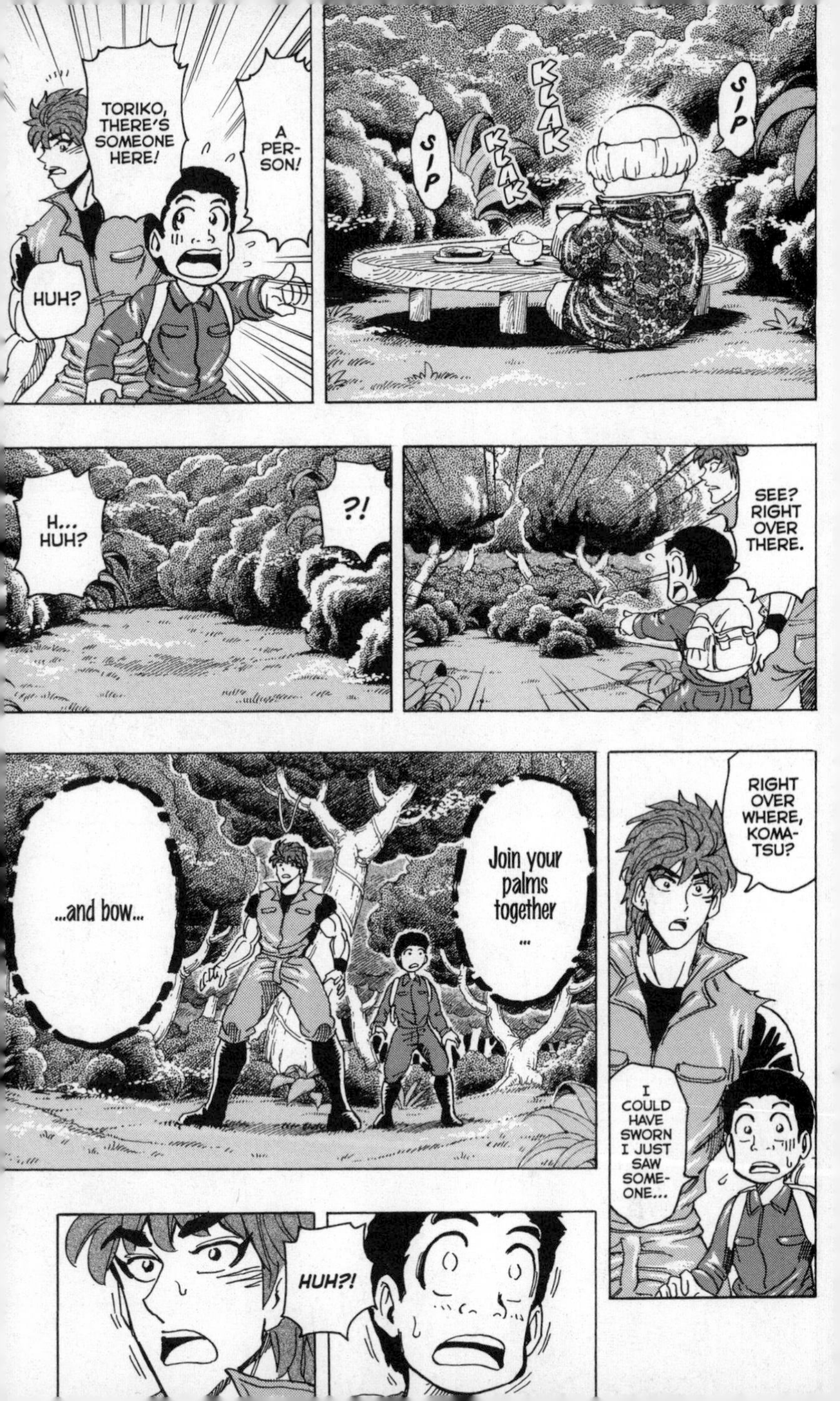
SIP
KLAK
KLAK
SIP
TORIKO, THERE'S SOMEONE HERE!
A PER-SON!
HUH?
SEE? RIGHT OVER THERE.
?!
H... HUH?
RIGHT OVER WHERE, KOMA-TSU?
I COULD HAVE SWORN I JUST SAW SOME-ONE...
Join your palms together ...
...and bow...
HUH?!

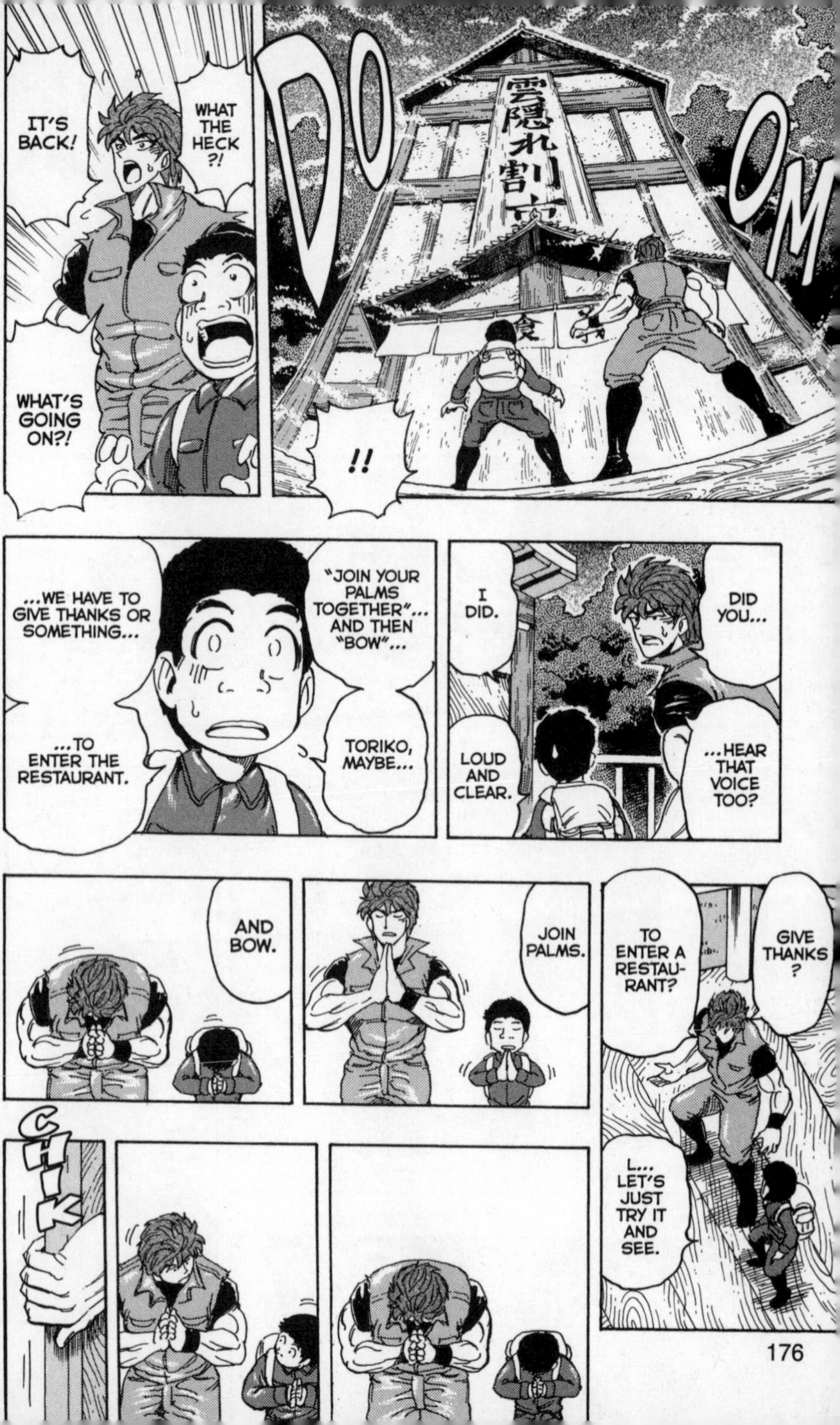
DO
OM
!!
WHAT THE HECK?!
IT'S BACK!
WHAT'S GOING ON?!
DID YOU...
I DID.
...HEAR THAT VOICE TOO?
LOUD AND CLEAR.
TORIKO, MAYBE...
"JOIN YOUR PALMS TOGETHER"... AND THEN "BOW"...
...WE HAVE TO GIVE THANKS OR SOMETHING...
...TO ENTER THE RESTAURANT.
GIVE THANKS?
TO ENTER A RESTAURANT?
L... LET'S JUST TRY IT AND SEE.
JOIN PALMS.
AND BOW.
CHIK

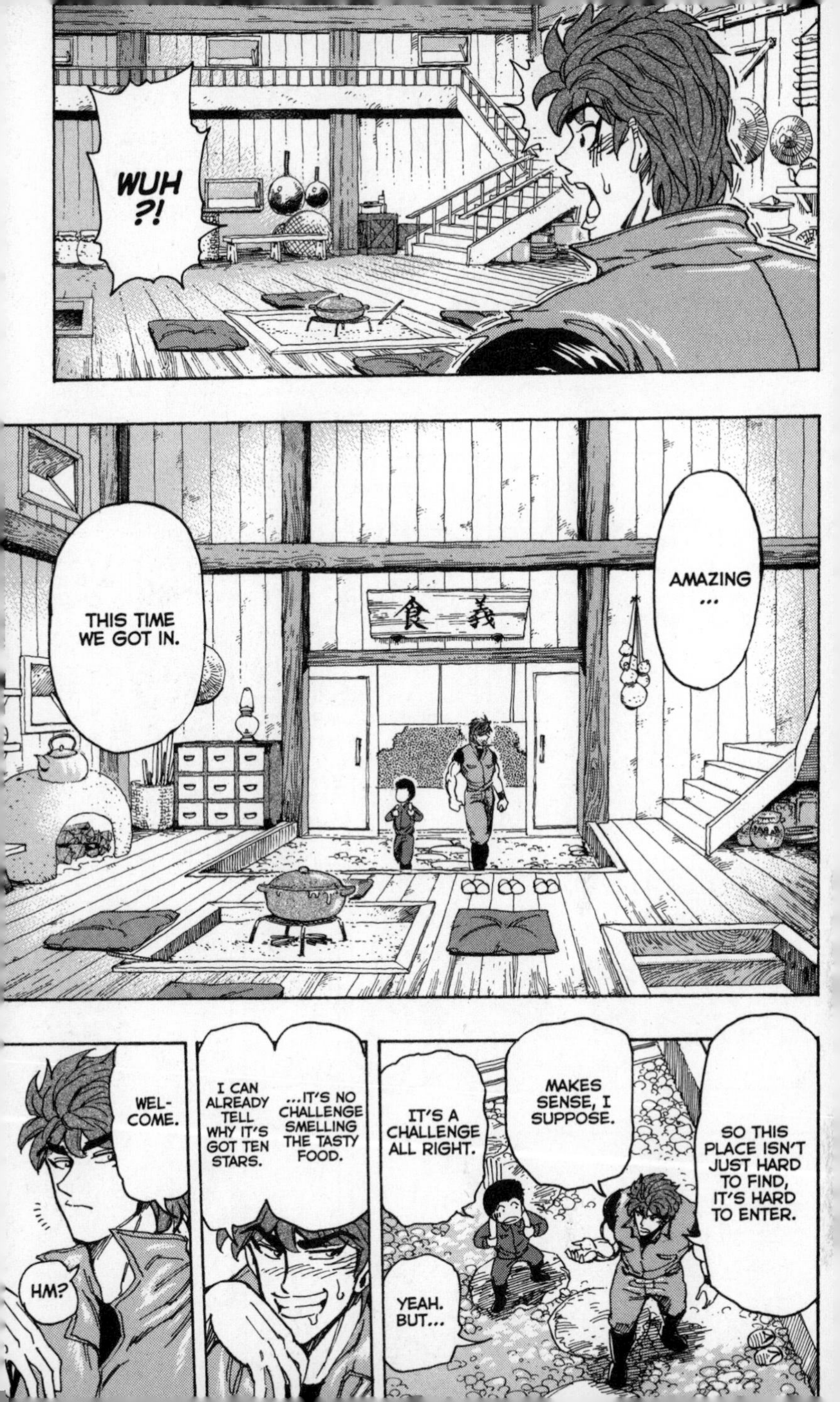
WUH ?!
AMAZING...
食義
THIS TIME WE GOT IN.
SO THIS PLACE ISN'T JUST HARD TO FIND, IT'S HARD TO ENTER.
MAKES SENSE, I SUPPOSE.
IT'S A CHALLENGE ALL RIGHT.
YEAH. BUT...
...IT'S NO CHALLENGE SMELLING THE TASTY FOOD.
I CAN ALREADY TELL WHY IT'S GOT TEN STARS.
WEL-COME.
HM?

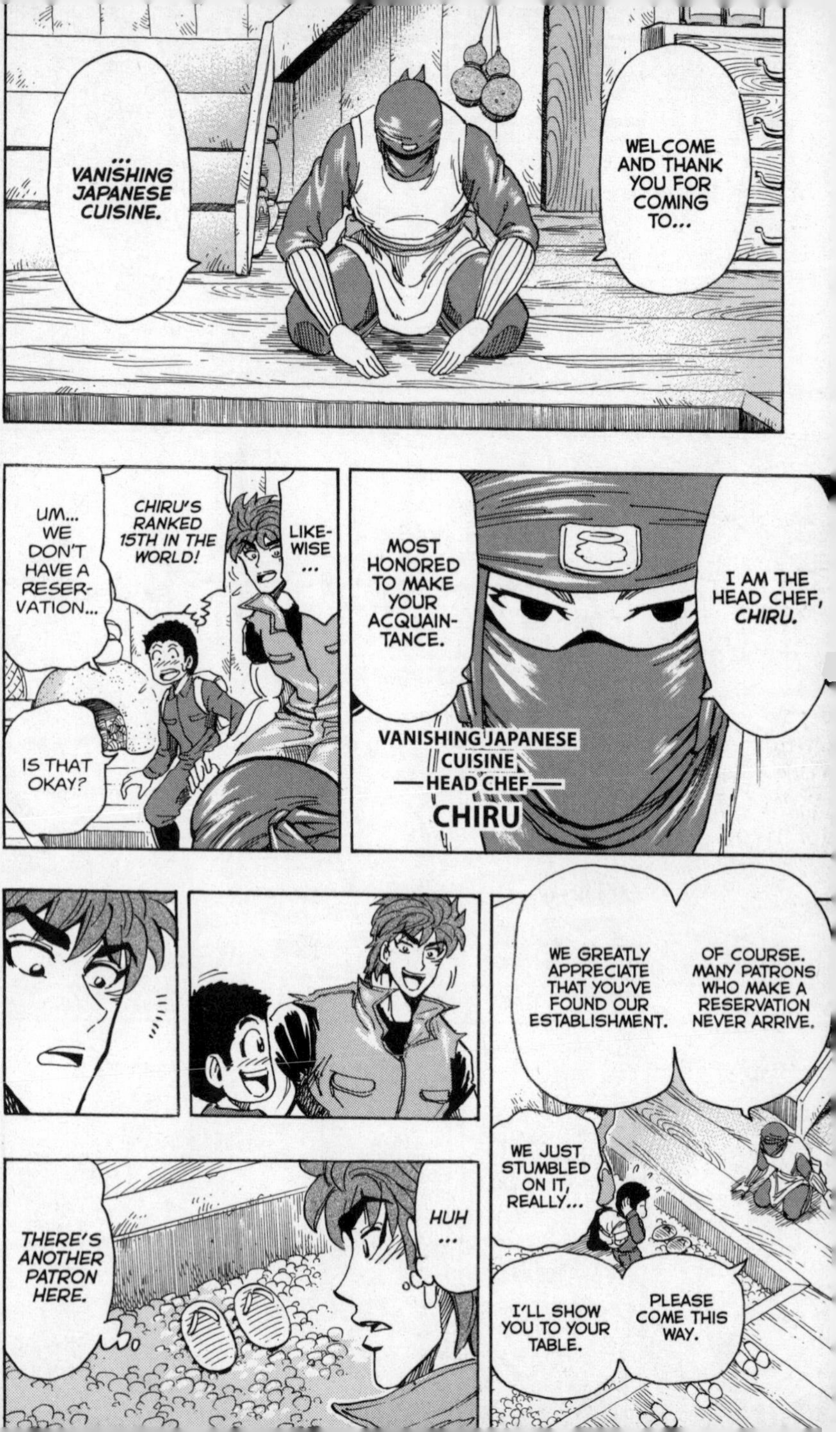
WELCOME AND THANK YOU FOR COMING TO...
... VANISHING JAPANESE CUISINE.
I AM THE HEAD CHEF, CHIRU.
MOST HONORED TO MAKE YOUR ACQUAIN-TANCE.
VANISHING JAPANESE CUISINE —HEAD CHEF— CHIRU
LIKE-WISE...
CHIRU'S RANKED 15TH IN THE WORLD!
UM... WE DON'T HAVE A RESER-VATION...
IS THAT OKAY?
OF COURSE. MANY PATRONS WHO MAKE A RESERVATION NEVER ARRIVE.
WE GREATLY APPRECIATE THAT YOU'VE FOUND OUR ESTABLISHMENT.
WE JUST STUMBLED ON IT, REALLY...
PLEASE COME THIS WAY.
I'LL SHOW YOU TO YOUR TABLE.
HUH...
THERE'S ANOTHER PATRON HERE.

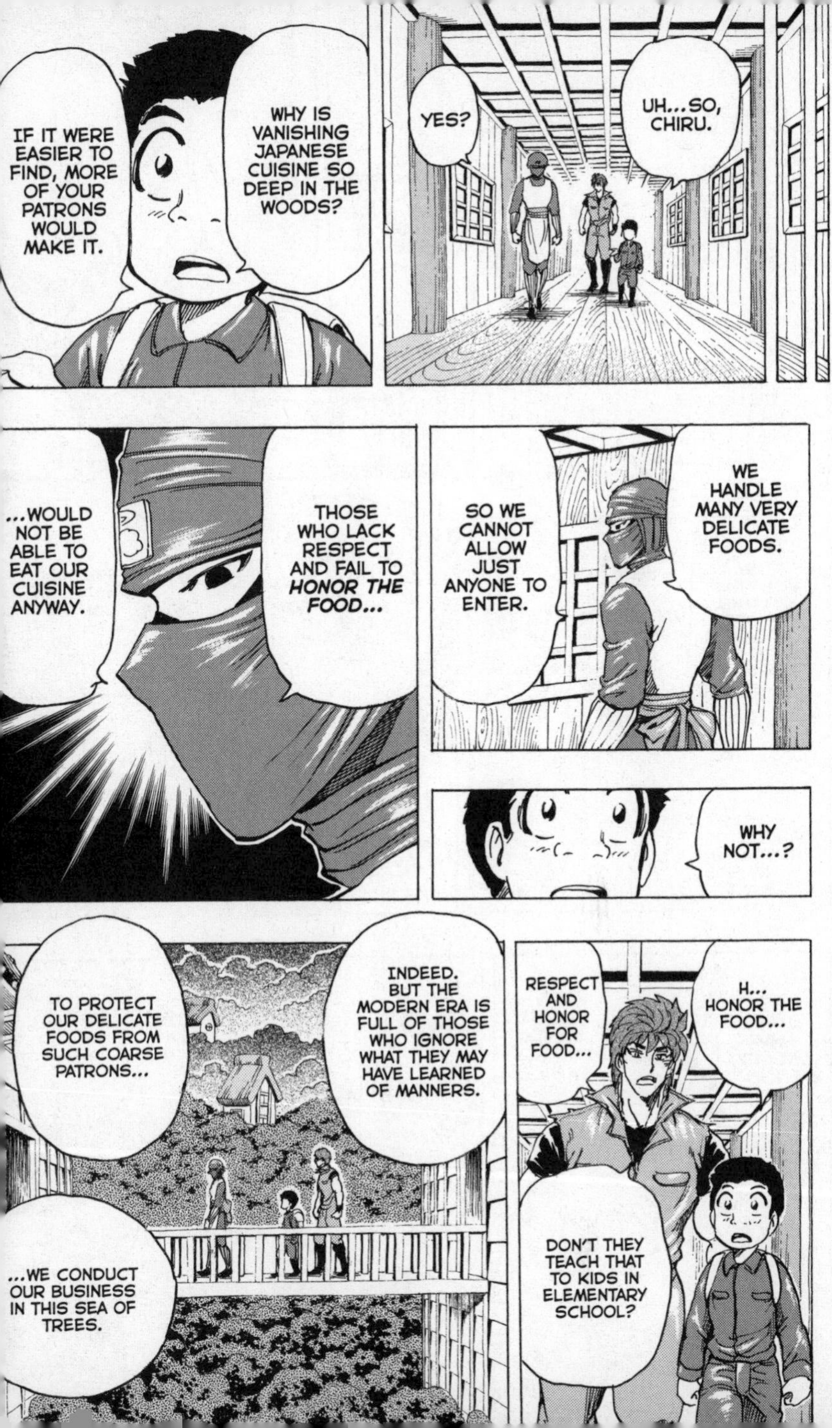
UH...SO, CHIRU.
YES?
WHY IS VANISHING JAPANESE CUISINE SO DEEP IN THE WOODS?
IF IT WERE EASIER TO FIND, MORE OF YOUR PATRONS WOULD MAKE IT.
WE HANDLE MANY VERY DELICATE FOODS.
SO WE CANNOT ALLOW JUST ANYONE TO ENTER.
WHY NOT...?
THOSE WHO LACK RESPECT AND FAIL TO *HONOR THE FOOD...*
...WOULD NOT BE ABLE TO EAT OUR CUISINE ANYWAY.
H... HONOR THE FOOD...
RESPECT AND HONOR FOR FOOD...
DON'T THEY TEACH THAT TO KIDS IN ELEMENTARY SCHOOL?
INDEED. BUT THE MODERN ERA IS FULL OF THOSE WHO IGNORE WHAT THEY MAY HAVE LEARNED OF MANNERS.
TO PROTECT OUR DELICATE FOODS FROM SUCH COARSE PATRONS...
...WE CONDUCT OUR BUSINESS IN THIS SEA OF TREES.

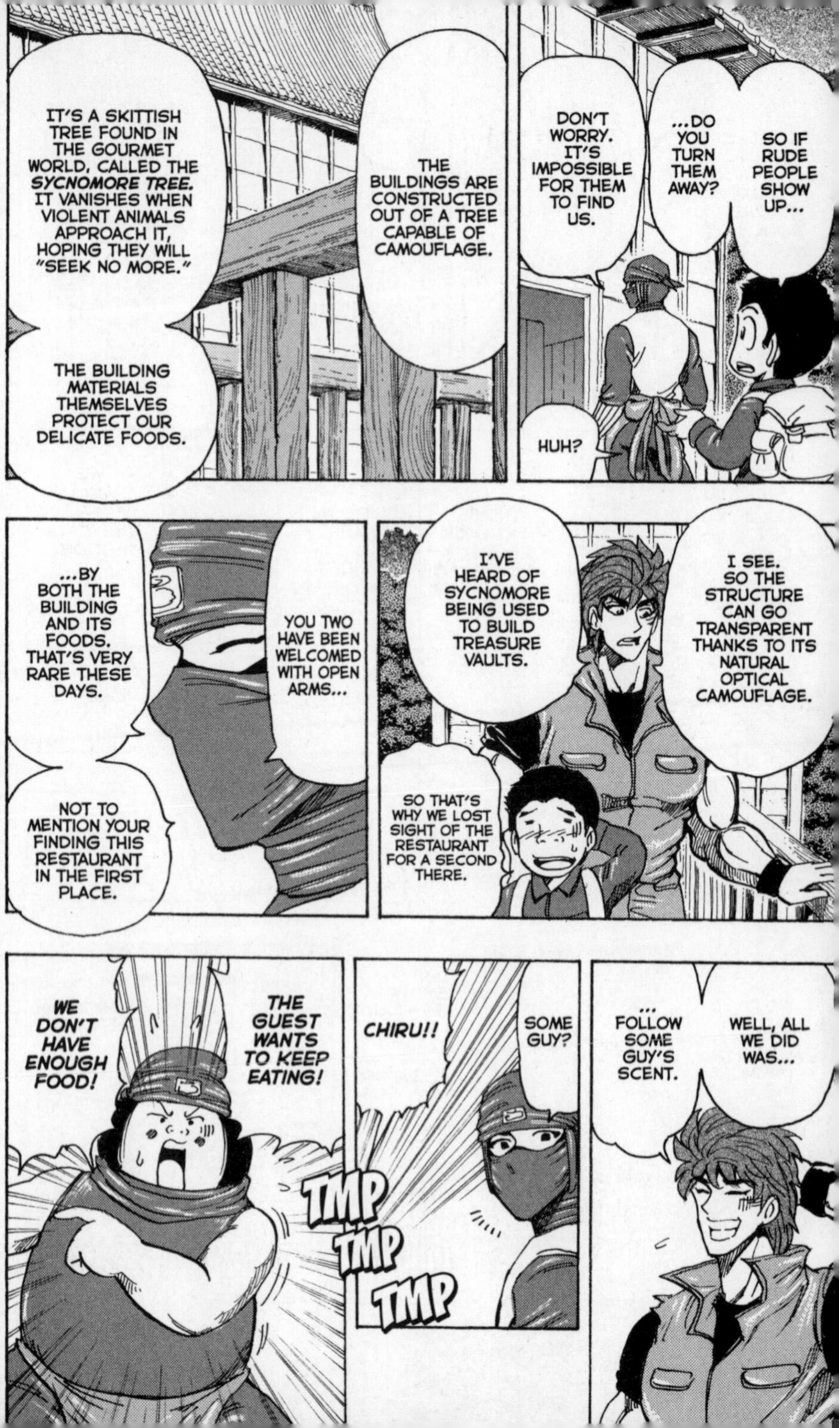
SO IF RUDE PEOPLE SHOW UP...
...DO YOU TURN THEM AWAY?
DON'T WORRY. IT'S IMPOSSIBLE FOR THEM TO FIND US.
HUH?
THE BUILDINGS ARE CONSTRUCTED OUT OF A TREE CAPABLE OF CAMOUFLAGE.
IT'S A SKITTISH TREE FOUND IN THE GOURMET WORLD, CALLED THE *SYCNOMORE TREE.* IT VANISHES WHEN VIOLENT ANIMALS APPROACH IT, HOPING THEY WILL "SEEK NO MORE."
THE BUILDING MATERIALS THEMSELVES PROTECT OUR DELICATE FOODS.
I SEE. SO THE STRUCTURE CAN GO TRANSPARENT THANKS TO ITS NATURAL OPTICAL CAMOUFLAGE.
I'VE HEARD OF SYCNOMORE BEING USED TO BUILD TREASURE VAULTS.
SO THAT'S WHY WE LOST SIGHT OF THE RESTAURANT FOR A SECOND THERE.
YOU TWO HAVE BEEN WELCOMED WITH OPEN ARMS...
...BY BOTH THE BUILDING AND ITS FOODS. THAT'S VERY RARE THESE DAYS.
NOT TO MENTION YOUR FINDING THIS RESTAURANT IN THE FIRST PLACE.
WELL, ALL WE DID WAS...
...FOLLOW SOME GUY'S SCENT.
SOME GUY?
CHIRU!!
TMP TMP TMP
THE GUEST WANTS TO KEEP EATING!
WE DON'T HAVE ENOUGH FOOD!

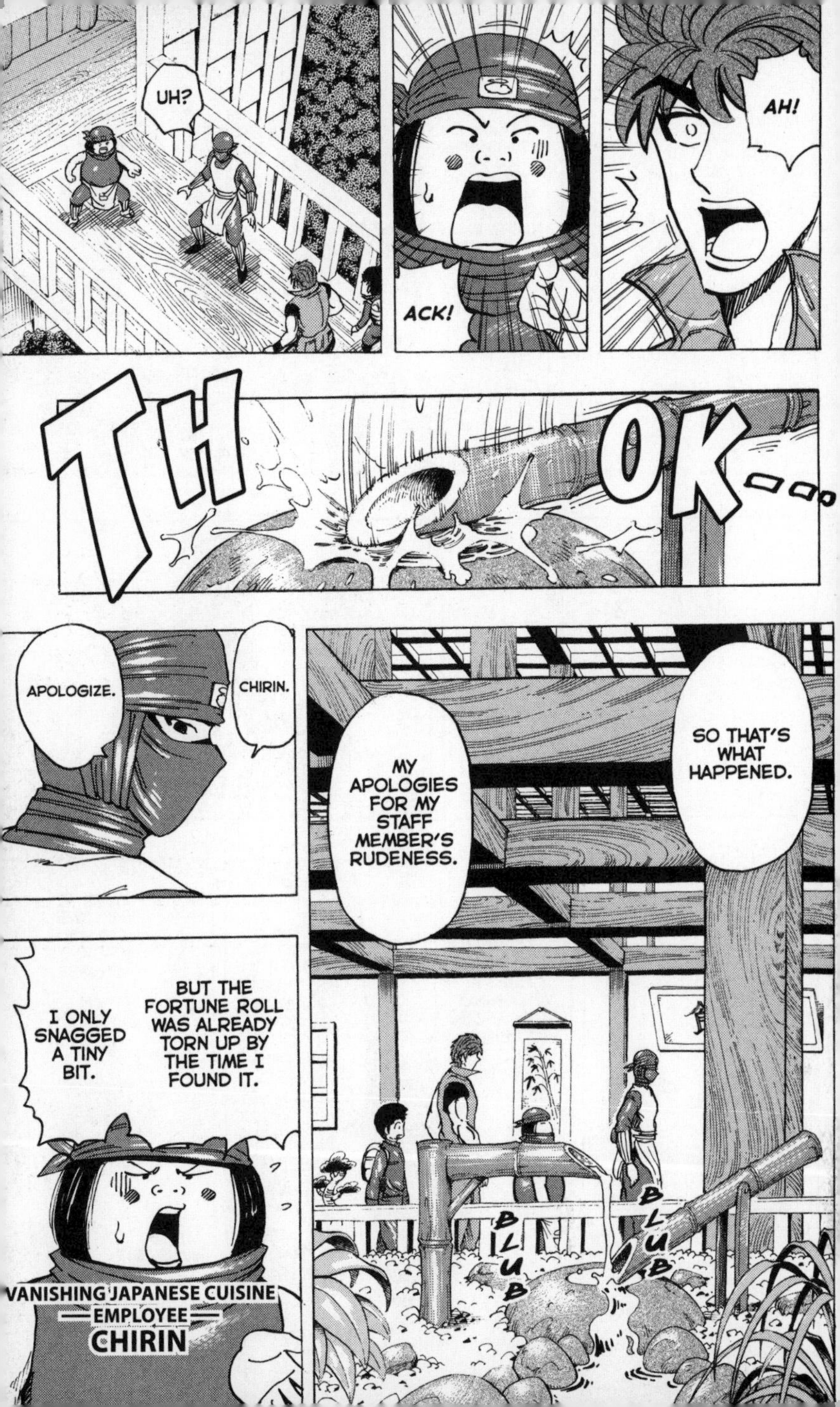
AH!
ACK!
UH?
THOK...
SO THAT'S WHAT HAPPENED.
MY APOLOGIES FOR MY STAFF MEMBER'S RUDENESS.
BLUB
BLUB
CHIRIN.
APOLOGIZE.
BUT THE FORTUNE ROLL WAS ALREADY TORN UP BY THE TIME I FOUND IT.
I ONLY SNAGGED A TINY BIT.
VANISHING JAPANESE CUISINE
—EMPLOYEE—
CHIRIN

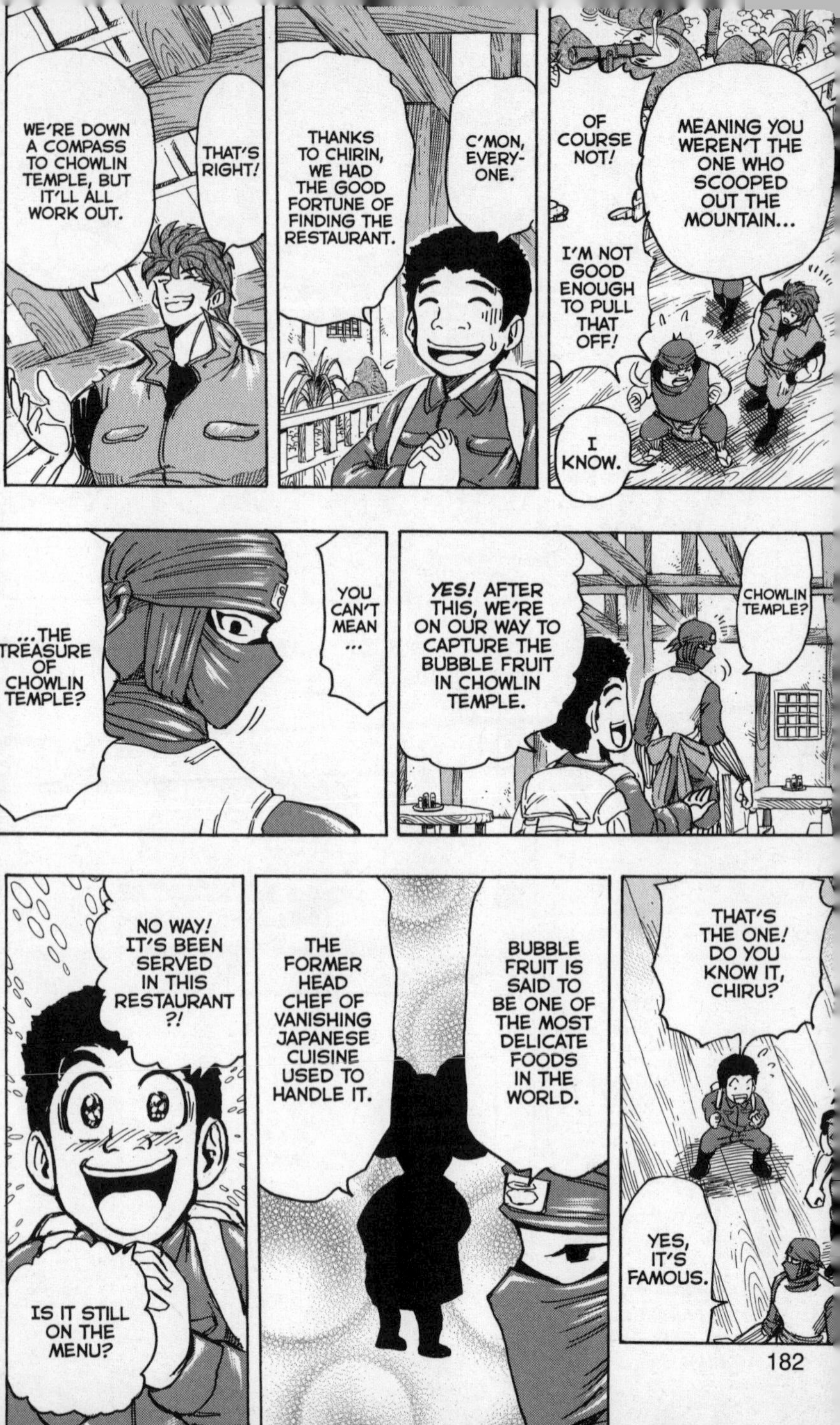

MEANING YOU WEREN'T THE ONE WHO SCOOPED OUT THE MOUNTAIN...
OF COURSE NOT!
I'M NOT GOOD ENOUGH TO PULL THAT OFF!
I KNOW.
C'MON, EVERY-ONE.
THANKS TO CHIRIN, WE HAD THE GOOD FORTUNE OF FINDING THE RESTAURANT.
THAT'S RIGHT!
WE'RE DOWN A COMPASS TO CHOWLIN TEMPLE, BUT IT'LL ALL WORK OUT.
CHOWLIN TEMPLE?
YES! AFTER THIS, WE'RE ON OUR WAY TO CAPTURE THE BUBBLE FRUIT IN CHOWLIN TEMPLE.
YOU CAN'T MEAN ...
...THE TREASURE OF CHOWLIN TEMPLE?
THAT'S THE ONE! DO YOU KNOW IT, CHIRU?
YES, IT'S FAMOUS.
BUBBLE FRUIT IS SAID TO BE ONE OF THE MOST DELICATE FOODS IN THE WORLD.
THE FORMER HEAD CHEF OF VANISHING JAPANESE CUISINE USED TO HANDLE IT.
NO WAY! IT'S BEEN SERVED IN THIS RESTAURANT?!
IS IT STILL ON THE MENU?

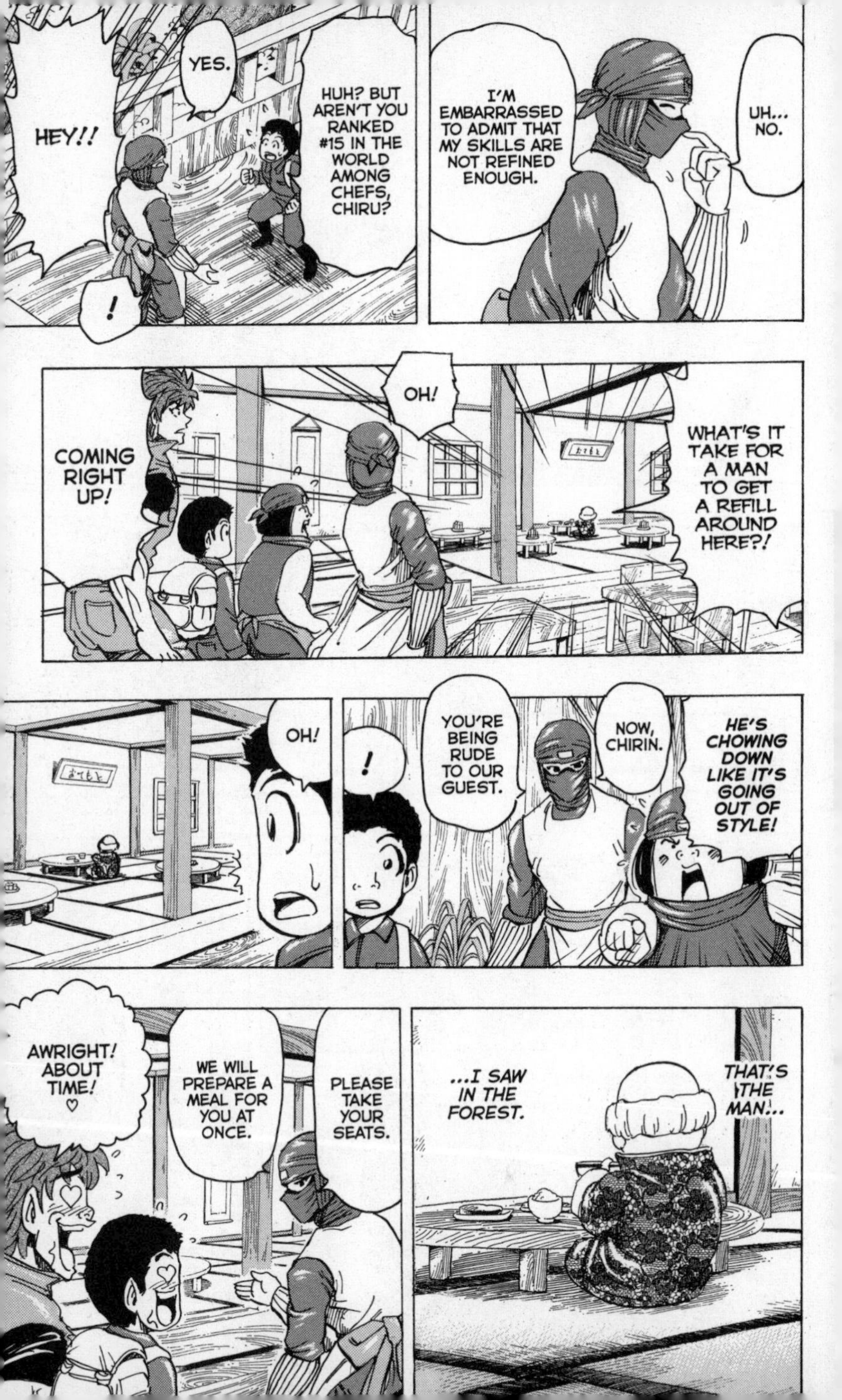
UH... NO.
I'M EMBARRASSED TO ADMIT THAT MY SKILLS ARE NOT REFINED ENOUGH.
HUH? BUT AREN'T YOU RANKED #15 IN THE WORLD AMONG CHEFS, CHIRU?
YES.
HEY!!
!
WHAT'S IT TAKE FOR A MAN TO GET A REFILL AROUND HERE?!
OH!
COMING RIGHT UP!
HE'S CHOWING DOWN LIKE IT'S GOING OUT OF STYLE!
NOW, CHIRIN.
YOU'RE BEING RUDE TO OUR GUEST.
!
OH!
THAT'S THE MAN...
...I SAW IN THE FOREST.
PLEASE TAKE YOUR SEATS.
WE WILL PREPARE A MEAL FOR YOU AT ONCE.
AWRIGHT! ABOUT TIME! ♡

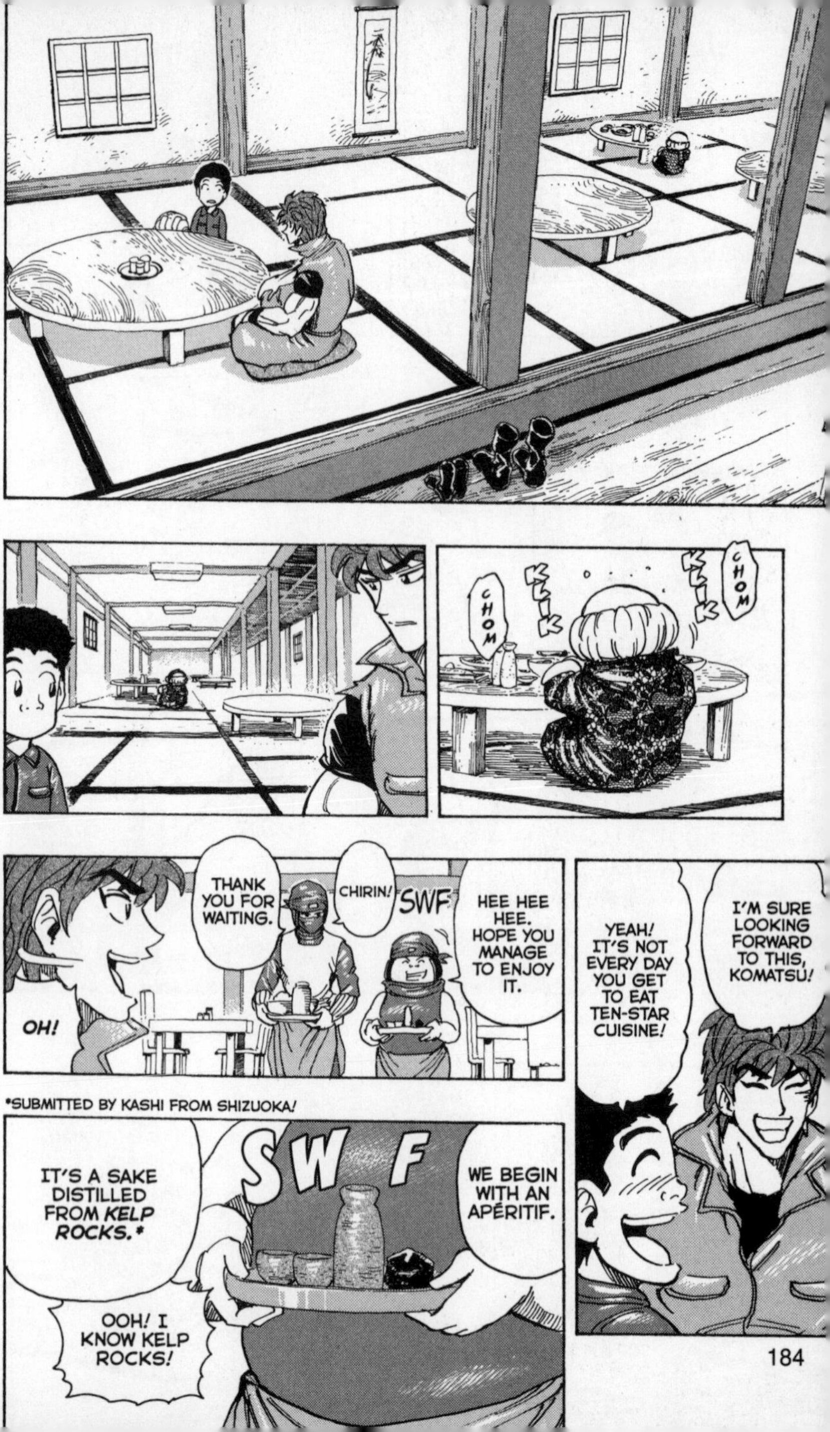
CHOM
KLIK
CHOM
KLIK
I'M SURE LOOKING FORWARD TO THIS, KOMATSU!
YEAH! IT'S NOT EVERY DAY YOU GET TO EAT TEN-STAR CUISINE!
HEE HEE HEE. HOPE YOU MANAGE TO ENJOY IT.
SWF
CHIRIN!
THANK YOU FOR WAITING.
OH!
*SUBMITTED BY KASHI FROM SHIZUOKA!
WE BEGIN WITH AN APÉRITIF.
SWF
IT'S A SAKE DISTILLED FROM *KELP ROCKS.**
OOH! I KNOW KELP ROCKS!

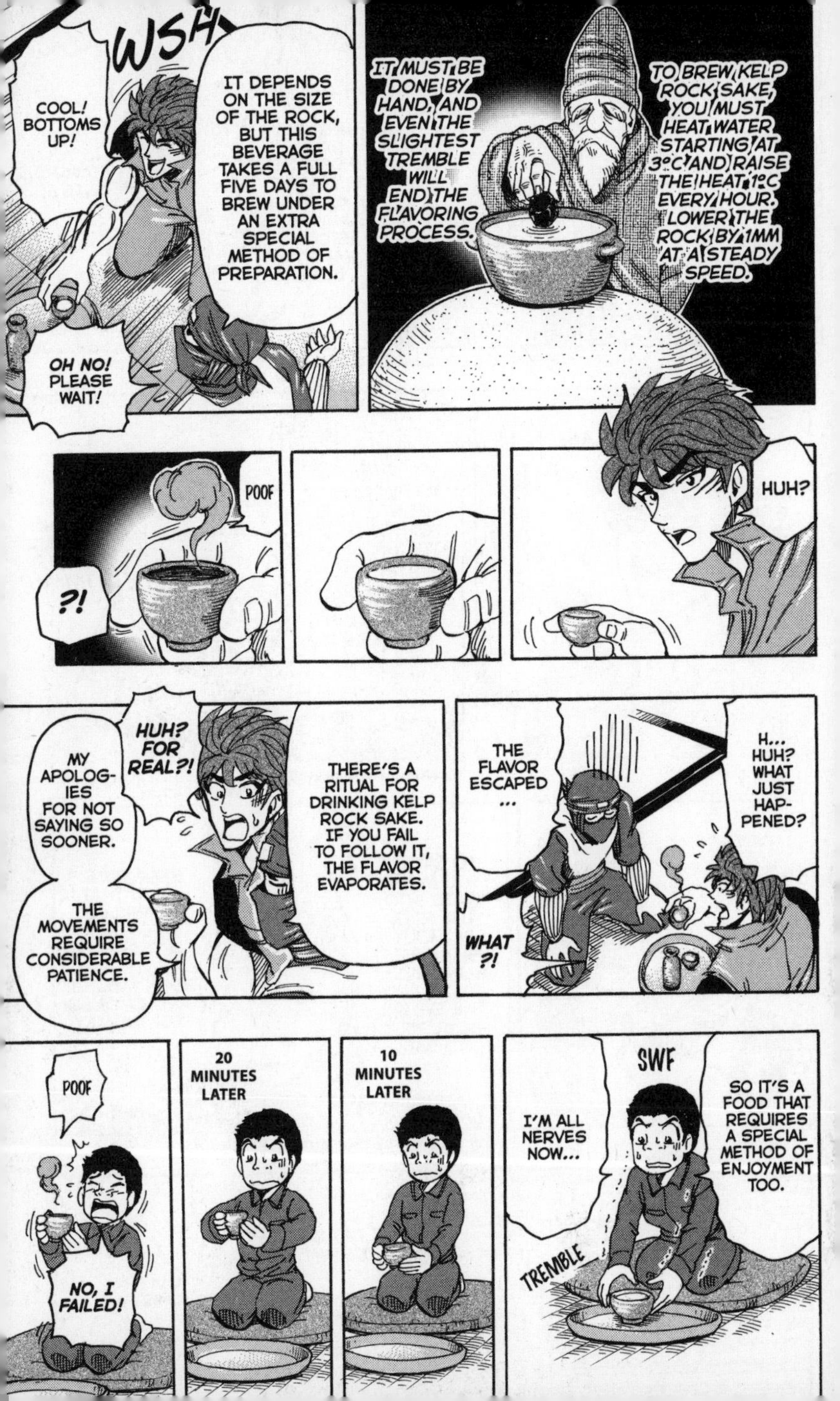

TO BREW KELP ROCK SAKE, YOU MUST HEAT WATER STARTING AT 3°C AND RAISE THE HEAT 1°C EVERY HOUR. LOWER THE ROCK BY 1MM AT A STEADY SPEED.
IT MUST BE DONE BY HAND, AND EVEN THE SLIGHTEST TREMBLE WILL END THE FLAVORING PROCESS.
WSH
IT DEPENDS ON THE SIZE OF THE ROCK, BUT THIS BEVERAGE TAKES A FULL FIVE DAYS TO BREW UNDER AN EXTRA SPECIAL METHOD OF PREPARATION.
COOL! BOTTOMS UP!
OH NO! PLEASE WAIT!
HUH?
POOF
?!
H... HUH? WHAT JUST HAP-PENED?
THE FLAVOR ESCAPED...
WHAT ?!
THERE'S A RITUAL FOR DRINKING KELP ROCK SAKE. IF YOU FAIL TO FOLLOW IT, THE FLAVOR EVAPORATES.
HUH? FOR REAL?!
MY APOLOGIES FOR NOT SAYING SO SOONER.
THE MOVEMENTS REQUIRE CONSIDERABLE PATIENCE.
SWF
SO IT'S A FOOD THAT REQUIRES A SPECIAL METHOD OF ENJOYMENT TOO.
I'M ALL NERVES NOW...
TREMBLE
10 MINUTES LATER
20 MINUTES LATER
POOF
NO, I FAILED!

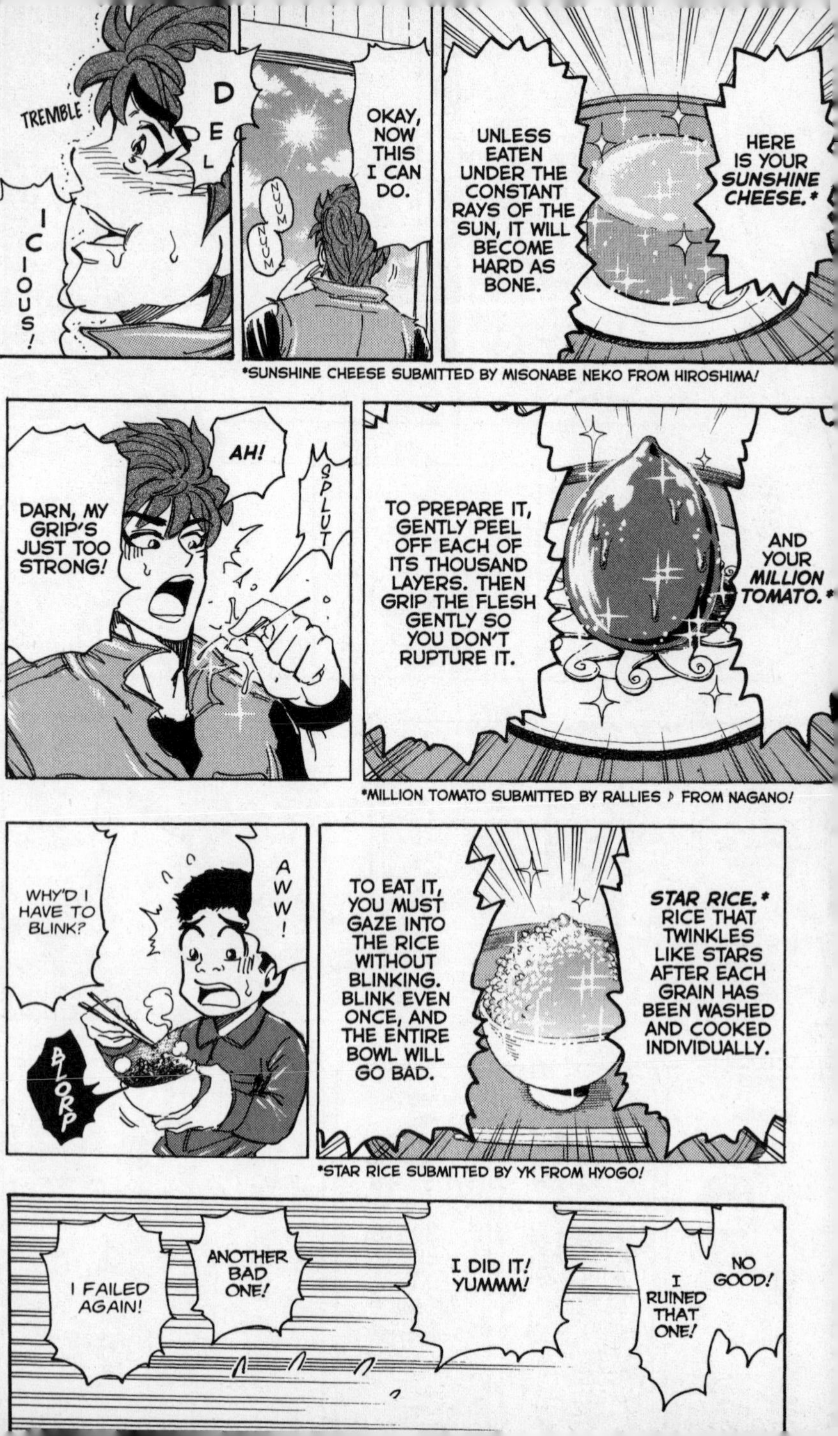
HERE IS YOUR SUNSHINE CHEESE.*
UNLESS EATEN UNDER THE CONSTANT RAYS OF THE SUN, IT WILL BECOME HARD AS BONE.
OKAY, NOW THIS I CAN DO.
NUUM NUUM
DEL
ICIOUS!
TREMBLE
AND YOUR MILLION TOMATO.*
TO PREPARE IT, GENTLY PEEL OFF EACH OF ITS THOUSAND LAYERS. THEN GRIP THE FLESH GENTLY SO YOU DON'T RUPTURE IT.
SPLUT
AH!
DARN, MY GRIP'S JUST TOO STRONG!
STAR RICE.* RICE THAT TWINKLES LIKE STARS AFTER EACH GRAIN HAS BEEN WASHED AND COOKED INDIVIDUALLY.
TO EAT IT, YOU MUST GAZE INTO THE RICE WITHOUT BLINKING. BLINK EVEN ONCE, AND THE ENTIRE BOWL WILL GO BAD.
AWW!
WHY'D I HAVE TO BLINK?
BLORP
NO GOOD!
I RUINED THAT ONE!
I DID IT! YUMMM!
ANOTHER BAD ONE!
I FAILED AGAIN!

*SUNSHINE CHEESE SUBMITTED BY MISONABE NEKO FROM HIROSHIMA!

*MILLION TOMATO SUBMITTED BY RALLIES ♪ FROM NAGANO!

*STAR RICE SUBMITTED BY YK FROM HYOGO!

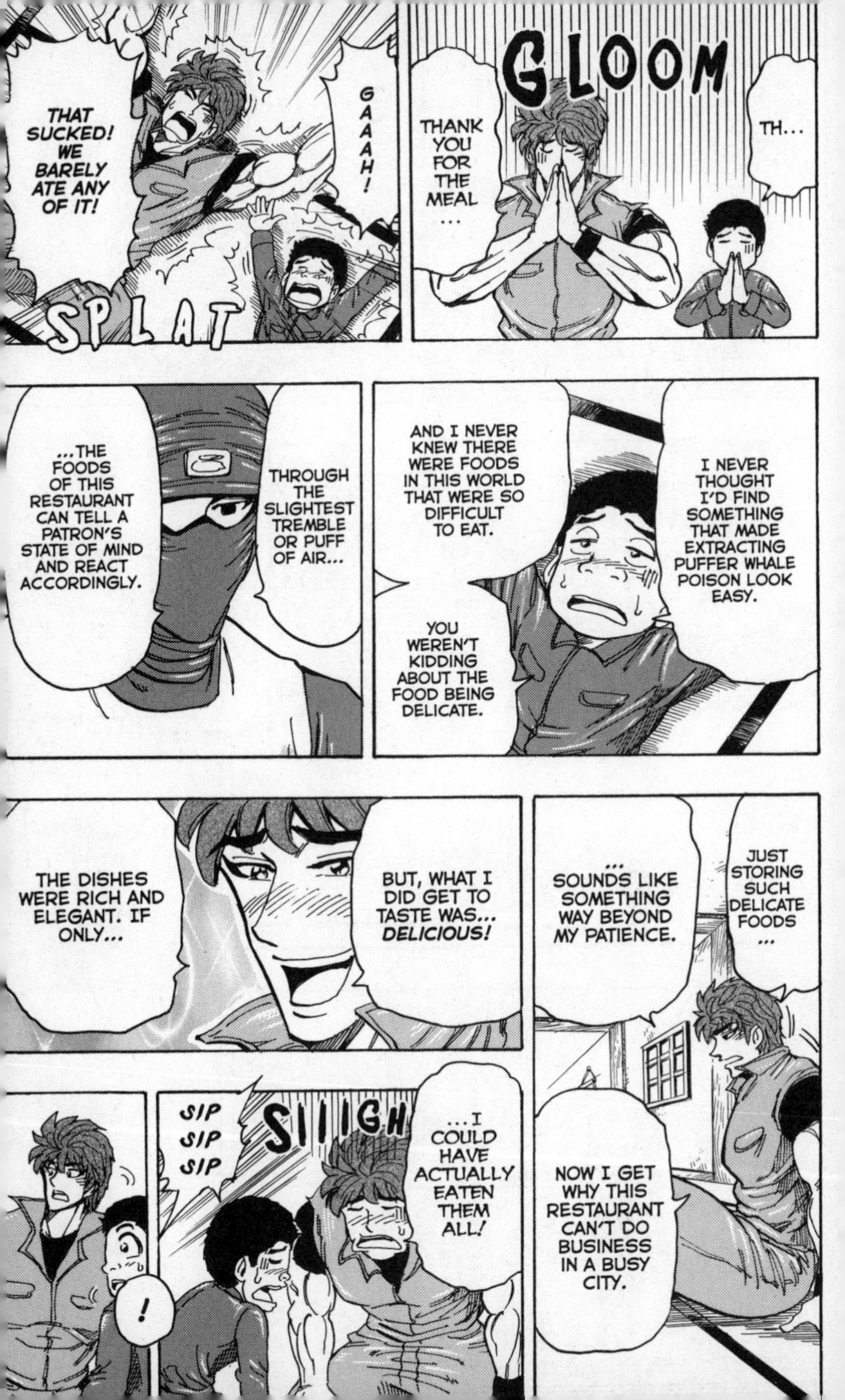
GLOOM
THANK YOU FOR THE MEAL ...
TH...
GAAAAH!
THAT SUCKED! WE BARELY ATE ANY OF IT!
SPLAT
I NEVER THOUGHT I'D FIND SOMETHING THAT MADE EXTRACTING PUFFER WHALE POISON LOOK EASY.
AND I NEVER KNEW THERE WERE FOODS IN THIS WORLD THAT WERE SO DIFFICULT TO EAT.
YOU WEREN'T KIDDING ABOUT THE FOOD BEING DELICATE.
THROUGH THE SLIGHTEST TREMBLE OR PUFF OF AIR...
...THE FOODS OF THIS RESTAURANT CAN TELL A PATRON'S STATE OF MIND AND REACT ACCORDINGLY.
JUST STORING SUCH DELICATE FOODS ...
... SOUNDS LIKE SOMETHING WAY BEYOND MY PATIENCE.
NOW I GET WHY THIS RESTAURANT CAN'T DO BUSINESS IN A BUSY CITY.
BUT, WHAT I DID GET TO TASTE WAS... DELICIOUS!
THE DISHES WERE RICH AND ELEGANT. IF ONLY...
SIIIGH
...I COULD HAVE ACTUALLY EATEN THEM ALL!
SIP SIP SIP
!

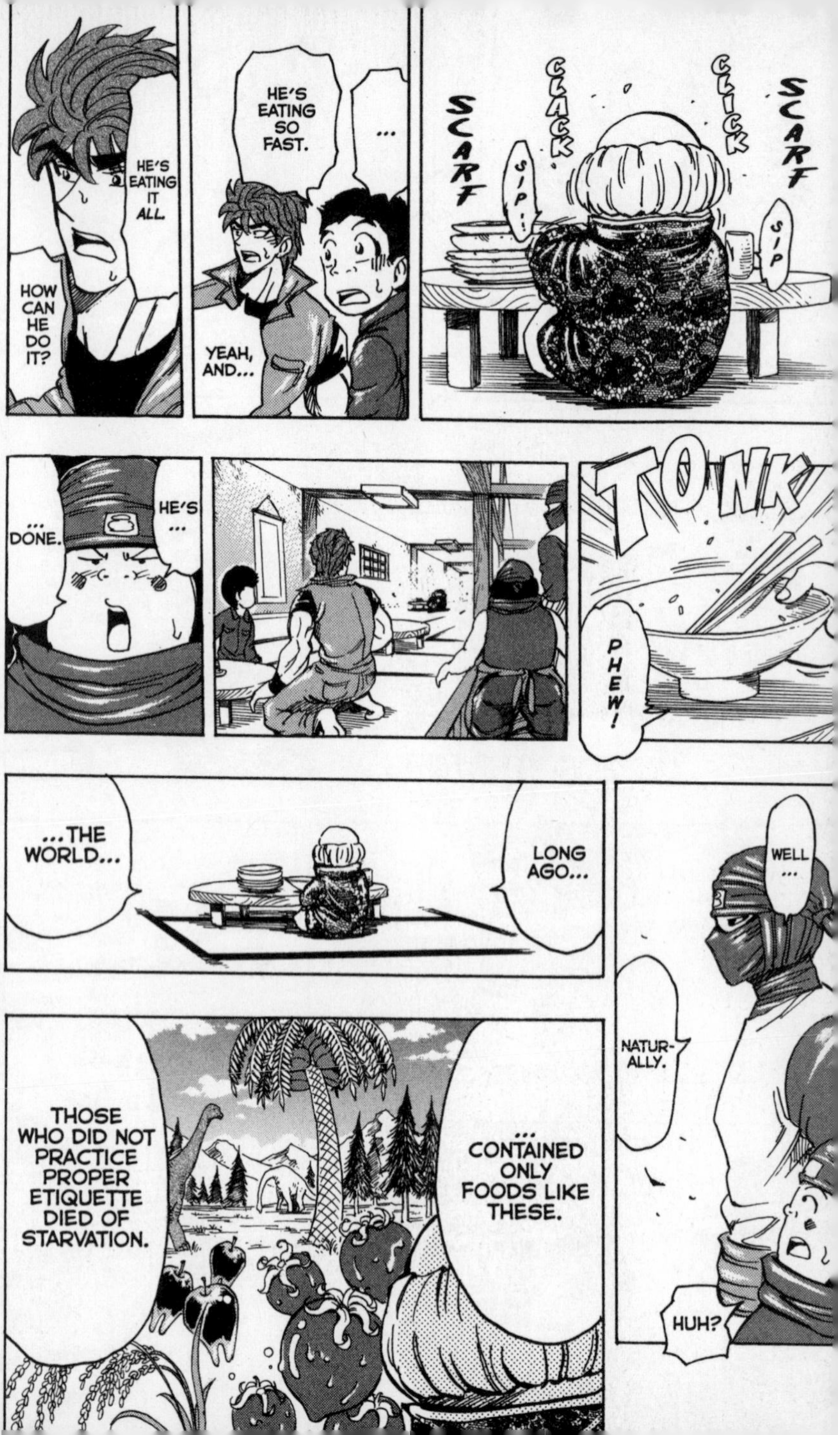
SCARF
CLICK
SIP
SCARF
CLACK
SIP!
...
HE'S EATING SO FAST.
YEAH, AND...
HE'S EATING IT ALL.
HOW CAN HE DO IT?
TONK
PHEW!
HE'S ...
... DONE.
WELL ...
NATUR-ALLY.
HUH?
LONG AGO...
...THE WORLD...
... CONTAINED ONLY FOODS LIKE THESE.
THOSE WHO DID NOT PRACTICE PROPER ETIQUETTE DIED OF STARVATION.

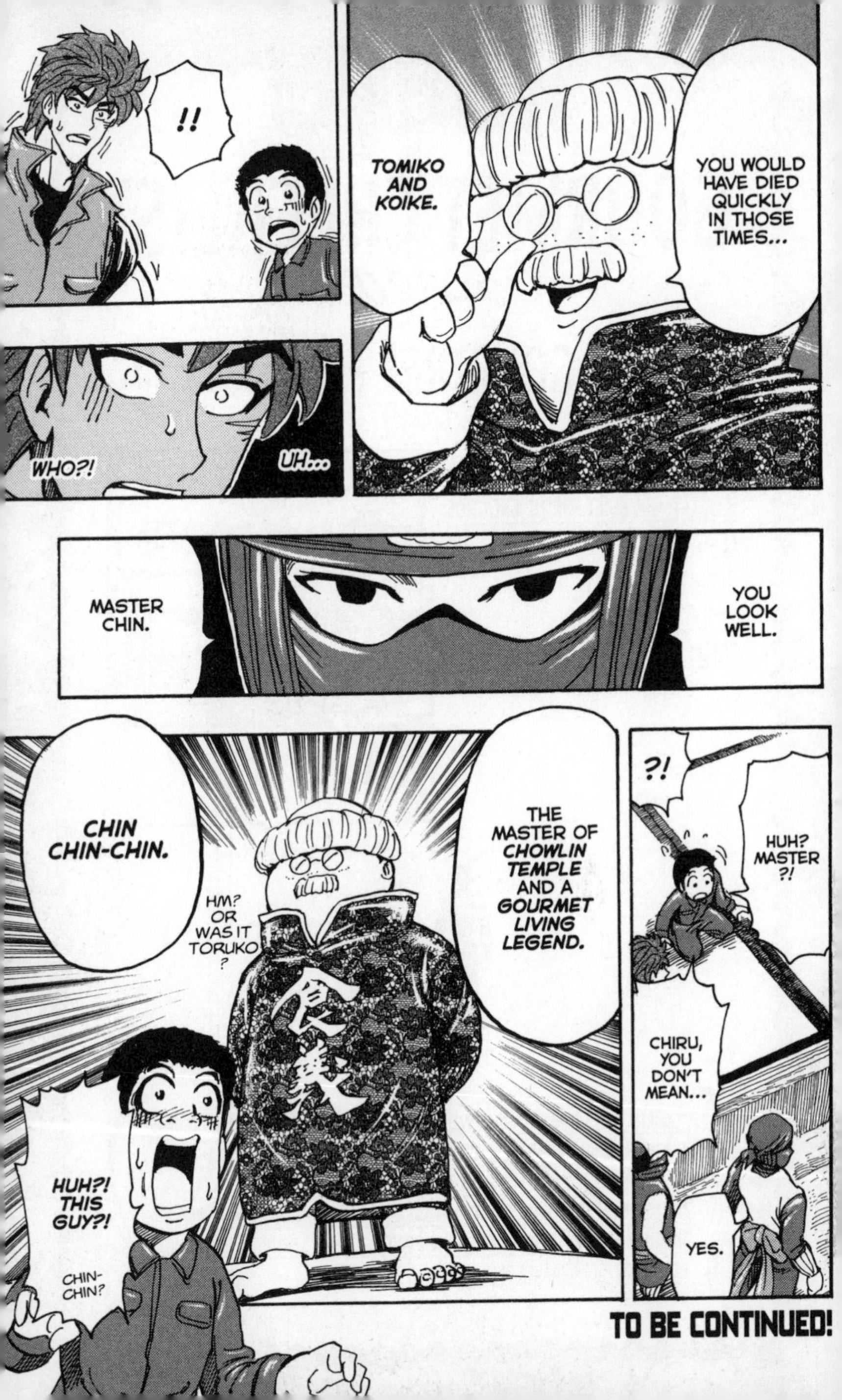
YOU WOULD HAVE DIED QUICKLY IN THOSE TIMES...
TOMIKO AND KOIKE.
!!
UH...
WHO?!
YOU LOOK WELL.
MASTER CHIN.
?!
HUH? MASTER ?!
CHIRU, YOU DON'T MEAN...
YES.
THE MASTER OF CHOWLIN TEMPLE AND A GOURMET LIVING LEGEND.
CHIN CHIN-CHIN.
HM? OR WAS IT TORUKO ?
HUH?! THIS GUY?!
CHIN-CHIN?
TO BE CONTINUED!

TORIKO

GOURMET CHECKLIST

Vol. 208

GOURTREE FRUIT

(FRUIT)

CAPTURE LEVEL: 1

HABITAT: GOURMET SHRINE GROUNDS

LENGTH: 10 CM

HEIGHT: ---

WEIGHT: 250 G

PRICE: 3,000 YEN PER FRUIT

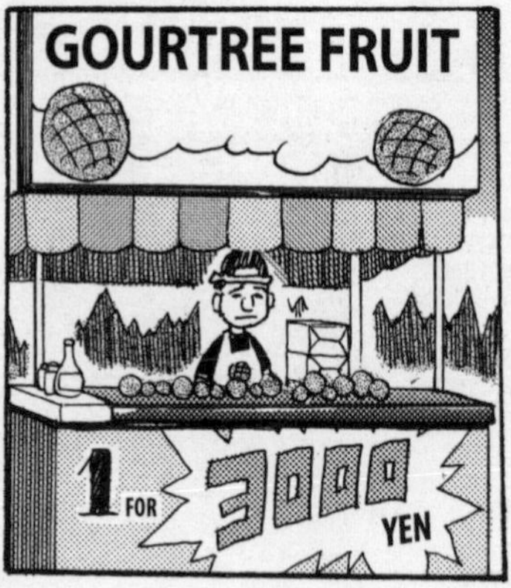
GOURTREE FRUIT
1 FOR 3000 YEN

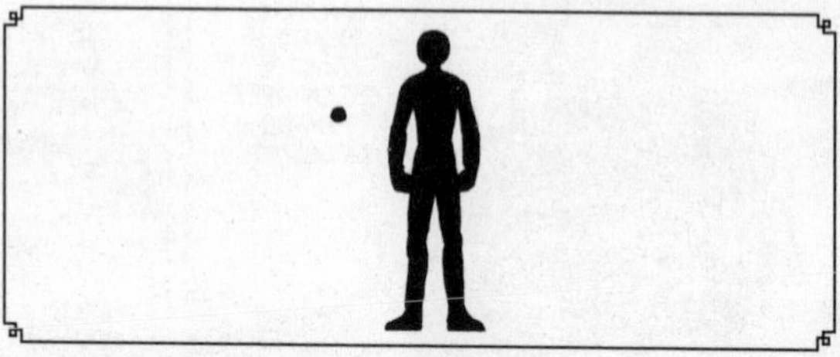

SCALE

"GOURTREE" IS THE NICKNAME OF THE HUNDREDS OF THOUSANDS OF GOURMET CEDARS THAT GROW ON GOURMET SHRINE GROUNDS. THESE EXCELLENT TREES ARE SAID TO HAVE BEEN USED BY GOURMET GOD ACACIA'S CHEF PARTNER, FROESE. EACH YEAR, THE "GOURMET MAN COMPETITION" AWARDS A PRIZE TO THE PERSON WHO FINDS THE SINGLE GOURTREE FRUIT CONTAINING A GOLDEN SEED. IT'S SOMETHING BEGGING PEOPLE TO TEST THEIR LUCK ON!

TORIKO

GOURMET CHECKLIST

Vol. 209

TAXSHEEP

(MAMMAL)

CAPTURE LEVEL: 4

HABITAT: RAISED AT GOURMET SHRINE

LENGTH: 4 METERS

HEIGHT: 3 METERS

WEIGHT: 1.5 TONS

PRICE: 1 HOUR RENTAL / 1,500 YEN

(NOT A FOODSTUFF)

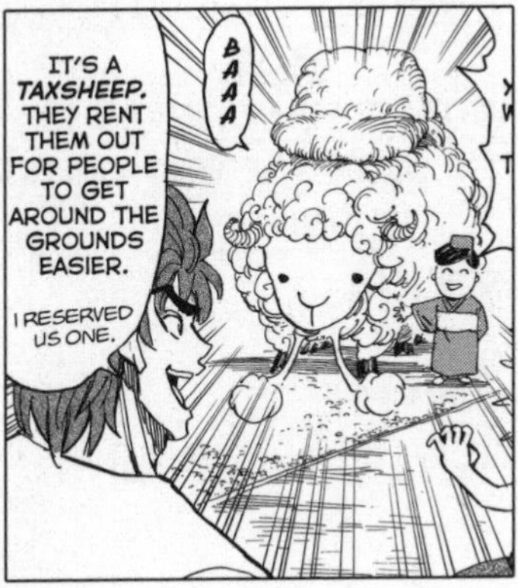
BAAA
IT'S A *TAXSHEEP.* THEY RENT THEM OUT FOR PEOPLE TO GET AROUND THE GROUNDS EASIER.
I RESERVED US ONE.

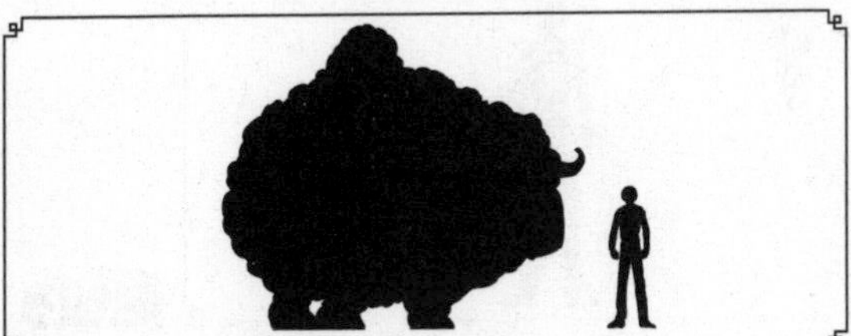

SCALE

THIS CONVENIENT SHEEP CARRIES WORSHIPPERS ACROSS THE 8-MILLION HECTARE EXPANSE OF GOURMET SHRINE AT SPEEDS UP TO 150 KM/HR. IT IS SMART ENOUGH TO AUTOMATICALLY TRANSPORT WORSHIPPERS TO THE NEXT FOOD HALL WITHOUT ANY SORT OF GUIDANCE. DON'T FORGET TO RENT YOUR OWN NEXT TIME YOU VISIT GOURMET SHRINE.

TORIKO

GOURMET CHECKLIST

Vol. 210

STUN APPLE

(FRUIT)

CAPTURE LEVEL: 1—88 (POSSIBLY EVEN HIGHER)

HABITAT: BATTLE ISLAND (THE IGO HAS RECENTLY SUCCEEDED IN ARTIFICIALLY CULTIVATING IT)

LENGTH: 18 CM

HEIGHT: ---

WEIGHT: 150 G

PRICE: 0—1 BILLION YEN PER FRUIT

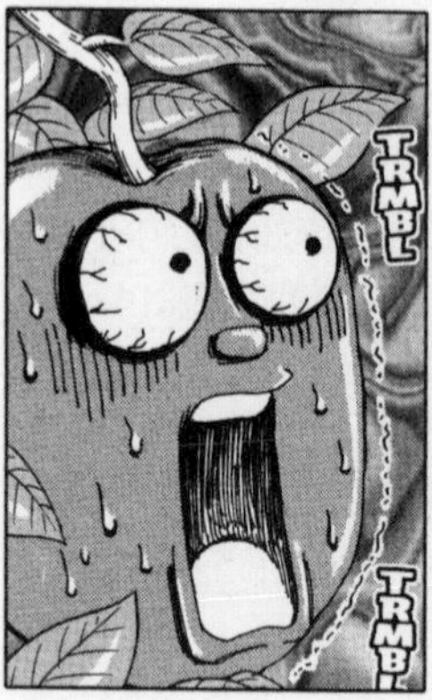
TRMBL
TRMBL

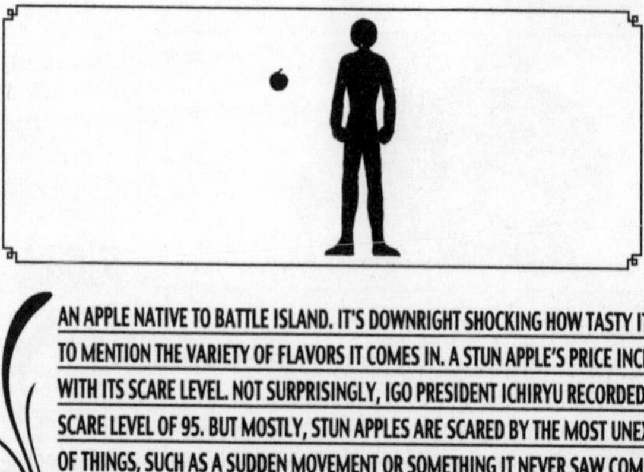

SCALE

AN APPLE NATIVE TO BATTLE ISLAND. IT'S DOWNRIGHT SHOCKING HOW TASTY IT IS, NOT TO MENTION THE VARIETY OF FLAVORS IT COMES IN. A STUN APPLE'S PRICE INCREASES WITH ITS SCARE LEVEL. NOT SURPRISINGLY, IGO PRESIDENT ICHIRYU RECORDED A SCARE LEVEL OF 95. BUT MOSTLY, STUN APPLES ARE SCARED BY THE MOST UNEXPECTED OF THINGS, SUCH AS A SUDDEN MOVEMENT OR SOMETHING IT NEVER SAW COMING. FOR EXAMPLE, ZONGEH'S RANCID FARTS ASTONISHED THE STUN APPLES MORE THAN TORIKO'S 17-FOLD SPIKED PUNCH. NOW THAT'S A STUNNER!

TORIKO

GOURMET CHECKLIST
Vol. 211

SHERBET APPLE
(FRUIT)

CAPTURE LEVEL: 3
HABITAT: GROWS VIRTUALLY EVERYWHERE (CAN ALSO BE ARTIFICIALLY CULTIVATED)
LENGTH: 12 CM
HEIGHT: ---
WEIGHT: 350 G
PRICE: 800 YEN PER FRUIT

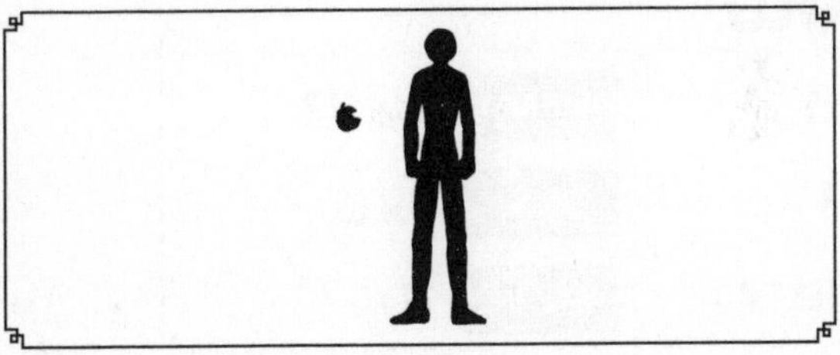

SCALE

AN APPLE THAT TASTES LIKE SHERBET. EATEN PLAIN IT IS TASTY ENOUGH, BUT ADDING A TOPPING TENDS TO ELEVATE THE FLAVOR EXPONENTIALLY. SHERBET APPLE IS A MILD, PLEASANT FOOD THAT CAN OFFER A DOSE OF COMFORT TO EVEN THE MOST TRYING GOURMET HUNTS.

CHARACTER PROFILE

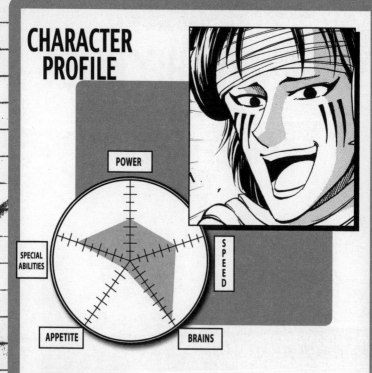

POWER

SPEED

SPECIAL ABILITIES

APPETITE

BRAINS

AIMARU

AGE:	25	**BIRTHDAY:**	MARCH 3
BLOOD TYPE:	A	**SIGN:**	PISCES
HEIGHT:	185 CM	**WEIGHT:**	77 KG
EYESIGHT:	20/8	**SHOE SIZE:**	28 CM

SPECIAL MOVES/ABILITIES: ● Eating Disease, Preshot Routine

Leader of the Gourmet Knights. He believes in the Gourmet Faith's teachings about entrusting your life to nature. He's also a "sicktarian" who can treat other people by eating their ailments. Recently, his sicktarian diet has turned on him and he is being eaten away by a severe illness himself. Regardless, there are still many young men who admire Aimaru for his iron willpower and wish to join the order of the Gourmet Knights. He's such close friends with Toriko that they'll fight over anything. It's been a contentious yet long-lasting friendship.

COMING NEXT VOLUME

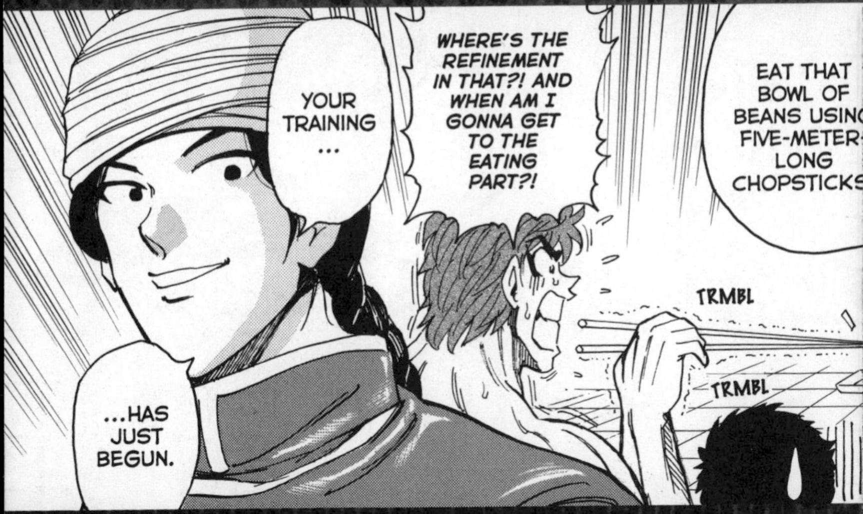
EAT THAT BOWL OF BEANS USING FIVE-METER-LONG CHOPSTICKS
WHERE'S THE REFINEMENT IN THAT?! AND WHEN AM I GONNA GET TO THE EATING PART?!
TRMBL
TRMBL
YOUR TRAINING...
...HAS JUST BEGUN.

SHOWDOWN AT CHOWLIN TEMPLE

Patience isn't one of Toriko's virtues, but to capture the elusive Bubble Fruit, Toriko and Komatsu undergo intense training at Chowlin Temple. Toriko struggles to quiet his rumbling stomach and show gratitude for food, but soon a bigger challenge arises—Gourmet Corp. sends sinister new agents to crush the temple. Can Toriko master Honoring the Food in time to save it?

AVAILABLE APRIL 2014!

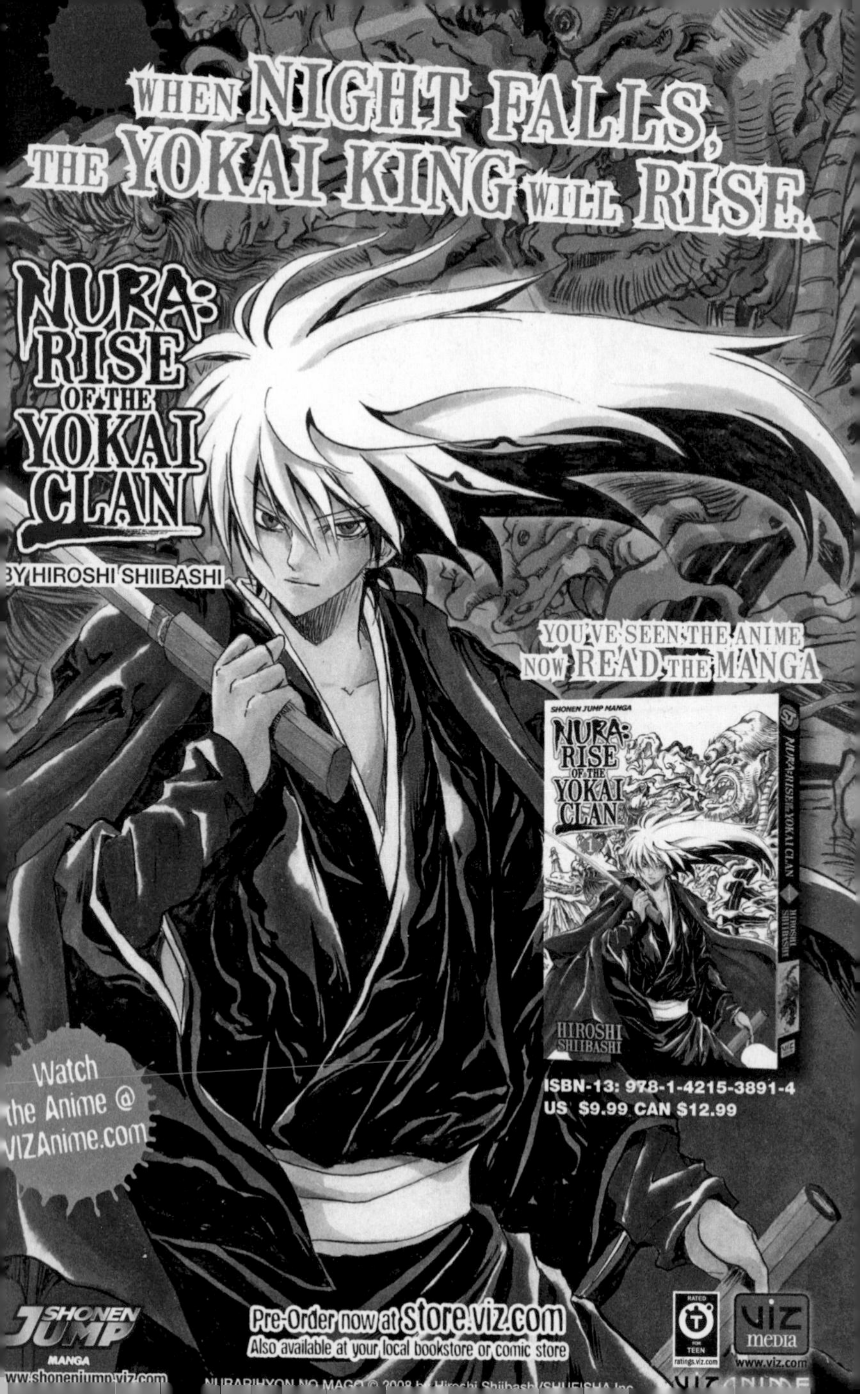

WHEN NIGHT FALLS, THE YOKAI KING WILL RISE.
NURA: RISE OF THE YOKAI CLAN
BY HIROSHI SHIIBASHI
YOU'VE SEEN THE ANIME NOW READ THE MANGA
SHONEN JUMP MANGA
NURA: RISE OF THE YOKAI CLAN
HIROSHI SHIIBASHI
ISBN-13: 978-1-4215-3891-4
US $9.99 CAN $12.99
Watch the Anime @ VIZAnime.com
SHONEN JUMP MANGA
www.shonenjump.viz.com
Pre-Order now at store.viz.com
Also available at your local bookstore or comic store
RATED T FOR TEEN
ratings.viz.com
viz media
www.viz.com

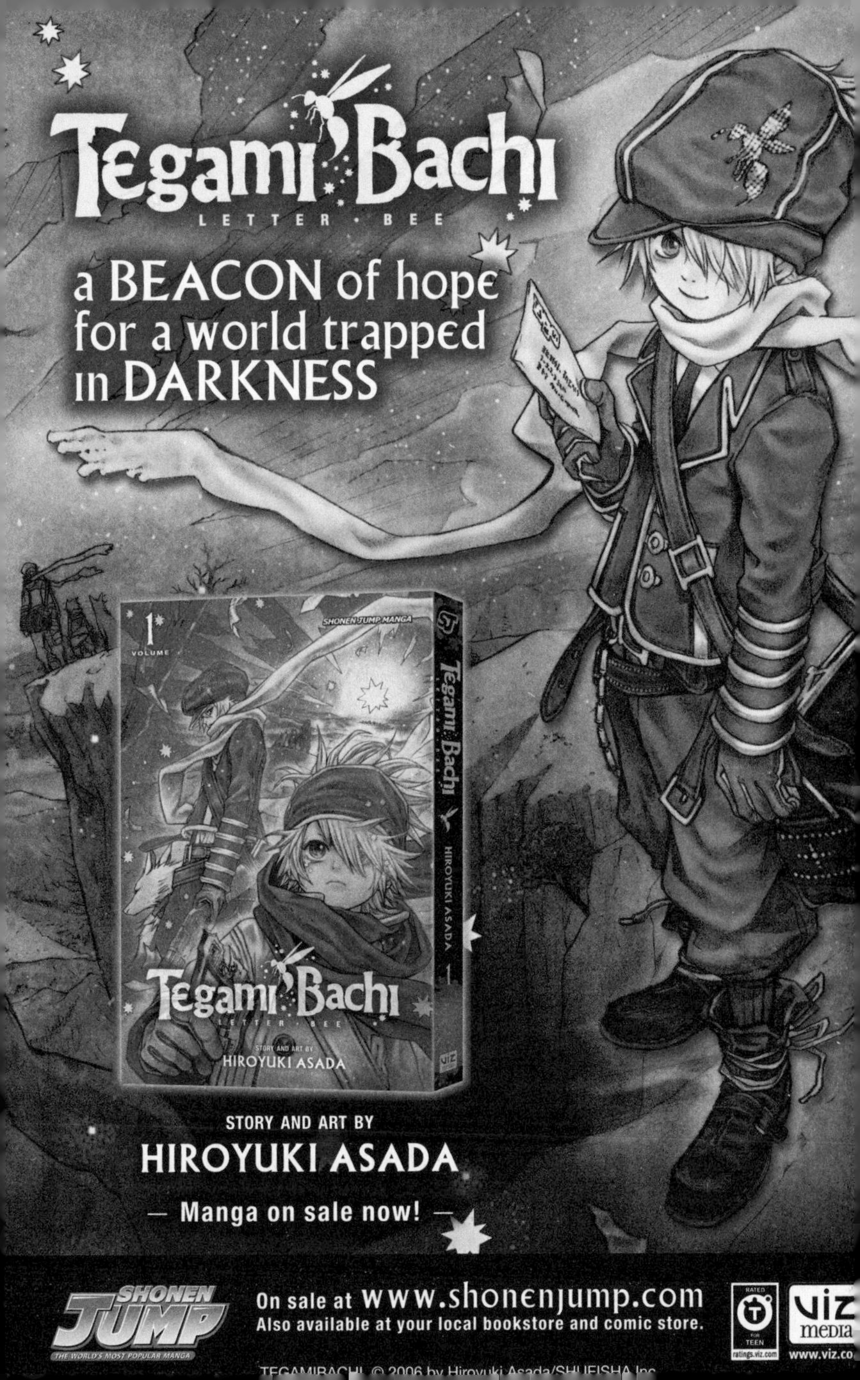
Tegami Bachi
LETTER • BEE
a BEACON of hope for a world trapped in DARKNESS
1
VOLUME
SHONEN JUMP MANGA
Tegami Bachi
LETTER BEE
STORY AND ART BY
HIROYUKI ASADA
Tegami Bachi
HIROYUKI ASADA
1
STORY AND ART BY
HIROYUKI ASADA
— Manga on sale now! —
SHONEN JUMP
THE WORLD'S MOST POPULAR MANGA
On sale at www.shonenjump.com
Also available at your local bookstore and comic store.
RATED T FOR TEEN
ratings.viz.com
viz media
www.viz.co
TEGAMIBACHI © 2006 by Hiroyuki Asada/SHUEISHA Inc.

You're Reading in the Wrong Direction!!

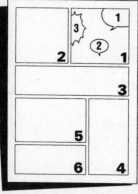

Whoops! Guess what? You're starting at the wrong end of the comic!

...It's true! In keeping with the original Japanese format, **Toriko** is meant to be read from right to left, starting in the upper-right corner.

Unlike English, which is read from left to right, Japanese is read from right to left, meaning that action, sound effects and word-balloon order are completely reversed... something which can make readers unfamiliar with Japanese feel pretty backwards themselves. For this reason, manga or Japanese comics published in the U.S. in English have sometimes been published "flopped"— that is, printed in exact reverse order, as though seen from the other side of a mirror.

By flopping pages, U.S. publishers can avoid confusing readers, but the compromise is not without its downside. For one thing, a character in a flopped manga series who once wore in the original Japanese version a T-shirt emblazoned with "M A Y" (as in "the merry month of") now wears one which reads "Y A M"! Additionally, many manga creators in Japan are themselves unhappy with the process, as some feel the mirror-imaging of their art skews their original intentions.

We are proud to bring you Mitsutoshi Shimabukuro's **Toriko** in the original unflopped format. For now, though, turn to the other side of the book and let the adventure begin...!

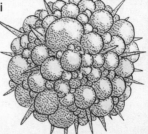

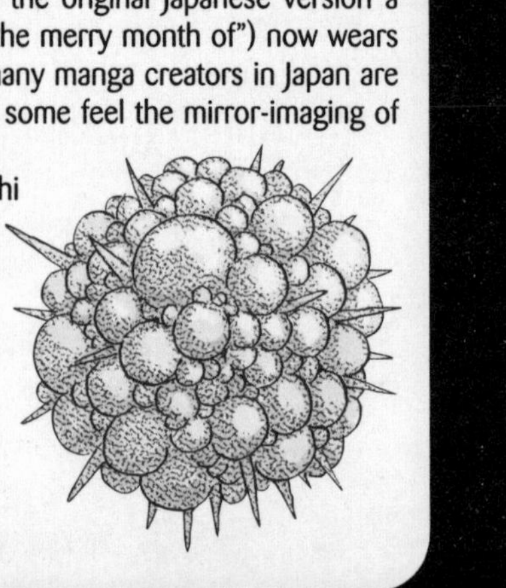

—Editor